BASHGALI DICTIONARY

BASHGALI DICTIONARY

AN ANALYSIS OF
COLONEL J. DAVIDSON'S NOTES ON THE BASHGALI LANGUAGE

STEN KONOW

GYAN

Published by

GYAN

Gyan Publishing House
5, Ansari Road
Daryaganj, New Delhi-110002
Phone: 011-47034999, 9811692060
E-mail: books@gyanbooks.com

Distribution Network
gyanbooks.com
India, USA, Canada, UK, Australia, France

ISBN : 978-81-212-4250-9 (HB)
First Published, Calcutta, 1913

2nd Impression 2020

Printed at: Gyan Press, Delhi.

Bashgali Dictionary
Author: Sten Konow

BASHGALI DICTIONARY

AN ANALYSIS OF

COLONEL J. DAVIDSON'S NOTES ON

THE BASHGALI LANGUAGE

BY

STEN KONOW

PROFESSOR OF INDIAN PHILOLOGY IN THE KRISTIANIA UNIVERSITY

PUBLISHED AS EXTRA NO. TO THE JOURNAL AND PROCEEDINGS OF THE ASIATIC SOCIETY OF BENGAL, N.S., VOL. IX, 1913]

CALCUTTA
PUBLISHED BY THE ASIATIC SOCIETY OF BENGAL
1 PARK STREET

PRINTED BY STEPHEN AUSTIN AND SONS, LTD.
HERTFORD, ENGLAND
1913

TO

SIR GEORGE A. GRIERSON, K.C.I.E.

WITH THE AUTHOR'S SINCERE REGARDS

PRELIMINARY NOTE

THIS vocabulary of the Bashgalī language is an attempt at a detailed analysis of the materials contained in Colonel J. Davidson's well-known Notes on the dialect.[1] A mechanical list of all the forms occurring in the grammatical sketch and the Bashgalī sentences published by that scholar was drawn up in Sir George A. Grierson's office for my use. I have gone through that list, arranged it, and worked it into the shape of a vocabulary, after comparing every single entry in the list with the original.

Alphabetical Arrangement.—Colonel Davidson, in the introduction to his Notes, has made some remarks on the difficulty he has experienced in rendering the sounds of Bashgalī by English letters. He has wisely refrained from attempting to introduce a consistent orthography, and has, in each single case, written the words as he heard them. The inevitable result is that one and the same word often occurs in different shapes. Most variations are found in the vowels, fewer in the consonants. In a vocabulary, however, one word should not be dealt with in more than one place, and the difficulty is to decide in which. Where the difference in form depends on consonant variations, the etymology of the word often solves the question. Thus the comparison with Greek ἐπί shows that the preposition *b*, *p* should be entered as *p*; *iwrakī*, *wrikī*, and *wrigī*, fox, should all be given under *wrikī*, compare Sanskrit *vṛika*; *jāṛ*, *zāṛ*, *zhāṛ*, to know, should come under *zāṛ*, while *jār*, to kill, is correctly written with *j*; compare Awestan *zan*, to know; *jan*, to kill. In numerous cases where the etymology of a word is not known, the decision is more difficult, and practical considerations such as the greater or smaller frequency of a certain form come into the field. In every case cross references will be necessary. The number of such references would be endless if all the variations in the representation of vowels should be registered in the same way. The spelling of the vowels varies to a much higher degree than in the case of consonants. It has therefore been

[1] Colonel J. Davidson, C.B., I.S.C., *Notes on the Bashgalī (Kāfir) Language* (published as Extra No. 1 to the Journal of the Asiatic Society of Bengal, vol. lxxi, pt. i, 1902), Calcutta, 1902. The author of this excellent work has kindly granted Sir George A. Grierson permission to utilize it for the following pages.

considered most practical to follow the same system of alphabetical arrangement as in Sir George A. Grierson's Kāshmīrī Dictionary, now under preparation: the arrangement is based on the alphabetical order of the consonants, without any regard to the vowels. The latter only come into consideration in cases where the same consonant or consonants are followed or separated by different vowels. Thus the different words containing the consonants *tr* will be found in the succession *trā, trai, trĕ, troi, tar, tăr, taṛ, taṛē, tarĭ, toṛ, tore, tur, tūr, turĕ.* Moreover, all words beginning with vowels are arranged together at the commencement, their mutual order being determined by the consonants. Long and nasalized vowels are not distinguished from short ones, except in cases where the difference between two words only depends on such variations. A similar principle has been followed in the case of diacritical marks. Thus *r* and *ṛ* have only been distinguished in cases such as *tar* and *taṛ*, where the diacritical sign constitutes the only difference between two words. Lastly, the consonants *v* and *w* are apparently used promiscuously, and they have not been treated as different letters in the vocabulary.

Nouns.—Under each word all instances of its use in Colonel Davidson's book have been quoted from the mechanical list mentioned above. In the case of nouns the different cases have been distinguished, mainly in accordance with Colonel Davidson's grammar. Thus the forms which are used to denote the case of the subject with the past tenses of transitive verbs, have been entered under the head of agent, though, in most cases, they do not differ from the corresponding nominatives. The forms used to denote the object with the same tenses have been entered under the head of accusative, though they are properly nominatives, such verbal tenses being formed from the past participle passive. All such cases as consist of a base followed by a postposition have been entered under the head of oblique base.

Verbs.—In the case of verbs I have thought it necessary to deviate from Colonel Davidson's arrangement in order to avoid bringing too many different forms together under one head. The following forms have been distinguished:—

Infinitive, the forms ending in *sth*; thus, *esth*, to go.

Verbal noun, the base, with or without the termination *n*; thus, *ē* and *en*, to go.

Present participle, ending in *l* or, sometimes, in *n*; thus, *jărl*, killing; *ettan*, going.

Past participle, ending in a vowel or in *st*, *ss*; thus, *uttā*, left; *bist*, become; *mṛiss*, dead.

Conjunctive participle, ending in *ī*, or usually in *tī*; thus, *aī*, *attī*, having come.

Present indefinite, formed by adding pronominal suffixes to the base; thus, *ēmå*, *ēmi<u>sh</u>*, we go.

Present, formed by adding an *n*-suffix; thus, *otinami<u>zh</u>bå*, if we remain.

2nd present, formed by adding a *t*-suffix; thus, *battami<u>sh</u>*, we can.

Present definite, formed by adding pronominal suffixes or the verb substantive to the present participle; thus, *kulom*, I am doing, I do.

Past, the past participle followed by pronominal suffixes; thus, *gā'm*, I went. In the case of transitive verbs, pronominal suffixes are not, as a rule, added; thus, *kaṛā*, I did, thou didst, etc.; in the paradigms in the grammatical sketch, however, they are commonly used.

Imperfect, formed by adding the past tense of the verb substantive to the present participle ending in *n*; thus, *kunazzam*, I was doing.

Perfect and pluperfect, formed by adding forms of the verb substantive *as* to the past participle; thus, *gāsam*, I have gone; *jăriss*, have, hast, has, killed. Pronominal suffixes are added in intransitive verbs, but, outside the paradigms in the grammar, not after transitives.

Causal and passive forms have been added in accordance with Colonel Davidson's grammar.

All forms of the individual verbs have been brought together under one head, which can, for practical purposes, be considered as the base. Compound verbs have been dealt with as bases, and the determination of the actual form of the individual bases has been made from practical and not from etymological considerations. Care has been taken, by means of numerous cross references, to make it easy to find each individual form occurring in Colonel Davidson's book in the vocabulary. The phonetical features and the grammatical system of the dialect have not been discussed. They will be dealt with in the Linguistic Survey of India.

STEN KONOW.

BASHGALI DICTIONARY

VOWELS

1 **Ā,** to come; the following forms of this base occur in the sentences:—

Infinitive, *aōsth*, to come, p. 58; *wā osth*, to come down, to descend, 341; *agal osthē dugā̆*, rain coming on account of, from the rain, 1401.

Verbal noun, *ā na balam*, I cannot come, go (to Drō<u>sh</u>), 1118.

Present participle, *al*, coming; *al-ossam*, I am coming, I shall dwell, 390.

Conjunctive participle, *aī*, having come, 1342; *pitur-ai-salam*, behind having come shall be, I shall follow, come after, 138; *attī*, having come, 396, 532, 547, 1090, 1251, p. 58; also used with postpositions, thus, *attī dugā̆*, on account of the coming, 604.

Present 2nd pers. sing. *anjībá*, if thou comest, 106, p. 48.

3rd pers. sing. *ann*, comes, is coming, 1336, 1338, 1391, 1527, 1624, 1697, 1702, p. 58; *luī annā*, does blood come? 1411.

Second present 3rd pers. *awettett*, he comes, p. 58; *attētt*, they come, p. 58; *awettett*, they have come, 74.

Present definite 3rd pers. sing. *kuī onzībá*, when it comes, 1166, 1466.

Past 2nd pers. sing. *o<u>sh</u>*, camest, p. 58; hast come, 389; *hāu*, camest, p. 58; *aiyo<u>sh</u>*, hast come, 769, 770; *aiyō<u>sh</u>*, camest, p. 58.

3rd pers. sing. *āya*, came, 623; *āyā*, came, 623, 895, 959, 1051; *āyo*, came, 758; has come, p. 15; *aiyo*, came, 50, p. 58; has come, 382, 388, 566, 694, 730, 810, 1169.

3rd pers. plur. *ayā*, they have come, 214, 279; *āyā*, came, 925; have come, 75, 600, 848, 932, 934, 1177; *aiyā*, they have come, 832, 873; *n'āio*, they have not come, 969; *āyū*, they have come, p. 58.

Perfect and pluperfect 1st pers. sing. *ayāsum*, I came, 134; *āyosam*, I have come, 1053; *aiyōsam*, I came, p. 58; *wār ossam*, I came, fell, down, 1488; *manoī nachētī ossum*, I have come having left my stick, 1111.

3rd pers. sing. *bar-anziss*, (sweat) has come out, he has sweated, 1446; *n'ais*, he did not come, 1147; *zīm n'aisī*, snow did not come, 1635; *ess*, he came, p. 58; *oss*, he came, 487, 1706; he has come, 1353; *kuī ossabā*, when he came, 1252; *osth*, (a fox) came, 1287; *azittā*, came-when, when he came, p. 4 (Abdul Hakim Khān); *ozess*, he has come, 1568; *n'ozz*, he did not come, 1615; *na ozz*, has not come, 1739; *haiss*, he has come, 537.

3rd pers. plur. *war-onstai*, (the teeth) have come, have fallen, out, 945; *n'aoght*, they have not come, 873; *osth*, they came, 552, 1386, 1429; they have come, 277, 1233, 1265, p. 58; *osthā*, they have come, 537; *osthai*, they have come, 1139, 1614, p. 48; *shtār ayasar*, thieves have come, 117.

Future 1st pers. sing. *ēlom*, I shall come, 704; *ēllom*, I shall come, 1734.

3rd pers. sing. *agal n'allon*, rain will not come, 1121; *allonn*, he will come, 672; cf. **AFZ** and **ATS**.

2 **ā**, interrogative particle added to the verb. It occurs both in simple and in disjunctive interrogative sentences.

(1) In simple sentences—

With the 1st pers. sing. *ōts shtār assum-ā*, (doest thou think that) I am a thief? 1105 (*assuma*), p. 17; *ī kuī tū vinoj-ā*, did I ever beat thee? 1312; cf. p. 11.

With the 2nd pers. sing. *afzōsh-ā*, art thou going? 38; *ajiss-ā*, didst thou sow? 1363; *ash-ā*, art thou? 1736; *ashi-ā*, art thou? 1307, 1366; *ēnj-ā* (*ētishi-ā*), art thou going? 1132; *ēttishi-ā*, art thou going? p. 17; *iyān-ā*, hast thou eaten? 87; *īdr-ā*, hast thou eaten? 85; *ktol n'kaṛs-ā*, hast thou not done thy belly? art thou not satisfied? 1232; *purjitish-ā*, doest thou think? 1105, p. 17; *n'pshusi-ā*, didst thou not sleep? 1733; *ragach-a*, doest thou request? 1149; *raganj-ā*, doest thou require? 1629; *vrāghuttas-ā*, hast thou received? 1136; *waṛains-ā*, hast thou seen? 546; *zā̃ṛch-ā*, doest thou know? 1277; *zā̃ṛlazh-ā*, doest thou understand? 1577.

With the 3rd pers. sing. *luī ann-ā*, does blood come? 1411; *ashtā*, is there? 1609; *ass-ā*, is? 58, 920, 1387, 1394, 1412, 1492, 1540, 1676, 1683, 1688, 1741; *ess-ā*, is? 1014; *azz-ā*, is? 1331, 1666, 1674; *kai awegut-ā*, what does he beg? 139; *iā̃ purugul bosell-ā*, is there leave to me? have I leave to depart? 36; *tu puṛṛ bissi-ā*, to thee smallpox became? hast thou smallpox? 1335; *zīm gūss-ā*, has the snow gone, melted? 1589; *kāchī ngālabas-a*, who can take? 1458; *katī less tui-ā*, is the harvest good? 621; *kū winozh-ā*, has anyone beaten thee? 1470.

With the 2nd pers. plur. *aduniyē azzir-ā*, are you well? 1659.

With the 3rd pers. plur. *asht-ā*, are there? 1006; *ess-ā*, are they? 64? *chok sē biss-ā*, how many years have become (to him)? how old is he? 19; *chō manchī-z-ā*, how many men are there? p. 19.

Instead of *ā* we apparently find *ē* or *ī* in *assē*, is? 763, 978; are there? 129; *tōtt kaikotē gos-ī*, why did thy father go? 1685; compare the suffix sh, shī of the 2nd pers. sing.

(2) In disjunctive interrogative sentences the interrogative particle is often added to both verbs; thus:—

With the 2nd pers. sing. *tū gatrā bissish-ā bradzowā ashi-ā*, art thou tired or ill? 1307; *tū kūro manchī aīsh kuchi-ā, ushp-o-sir manchī aīsh kuch-ā*, doest thou want a footman or horseman? 510; *tinj bītī kaṛs-ā parmarshtētī kars-ā*, hast thou done it on purpose or forgetfully? 951.

With the 3rd pers. sing. *wishtrī ass-ā aṛin ass-ā*, is it wide or narrow? 1686; *chakūr assā uchan-gust ass-ā*, is it a gentle slope or a steep slope? 1331; *iā̃st assē warants assē tinch n'bā*, there is no proof: is it mine or another's? I have no proof that it is mine, 1078; *kāno-wā azz-ā giyān azz-ā*, is it shady or devoid of trees? 1713; *tū skillē biss-ā tu ranzol ass-ā*, is there cold or fever to thee? art thou cold or hast thou got fever? 1290; *tarwoch prōr bissizh-ā tapkiē pondrik prōr bissish-ā*, has there become a sword wound or a bullet wound to thee? 1724; *aō parē kaṛs-ā zū parē kaṛs-ā*, has it been filled with water or milk? 544.

With the 1st pers. plur. *sū chunzlī pōr ētimish-ā nai sū puēli pōr ētimish-ā*, are we going sunrise way or sunset way? 402.

With the 3rd pers. plur. *āṛu attī mēsh botasal-ā giṭu kaṛbá botasal-ā*, do peaches come from seed or do they come when one does grafting? 577; *khazonn ngand-a wārē dorē tuch ngand-ā*, do they take treasure or gunpowder and bullets? 1550.

Sometimes the interrogative particle is only added after the first verb; thus, *tū parkī afzōsh-ā tū brá dī afzio*, dost thou go alone or does thy brother also go? 38; *ranzul ass-a shillā biss*, hast thou got fever or cold? 1552.

In other cases the interrogative particle is only added after the last verb; thus, *Chandrāl pōr gwā to Ashrett pōr gūss-ā*, did he go Chitral way or has he gone Ashrett way? 1538; *pēr ēmish īr emish-ā*, shall we go that side or this side? 1305; *dalkiē ētimish attrī ētimish-ā*, shall we go to-morrow or next day? 1030.

In numerous cases, and especially when there is an interrogative pronoun or adverb in the sentence, no interrogative particle is added; compare 38, 51, 80, 150, 177, 227, 234, 270, 278, 291, 309, 362, 369, 389, 408, 420, etc. On the other hand, forms ending in *ā* are frequently used in affirmative sentences; compare *assā* (base *AS*), *bissā* (base *BŪ*), etc. In such cases this particle is perhaps identical with the *ā* which is used as a copula. Compare also *kōrā*, where? 1300.

8 **ā, ai,** is, are. *ā* is used as a copula after an adjective in *digar-ā*, they are bad, 63, p. 19; *ai*, is, are, p. 19; *ai*, is, are, is used as a copula in 116, 253, 368, 391, 425, 471, 486, 502, 514, 529, 572, 622, 639, 938, 1096, 1100, 1151; compare also

bradsw-aio, he is ill, 1236; *bradsow-ai,* he is ill, 589; *tapik-na-w-âi,* gun not having are, they have no guns, 627; *zor-w-ai,* strength having are, they are strong, p. 19; *zūr-w-ai,* strength having are, they are strong, 181; *katī less tuiā,* i.e. probably *lesst-ui-ā,* is the harvest good? 621; *ai* also means is, are existing; thus, 293, 478, 530, 609, 894, 947, 1192; *n'ai,* is not, 427, 428, 485, 570, 706, 845, 868, 1184, 1705, 1721; *nā ai,* is not, 1657; *n'āio,* are not, 969.

4 **ā, ai, ē, ī, o,** a termination of the oblique form added to the infinitive in *sth.* In some cases *ā* is apparently added without modifying the meaning; thus, *akī gusthā kai ōd bā,* what is the use of going there? 10; *ā* and *o* usually denote purpose; thus, *kusthā less,* good for making (a fight), 336; *nizhisthā,* for sitting on, 241, p. 15; *ano peṭasthā,* in order to cut meat, 746; *krujā shisthā,* for cultivating, 310; *yosthā,* for the sake of eating, p. 15; *yusthā,* for the sake of eating, p. 62; *sūī postho,* in order to make a bridge, 465; *ai, ē,* and *ī* are used before postpositions; thus, *jāristhai dugā̃,* in order to kill, 1011; *mishisthai dugā̃,* for playing, 1040; *agal osthē dugā̃,* from the coming of rain, 1401; *achūnisthē dugā̃,* on account of running, 1604; *kusthē dugā̃,* in order to make, 778; *shusthē dugā̃,* in order to sew, 1138; *yusthē dugā̃,* for eating, 1167; *sū garo yaristhē dugā̃,* on account of an eclipse eating the sun, 325; *lunishtī mēsh,* by the falling, p. 15.

1 **ai,** is, are, see 3 **ā.**

2 **ai,** termination of verbal noun, see 4 **ā.**

âo, subst., water; sometimes also written *āo*; nom. *âo,* 412, 533, 534, 912, 1183, 1212, 1227, 1272, 1379, 1418, 1421, 1465, 1506, 1641, 1643, 1645, 1698; *āo,* 755; acc. *âo,* 173, 313, 377, 378, 413, 414, 1067, 1380, 1555, 1642, 1644; *āo,* 1052; *âo para kshi,* water full make, fill it with water, 474; *aō parī kshī,* water full make, fill it with water, 1052; *âo parē karsā,* has water been filled in? 544; oblique *âo mish,* with water, 1442, 1561; *āo mish,* with water, 874; *âo p'mich,* in the water, in the river, 284, 1227 (*p'mich*); *âo tā̃,* in water, 1321, 1636; *âo tā̃ ī̃r,* this side the water, 1305; *âo tã pãr*, yonder side the water, across the river, 1702; *âo tã pẽr*, yonder side the water, across the river, 1305; *âo tã p'mich*, into the water, 1316; *âo tawarẽ*, near the water, on the bank of the river, 116.

gol âo, nullah water, river, 500, 728 (nom.); *golo āo*, nullah water, river, 518.

âo-duk, a well, 1657.

âo kūsth, to make water, urinate, 1592.

âo-matsa, a fish of the water, a fish, 488, 1451 (*matsī*).

âo pig, thirsty, 377, 866, 1041; *âo pik*, thirsty, 1496.

âo-tre, a ford, 518 (acc.).

âo-tr-mir, an inflated skin for crossing a river; *âotrmir mēsh*, by means of such a skin, 1452 (*mish*), 1702, 1704; *âotarmir mīsh*, by means of such a skin, 1321.

1 **Ē**, to go, see 1 **I**.

2 **ē**, termination of verbal noun, see 4 **ā**.

3 **ē, eo, yō, yu**, numeral, one, p. 63; the form *ē* is used as a numeral, one, 205, 219, 327, 537, 590, 673, 677, 793, 794, 815, 846, 907, 934, 956, 957, 1063, 1077, 1136, 1149, 1158, 1164, 1175, 1209, 1210, 1214, 1282, 1285, 1286, 1352, 1355, 1474, 1477, 1619, 1693, 1717, pp. 3, 11, 63, 64; in many cases it can be translated as an indefinite article; thus, 121, 283, 287, 365, 379, 501, 613, 648, 683, 712, 797, 829, 1014, 1069, 1216, 1222, 1225, 1258, 1294, 1467, 1566.

ē brobar, one like, the same, 1282.

ē chillai, one half, 607.

ē dī, one even, 645, 875, 914, 1040, 1112, 1183, 1184, 1187, 1253, 1309, 1439, 1482, 1551, 1657, 1690.

ē pōr, ē pur, one way, one direction; *ē pur butta tã*, one way becoming at, at the junction (of two rivers), 728; *dū ē pōr*, two one way, twofold, p. 64; *duts ē pōr*, tenfold, p. 64.

ē purstha, one kind, alike, 1151.

ē var, another, 50.

ē wōr, at one time, once, 954, p. 60; together, 1529, p. 60.

ē yōr, one like, exactly alike, 808.

eo, one, is used as a numeral, 42, 255, 473 (one and the same, alike), 578, 845, 1144, p. 63; *eo dī*, one even, 427, 538, 719, 823, 1133; *eo gujrē̃*, in one day, each day, 327, 1056, 1061, pp. 5, 60; in *eo naṛgī*, each separately, one at a time, 1718, *eo* seems to mean one each, each, cf. Sanskrit *ēkaika*. In this sense the forms *yo*, *yō*, *yu* are commonly used; thus, *yo chok prē*, each bit give, give each (coolie) one portion, 1049; *yo kūrē*, each separately, one by one, pp. 14, 64 (*yō kūrē*); *yu kūrē*, each separately, one by one, 953; *yo narē*, one each, p. 14; *yō narī kutt*, one tower each, 1609; *yō narik*, each separately, one by one, p. 64; *yo nirikē̃*, each separately, one by one, 1235 (*niṛikē*), p. 60; *yō do-dun*, each two-two, two by two, p. 64; *yō trā-trē*, three by three, p. 64; *yō cha-s̲h̲ton*, four by four, p. 64.

eo. one, see 3 **ē**.

1 **I**, to go; this base is often used as an auxiliary with other verbs, especially in order to form a kind of passive. *I* is then sometimes added to the past participle passive; thus, *shá jāra elār*, you will be killed, p. 59; *angā yassa ettā*, the fire is extinguished, 1142. In other cases *I* is added to a participle or verbal noun ending in *n*; thus, *waṛon enn*, he is seen, he appears, 1607; *waṛon ett*, he is seen, is visible, 1180, 1434; *waṛon ettā*, he is seen, is visible, 1212; *waṛon end*, they are visible, 1392; *peṭang ellā*, will be broken, p. 59, should probably be corrected to *peṭan gellā*, see **GŪ**; most forms of *LUSHT*, to be frost-bitten, are apparently formed by adding *I* or *GŪ*.

The following forms of the base *I* occur in the sentences:—

Infinitive, *ē̃sth*, to go, 1031, 1355, 1382, 1629, p. 22; *esth*, to go, p. 22; *ēsth*, to go, 1092; *ptiwar esth*, to go behind, to cross, 1023; *sū pū esth pōr*, sun behind going direction, sunset way, west, 1663, p. 65 (*pu-esth*).

Verbal noun, *ē*, to go; *ē na bam*, we cannot go, 639; similarly, 907, 1054, 1174, 1483, 1704; with *banam*, I can, we also find *iam*; thus, *n'iam banam*, I cannot go, p. 58; *n'ai iam banam*,

I cannot go, 263 (but *ē n'banam*, 1704); in *en n'battam*, I cannot go, 674, p. 58, *en* is used instead; *en, ien*, going, is also used before the postposition *dā, tā*; thus, *ī en dā* (*tā*), I going in, at the time of my going, p. 17; *ien-dā, ien-tā*, at the time of going, 1057.

Present participle, *ēl*, going; *sū pu-ēlī*, sun behind going, sunset, p. 65; *sū pu-ēlī pōr*, sunset way, west, 402 (*puēli*), 403, p. 65; *ōts ba-dō eila bim-bā*, I on-hill going become-if, if I climb the hill, 952; *ettan*, going; *sū pū-ettann pōr*, sun down going way, west, 1662; *sū pu-ettan pōr*, sun down going way, west, p. 65.

Indefinite present 1st pers. sing. *n'aim*, I shall not go, 1119.

2nd pers. sing. *tū n'ai*, if thou dost not go, 1704; *izhībā*, thou mayest go, 1157.

1st pers. plur. *ēmā*, we shall go, 398, 403, 714, 785, 1092, 1324, 1370, 1498, 1530, 1588, 1618, 1648, 1702, p. 22; *ēmish*, we go, p. 22; we shall go, 16, 32, 562, 1305, p. 22.

2nd pers. plur. *ēr*, you go, you will go, p. 22.

Present 1st pers. sing. *anam*, I shall go, 1249; I go, p. 22; *n'annam*, I cannot go, 1301; *ennam*, I am about to go, 1524; I will go, 1625; I can go, 1704; I go, p. 22; *n'ennam*, I cannot go, 1704; *na ennam*, I won't go, 1582; *ennom*, I will go, 1162.

2nd pers. sing. *n'anjī*, dost not go, 952; *enjā*, wilt go, p. 22; *ēnjā*, art thou going? 1132; *ēnjī*, goest, wilt go, 1134, p. 22; *so enjī*, farewell, 1162, p. 63; *enjī-bā*, if goest, 702, 1582.

3rd pers. sing. *ann*, goes, p. 22; *enn*, goes, 491, 1607, p. 22; *ennā*, will go, p. 22.

3rd pers. plur. *end*, go, 981, 1125, 1392, p. 22; *enda*, they will go, 563; *tīnch n'ess korē enda-bā*, there is no knowing where they may go, 1125.

Second present 1st pers. sing. *aietam*, I go, p. 22; *n'aietam*, I do not go, 40; *aiētum*, I am going, 180; *aīetum*, I intend to go, 327; *ettam*, I am going, 922, p. 22.

2nd pers. sing. *ētish*, goest, p. 22; wilt go, 439, 1134; *ettishīā*, art thou going? 1132, p. 17.

3rd pers. sing. *ett*, goes, 298; *waṛon ett*, is visible, 1180, 1434; *na zhi ett* (read *nazhi ett*), is spoiled, 1522; *waṛon ettā*, is visible, 1212; *yassa ettā*, gets extinguished, 1142; *gūrūm ettā*, cock crow goes, dawn, p. 64; *kōr etta-bá*, they go somewhere, 1244; *n'aiett* (read perhaps *nai ett*), does not go, 911; *pshutī n'yett*, sleeping not goes, he cannot sleep, 928; *ettett*, he goes, p. 22.

1st pers. plur. *ētimish*, we are going, we shall go, 1030, p. 22; *ētimish-ā*, shall we go? 402, 1030.

3rd pers. plur. *ettett*, they go, 374, 573, 965, p. 22; *p'ochen ettett*, they go to eyes, come to light, 890; *etassal*, they may be going, 890; *ettessel*, they go, p. 22.

Imperfect 1st pers. sing. *enazzam*, I was going, 1208; *ēnazzam*, I was going, p. 22.

2nd pers. sing. *ēnazzish*, thou wast going, p. 22.

3rd pers. sing. *ēnazzī*, he was going, p. 22.

1st pers. plur. *ēnazzamish*, we were going, p. 22.

2nd pers. plur. *ēnazzār*, you were going, p. 22.

3rd pers. plur. *ēnazzī*, they were going, p. 22.

Future 1st pers. sing. *ēlam*, I shall go, p. 22; *ēlom*, I shall go, 37 (I am off), 40 (I go), 329, 560, 702, 753, 923, 1003, 1120, 1278, 1619, p. 22; *ne ēlom*, I won't go, 47.

2nd pers. sing. *ēlosh*, thou wilt go, 561, 863, 1181, 1531, p. 22.

3rd pers. sing. *allon*, he will go, p. 22; *ushp ailī*, a horse will go, 788; *ēlā*, he will go, p. 22; *ellā*, he will go, p. 22; *peṭang ellā*, it will be broken, p. 59; read probably *peṭan gellā*.

2nd pers. plur. *elār*, you will go, p. 59 (read *elãr*).

3rd pers. plur. *allā*, they will go, p. 22; *ellā*, they will go, 1270, p. 22.

Imperative 2nd pers. sing. *ī*, go, 564, 974, 1085, 1202, 1256, 1332, 1539, 1563, 1671, p. 23; *ĩ*, go, 1181, 1476; *iē*, go, p. 23; *īē*, go away, 646; *n'ai*, don't go, 158, 324, 407, 440, 542, 1107, 1137, 1410, 1462, 1476, 1525; *na ī*, don't go, 1410; *n'iyē*, don't go, 261, 355.

3rd pers. sing. *ellā*, let him go, p. 23.

1st pers. plur. *ēmá*, let us go, 340 (*emá*), p. 23; *ūm*, let us go, 262, p. 23; cf. 1 **Ū**.

2nd pers. plur. *iēr*, go ye, p. 23.

3rd pers. plur. *ellā*, let them go, 565, p. 23.

Other tenses are formed from the base *GŪ*. Compare also 1 **Ā**. The initial *a* of some of the forms registered above is perhaps due to a confusion with this base.

2 **ī**, suffix, my; occasionally added to nouns; thus, *akl-ī*, my chin, 252; *akilatt-ī*, my jaw, 723; *jū-ī*, my daughter, 194; *sha-ī*, my head, p. 12; *tōtt-ī*, my father, p. 11; my uncle's, 293; *tōtt-i*, my father's, 545, 605; *tōtt-i-a*, to my father, 24; *tōtt-i-o*, to my father, 749.

3 **ī**, termination added to the infinitive, see 4 **ā**.

1 **ī, iā, īo**, pronoun, this, he; *īo tarāzho*, drive it out, 379; *īo*, his, p. 11; *iā-dugá*, therefore, 849; *iā dugā*, therefore, 314, 399; often used with nouns, thus, *iā krūī*, this dog, 1378; *iā postao*, this on hearth, on the hearth, 636; *ī poshtrē*, on the hill, 499; plural *am*, these; *am bazisná*, these clothes, 476; cf. **iyi**.

2 **ī, iā, o**, pronoun, I; several different forms are in use; the nasalization is often dropped, perhaps owing to the breaking off in the press of the sign of nasalization. The following forms occur in the sentences:—

Nom. *ī*, I, p. 10; *ī*, I, 469, 1029, 1301, 1472, pp. 12, 17; *iā*, I, p. 10; *iá*, I, 46, 495, 866, 939, 1091, 1111, 1143, 1320, 1486, pp. 10, 13; *o*, I, 699, 1106, 1370 (read *starak shá o anī wisilom*), 1495, 1740; *ō*, I, p. 4; *ō*, I, 531, 593; *ó*, I, 143, 300, 367, 401, 452, 591, 617, 619, 702, 731, 738, 750, 775, 776, 828, 839, 916, 968, 983, 984, 987, 1012, 1037, 1080, 1093, 1101, 1105, 1115, 1121, 1122, 1137, 1143, 1144, 1149, 1173, 1179, 1181, 1203, 1212, 1246, 1249, 1254, 1257, 1276, 1281, 1313, 1323, 1326, 1335, 1375, 1425, 1437, 1441, 1582, 1615, 1736, pp. 4, 10; *óst*, I, 1523 (probably misprint for *ōts*); *ots*, I, 57, 83, 100, 201, 263, 656, 814, 1042, 1109, 1140, 1210, 1219, 1252, 1297, 1301, p. 10; *ōts*, I, 187,

244, 1065, 1513, pp. 10, 59; *ôts*, I, 526, 539, 582, 803, 952, 1451, 1606; *ỗts*, I, 40, 44, 84, 132, 138, 185, 281, 391. 456, 459, 555, 560, 665, 690, 704, 709, 751, 852, 975, 1013, 1015, 1061, 1153, 1171, 1172, 1208, 1235, 1260, 1273, 1293, 1303, 1328, 1332, 1361, 1395, 1413, 1422, 1444, 1477, 1496, 1524, 1532, 1540, 1547, 1558, 1574, 1594, 1625, 1660, 1693, 1695, 1704, 1729, pp. 10, 13, 17.

Case of the agent, *ī*, I, 1271; *ī̃*, I, 205, 794, 841, 932, 1255, 1312, 1327, pp. 4, 10, 11; *iā*, I, 1246; *iā̃*, I, 86, 347, 385, 420, 466, 556, 783, 833, 873, 921, 969, 1126, 1149, 1252, 1579, 1644, p. 11; *o*, I, 52, 1253; *ō̃*, I, 52; *ots*, I, 614, 711, 1725; *ōts*, I, 1619; *ō̃ts*, I, 85, 516, 1091, 1234, 1570, 1620, pp. 3, 11.

Accusative (case of direct object), *ī*, me, 459, p. 10; *ī̃*, me, 652, 1467, p. 13; *iā̃*, me, 83, 630, 738, 881, 941, 1093, 1105, 1608, p. 10; *ō̃*, me, p. 10; *ōts*, me, p. 12; *ō̃ts*, me, 1169, 1671, pp. 10, 12.

Dative (case of indirect object), *ī*, me, to me, 1278; *ī̃*, me, to me, 185, 518, 841, 1163, 1300, 1301, 1481; *iā*, me, to me, 731; *iā̃*, me, to me, 84, 678, 679, 812, 822, 1003, 1010, 1264, p. 11; *ō*, me, to me, 794; *ō̃ts*, me, to me, pp. 11, 12; these forms are often used with verbs meaning 'to be', thus, *ī̃ non angur ai*, to me nine fingers are, I have nine fingers, 478; similarly, *iā*, to me, 957; *iā̃*, to me, 36, 120, 530, 589, 739, 749, 792, 830, 921, 1140, 1285, p. 58; *iā̃st*, to me, 1025, 1293.

Genitive; the same forms are used with all genders, numbers, and cases; before a noun in the nominative or accusative we find *ī*, my, 175, 436; *i*, my, 1090, p. 10; *ī̃*, my, 547, 602, 1334, p. 10; *iā*, my, 48, 295, 593, 663, 716, 726, 754, 773, 973, 1314; *iā̃*, my, 1545; *iā̃*, my, 8, 12, 20, 21, 25, 28, 31, 39, 48, 49, 66, 100, 102, 103, 110, 123, 148, 169, 186, 188, 194, 212, 223, 225, 242, 248, 249, 250, 254, 267, 269, 283, 288, 300, 315, 319, 352, 354, 361, 391, 428, 431, 444, 446, 451, 454, 486, 508, 509, 550, 567, 585, 588, 595, 599, 659, 661, 665, 685, 737, 748, 759, 760, 809, 811, 816, 821, 831, 836, 849, 850, 856, 859, 916, 943, 960, 961, 977, 980, 984, 1004, 1017, 1038, 1075, 1076, 1095, 1098, 1113, 1116, 1122.

1128, 1133, 1152, 1164, 1165, 1190, 1199, 1213, 1218, 1289, 1296, 1317, 1318, 1341, 1342, 1358, 1398, 1426, 1427, 1446, 1450, 1451, 1454, 1459, 1460, 1493, 1577, 1637, 1691, 1742, pp. 2, 3, 10, 59; *iãs*, my, 504; *iā̃s*, my, 45, 50, 147, 1009, 1528, 1622; *iãsī*, my, 612, 624; *iā̃si*, my, 462; *iāsī*, my, 204; *iā̃sī*, my, 202, 206, 317, 351, 468, 622, 703, 765, 1255, 1703; *iā̃st*, my, 308, 330, 455, 456, 461, 503, 529, 536, 596, 616, 696, 1567; *iāst*, my, 797; *iā̃st*, my, 72, 270, 301, 331, 371, 377, 381, 383, 396, 411, 597, 598, 604, 706, 744, 791, 817, 860, 870, 884, 895, 1078, 1081, 1084, 1087, 1144, 1173, 1190, 1194, 1203, 1246, 1248, 1251, 1261, 1263, 1276, 1280, 1291, 1295, 1306, 1322, 1328, 1346, 1359, 1393, 1396, 1400, 1417, 1420, 1444, 1469, 1471, 1489, 1491, 1504, 1535, 1573, 1591, 1621, 1628, 1679, 1699, 1706, 1709, 1728, pp. 3, 12; *iā̃'st*, my, p. 10; *ĩsta*, my, pp. 3, 4, 8, 10.

Before nouns in oblique cases, governed by postpositions, we find *i*, my, 676; *ī*, my, 772; *ĩ*, my, 925, 1230, 1343; *iã*, my, 307, 635, 687, 826, 962; *iẵ*, my, 505, 1551; *iā̃*, my, 24, 157, 184, 193, 198, 240, 245, 251, 289, 290, 326, 349, 432, 433, 445, 545, 553, 566, 576, 580, 581, 585, 601, 615, 629, 631, 640, 662, 672, 674, 691, 743, 804, 830, 844, 845, 871, 896, 911, 918, 935, 976, 996, 1033, 1076, 1094, 1104, 1112, 1115, 1123, 1138, 1148, 1157, 1191, 1196, 1198, 1204, 1222, 1241, 1297, 1464, 1501, 1615, 1680, p. 9; *ĩā̃*, my, 1622; in *inā p'amū*, at my house, 70, 71, 237, 958, *inā* seems to be developed from *iā̃*; *iãs*, my, 505; *iā̃s*, my, 1507; *iā̃sī*, my, 189; *iăst*, my, 473, 512, 613, 641, 902; *iāst*, my, 736, 1339, 1562, 1720; *iā̃st*, my, 67, 68, 379, 584, 706, 736, 899, 1012, 1185, 1237, 1260, 1261, 1329, 1386, 1399, 1403, 1405, 1445, 1447, 1449, 1455, 1457, 1481, 1506, 1514, 1576, 1578, 1627, 1638, 1657, 1694, 1722; *ots*, my, 1292.

Oblique case, before postpositions, *iã dugĕ*, for me, for my sake, 514; *iã dugẵ*, for me, for my sake, 200; *iā̃ dugā*, for me, for my sake, 1320, 1735; *iā̃ dugã*, for me, for my sake, 211, 314, 316, 320, 359, 422; *iā̃ dugā̃*, for me, for my sake, 307, 987, 995, 1043, 1082, 1216, 1286, 1484, 1636, 1696, 1729; *iā̃ dugĕ*, for me, for my sake, 119, 558, 575; *iā dugē*, for me, for my sake, 160, 733; *iāst dugā*, for me, for my sake, 1511, 1669, p. 11.

ī-gē, for me, p. 3.

ī mēsh, with me, 703; *iā mēsh*, to me, 644, 1702; from me, p. 10.

ī purstha, like me, 1174.

iā ptiōr, after me, 14; *iā ptiora*, behind me, 141; *iā tā*, to me (indirect object), 524, 905, 906, 1077, 1471, 1474, 1542, pp. 10, 11, 12; *iā tā*, to me, me (direct object), 89, 933, 1169; *iā tā*, to me, for me (dativus commodi), 104, 130, 671, 1336, 1508; *iā tā kai n'asht*, to me nothing is, I have nothing, 933; similarly, *iā tā*, to me (is, I have), 1116, 1423; *iā tā*, to me, 415; near me, 911; with me, 1101, 1553, 1667.

iā, iā, iā, I, see 2 **ī.**

iā, this; **īo,** him, his, see 1 **ī.**

1 **o,** termination added to the infinitive, see 4 **ā.**

2 **o,** up, out, see 2 **ū.**

3 **o, ō, ō, ō,** I, see 2 **ī.**

1 **Ū,** to go up, to climb; *ba-dō ū n'bann*, he cannot climb on the hill, 1397; *ūm*, we will climb, 262; cf. 1 **I** and **UWE.**

2 **ū,** adv., out; *dusht ū kshī*, hand out make, show your hand, 1308; *achē o-ksh*, show thy eye, 434; *u-kshosth dugā*, in order to drag out, 1008, 1098; *padrē ū prētt*, the bowels (?) go out, there is diarrhœa, 349, 350; *pīsh ū osthai*, the flowers have come out, 1614; see 1 **wā.**

ābâd, adj., cultivated; *bhīm ābâd assett*, is the land cultivated? 762.

ublindī, adj., big, high; *bās ublindī enn*, the flames go high, 491.

abas, adj., useless; *kudūm abas azzā*, the work is useless, 1595.

absiss, there is a boil, 491; see **APS.**

achē, subst., an eye; nom. sing. *achiē*, eye, 432; acc. sing. *achē*, eye, 434; nom. plur. *achiē*, eyes, 980, 1346; oblique, *p'ochen ettett*, they go to-eyes, they have become visible, 890; *tū achē tā*, in thy eyes, 1470; *achē vrē*, with the eyes, 667; *achē warē*, with the eyes, 1579, 1624; *achēn warē*, with the eyes, 1126.

achē̃-ktelik, an eyelid, 434.

achē̃-paṭṭā, an eyebrow, 433.

1 **achu,** subst., a tear, 1470 (nom. plur.).

2 **achu,** adj. (?), good (?); *tū achu kalom*, I shall make thee well (?), I shall give thee a back, 107, 457.

UCHA, to raise, to pitch.

Infinitive, *uchasth*, to pitch (tents), 893, 1019 (*uc͟hasth*), 1713 (*uc͟hasth*); *assalā́ uchasth dugā́*, in order to raise, bring out, the poppinjay, 1047; *uchaiesth*, to pitch (a tent), 594.

Passive participle, *uchangust*, raised-gone, high, steep, 1331 (pred.); *uchangiest*, steep, 1397; cf. **OS͟HT.**

achok, adj., (1) some, a little, p. 14; used as an attribute; thus, 156, 320, 734, 812, 1010, 1065, 1135, 1225; as a predicate; thus, 1697; and as an adverb, somewhat, a little, 1143, 1480, 1523 (*ac͟hok*), p. 61.

(2) Little, not much, 796, 811; used as a predicate, 391; as an adverb, to a small extent, p. 61; *achok*, few, not many, 470 (attribute); 416, 417, 938 (predicate); *achok wokta*, few times, rarely, 1124, p. 60.

Instead of *achok* we also find *chok*; thus, *chok brē*, some flour, 1353; *yo chok prē*, give each a little, 1049.

ACHŪN, to run; the following forms occur in the sentences:—

Infinitive, *achūnasth*, to run, pp. 18, 36; *achūnisthē̃ dugā́*, on account of the running, 1604.

Verbal noun, *achūn na banam*, I cannot run, 1208; *ac͟hūn na banch*, thou canst not run, 1534; *achūn na banj*, thou canst not run, p. 58; the base is identical with this verbal noun, p. 18.

Conjunctive participle, *achūnam*, running, quickly, fast, soon, 337, 1107, pp. 18, 36, 60; *achūndī*, having run, pp. 18, 36.

Indefinite present 1st pers. sing. *achūnam*, I run, pp. 18, 36; *achūnambā́*, if I run, pp. 18, 37.

2nd pers. sing. *achūnas͟hbā́*, if thou runnest, p. 37.

3rd pers. sing. *achūnabā́*, if he runs, p. 37.

1st pers. plur. *achūnamish*, we run, p. 36; *achūnamishbá*, if we run, p. 37.

2nd pers. plur. *achũr*, you run, p. 36; *achũrbá*, if you run, p. 37.

3rd pers. plur. *achūnabá*, if they run, p. 37.

Present 2nd pers. sing. *achūnanj*, thou runnest, p. 36.

3rd pers. sing. *achunann*, he runs, p. 36.

Imperfect 1st pers. sing. *achūnazzam*, I was running, pp. 18, 36.

2nd pers. sing. *achūnazzish*, thou wast running, p. 36.

3rd pers. sing. *achūnazzī*, he was running, p. 36.

1st pers. plur. *achūnazzamish*, we were running, p. 36.

2nd pers. plur. *achūnazzãr*, you were running, p. 36.

3rd pers. plur. *achūnazzī*, they were running, p. 36.

Past, *achūniā*, ran, p. 18.

1st pers. sing. *achūniā'm* (?), I ran, p. 36.

2nd pers. sing. *achūniā'sh* (?), thou rannest, p. 36.

3rd pers. sing. *achūniā* (?), he ran, p. 36.

1st pers. plur. *achūniāmish*, we ran, p. 36.

2nd pers. plur. *achūniãr*, you ran, p. 36.

3rd pers. plur. *achūniā*, they ran, p. 36.

Perfect and pluperfect, 1st pers. sing. *achūnissam*, I have run, 1496; I had run, p. 36; *achūnissum*, I had run, p. 18.

2nd pers. sing. *achūnissish*, thou hadst run, p. 36.

3rd pers. sing. *achūnissī*, he had run, p. 36.

1st pers. plur. *achūnissamish*, we had run, p. 36.

2nd pers. plur. *achūnissãr*, you had run, p. 36.

3rd pers. plur. *achūnissī*, they had run, p. 36.

Future 1st pers. sing. *achūnlom*, I shall run, pp. 18, 36.

2nd pers. sing. *achūnlosh*, thou wilt run, p. 36.

3rd pers. sing. *achūnlā*, he will run, p. 36.

1st pers. plur. *achūnlammá*, we shall run, p. 36.

2nd pers. plur. *achūnlṛ* (sic), you will run, p. 36.

3rd pers. plur. *achūnlā*, they will run, p. 36.

Imperative 2nd pers. sing. *achūnō*, run, pp. 18, 37.

3rd pers. sing. *achūnlā*, let him run, p. 37.

1st pers. plur. *achūnlammá*, let us run, p. 37.

2nd pers. plur. *achūnlār*, run ye, p. 37.

3rd pers. plur. *achūnlā*, let them run, p. 37.

ochen, eyes, see **achē.**

uchangust, uchangiest, steep, see **UCHA.**

uchpo, uchpu, adv., up and down, forwards and backwards, hither and thither; *ushp amu uchpo afzett*, the horse is going hither and thither (loose) in the stable, 633; *ushp uchpu palangett*, the horse is rolling (on the ground) from side to side, 393.

uchar, adj., emptied, poured out; *áo uchar kusth*, to make the water emptied, to empty the water out, 413, 414.

achutt, adv., the second day after to-morrow, 1530, p. 60 (translated 'two days hence').

adu, adj. (?), well, in good health, proper; occurs in the following compounds:—

adu-gē assum, I am well (in good health), 767.

adu-gosā, he has gone right, *shtār ess adu-gosā tinch n'ess*, there is no certainty, is he a thief or has he gone all right? I have a doubt whether or not he is a thief, 343.

aduniyē, well; *aduniyē azzirā*, are you well? 1659; *aduniyē ashā? ō aduniyē assum*, art thou well? I am well, 1736.

ōd, ūd, use, profit, see **ōt.**

adugē, adugosā, well, all right, see **adu.**

odh, adj., merciful; *odh bō*, be merciful, 863.

áoduk, subst., a well, 1657, see **áo.**

aduniyē, well, see **adu.**

adap, subst., respect; *adap kund*, they respect him, 1154.

1 **adr, aḍr,** subst., a box; nom. *adr*, 188; *aḍr*, 960; acc. *adr*, 1591; *aḍr*, 961; *adrē*, 186, 733; gen. *adrē*, 736; oblique, *adrē tā atēr*, inside the box, 713; nom. plur. *adar*, boxes, 1201.

2 **aḍr,** adj., yellow, pale; *aḍr rang*, yellow-coloured, 1378; *miok aḍrā biss*, (thy) face is pale, 983.

uḍeṛl, subst., thundering, 807 (acc.); compare **wodaranchut.**

adsā, he has come, see **ATS.**

odsī, came, went, see **ATS.**

edsam, I am, see **AS.**

adzum, I am, see **AS.**

AFZ, to come. The few forms of this base perhaps belong to 1 *Ā*; cf. *awettett,* he is coming, etc. The following forms occur:—

Present time. 3rd pers. sing. *afziā,* it comes, it will come, p. 58; *ão be afziā,* water out comes, leaks out, 412; *ão bilugh afziā,* water much comes, the river is in flood, 500; *gun afziā,* smell comes (to me), I smell, 1001; *as͟hpā afziā,* perspiration comes, he is in perspiration, 1004; *zīm afziā,* snow comes, it snows, 1147; *z͟huk Peshâr stē afziā,* the salt comes from Peshawar, 1223. This form is perhaps also used as a plural; thus, *bāghrē lē afziā,* owls many·came, owls are numerous, 976. Another form is *afzio,* he will go, 38, 39, p. 22. A present definite is *afsett,* he is going, 633.

Past time. The same and similar forms are also used in the past tenses.

2nd pers. sing. *ạfzōs͟hā,* didst thou come? 38.

3rd pers. sing. *afziā,* he came, p. 58; *bru afziā,* indigestion came, it has not been digested, 356; *afzio,* he has come, 88.

3rd pers. plur. *afziā,* they have come, 75, p. 58; *vōtt lē afziā,* stones many came, many avalanches fell, 96; *diz͟ho dom tittī afziā,* goats herding have come, a flock of goats has come, 499.

igē, igē̃, igiē̃, that, he, see 1 **akī.**

īgē̃, for me, see 2 **ī.**

ūgh, subst., water, 909. This is a Khōwār word. It also occurs in *golog͟h* or *golūg͟h,* water of a river, 1182.

aoghān, adj., Afghan, 150. Usually *aog͟hānī,* 63, 69, or *aog͟hānī,* 108, 552, 625, 669, 710, 1430. This latter form is also used as a noun, 995, p. 3.

egiak, so many, 1717, see **ajik.**

igiak, this much, p. 61, see **ajik.**

agal, agol, subst., rain. The usual form is *agal*, 1002, 1117, 1118, 1119, 1120, 1121, 1166, 1401, 1527. It only occurs in the nominative. The form *agol* is used in the nominative, 268, 302, 401, and before a postposition, *agol tā*, from, on account of, rain, 239. Various verbs are used with this word; thus several forms of the base *Ā*, to come (*ann*, 1527; *allon*, 1121; *onzībā*, 1166; *osthē*, 1401); the forms *bōlan* (268) and *bibā* (1119, 1120) of the base *BŪ*, to become, further *prētt*, comes (302, 1117); *ptā*, came (441); *prēlā*, will come (1002); and *pittabā*, if falls (1118).

agar, subst., Friday; the Sabbath or day of rest, 1215, p. 65.

agūr, adj. (?), like to, p. 61; *agyūr*, like to, pp. 9, 61 · also written *ayūr* and *yōr*; thus, *iwrakī ayūr*, fox-like, cunning, 312, p. 9 (*wrikī*); *ē yōr asht*, they are one like, exactly alike, 808.

ugrē, subst., a beam, 1085 (acc.); see **argru.**

ugrām, subst., step, stair, 1399 (acc. plur.).

agyūr, like, see **agūr.**

ajē, ojē, je, jē, conjunction, and; *ajē*. 1277; *ojē*, 643, 647, 1464; *je*, 576, 1293, 1310, 1640; *jē*, p. 62.

AJHO, to whisper:—

Future 1st pers. sing. *ajholam*, I shall whisper, 649 (perhaps 'I shall throw the word into thy ear', cf. **ASH**).

ajik, adj., so much, 789, 796; so many, p. 14; also used as an adverb, like this, p. 61; different forms of the same word are *egiak*, so many, 1717; *igiak*, so much, p. 61; *azhik*, so much, 79, p. 14; so many, 674, p. 61.

ajistuk, adj., so big; *ajistuk āl argru*, such a big log, 815, *azhisto*, so big, 435; so much, p. 61.

ajissi, I have sown; *ajissā*, hast thou sown? See **ASH.**

i **akī, ika, iki, ikīā, ikīē,** pronoun, he, that. The remote demonstrative pronoun is formed by adding *ki*, or sometimes *gi*, to *a* or *i*. There does not seem to be any difference whether *a* or *i* is used. The plural is formed by adding *ki* to *am*. The following forms occur:—

Nom. sing. *akī*, he, that, pp. 10, 11; *ika*, he; *ika winagan ungalazī*, he would have been beaten, p. 59; *ikī*, he, 506; *ikī shtī*, that cliff, 261; *ikī purdik*, that old woman, 1708; *ikī jugūr*, that woman, 1707; *ikia*, he, that, p. 11; *ikīa*, he, p. 13; *ikīā*, he, that, 1, 1333, 1374, 1683, 1731, pp. 10, 11; *ikya*, he, that, p. 11; *ikīā argrū*, that beam, 127; *ikīā aṛūnī gol*, that defile, 336, 574 (translated 'this'); *ikīā ashṭar*, the hill, 1331; *ikīā ushp*, that horse, 1666, 1689; *ikīā ushtiwā*, that precipice, 1062; *ikīā dō*, that mountain, 655; *ikīā dāo*, that stick, 1499; *ikīā gōl*, that valley, 1598; *ikīā jugūr*, that woman, 1688; *ikīā kachwach*, the fruit, 1448; *ikīā kutt*, the tower, 1575; *ikīā manchī*, that man, he, 97, 139, 140, 226, 312, 345, 359, 372, 498, 571, 689, 705, 1087 (*ikīā manjī*, this man), 1089, 1251, 1368, 1390, 1462, 1472; *ikīā marangats*, that bird, 133; *ikīā maṛiṛ*, that boy, 309 (*ikyā*), 583, 1389 (*ikiā*); *ikīā nizhā*, that wood, 1711; *ikīā purdik*, that old woman, 1654; *ikīā parmen*, that child, 529; *ikīā tol*, that cauldron, 412; *ikīā wāo mushtar*, that hunchbacked man, 692; *ikīē*, he, that; *ikīē manchī*, that man, he, 1313.

Acc. sing. *akī*, him, that, p. 10; *ikī*, him, p. 12; it, 1513; *ikīā*, him, 1087, 1156; that, it, 859, 860, 1454; *ikīā drun tapē*, that pistol, 1016; *ikīā kudūm*, that work, 1597; *ikīā manchī*, that man, him, 537, 1412; *ikīā mārоī*, that stick, 1508; *ikīā mṛishta*, that corpse, 216; *ikīā pīsh*, that flower, 1735; *ikīā shtan*, that stick, 215; *ikiē*, him, p. 15; *ikiē*, it, 1303; *ikīē*, him, 1089, 1326, 1398, 1549, pp. 12, 13; *ikīē*, it, 858, 1556, 1561; *ikīē manchī*, that man, him, 1246; *ikyē*, it, 1221; *ikīō*, it, 826.

Case of the agent, sing. *akī-ē*, by him, by that, p. 11; *ikī*, he, by him, p. 12; *ikīā manchī*, that man (agent), 768; *ikīā maṛiṛ*, that boy (agent), 1408, 1469; *ikīē*, by him, p. 12.

Dat. sing. *akīyē*, to him, to that, p. 11; *ikī*, to him, 556, p. 12; *ikiē*, to him, 1009; *ikīē*, to him, 1333, 1393, p. 12; *ikīē zān biss*, to her damage became, she is hurt, 1281; *ikīō*, to him, 1014.

Gen. sing. *akīo*, of him, of that, p. 11; *igē*, of that; *igē karē pa ptī*, on the back of that donkey, 370; *igiē*, his, 661; *ikī*, his, 12, 1334, p. 11; *ikī mṛi<u>sh</u>t krūī*, of that dead dog, p. 14; *iki <u>sh</u>tom*, of that tree, 179; *ikīā*, his, 143; *ī ikīā tīch na bunn*, to-me of-him certainty not is, I do not believe him, 1472; *ikīā ano*, of that meat, 1145; *ikīā brē*, of the flour, 1278; *ikīā kāna*, of that tree, 616, 1193 (*kāno*); *ikīā manchī*, of that man, 11, 161, 473; *ikīē*, his, 1303, 1408; *ikīē*, of that, its, 1283; *ikyē*, his, 1239; *ikyē u<u>sh</u>pē la<u>zh</u>om*, that horse's bridle, 231; *ikiēst*, his; *ikiēst basnā tā*, in his clothes, 1412; *ikīost*, his, of that, p. 11; *ikīost puṭriness*, his sons, 1398; *ikio'st gun*, the smell of it, 1195.

Almost all these forms are also used as oblique cases before postpositions, adverbs, etc., both as nouns and as adjectives. When *akīā*, *ikīā*, that, qualifies a word ending in *m* it often likewise takes the same termination; thus, *ikiam bagrām*, in that village, 1163; cf. p. 11.

In some cases no postposition is added; thus, *akīō bhīmā*, in that ground, there on the ground, 803; *akī pōr*, that way, in that direction, 1331 (on yonder side, on the far side), 1647, 1648, p. 61; *akīā pōr*, that way, 1476; *ikyē pāṛ*, in that ravine, 1126; *ikīā psōn*, in this (?) forest, 825. No postposition is, further, added when *pristha*, *pursth*, like, equal, follows; thus, *ikīā argru pristha*, like this beam, 422; *ikyē basnā pursth*, like this cloth, 1225.

The following prepositions and postpositions occur in connexion with the singular forms of this pronoun :—

ba, *b*, *p*, in; *ikīā ba-do*, on that hill, 125; *ikiā ba-grām*, in that village, 1163; *ikīā ba-grām*, in that village, 343, 358, 368 (*ba-grom*), 609 (*bagrom*), 1155, 1156, 1163 (*ikiā*); *ikiam ba-grām*, in that village, 1163; *ikya ba-grom*, in that village, 227; *ikiā p'amu*, in that house, 76.

dugā, for the sake of; thus, *ikiā dugā*, therefore, 1154; *ikīā dugā*, therefore, 380 (*dugā*), 1238 (*ḍugā*); for the following reason, 1178; *ikiē dugā̆*, therefore, p. 61; *ikīē dugā̆*, therefore, 1435 (*dugā*), 1440, 1608, 1616; *ikīē dugā*, for the following reason, 1179; *ikiyē dugā̆*, therefore, 1228; *ikīō dugā̆*, for his sake, for him, 856, 1075; *ikīē badisnā̆ dugā̆*, for that cloth, 1068.

mē̆sh, with; thus, *akīō mē̆sh*, with him, with that, from him, from that, p. 11; *ikīā mish*, from it, out of it, 1595; *ikīo mē̆sh*, with him, towards him, 1611.

pgūro, under; *ikīā pkūsh pgūro*, under that willow-tree, 1485.

p'mish, in among; thus, *ikīā p'mīsh*, in it, among the (reeds), 1137; *ikīē p'mish*, in it, 1485.

tā̆, in, on, to; thus, *akīo tā*, to him, to that, p. 11; *ikīā tā*, in it, 803; *ikīē tā̆*, on it, 1537; *ikīo tā biss*, to him is, he has, 1203; *ikē angā tā̆*, on that fire, on the fire, 1380; *ikīē bannē tā̆*, in that wood, 1712; *ikīā bzul tā̆*, in that jungle, 1485; *ikē pashī tā̆*, on that hill, 950; *ikīā pashī tā̆*, on that hill, 845.

tibar, on the other side of, beyond; *igē̆ kazhīrī pit tibar*, on the other side of that white hillock, 659.

tawarē̆, near; thus, *akīō tawarē*, near it (the rushes), 1212; *akīā watla wōtt tā̆r torē̆*, near those falling stones, 1410; *ikī shur tawarē̆*, near that swamp, 1137.

The following forms of the plural occur:—

Nom. plur. *amgī*, they, p. 11; *amgīān*, they, p. 11; *amkī sundī manchī*, those all men, all those men, 1502.

Acc. plur. *amkīān*, they, p. 11.

Case of the agent plur. *amkī*, they, p. 11; *amkīān*, they, p. 12.

Dat. plur. *amkīān tā̆*, to them, p. 11; *amkī manchīān*, to those men, to them, 1245.

Gen. plur. *amkīān*, their, 1478; *amshīest*, their, 825, 1301, p. 11; *amshīo'st*, their own, p. 13.

The forms *amkīān* and *amshiā* occur before postpositions; thus, *amkīān mē̆sh*, from them, p. 11; *amshiā p'mish*, amongst themselves, 901; cf. **ikiā'st.**

2 **akī,** adv., there, 10, 1173, 1178, 1212, 1301, 1465, 1482, 1723, p. 61; also used as a correlative with the meaning 'then', 1671. Other forms are *akiē*, there, 1664; *akīē stē*, there from, thence, 1481; *akīyē*, there, p. 61.

akīā, that, see 1 **akī.**

1 **akīē,** by him, see 1 **akī.**

2 **akīē,** there, see 2 **akī.**

akīō, his, of that, see 1 **akī.**

ika, he, see 1 **akī.**

ikē, he that, see 1 **akī.**

ikī, he that, see 1 **akī.**

ikīā, he, that, see 1 **akī.**

ikīē, he, that, see 1 **akī.**

ikīō, he, that, see 1 **akī.**

akl, subst., chin; *aklī*, my chin, 252.

akilatt, subst., jaw; *akilattī*, my jaw, 723.

ikiam, that, see 1 **akī.**

aikūn, subst., egg, 9 (nom.).

okra, subst., porridge, 1048 (acc.).

ukaṛ, adj., steep; *ktī ukaṛ ess*, the crag is steep, 296; *do ukṛī ess*, the hill is steep, 548; cf. *urkrī n'assiā*, (this hill) is not steep, 653.

oksh, imper., out-make, show, 434, see 2 **ū.**

ukshosth, to drag out, see 2 **ū.**

ikiā'st, such; *ikiā'st ål bor*, so large loads, 1349. Formed from the demonstrative pronoun *akī*, *ikiā*, he, that.

ikīest, ikīost, his, its, see 1 **akī.**

UKTS (?), to let fall, to drop; *jil wō uktsess*, he has dropped a blanket, 1009.

ikya, he, that, see 1 **akī.**

1 **akīyē,** to him, to that, see 1 **akī.**

2 **akīyē,** there, see 2 **akī.**

ikyē, he, that, see 1 **akī.**

ikiyē, that, see 1 **akī.**

âl, adj.

(1) high, big, large, great, p. 8; used both as an attribute and as a predicate; qualifies human beings; thus, *âl mosh*, a big man, p. 7; *iâ piṭr âl biss*, my boy has grown big, 595; very often it is used about animals, as an attribute in 154, 765, 795, 959, 1043, 1125, 1342, 1493, and as a predicate in 585, p. 9; it also qualifies inanimate objects, as an attribute in 120, 233, 308, 490, 523, 819, 888, 1189, 1298, 1349, 1376, 1590, 1628, p. 7; likewise as a predicate in 892, 996, 1218, 1499, 1500. Note *âl ktol*, a big belly; *iâ brâ âl ktol oss*, my brother has a big belly, 288; *âl ktol manchī*, a big-belly man, a fat man, 190; *âl ktolwā*, big-bellied, stout, 1050, 1415; greedy, 586; *âl muzzā*, big mouse, rat, 1125.

(2) high, steep, 655, 886 (pred.), 697 (attr.).

(3) mighty, exalted; *Imrā âl ess*, God is great, 567; *tū âl ashī*, thou art master, 852; *âl manchī*, a great man, a nobleman, a well-bred man, 926, 968, 985, 1045; *âl bidi-o*, of large mind, of noble disposition, generous, 927; *âl bidīwā*, of great heart, of noble disposition, generous, 361, 550 (*bidiwā*), 1055, p. 5.

(4) high, loud, *âl vrī*, loud words, 1680.

Instead of *âl* we also find *âla* or *âlla*, and, in the examples contributed by Abdul Hakīm Khān, *ōla*; thus, *amu âla ess*, the house is large, 1334; *âlla amu*, a big house, p. 7; *ktol âlla bā*, my stomach is swelled, 857; *ōla aṛi*, the big boy, p. 8.

Another form, *âlī* or *âllī*, is perhaps feminine; thus, *dros âli pul ess*, the grapes (in my garden) are big corn, are big, 580; *âlī ushp*, a large horse, 1424; *âllī ushp*, a big horse, p. 7 (but *âl ushp*, 765, 1043, 1493); *âlī paṛṛ*, a big apple, 607; *âllī paṛṛ*, a big apple, p. 7.

alo, subst., generation, age; *shtowa alo*, four generations, 549.

ālo, subst., a pumpkin, 1086, 1087.

ailī, he will go, see 1 **I**.

ēlā, he will go, see 1 **I**.

eila, going, see 1 **I**.

īlā, subst., sour milk, 1362 (acc.).

ōla, big, see **ál.**

alek alok, to wrestle; pres. 3rd plur., *alek alokand,* they are wrestling, 1726.

alkūr, adv., separately, alone; cf. *kūr*; *kuī tū alkūṛ gujbá,* when you go to stool, 1411.

allā, they will go, see 1 **Ā.**

álla, álli, large, big, see **ál.**

ellā, he, they will go, let him, them, go, see 1 **I.**

ēllom, I shall go, see 1 **I.**

allon, he will come, see 1 **Ā.**

allangā, adj., heavy, 1478 (pred.), 1732 (attr.); *dumī allangitī,* a violent (?) wind, a gust of wind, 602. Both adjectives are formed from a verbal noun *allan* by adding *gā, gitī,* respectively.

allonn, he will come, see 1 **Ā.**

ēlam, ēlom, I shall go, I go, see 1 **I.**

elār, you will go, see 1 **I.**

alūrī, adj., dirty; *áo bilugh alūrī ess,* the water is very dirty, 1645.

ulēr, adv., up, cf. **ū**; *ulēr kshī,* pick it up, 1009.

ēlosh, thou wilt go, see 1 **I.**

alossam, I am coming, I shall dwell, 390, see 1 **Ā.**

aluts, subst., quoit-playing; *aluts kutt,* he plays quoits, 1113.

uleṭṭ, adj., heaped up; *anī bilugh tsū uleṭṭ biss,* here much manure heaped up has become, 634.

am, plural of the demonstrative pronoun **ī**, this; *am bazisná,* these clothes, 476.

ami, adj., stale; *stā kazhwajh ami istai,* this fruit is stale, 535.

1 **amo,** his own, p. 13; *amu piṭr,* his own son, p. 4; *amo tarwochī mēsh,* with his own sword, 1074; *amo'st,* his own, p. 13; *amost damtōl mochis widarthī,* his own strong master having feared, from fear of his cruel master, 1325.

2 **amo,** house, see **amu.**

amu, subst., house; said to be a feminine, p. 1, but cf. *álla* *amu*, p. 7, and *ikī amu sundī amu tā̆ âla ess*, his house is the largest of all the houses, 1334. Instead of *amu* we find *amū*, 70, 71, 76, and *amo* in *amo-wārī*, house-man, the owner of the house, 979. Note *to pamu sirtan tā̆ sett s͟hor tā̆ assē*, is your at-home on the high lands or low lands? 763, where we should expect *amu*; the *p* has perhaps been transferred from 762, whēre it is a preposition. The same form *amu* is used in all cases and numbers. The following instances occur:—

As a subject, 391, 475, 659, 685, 687, 944, 1173, 1334, 1674, p. 4; as a plural, 572, 609, 686.

As an object, 211, 982, 1409.

As a genitive, 1012, 1115, 1303, 1399.

With postpositions, *amu beṛu*, outside the house, 1091; *iā̆st amu dugā̆*, for my house, 1694; *iā̆ amu dugē̆*, for my house, 193; *yost amu dugā̆*, for your house, 1605; *iā̆st amu tā̆*, in my house, 1339; *sundī amu tā̆ âla*, all houses than large, the largest house, 1091.

With the preposition *pa*, in, to, it becomes *p'amu* or *pamu*, in the house, 237, 251, 493, 646, 674, 763, 804, 1051, 1053, 1094, 1157, 1191, 1192, 1357, 1481, 1622, 1720; to the house, 925, 1671; *inā p'amū*, at my house, 70, 71; *ikiā p'amū*, to that house, 76.

The forms *p'amu* and *pamu* are often used before postpositions; thus:—

p'amu attā, into the house, 420, 423; inside the house, 706.

pamu bē, out of the house, 974; *pamu begū*, out of the house, 964.

p'amū barēla, around the house, 70.

pamu pabanūr, round the houses, 1202.

p'amu ptior, around the house, 762; near the house, 772.

p'amu stē, from in the house, out of the house, 410, 1568; *p'amu stē*, from in the house, out of the house, 517; *pamu stha*, from in the house, out of the house, 160.

p'amu tā̆ nirgo, in front of the house, 386.

p'amu tā̆r, at the house, 1413.

p'amu torĕ, near the house, 844; *pamu tawarĕ*, near the house, 958; *pamu torĕ tā*, near the house, 1562.

The word *amu* is also used with the meaning 'a small house within a house', 'a compartment, room'; thus, *tū pamu chè amo ai*, how many rooms are there in your house? 1192.

Note also *amu* or *ushp-amu*, a stable, 633, 1385; *burī kutan amu*, bread-making house, kitchen, 743; *parmenstuk amu*, a small house, a trap for catching hawks, 1543.

amu-vishī, a neighbour, 917.

amo-wārī, a householder, the owner of a house, 979.

aim, I shall go, see 1 1.

ēm, postposition, with by means of; *tarwāz-ēm*, with a sword, 1703.

emâ, pron., we. This form is used in all cases. The following instances occur:—

Nom. *emâ*, we, 16, 32, 398, 513, 562, 608, 639, 777, 779, 785, 819, 1044, 1086, 1099, 1238 (*emâ manchīān*, we men, we), 1305, 1345, 1483, 1498, 1530, 1580, 1588, 1618, 1649, 1702, 1737, pp. 10, 58, 59; *emâ yōtzara*, we ourselves, p. 13; *emā*, we, 519.

Acc. *emâ*, us, 1429, p. 10.

Case of the agent, *emâ*, we, by us, 590, pp. 3, 10, 12.

Gen. *emâ*, our, 344, 365, 410, 417, 450, 488, 515, 639, 757, 805, 914, 915, 938, 972, 1086, 1202, 1282, 1375, 1521, 1566, 1600, 1713; instead of *emâ* we occasionally find *ēmâ*, 1020, 1223. Note *emâ biluk zur bā*, our much oppression became, we were much oppressed, 1430. The form *emâ* often has the meaning 'my'; thus, 27, 197, 256, 292, 348, 520, 546, 549, 552, 570, 917, 1097, 1139, 1168, 1357. The same form is used whether the word qualified is in the nominative or another case, and without change for gender or number. The same is the case with other forms, *emâ'st*, our, 944; *emâs't*, our, p. 10; *emâst*, our, 335, 1610; *emâ'st*, my, 1139; *imāsta*, our, in *imāsta ushpa*, our horses, p. 8.

Oblique base before postpositions, *emâ dugā*, for our sake, 1593.

emá mēsh, from us, with us, 965, p. 10.

emá tã, towards us, to us, 1430, 1571, p. 10; *emá tã churī n'aiesht*, we have no sickles, 1304.

ēmâ, we shall go, let us go, see 1 **I**.

iam, to go, see 1 **I**.

ūm, we will climb, let us go, see 1 **I** and 1 **Ū**.

UMA, to keep; *katā marē na umattett*, the Kāfirs do not keep hawks, 628.

AMCHO, to fasten the shoes of a horse; present participle, *amchol* or *amchōl*; *ushup wetsá amchol*, horseshoe fastener, a farrier, 450, 571 (*ushp watsá*); *ushp wetsu amchōl*, horseshoe fastener, a farrier, p. 15. Probably connected with *amjōsth*, to clothe, see **AMJI**.

amgī, they, see 1 **akī**.

AMJI, to put on clothes, to wear. The following forms occur:—

Infinitive, *amjisth*, to put on, pp. 18, 48.

Verbal noun, *amji* and *amjī*, to put on; *amjī na banam*, I cannot put on, 1513; *amji n'battam*, I cannot put on, 1095.

Present participle, *amjil*, putting on, p. 48.

Conjunctive participle, *amjītī*, having put on, p. 48.

Present 1st pers. sing. *amjinam*, I put on, p. 48.

2nd pers. sing. *amjinj*, thou puttest on, p. 48.

3rd pers. sing. *amjinn*, puts on, p. 48.

1st pers. plur. *amjimish*, we put on, p. 48.

2nd pers. plur. *amjīr*, you put on, p. 48.

3rd pers. plur. *amjind*, they put on, 824, 1651, p. 48.

Second present 3rd pers. sing. *amjitt*, he puts on, p. 48.

3rd pers. plur. *amjittett*, they are wearing, 1097.

Imperfect 1st pers. sing. *amjinazzam*, I was putting on, p. 48.

2nd pers. sing. *amjinazzish*, wast putting on, p. 48.

3rd pers. sing. *amjinazzī*, he was putting on, p. 48.

1st pers. plur. *amjinazzamish*, we were putting on, p. 48.

2nd pers. plur. *amjinazzār*, you were putting on, p. 48.

3rd pers. plur. *amjinazzī*, they were putting on, p. 48.

Past indefinite 1st pers. sing. *amjiā'm*, I put on, p. 48.

2nd pers. sing. *amjiā'sh*, thou puttest on, p. 48.

3rd pers. sing. *amjiā*, he put on, p. 48.

1st pers. plur. *amjiāmish*, we put on, p. 48.

2nd pers. plur. *amjiār*, you put on, p. 48.

3rd pers. plur. *amjiā*, they put on, p. 48.

Perfect and pluperfect 1st pers. sing. *amjissim*, I had put on, p. 48.

2nd pers. sing. *amjissish*, thou hadst put on, p. 48.

3rd pers. sing. *amjiss*, he has put on, 1687; *amjissī*, he had put on, p. 48; *amjistai*, he has put on, he is wearing, 1014; he had put on, p. 48.

1st pers. plur. *amjissimish*, we had put on, p. 48.

2nd pers. plur. *amjissār*, you had put on, p. 48.

3rd pers. plur. *amjissī*, *amjistai*, they had put on, p. 48.

Future 1st pers. sing. *amjilom*, I shall put on, p. 48; *amjilam-bá*, if I put on, p. 49.

2nd pers. sing. *amjilosh*, thou wilt put on, p. 48; *amjilosh-bá*, if thou puttest on, p. 49.

3rd pers. sing. *amjilā*, he will put on, p. 48; *amjila-bá*, if he puts on, p. 49.

1st pers. plur. *anjimmá*, we shall put on, p. 48; *amjimma-bá*, if we put on, p. 49.

2nd pers. plur. *amjīlr*, you will put on, p. 48; *amjīlr-bá*, if you put on, p. 49.

3rd pers. plur. *amjilā*, they will put on, p. 48; *amjila-bá*, if they put on, p. 49.

Imperative 2nd pers. sing. *amjū*, put on, p. 49.

3rd pers. sing. *amjīlā*, let him put on, p. 49.

1st pers. plur. *amjimmá*, let us put on, p. 49.

2nd pers. plur. *amjūlār*, put on ye, p. 49.

3rd pers. plur. *amjīlā*, let them put on, p. 49.

Causative, *amjōsth*, to cause to put on, to clothe, p. 18.

Imperative, *amjīō*, clothe, put the clothes on (me), 1095; cf. **AMCHŌ.**

amkī, they, those, see 1 **akī.**

amnā, amnâ, these, they, see 2 **anī.**

1 **amnī,** adv., here, 30, 53, 56, 165.

2 **amnī, amnīē,** these, they, see 2 **anī.**

amnio, these, them, see 2 **anī.**

amniō (?), imper. in *kai n'amniō*, anything not attack, don't attack him, 90.

amno, these, them, see 2 **anī.**

amir, subst., the Amir; case of the agent, *amir*, 1394; genitive, *amīro*, 600.

imrā, subst., God, 526, 567, 1002; used as an imprecation, 1244.

iamru, subst., walnut-tree; *iamru kāno*, walnut-tree, 1628; *iamru mana*, a walnut, 1628.

Umrā K͟hān, subst., name of a person, 751.

amāṛts, subst., pomegranate, 1041.

emis͟h, we shall go, see 1 **I.**

ams͟hī, ams͟hiā, ams͟hīest, ams͟hio'st, they, their, see 1 **akī.**

amost, his own, see 1 **amo.**

emâst, our, see **emâ.**

imāsta, our, see **emâ.**

umattett, they keep, see **UMA.**

AN (?), to bite.

Future 3rd pers. sing. *analā*, (the horse) will bite, bites, 158.

1 **anī,** subst., a side; *iâst anī winā'm, anī brazott*, he beat my side, my side aches, 1306.

2 **anī, inā, in,** this, he, the near demonstrative pronoun, formed from the base *a*, or, more commonly, *i*, by adding *nī*, *nā*. The plural is formed by adding *nī* to *am*. The form *inā* often becomes *inām* when added to a word ending in *m*; see p. 11. The following forms occur:—

Nom. sing. *anī*, he, this, p. 10.

inā, he, this, p. 10; this, 607, 977, 979, 1056, 1250, 1269, 1435, p. 10; very commonly used as an attribute with nouns; thus, 41, 61, 82, 170, 218, 242, 266, 321, 429, 487, 489, 492, 520, 548, 618, 655, 765, 801, 820, 908, 909, 910, 922, 923, 924, 971, 1019, 1022, 1078, 1127, 1128, 1187, 1351, 1425, 1468, 1492, 1499, 1522, 1537, 1584, 1587, 1595, 1601, 1623, 1633, 1641, 1730, 1731. Sometimes, probably wrongly, translated 'that'; thus, *inā spāhī*, that sepoy, 29; *inā thuṛus*, that precipice, 324; *inā taman*, those pyjamas, 1513. Note *inām grām*, this village, 1500.

Acc. sing. *anī*, him, this, p. 10.

enā kudūm, this work, 951.

inā, this; used as an attribute with nouns, 91, 92, 176, 236, 364, 366, 474, 733, 874, 986, 1024, 1094, 1185, 1267, 1279, 1283, 1442, 1458, 1505, 1511, 1642. In one example we find *inī* instead of *inā*; thus, *inī bangut <u>sh</u>to ptistuk k<u>sh</u>īr*, make this wall square, 1384. Note *īn-az*, this is it, p. 19; *inā barwai yo chok prē*, give each coolie one share, 1049; *inānī jagā skā*, clean this place, 199.

Case of the agent sing. *anī*, by him, by this, p. 10; *inā*, by him, 51, p. 12; *inā manchīē*, by this man, 1362.

Gen. sing. *anīo*, his, of this, p. 10.

inā, his, 971, 1350; *inā gum pul*, the grain of the wheat, 1668; *inā maṛiṛē major*, the age of this boy, 177; *inā yū ḍo*, the water of this water-cut, 1643.

anī is used with a substantive in *anī pōr*, this way, in this direction, 1476, 1647, 1648, p. 61.

inā is used in the same way in some idioms; thus:—

in-īa<u>sh</u>, this morning, 287.

inā sē, this year, 6, 65, 95, 118, 212, 247, 286, 390, 399, 538, 541, 698, 727, 997, 1012, 1032, 1167, 1170, 1179, 1221, 1228, 1240, 1428, 1628, 1668, p. 9.

inā wazdōr, this summer, 1371.

When postpositions follow, *anī* seems to be used if the

pronoun is a noun, and *inā* is the form used as an adjective qualifying nouns governed by a preposition or postposition.

As a noun, *anī mẽsh*, from this, from him, with this, with him, Hindī *is sē*, p. 10; *anī pagur*, under it, 1350; *anī tā̃*, to him, to this, p. 10.

The form *inā* is common with nouns preceded by the postposition *p*, *ba*; thus :—

inā bado, on this hill, 648, 1397.

inā b'gul, in this valley, in this district, 363 (*b'gol*), 871, 1418, 1698; *inā b'gul tā̃*, in this river, in this valley, 1183, 1224.

inā bagrām, in this village, 425, 609, 1159, 1433; *inā bagrom*, in this village, 549, 686, 823, 1050; *inā bagrom p'mich*, in the midst of this village, 427; *inā bragom*, in this village, 232, 322. Note *inām bagrām*, in this village, 62, 1650, p. 11.

inā p'nilē, in this pond, 1272.

In numerous instances *inā*, this, qualifies a noun followed by a postposition, thus :—

inā ushp dugā̃, for this horse, 1211; *inā undsáo p'mish*, in this spring, 1379; *inā kudūm p'mish*, in this affair, 1160, 1701; *inā vott p'sïr*, on this stone, 1319; *inā gum sē tā̃*, from, out of, this wheat, 1049; *inā ushp tā̃*, in this horse, to this horse, 1424; *inā bhīma tā̃*, on this ground, on the ground, 213; *in dunyā tā̃*, in this world, in the whole world, 1721; *inā gol tā̃*, in this river, 534; *inā gula tā̃*, in this valley, 304; *inā pashku tā̃*, in this ewer, from this ewer, 413; in that (?) ewer, 544; *inạ̄ prushtī tā̃*, in this bed, 210; *inā sē tā̃*, in this year, 472; *inā shē tā̃*, into this pit, 1017; *inā watan tā̃*, in this country, 575.

The following forms of the plural occur :—

Nom. plur. *amná*, these, they, 563, 1738, p. 10; *amná yōt zara*, they themselves, p. 13; *amnī*, they, 1656.

The following forms occur with nouns :—

amnā manjī, these men, 1483; *amnī dū brá*, these two brothers, 808; *amnī dū manchī*, these two men, 353 (translated 'those'), 362; *amni manchī*, these men, the people, 1047; *amnīẽ dū brá*, these two brothers, 1114.

Acc. plur. *amnīān*, these, them, p. 10; *amno*, them, 1479; *amnī dū brásan*, these two brothers, 1102; *amnī s̲h̲to bōr*, these four loads, 1458.

Case of the agent plur. *amná*, by these, by them, pp. 10, 12.

Gen. plur. *amnīān*, their, of these, p. 10.

Oblique bases before postpositions—

amná in *amná dugă*, for them, 1536.

amnio in *amnio p'mich*, among them, 42; *amnīō tă*, to them, 1418.

amno in *amno tă*, to them, 516.

amnīān in *amnīān mes̲h̲*, from, with, them, these (Hindī *in sẽ*), p. 10; *amnīān tă*, to them, to these, p. 10.

s **anī,** adv., here, 59, 105, 110, 112, 148, 211, 255, 257, 389, 431, 485, 601, 634, 649, 651, 684, 697, 710, 784, 835, 894, 1100, 1120, 1153, 1370, 1395, 1404, 1503, p. 60; translated 'there', 1046.

anio, here, p. 60; *anīo*, here, 17, 507, 608, 644, 1076, 1143, 1632.

anīō, here, 400, 893, 1206, 1624.

ano, subst., (1) flesh, meat. The following forms occur:—

Nom. sing. *ano*, 987, 1128.

Acc. sing. *ano*. 99, 394, 620, 746, 855, 1001, 1010, 1048, 1185, 1574.

Gen. sing. *ano*, 1145.

Oblique base, *ano tă*, of meat, 1001; *ano mẽs̲h̲*, with meat, 1372.

(2) clarified butter, *ghi*. In this meaning *ano* occurs in the nom. sing., 858; the acc. sing., 551, 638, 688, 796, p. 3, footnote; and the gen. sing., 1201. No. 1594 shows that the *ghi* is also used as an ointment.

ano kchāl, meat-maker, cook, 647. Cf. **anji.**

en, to go, see 1 **I.**

enā, this, see 2 **anī.**

in, inā, this, see 2 **anī.**

inā, my. This form occurs in *inā p'amū*, around my house, 70, 71; *inā p'amu*, in my house, 237; *inā pamu tawarē̃*, near my house, 958. Perhaps mistake for *iā̃*.

inā, adv., here, 121, 500.

inī, this, see 2 **anī.**

ien, going, in *ien-dā̃*, at the time of going, see 1 **I.**

end, enda, they go, see 1 **I.**

andhaṛ, adj., dark, 325, 804, 1485. In all these examples *andhaṛ* is used as a predicate, and it is everywhere possible to translate 'darkness'. The word is, however, clearly an adjective in *miok andhṛ kunn*, face dark makes, he is scowling, 1246. Instead of *andhaṛ* we also find *andṛ* in *miok andṛ kṛiss*, face dark is made, you are frowning, 544.

andṛ, adj., dark, see **andhaṛ.**

inḍrōn, subst., rainbow, 1121; cf. *drōn*, bow, and Sanskrit *indradhanus*, rainbow,

ūndrēparu, subst., wing feather, 1696 (acc.).

indrish, subst., an earthquake; *indrish ptā*, an earthquake fell, occurred, 401, 1717; gen. *indrisht*, in *indrisht tū shū bā*, of earthquake you knowledge became? did you feel the earthquake? 1510.

ONDS, to shiver, to have fever. The actual form of this base cannot be determined. The final consonants occur in various forms such as *nds, nts, ns*, and probably also *nz*. An *r* is often prefixed, and may belong to the original base. The following forms occur:—

Present participle, *ondsil ī andsitī*, feverish I having shivered (?), fever having had hold of me, 469; *randsōl bitī*, having had fever, 467, 470; *tu ranzol assā*, have you got fever? 1290; *ranzul assa*, have you got fever? 1552; *iā̃ su tā̃ shtarak ranzul biss*, my sister has got fever to-day, 1317.

Second present 3rd pers. sing. *onsatt*, he has fever, 468;

tū brá ontsatt, thy brother has fever, 203 ; *jidd kai dugā ranzott ?* why is your body shivering ? 1552.

undsâo, subst., a spring of water, 1379.

angā, subst., fire ; also signalling fire, beacon, 124, 125. The following forms occur :—

Nom. sing. *angā*, fire, 481, 483, 1128, 1142, 1633, 1645. Note *iāst yūs goṭṭ angā taṛā*, to my grass stack fire was put, 1386.

Acc. sing. *ungā*, fire, 166, 484, 485, 729, 806, 1710, 1714 ; *ango*, a beacon, 124, 125.

Gen. sing. *askā angā bās*, the flames of that fire, 491.

Base used with postpositions, *angā tā*, on the fire, 1380 *ango p'tsiru watē*, put it on the fire, 233 ; *ango tā assā gaiē*, take away the ashes in the fire, 78.

ango, fire, see **angā.**

UNGA (?). This base occurs in the following forms :—

Imperfect 3rd pers. *ika vinagan ungalazī*, he would have been beaten, p. 59.

Pluperfect 3rd pers. *emá vinagan ungutussī*, we have been beaten, p. 59.

Future 2nd pers. sing. *tu vinagan ungalosh*, thou wilt be beaten, p. 59 ; probably connected with *NGĀ*.

ingol kā, adv., perhaps, 268, p. 61.

ungalosh, ungalazi, see **UNGA.**

Angṛ, subst., name of a place, Aigūn, 1406 ; also written *Angār*, 551, 719.

angur, subst., a finger. Nom. plur. *angur*, the fingers, 478, 936. Base with postpositions *angur warē*, with the finger, 1037 ; *jasht angur*, the thumb, 1509, 1634 ; *kāir angur*, foot finger, toe, 1528.

angrēzi, adj., English, 1211.

angushti, subst., a ring ; nom. sing. *inā angushtūn*, this ring, 1601 ; acc. sing. *angushtī*, a ring, 1177 ; nom. plur. *angushtīēn*, the rings, 1177.

ungutussi, see **UNGA.**

anji, subst., food, 479, 743, 1322. In all these instances the word is used in the accusative. Cf. **ano.**

anjī, thou goest, see 1 **I.**

enjā, enjī, wilt go, see 1 **I.**

anjībá, if thou come, see 1 **Ā.**

enjībá, if thou go, see 1 **I.**

analā, he will bite, see **AN.**

anam, I shall go, see 1 **I.**

inām, this, see 2 **anī.**

ann, comes, see 1 **Ā.**

enn, he goes, see 1 **I.**

inānī, this, 199, see 2 **anī.**

annam, ennam, ennom, I go, see 1 **I.**

ons, in *pețț ons,* is broken, 189, read *pețțons*; see **PEṚ.**

unsatt, ontsatt, he has fever, see **ONDS.**

īnaz, this is it, p. 19; see 2 **anī.**

onzibá, if it comes, see 1 **Ā.**

īnzarin, subst., a glacier, 557 (nom.).

ēnaẓzī, was going, see 1 **I.**

EPA, to make. Imperative 1st pers. plur. *epamá,* let us make, 717; see **PO.**

opigná, adj., high, lofty; *iyē bado bilugh opigná ess,* on this mountain it is very lofty, 818.

upoh, subst., a scorpion; nom. plur. *upoh,* scorpions, 1244.

epol, adj. or part., flat; *epol toch,* a flat bullet, 213.

epor, subst., the rutting season (for markhors); *epor bibā,* when the rutting season comes, in the rutting season, 1214.

1 **APS,** to fetch. Imperative, *dār apsio,* fetch firewood, 484; cf. **AFS.**

2 **APS,** to be swollen. Perfect 3rd pers. sing. *apsiss,* is swollen, 1449; *dodmōss apsiss,* my gum is swollen, 599; *iās garak tā apsiss,* there is a boil on my throat, 1507; *kūr apsiss,* my leg has a boil, 172; *ktol apsiss,* my stomach is swollen, 275; *naskor absiss,* on the cheek is a boil, 245; *nasur tā atēr apsiss,* inside

the nostril is a boil, 931; *p'shai p'mīju apsiss*, on the head is a boil, 949; *patōs apsiss*, on the shoulder is a boil, 1297; *apsisst*, a boil, 1537. In *apsiss stē witlosth dugā*, in order to cut a tumour, 1560, *apsiss stē* is perhaps miswritten for *apsisstē*.

epos diktī, adv., presently, in a short time, 1065. The final *ktī* in *diktī* is perhaps the conjunctive participle of *KṚ*.

apshē, subst., a grinding mill; *apshiān n'ai*, there is no mill, 868; *apshiān wāṛ*, the stone of the mill, 869; *p'apshē*, at the mill, 590; *chuk apshē asht*, how many mills are there? 1646; *apshiān manchī*, a miller, 869. Cf. **PSHI**.

apsiss, apsisst, see 2 **APS**.

āṛi, subst., a boy, p. 8. This form occurs in a sentence contributed by Abdul Hakīm Khān; cf. **maṛiṛ**.

aṛu, subst., silver, 1310.

āṛu, subst., a peach; nom. plur. *āṛu*, peaches, 577, 996.

ēr, you go, you will go, see 1 **I**.

īr, adv., on this side, 1305, p. 61; cf. **pēr** and 3 **ī**.

iār, iārā, iāro, eaten, see **YŪ**.

iēr, go ye, see 1 **I**.

ōr, subst., the chest; *iā ōr wishtr ass*, my chest is big, 254.

ŏr, subst., a dwarf; *ŏr manchī aiyo*, a dwarf has come, 388.

uṛā, uru, or **uṛu**, subst., the headman of a Chitral village, the charbū; nom. sing. *uṛā*, 1050; *uru*, 1156, 1163; *uṛu*, 333.

URU, to reap. Verbal noun *urusth*, to reap, 1133; future 1st pers. plur. *ruimā*, (how) can we cut? 1304; imperative 1st pers. plur. *erwemā*, let us reap, 94.

iārabā, if it is eaten, see **YŪ**.

Argich, subst., name of a place, Urgūch, 523; also *Arguich*, 889.

argru, subst., a log, beam, 376, 819, 820, 1198; the ceiling of a house, 237, p. 1; *argrū*, a beam, 127, 422, p. 7; *urgru*, the timbers of a roof, 1191. The word is stated to be feminine, p. 1; cf. *inā p'amu argru digrī biss*, the ceiling of my house is bad, 237; *drgrī argrū*, a long log, p. 7; *argru drigrī ass*, the log is long, 820. Cf. **gāṛ**, **ugrē**.

arkien, adj., undermined; *ikīā kutt arkien biss,* the tower is undermined, 1575.

urkrī, adj., steep; *in dō urkrī n'assiā,* this hill is not steep, 653. Cf. **ukaṛ.**

ũrktī, having inflated; *ktol ũrktī nosh kõṛ,* he floats having inflated his stomach, 498; *ktī* is the conjunctive participle of *kusth,* to do. It is possible that the translation given is wrong, and that *ũr* is = *wãr,* downwards, so that *ũrktī* means "putting downwards".

iãramish, we ate, see **YŪ.**

aṛin, adj., tight, narrow; *gōl aṛin assā,* the valley is narrow, 1598; *puṭṭ aṛin assā,* is the road narrow? 1686; *shugā aron butt,* the choga is tight, 254; *aruṇī gol,* a narrow valley, a gorge, defile, 336 (*arūṇī*), 574, 728; *puṭṭ aruṇī ess,* the road is narrow, 907. The *ṛ* has been doubled in *iāst tarwach parōsh tā aṛṛīn biss,* my sword belt in tight became, my sword belt is very tight, 1455. The word *aṛaṛ,* tight, is perhaps identical; thus, *inā taman aṛaṛ ass,* those pyjamas are tight, 1513.

arṇa, subst., mange, 1203.

iãron, I ate, see **YŪ.**

oṛen wisth, to push; *tū iā kai dugā oṛen vich? tū iā oṛen vichībá,* why art thou pushing me? if thou pushest me, 1093.

erangst, adj., equal, like; *ē giḍr gum ē sir zū erangst ess,* one sheaf of corn (and) one seer of milk are equal (in price), 1282; *iā krūī to krūī erang'st asht,* my dog (and) thy dog are alike, 1152. On p. 64 *erangst* is translated 'a pair'. The word is formed by adding the suffix *st* to *e-rang,* one colour, and properly means 'of one colour'.

aṛaṛ, adj., tight, 1513; see **aṛin.**

Aror, subst., Aror, name of a man, 906; *aror varī chut,* Aror's voice, 1615.

uṛṛ, subst., (1) a hill partridge, chakor, 744, p. 3; gen. *uṛṛē,* 987; the word is said to be feminine, 744, p. 3; (2) wing of a bird; gen. *uṛṛ,* 1696; cf. *ūndrē-paru,* wing feather.

URR, to fall; *chá urriss,* the wall fell down, 1627.

arrin, tight, see **aṛin.**

urriss, fell down, see **URR.**

arorwē, subst., an orial; gen. *arorwē,* 394.

AṚS, to low; second present 3rd pers. plur. *gá aṛsett,* cows are lowing, 833.

iārs, he has eaten, see **YŪ.**

arshum, subst., silk, 1310.

iāriss, etc., has eaten, see **YŪ.**

urusth, to reap, see **URU.**

aṛsett, they are lowing, see **AṚS.**

erwemá, let us reap, see **URU.**

arwaṛā, brought, **arwaṛissam,** I had brought, **aṛwristai,** they have brought; see **AWĒ.**

aruz, adj., sweet; *inā paṛṛ aruz ess,* this apple is sweet, 61; *kachwach arūzdo ess,* the fruit is sweet, 1448; *Katō warī aruzwā essā,* the Kafir language is sweet, 764; *paṛṛ aruzwai n'bistā,* the apples are not juicy, 727; *inā kajwaj aruzwai n'asht,* this fruit is not luscious, 910.

AS, to be. The following forms occur:—

Infinitive, *esth,* to be, pp. 19, 29.

Present tense 1st pers. sing. *edsam,* I am, 456 (copula); *adzum,* I am, p. 19; *ashim-bá,* if I am, p. 19; *assum,* I am, p. 19; used as a verb substantive, 23, 300, 314, 391, 539, 617, 690, 709, 767, 852, 875, 1061, 1109, 1140, 1171, 1172, 1231, 1252, 1486, 1608, 1736; cf. *dām assum,* I owe, 975; in interrogative sentence *assum-ā,* am I? 1105, p. 17; *issam* in *nishin-issam,* I am sitting, I live, 814; *azzum,* I am, pp. 19, 26; copula, 617; *al-ossam,* I am coming, I shall dwell, 390.

2nd pers. sing. *ashī,* thou art, p. 19; used as a verb substantive, 707, 852, 1054, 1335, 1534, 1692, 1693; in interrogative sentences *ashā,* art thou? 1736; *ashiā,* art thou? 1307, 1366; *ashī-bá,* if thou art, 617, p. 19; *oshī,* thou art, p. 19; used as a verb substantive, 703; *oshī-bá,* if thou art, 617; *oshish,* thou art, p. 19; *assī*, thou art, p. 19; *ess*, thou art, used as a verb substantive, 87, 477; *oss*, 701 (*tū biliuk pshuik oss*, thou much sleeping art, thou art very lazy); *osish*, thou art, 99 (copula); *assish*, thou art, used as a copula, 105, 190, 224, 457, 525, 586, 611, 670, 700, 708, 720, 740, 919, 927, 940, 968, 974, 983, 994, 1000, 1018, 1080, 1088, 1103, 1171, 1176, 1262, 1273, 1275, 1311, 1486; *azhichī*, art, *kai dugā chusht azhichī*, why are you silent? 1366; *azzish*, art, p. 19; *sâch*, dwellest, 389.

3rd pers. sing. *ass*, is, 149 (is with us, we have), 772, 957 (is to me, I have), 1183 (*n'ass*), 1273 (*tū n'ass*, is not to thee, hast not), 1293 (*iāst tapk n'ass*, I have no gun), 1673, p. 19. This form is also used with a fuller meaning 'it is appropriate' in *ikūā* (*ikiē*) *vīsth ass*, him to-beat is appropriate, he should be punished, 1156, p. 15. It also occurs in connexion with participles so as to form a kind of compound tense; *dūr bitī ass*, bent, having-become is, he got cramp, 297. In most cases *ass* is used as a verb substantive, thus, 41, 178, 254, 292, 527, 559, 631, 636, 680, 684, 685, 703, 728, 755, 791, 820, 821, 837, 917, 946, 1141, 1156, 1158, 1184, 1187, 1188, 1242, 1253, 1263, 1264, 1269, 1272, 1296, 1330, 1378, 1382, 1383, 1388, 1435, 1448, 1475, 1493, 1499, 1513, 1520, 1544, 1559, 1623, 1643, 1664, 1668, 1682, 1689. Sometimes *assa* is used instead. It occurs as a copula 361, p. 8, and in an interrogative sentence, 1552. Doubtful is *iā barē assabū*, I hope, 589; *korār assabá*, where it may be, 1357. More usual is the form *assā*, is, 532, 642, 722, 899, 1212, 1234 (there is to him, he has), 1239, 1285 (there is to me, I have), 1290, 1345, 1576, p. 19. This form is also used as a copula, 732, 765, 781, 900, 959, 1021, 1028, 1046, 1050, 1056, 1062, 1153, 1174, 1175, 1188, 1197, 1218, 1221, 1226, 1246, 1280, 1292, 1313, 1315, 1333, 1339, 1355, 1359, 1368, 1397, 1407, 1418, 1424, 1450, 1456, 1457, 1491, 1557, 1559, 1572, 1585, 1587, 1598, 1621, 1632, 1709, 1711, 1731, 1742, pp. 8, 9; *assā* is also used in interrogative sentences, where the final *ā* is perhaps an interrogative particle, thus, 58, 920, 1331, 1387, 1394, 1412, 1492, 1540. 1676, 1683, 1686, 1688, 1741. Other fuller forms of *ass* are *asē*, is there ? 227 (read *sell asē*) ; *assē*, 129 (translated 'are there ?'), 763, 978 (*tu mēsh assē*, is there with you ? have you ?), 1078, p. 19. All these forms occur in interrogative sentences ; further, *assī*, 550 (translated 'was'), 955 (*n'assī*, was not to be had), 1104 (with a feminine subject) ; and *assiā*, used as a copula, 653, 695, 836, p. 19.

The most common form of the person singular is *ess*, is, 34, 42, 81, 146, 148, 177, 178, 257, 272, 315, 338, 342, 365, 373, 386, 400, 430, 435, 443, 445, 449, 453, 458, 483, 541. 542, 609, 625, 637, 659, 666, 670, 672, 684, 685, 714, 716, 728, 749, 770, 792, 799, 803, 830, 834, 843 (*tū ness*, there is not to thee, hast not), 846, 847, 870, 871, 878, 887, 893, 912, 921, 930 (*nasur n'ess*, nose is not, he has no nose), 942, 950, 962, 991, 992, 993, 1013, 1069, 1107, 1109, 1111, 1112, 1125, 1128, 1147, 1160 1173, 1179, 1181, 1194, 1204, 1324, 1357, 1404, 1518, 1521, 1597, 1599, 1645, pp. 14, 19. This form is often used in connexion with participles in order to form compound tenses ; thus, *otin ess*, remaining is, is left, 934 ; *utin ess*, remaining is, is left, 1144 ; *oz ess*, he came back, 1568 ; *bal-ess*, he can, 773 ; *kai dugă n'dai ess*, why has it not been cooked ? 1127 ; *ladēl ess*, lying is, he lies, 862 ; *nishīn ess*, is sitting, 217, 235 ; *nizin ess*, are sitting, 1617 ; *peṭang ess*, is broken, 196, 599, probably miswritten for *peṭan-gess*, cf. 198, 307, 615, 1033, 1138 ; *dom tin-ess*, was herding, 648 ; *shē tin ess*, it is frozen, 534, 858, 1034 ; *tip-ess*, it has been warmed, 1644 ; *wopsin ess*, he is left, 790. *Ess* is in such connexions sometimes shortened to *s* ; thus, *pēr's*, is across, 7 ; *peṭṭon-s*, it is broken, 189 ; *wanā's*, has beaten, 630 ; *n'waṛoin-s*, cannot be seen, 657. The most common use of *ess* is as a verb substantive, 1, 2, 8, 11, 12, 18, 20, 24 (*nēss* = *n'ess*), 29, 61, 77, 82, 90, 97, 113, 120, 123, 127, 140, 163, 170, 206, 208, 212, 222, 226, 238, 260, 261, 266, 272, 295, 296, 298, 306, 311, 312, 321, 324, 332, 333, 340, 345, 355, 359, 365, 366, 369, 372, 373, 405, 410, 419, 426, 428, 429, 446, 451, 454, 455, 464, 468, 475, 481, 488, 489, 492, 504, 508, 518, 520, 533, 536, 540, 548, 557, 567, 571, 574, 575, 576, 580,

585, 594, 598, 603, 607, 618, 632, 647, 655, 675, 676, 680 681, 682, 687, 692, 700, 705, 724, 725, 741, 760, 761, 765, 773, 774, 818, 836, 837, 840, 846, 862, 870, 885, 886, 889, 892, 893, 907, 908, 909, 915, 960, 971, 977, 987, 988, 989, 1019, 1021, 1022, 1025, 1032, 1036, 1043, 1055, 1061, 1070, 1071, 1086, 1127, 1128, 1163, 1167, 1170, 1182, 1187, 1200, 1215, 1220, 1250, 1263, 1269, 1272, 1282, 1295, 1303, 1313, 1334, 1341, 1398, 1405, 1438, 1448, 1464, 1468, 1485, 1486, 1490, 1493, 1499, 1500, 1548, 1567, 1584, 1641, 1645, 1668, 1717, 1723, 1730, 1743, 1744, pp. 7, 9. A fuller form *essā* is used as a copula in 764, 1373, 1374, 1719, p. 19, and in an interrogative sentence, 1014.

oss, is, is used as a copula in 280, 288, 411, 790, 1324, and in connexion with a participle in *mizhongai oss*, he has lied, he has played a trick, 1553. The fuller form *ossā* occurs as a verb substantive, 970.

All these forms of the third person singular contain the base in a form ending in *s*. Instead of *s* we also find *z* in several forms, viz.:

az, is, in *īn-az*, this is it, p. 19; with the fuller forms, *aza*, is, p. 8 (verb substantive, she is), and *azia*, p. 8 (verb substantive, he is).

ezā, is, p. 19.

izhā, is (the cow white)? 294; *azhī-bá*, if he is, p. 19; if there is, 1381.

azs, is, 706, p. 19.

azz, is, used as a verb substantive, 1195, 1596, 1613, 1701, pp. 9, 14. A fuller form is *azzā*, is, 1355, 1379, 1590, p. 19; also used in interrogative sentences, 294, 1331, 1666, 1674, 1713, and as a verb substantive, 536, 1378, 1595, 1601.

ezz, is, 278, 683.

A variety of these forms is perhaps *aiets*, is, 133 (verb substantive).

A compound form is *assett*, 762 (interrogative sentence, verb substantive), p. 19; *sett*, 763.

Several forms of the 3rd pers. sing. are orginally plural, but are also used in the singular, viz.:

a͟s͟ht, is, 109, 251, 289, 538, 891 (*Mirak guchī a͟s͟ht Bastīe guchī n'a͟s͟ht*, Mirak has mustachios and Basti has not), 933 (*iă tă kai n'a͟s͟ht*, I have nothing), 1393; used as copula, 243, 250, 568, 570, 910, 1224, 1351. In an interrogative sentence, *a͟s͟htā*, is there? 1609.

n'ae͟s͟ht, there is not, 1133, 1482.

n'aie͟s͟ht, there is not, 135, 149, 151, 285, 289, 437, 719, 769, 823, 875, 957, 1040, 1116, 1140, 1209, 1301, 1304, 1423, 1424, 1551.

n'aie͟s͟hta, there is not, 153.

n'aiest, there is not, 914.

n'aiesth, there is not, 1206.

1st pers. plur. *assumi͟s͟h*, we are, 1044 (copula); *azumi͟s͟h*, we are, p. 19; *azumi͟s͟h-bá*, if we are, p. 19; *azzami͟s͟h*, we are (copula), 1580, 1649; *wichá-zmi͟s͟h*, we are travellers, we shall travel, 1059.

2nd pers. plur. *azăr*, you are, p. 19; *azĕr-bá*, if you are, p. 19, *azzirā*, are you? 1659.

3rd pers. plur. Several forms are used. The most common is—

a͟s͟ht, are, 53, 56, 197, 210, 249, 255, 291, 353, 363, 372, 674, 772, 891, 897, 903, 931, 935, 958, 1037, 1168, 1172, 1196, 1285, 1293, 1318, 1367, 1377, 1485, 1515, 1646, 1652, 1690, 1712, p. 58. This form is often used as a copula, 6, 108, 136, 256, 304, 343, 344, 418, 437, 473, 493, 588, 658, 805, 808, 823, 845, 861, 888, 896, 900, 903, 932, 938, 966, 985, 996, 998, 1007, 1027, 1123, 1152, 1155, 1191, 1198, 1199, 1201, 1228, 1240, 1291, 1348, 1367, 1478, 1502, 1590, 1650, 1720, pp. 9, 19. A fuller form, *a͟s͟hta*, are, is used as a copula on p. 8; interrogative is *a͟s͟htā*, are there? 1006. Other forms are—

ae͟s͟ht, are, 1130 (verb substantive).

ai͟s͟ht, are, p. 19.

aiesht, always used with a negative; *n'aiesht*, are not, 155, 497, 691, 958, 1007, 1196; used as a copula, 358, 891.

ashth, are, 926 (copula).

ista, are, p. 19; *istai*, are, 535 (copula), and in forms such as *nishīn-istai*, they are sitting, 385; *wasanṛ-istai*, they are assembled, 545, 849.

asth, are, 447, 668, p. 19; used as a copula, 421, 658, 1027.

aesth, are, used as a copula, 416, 417.

n'aiasth, there are not, 450.

aiesth, are, 645, 668, 697.

hōst, are, 528; *hosth*, are, p. 19.

A compound form is *etasal*, are, p. 19.

Other forms are identical with those used in the singular, viz. *assā*, are, 876 (*nāru-ssā*), 1434.

ess, are, 128, 268, 662, 1266, 1392, 1617 (*nizin ess*, are sitting); also used as a copula, 64, 580, 588.

essā, there are, 69.

azā and *aziā*, are, in *chō manchī-zā*, how many men are there? 62, p. 19; *wiaziā*, they are falling, 787.

azza-bá, if they are, p. 19.

Past tense 1st pers. sing. *assium*, I was, 390, 1327, p. 19; used as a copula, 767.

2nd pers. sing. *azzī*, wast, 1335; *azzush*, wast, p. 19.

3rd pers. sing. *n'aisī*, was not, p. 19; cf. 1635 and base *Ā*; *essī*, was, 404 (copula), p. 19; *azzī*, was, 1148, 1206, 1429, p. 19; *azziā*, was, 1148.

1st pers. plur. *azzumish*, we were, p. 19.

2nd pers. plur. *azār*, you were, p. 19.

3rd pers. plur. *azzī* and *azammē*, they were, p. 19.

Future 1st pers. sing. *pitur-ai-salam*, behind coming shall be, I shall follow, 138.

3rd pers. sing. *asēl*, is, p. 19; *chaṭṭa assel*, (I think) he may be mad, 839; *marangatsē noshpā kai etsal*, what may be in the bird's beak? 126; *ī nasib n'azila-bá*, if there is not luck to me, if my luck is bad, 436.

3rd pers. plur. *assēl*, they are, p. 19; *tīch n'bunn kōr assela-bā*, there is no certainty where they may be, 1417; *chok amu assil*, how many houses may there be? 686.

Imperative, *osh*, be, 1108, pp. 19, 63; *ōshī*, be, 25; cf. also *chusht eshtinājē*, be silent, hide, 650, probably from *esht*, to be, and *tinājē*, i.e. *tinj-ē*, there is necessity; *azhō*, be; *chusht azhō*, be silent, 1308, 1309; *grām pabunor azhō*, be around the village, surround the village, 1439.

3rd pers. sing. *azhalā*, may it be; *shtalē ōts p'mishtalom Imrā bapdī azhalā*, perhaps I shall forget, let it be in God's mind, if I forget may God give me punishment, 526

ais, aisī, came, see 1 **Ā.**

iās, iāsī, my, see 2 **Ī.**

asuch, in *raganasuch*, see **RAG.**

aischitt, it is useful; *ashu barā n'aischitt*, it is no good to plough, 1034.

ASH, to throw; *bī ash*, to throw seed, to sow; the consonant of this base also occurs in the forms *zh*, *z*, and *j*. The following forms occur in the sentences:—

Infinitive, *bī azhisth dugā*, for sowing, 1516; *krujā shisthā* (i.e. perhaps *kruzhī ashisthā*), for sowing, 310.

Present 2nd pers. sing. *baron azinj*, thou art throwing out, vomiting, 1616.

3rd pers. plur. *ba-biā azhind*, they throw into seed, they are winnowing, 1697.

Past 3rd pers. plur. *tuṛ azhā*, they have thrown out, ejected, 1135.

Perfect 1st pers. sing. *bī ashiss*, I have sown the seed, 835; *bī ajissī*, I have sown the seed, 1253; *azhiss*, I have thrown up, made (steps), 1399.

2nd pers. sing. *bī ajissā*, hast thou sown? 1363.

Future 1st pers. sing. *toṛ azhēlam*, I shall throw out, dismiss, 1205; *tōṛ azhēlom*, I dismiss, 1262, 1375.

Imperative 2nd pers. sing. *azhō*, throw, sprinkle, 1380; *tar-ázho*, drive him out, 379.

2nd pers. plur. *taṛ-zhăr*, turn him out, 517; cf. also **AJHO.**

ãsh, subst., meat food; *buṛī ăsh kūrik*, to make bread and meat, to cook the food, 283. Cf. **anjī.**

ashā, ashī, ashiā, art, see **AS.**

ashī, subst., mouth, 892; *ashī*, into the mouth, 157; *p'ashī*, in the mouth, 174: *azhī tă*, from the mouth, 1532; *tapkiē ashī*, the muzzle of a gun, 902.

ashī bradsī, the reins of a horse, 1138.

ashīā, him, misprint for *askīā*, see **askā.**

ashu, subst., a bull, 1490; nom. plur., *ashu*, bulls, 212, 293; *ashē kū n'aiesht*, bulls have no humps, 691; *ashu baṛā*, a bullock plough, 1033, 1034. Another form is *azhē*, bull, p. 8 (Abdul Hakīm Khān); *azhē n'karolam*, I will not work the bull, I will not plough, 1586.

aīsh, aish, subst., seeing, beholding, perceiving. This noun is used in connexion with the verb *kusth*, to do, in some slightly different meanings—

(1) To see, behold, perceive; *aīsh kshī*, look, 344, 822; *aīsh kshī*, look, 88, 851, 1113; be on the watch, take care, 964, 1083. In 298 we have *aīshī*, see, probably an abbreviation of *aīsh kshī*.

(2) To investigate, to ascertain, to examine; *aīsh kṛā*, I have ascertained, 75; *aīsh kshī*, ascertain, 74, 76.

(3) To take into account, to care for; *tū barwai aīsh n'kutish*, you have no pity on the coolies, 1018; *wokshhal giats, aish kshī kom*, call a doctor, I will say 'look after me', 314.

(4) To try, to make arrangements for; *Chălū iă kudūm nashisth dugă aīsh kutt*, Chānlū seeks an opportunity to harm my work, 963.

(5) To look out for, to wait for; *iă aīsh kshī*, expect me, 431; *piṭr aīsh kuttam*, I await my son, 100.

(6) To ask, demand, want; *buṛī aīsh kutt*, he asks for food,

388; *kai aīsh kuch*, what are you asking? 80; *tū kūro manchī aīsh kuchiā ushp-o-sir manchī aīsh kuchā*, do you want a footman or a horseman? 510.

A slightly different form, *osh, ōsh*, is used in the same way—

(1) To see, behold; *ōsh kulom*, I see, 1540, 1541, 1547 (*kalom*); *ōsh kṛā*, I have seen, 1126; *ōsh kshī*, look, 1092, 1714; *ōsh ktī*, having seen, beheld, 1241.

(2) To examine, to inspect; *ōsh kulom*, I will examine (your tongue), 1532; *tū kudūm ōsh kaṛsā*, I have inspected your work, 1231; *ikīest basnā tā ōsh kshī shtār assā*, examine in his clothes if he is a thief, search him to see if he is a thief, 1412; *paṛhī ōsh kusth*, books to inspect, to read books, 1129.

(3) To reflect, think; *ōts ōsh kaṛosh tū lesst manchī ass*, I thought about you that you are a good man, 1273.

(4) To look out for, to wait for; *iāst dugā ōsh kaṛsam*, didst thou look out for me? 1669; *tū iāst dugā ōsh kaṛsam*, thou hast looked out for me, p. 11; *pachanwarī ōsh kusth dugā*, in order to look out for the enemy, 1143; *shtār poh ōsh kusth dugā*, to track the thief's way, 1542.

(5) To search for, to provide; *ē manchī ōsh kshī*, get me a man, 1467; *chik ōsh kshī* (or *ōshē*) *ō dī ōsh kusth dugā zapp anam*, search for a ladder, I shall myself go shortly to search, 1249.

(6) To demand, to want; *chimr ōsh kotam*, I want an axe, 718.

ishā, subst., food, 507; see **shō**.

īash, subst., morning; *in-īash*, this morning, 287; *dalkiē piash*, to-morrow in the morning, to-morrow morning, 1048; *starak piāsh*, to-day in the morning, this morning, 1038. Also written *yazhī*; thus, *yazhī wēl*, morning, p. 65; *yazhī wēl tā*, in the morning, 881, 1147. Cf. *mizhim* in *dalkiē mizhim ēmā*, we shall go to-morrow morning, 1324.

1 **osh**, camest, see **1 Ā**.

2 **osh, oshi**, art, be, see **AS**.

ōsh, ōsh, seeing, see **aīsh.**

OSHI, to knit.

Indefinite present 2nd pers. sing. *oshich*, knittest, 747.

Present 1st pers. sing. *oshinam*, I am knitting, 747.

ushā, subst., medicine, 856. The following slightly different forms of this word occur: *ushu*, 290; *uzha*, 1480; *uzhā*, 1593; *azhur*, 703; *wish*, p. 3; *wushē*, 874; all these are instances of the object case. In an example taken from Sir G. Robertson's papers we have *uzhur dugā*, for medicine, p. 3*.

ushu-kul, medicine making, clever (of a doctor), 695.

ushī, adj., torn; *iā bazisnâ ushī bistai*, my cloth is torn, 859; cf. **SHU.**

ushu, medicine, see **usna.**

ashībâ, oshībâ, if thou art, see **AS.**

oshich, art knitting, see **OSHI.**

ashimbâ, if I am, see **AS.**

oshinam, I am knitting, see **OSHI.**

ashpā, subst., sweat; *ushp ashpā biss*, my horse is dirty with sweat, 592; *ushp ashpā afziā*, to the horse sweat has come, 1004; *iāst ushp ktol pagiur bilugh āshpā biss*, under my horse's belly there is much sweat, 1445; *iā ushpē bilugh ashpā baranziss*, on my horse much sweat has come out, 1446; *ashpē dugā*, owing to sweat, 1402. The word is apparently only used about horses' sweat.

ushp, subst., a horse. The word is often apparently a feminine; thus, 159, 341, 451, 504, 678, 679, 773, 788, 1184, 1424, 1425, 1450, 1460, pp. 1, 2, 3, 7, 11, 15. In other cases it is used as a masculine; thus, 223, 330, 352, 851, 1545, 1611, p. 2. *Ushp* accordingly simply means 'horse', and is not in itself feminine. 'A male horse' is *nāh ushp*, 675, 680, 682, or *neh ushp*, 677, p. 1. 'Mare' is *ushpē ishtrī*, 503; *ishtrī ushp*, 677, p. 1; *ishtri ushpa*, p. 8; *shtarī ushp*, 676, 680, 681. The following forms occur in the sentences :—

Vocative, *hē ushp*, O horse, O horses, p. 6.

Nom. sing. *ushp*, horse, 8, 158, 159, 191, 223, 296, 330, 341, 352, 377, 451, 454, 504, 548, 589, 593, 633, 661, 663, 665, 675, 676, 680, 681, 682, 757, 765, 773, 788, 851, 957, 977, 1075, 1098, 1173, 1184, 1203, 1385, 1425, 1426, 1427, 1450, 1492, 1493, 1545, 1548, 1611, 1666, 1683, 1689, pp. 2, 5, 6, 8, 58; *ushup*, horse, 123, 916; *ushpa*, horse, 1666, p. 8; *ishtri ushpa*, mare, p. 8; *ushpe*, horse, p. 4.

Acc. sing. *ushp*, horse, 503, 661, 663, 677, 678, 679, 765, 992, 1043, 1190, 1219, 1424, 1460, 1592, 1629, pp. 2, 3, 5, 11; *ushpē*, horse, 584, 737, 1453, pp. 5, 6. The same forms are also used to denote the indirect object; thus, *ushp n'ētē*, don't give to the horse, 811; and as a dativus commodi; thus, *ushp*, 592, 1004; *ushpē*, 1446.

Case of the agent sing. *ushap*, horse, 1365; *ushpe*, horse, 4; *ushpē*, horse, p. 6; *ushpē ishtrī*, mare, 503.

Gen. sing. *ushp*, of a horse, 157, 522, 571, 591, 662, 826, 885, 937, 993, 1037, 1096, 1138, 1173, 1174, 1385, 1402, 1445, 1457, 1488, 1541, 1604, 1617, 1625, 1678, pp. 4, 9, 15, 40; *ushpē*, of a horse, 231, 278, 375, 633, 1292, p. 6; *ushpo*, of a horse, 510, 889, p. 6.

The same forms are also used with postpositions; thus, *ushp, dugã*, for the horse, 200 (*dugā*), 505 (*dugē*), 581, 613, 1211; *ushpo mẽsh*, by means of a horse, on horseback, 40; *ushpē stē*, from a horse, p. 6; *ushp tã*, on the horse, 1219; *ushp tã wāo*, down from a horse, 340 (*wāwo*), 360, 775; *ushp tã*, to a horse, dativus commodi, 198, 307, 553, 842, 1405, 1424; *tū ushp tã shataramī*, quicker than your horse, 1450; *ushpa tã*, on the horse, 141; *ushpē tã*, to a horse, p. 6; dativus commodi, 593.

Nom. plur. *ushp*, horses, 757, 1443, p. 6; *ushpa*, horses, and *ishtri ushpa*, mares, p. 8.

Acc. plur. *ushp*, horses, 31, 279, 1114, 1256, 1354, 1555; *ushpān*, 825, p. 6.

Case of the agent plur. *ushp*, horses, p. 6.

Gen. plur. *ushp*, of horses, 1583; *ushpān*, of horses, p. 6.

Plur. base with postpositions, *ushp dugē*, for the horses, 149 ; *ushpē dugā̃*, for the horses, 578 ; *ushpā̃ dā̃*, from the horses, p. 8 ; *ushpān tā̃*, to horses, p. 6 ; *ushpān stē*, from horses, p. 6.

Note the following expressions :—

ushp amu, horse's house, stable, 1385 ; *ushp bradzī*, horse-whip, 1678 ; *ushp kudūm*, horse business, grooming, 591, p. 40 ; *ushpē nāl*, a horse's shoe, 1292 ; *ushp p'ptī tā̃*, from on the back of the horse, 1583 ; *ushp patso*, a groom, 591 ; *ushp sir manchī*, horse-top-man, horseman, 1037 ; *ushp-o-sir-manchī*, horse-top-man, horseman, 510, 889 ; *ushp sir nishishth dugā̃*, for sitting on horseback, 1096 ; *ushp psir*, on horseback, 1625 ; *ushp p'sir nishī*, sit on horseback, mount your horse, 885 ; *ushp p'sir nishel*, a rider, equestrian, 1174 ; *ushp p'tsir nishēl*, a rider, equestrian, p. 9 ; *ushp p'sir nizhisth*, to ride, 1173 ; *ushp p'tsir*, upon the horse, on the horse's carcase, 1617 ; *ushp p'tsir stē wā̃r*, down from a horse, 1488 ; *ushp wārī manchī*, a horseman, 1092 ; *ushp watsá amchol*, horseshoe fastener, a farrier, 571 ; *ushp wetsu anchōl*, a farrier, p. 15 ; *ushup wetsá amchol*, a farrier, 450 ; *ushpe wetzá*, a horse's shoe, 1292.

ūshpik, subst., a wasp, 1637 (case of the agent).

ashperuk, adj., sunny ; *inā ashperuk grām ass*, this is a sunny village, 1435.

ASHURĀ (?), to eat. Future 1st pers. sing. *ashurālom*, I shall eat, 1048; cf. **shō̃.** Perhaps *okra ashu* = porridge, and *rālom* for *yūlom*.

Ashrett, subst., Ashrett, name of a place, 1538, 1661 ; *Asrett*, 471.

oshish, art, see **AS.**

ashiss, I have sown, see **ASH.**

asht, aesht, aisht, aiesht, is, are, see **AS.**

aosht, they have come, see 1 **Ā.**

isht, subst., a spear, 1367 (nom.).

iāsht, I ate, see **YŪ.**

1 **OSHT, USHT,** to rise, stand up; to blow. The following forms occur in the sentences :—

Infinitive, *oshtasth dugă,* for rising, for starting, 1383.

Conjunctive participle, *oshtī,* having risen; *oshtī giats,* having risen fetch, rise and call, 283.

Present 3rd pers. sing. *damu ushtenn,* a wind gets up, is blowing, 1612; *damu ushtinn,* a wind is blowing, 1663.

Second present 3rd pers. sing. *dumī n'ishtatt,* there is no wind, 27 ; *dumī ishtett,* the wind blows, 167 ; *damu ushtett,* the wind blows, 1178, 1228 ; *dumī shtett,* the wind blows, 387.

Past 3rd pers. sing. *damu ushtiă,* a wind blew, 162, 1414.

Imperative, *ushtă,* rise, get up, 1180; *ushto,* stand up, 1391.

Forms such as *kai dugă n'otich,* why doest thou not rise ? 1180 ; *kai dugă n'utinshess,* why art thou not getting up ? 1232, are perhaps miswritten for *oshtich, ushtinshess,* respectively ; cf. **OTI.**

Causal verb, past, *utēa,* caused to rise ; *tŭ utēash,* I have caused thee to rise, 1180. Seems to be formed from *OTI.*

2 **osht, usht,** numeral, eight, 1318, 1709 (*osht*), pp. 12, 63.

ushtī, subst., a built-up precipice road, a pari. Nom. *ushtī,* 1184 ; *ushtiwa,* 1221 ; *ushtiwă,* 1062. Gen. *ushtī,* 407 ; *ushtiwă tă pĕr,* across the pari, 1181.

ashth, are, see **AS.**

eshtinājē, it is necessary to be, be, see **AS** (imperative).

ushtenn, ushtinn, is blowing, see 1 **OSHT.**

ashtr, subst., hill. Nom. *ashtr,* 655 ; *ashtar,* 1331. Oblique base, *ashtrē* or *oshtrē* ; *ī poshtrē,* on the hill, 499 ; *ashtrē p'sir,* on the top of the hill, 887 ; *ashtrē tă,* on the hill, 436.

ishtrī, subst., a woman, a wife. The word also occurs in the forms *istrī, shtrī,* and *shtarī.* The following forms occur : *ishtrī,* woman, pp. 1, 2 ; *istrī,* woman, 1281 (nom.) ; *ishtrī,* wife, 1691 (nom.) ; *shtrī,* wife ; *mehr shtrī awaṛiss,* the ruler has taken a bride, 742, p. 3 ; *shtrī kusth,* to contract a marriage, 1584 ; *shtarī,* wife ; *iă nawōs jus shtarī kṛiss,* he has married my nephew's daughter, 918; *shtri-ss-ē* or *ishtrī-s-ē*, to his wife, 726.

In connexion with the names of animals this word is used to denote the female, p. 1; *ishtrī ushp*, a mare, 677, p. 1; *ishtri ushpa*, a mare, mares, p. 8; *ushpē ishtrī*, the mare (agent), 503; *shtarī ushp*, a mare, 680, 681; *ishtrī kakkuk*, a hen, 645; hens, 754; *istrī kakok duts kuṛ asht*, the hen has ten chickens, 249; *ishtrī krūī*, *shtarī krūī*, a bitch, 369.

ushtar, subst., a camel, 1184; *shtur*, a camel, 222; *shtur*, camels, 1124; *shturē dugā̆*, for camels, 924.

ishtrak, now, see **shtarak.**

ashtrith, subst., bedclothes, bedding, 135.

ashtrutt tuch, subst., lead-stone; *ashtrutt tuch kōn*, a mine of lead-stone, 871.

oshtasth, to get up, to set out, see 1 **OSHT.**

ashtits, numeral, eighteen, p. 63.

ishtatt, ishtett, ushtett, is blowing, see 1 **OSHT.**

ushtiwā, a pari, a built-up precipice road, see **ushtī.**

askā, pronoun, he, that, pp. 10, 11; cf. 1 *akī*. The following forms occur, all belonging to the singular: *askā*, he, 1475; *aska*, he, p. 59; *askā*, that, is common as an attribute with nouns, and does not change for gender; cf. *askā manchī*, that man, he, 536, 1257, 1687; *askā purdā̆*, that old man, 1352; *askā istrī*, that woman, 1281; *askā jugūr*, that woman, 696; *askā vōtt*, that stone, 1189. In Abdul Hakīm Khān's examples on p. 8 *aske* is used instead.

Acc. *askē*, him, that, 1565, p. 11; *ashīā*, i.e. *askīā*, him, 1090; *askīā*, it, 1506; *askīē*, him, 1091, p. 13; *askīō*, it, 1241. As an attribute with nouns *askā* is used instead, 517, 524, p. 12. Case of the agent, *aske*, by him, pp. 3, 4; by her, p. 3; all three in examples written down by Abdul Hakīm Khān.

Gen. *askesta* (*jus*), his (daughter), p. 4 (written down by Abdul Hakīm Khān). As an attribute with nouns, *askā*; thus, *askā angā*, of that fire, 491; *askā maṛiṛ*, of that boy, 357; *askā purdikē*, of that old man, 1727; but *askē marangatsē*, of that bird, 1696.

With a noun preceded by a preposition we find *askē* in *askē badō*, on that hill, 34. *Askē* is also used before a postposition in *askē dugā*, therefore, 701.

With nouns followed by postpositions we find *askā*, *askē*, *askī*; thus, *askā potta tā*, by that road, 355; *askā pashuī tā*, in that forest, 668; *askā pazhu tā*, in that place, 1301; *askē wōs tā*, on that day, at that time, 1161; *askī wokt tā*, at that time, then, 1480.

askuē, subst., a key, 736.

asēl, he will be, he is, see **AS.**

asangā, adj., deaf; *asangā biss*, he has become deaf, 331; cf. **SANGA.**

esop, isop, subst., justice; *esop kutt*, he does justice, 1154; *isop kshī*, do me justice, 731.

Āsrett, subst., name of a place, see **Ashrett.**

ass, assa, assā, is, see **AS.**

assā, subst., ashes, cinders, 78, 636; *assē*, ashes, cinders, 79, 80.

assē, assī, assiā, is, see **AS.**

ess, essā, essī, is, was, see **AS.**

1 **oss,** subst., a day, 879; see **wōs.**

2 **oss, ossā,** is, see **AS.**

assalā, subst., a popinjay, 1147 (acc.).

assel, he may be, see **AS.**

assēl, assil, asselabā, they are, they may be, see **AS.**

assium, I was, see **AS.**

assum, I am, see **AS.**

ossam, ossum, I came, see 1 **Ā.**

assumish, we are, see **AS.**

assish, thou art, see **AS.**

assett, is, see **AS.**

aiest, is, see **AS.**

iāst, iāst, my, see 2 **Ī.**

ista, istai, they are, see **AS.**

īsta, my, see 2 **ī.**

asth, aesth, aiesth, they are, see **AS.**

aōsth, to come, see 1 **Ā.**

esth, ēsth, to go, see 1 **I.**

ėsth, ēsth, to be, see **AS.**

iasth, iăsth, to eat, see **YŪ.**

osth, osthā, osthai, they come, see 1 **Ā.**

osthē, coming, see 1 **Ā.**

istrī, woman, see **ishtrī.**

ATI, to pour out; imperative, *zū ptol tă atiōsh*, pour milk into the pot, 1052.

ētē, give; *iă ushp pul lē n'ētē,* don't give my horse much grain, 811; see 2 **PRE.**

ōt, subst., use, profit; *mizhosth kai ōt ess,* what is the use of telling lies? 799; commonly written *ōd, ūd*; thus, *iă bilugh ūd bissam,* to me much use has been to me, it has been of great use to me, 1264; *kai ōd bā,* what is the use of? 10; *kā ūd n'ess,* there is no use, it is not wanted, 912; *kai ūd n'ess,* there is no use, it is not wanted, 81, 1111; cf. **UT**; see also **utkor.**

OTI, UTI, to stay, to remain. The following forms occur:—

Infinitive, *otisth, utisth,* to remain, p. 38.

Verbal noun, *otī na batt,* he cannot stand still, 665; *uttī na battam,* (my legs are asleep) I cannot remain standing, 1328.

Present participle, *otin, utin,* remaining, p. 38; *ptior otin ess,* he is remaining behind, he is left behind, 934; *ptiwor utin ess,* he is remaining behind, he is left behind, 1144; *ptiwar utiness,* he is left behind, 1209.

Past participle, *uttā,* that which is left, leavings, p. 38; *ajik yash uttā bistai,* this much meat is left, 789; *ikīā ano uttā bistai ngātī gyē,* that meat left became, taking go, take away the remains of that meat, 1145; *du gōr rīts uttā biss,* two handfuls of barley are to spare, 1363; *uttā bistai sōn giats,* bring me the remains of the cloth, 1146.

Conjunctive participle, *otītī, utītī, uttī*, having remained, p. 38.

Indefinite present 1st pers. sing. *otim*, I shall stay, 1120.

2nd pers. sing. *kai dugā n'otich*, why doest thou not rise? 1180; seems to belong to *O<u>SH</u>T*.

1st pers. plur. *otimmi<u>sh</u>, utimmi<u>sh</u>*, we remain, p. 38.

2nd pers. plur. *otār, utār*, you remain, p. 38; *otīrba, utīrbá*, if you remain, p. 39.

Present tense 1st pers. sing. *otinam, utinam*, I remain, p. 39; *utinam*, I am done (?), 1332; *wotinam*, I am dead beat, 1276; *otinambá, utinambá*, if I remain, p. 39.

2nd pers. sing. *otinj, utinj*, thou remainest, p. 38; *otino<u>sh</u>*, thou art dead beat, 1523; *otina<u>zh</u>bá, utina<u>zh</u>bá*, if thou remain, p. 39.

3rd pers. sing. *otinn, utinn*, remains, p. 38; *otinabá, utinabá*, if he remain, p. 39.

1st pers. plur. *otinami<u>zh</u>bá, utinami<u>zh</u>bá*, if we remain, p. 39.

3rd pers. plur. *otind, utind*, they remain, p. 38; *otinabá, utinabá*, if they remain, p. 39.

Imperfect 1st pers. sing. *otinazzam, utinazzam*, I was remaining, p. 38.

2nd pers. sing. *otinazzi<u>sh</u>, utinazzi<u>sh</u>*, thou wast remaining, p. 38.

3rd pers. sing. *otinazzī, utinazzī*, he was remaining, p. 38.

1st pers. plur. *otinazzami<u>sh</u>, utinazzami<u>sh</u>*, we were remaining, p. 38.

2nd pers. plur. *otinazzār, utinazzār*, you were remaining, p. 38.

3rd pers. plur. *otinazzī, utinazzī*, they were remaining, p. 38.

Past 1st pers. sing. *otiniā'm, utiniā'm, uttā*, I remained, p. 38.

2nd pers. sing. *otiniā'sh, utiniā'sh*, remainedest, p. 38.

3rd pers. sing. *otiniā, utiniā*, remained, p. 38.

1st pers. plur. *otiniāmish*, *utiniāmish*, we remained, p. 38.

2nd pers. plur. *otīr*, *utīr* (?), you remained, p. 38.

3rd pers. plur. *otiniā*, *utiniā*, they remained, p. 38; *gā̃ṛ utinā*, logs are stranded, 1227.

Pluperfect and perfect 1st pers. sing. *otinassam*, *utinassam*, I had remained, p. 38.

2nd pers. sing. *otinassish*, *utinassish*, hadst remained, p. 38; *kai dugā̃ n'utinshess*, why hast thou not risen? 1232, seems to belong to the base *OSHT*.

3rd pers. sing. *otinassī*, *utinassī*, had remained, p. 38.

1st pers. plur. *otinassamish*, *utinassamish*, we had remained, p. 38.

2nd pers. plur. *otinassā̃r*, *utinassā̃r*, you had remained, p. 38.

3rd pers. plur. *otinassī*, *utinassī*, they had remained, p. 38.

Future 1st pers. sing. *otilom*, *utilom*, I shall remain, p. 38.

2nd pers. sing. *otilosh*, *utilosh*, wilt remain, p. 38.

3rd pers. sing. *otilā*, *utilā*, he will remain, p. 38.

1st pers. plur. *otimmá*, *utimmá*, *otīlammá*, *utīlammá*, we shall remain, p 38.

2nd pers. plur. *otilr*, *utilr*, you will remain, p. 38.

3rd pers. plur. *otilā*, *utilā*, they will remain, p. 38.

Imperative 2nd pers. sing. *otī*, *utī*, remain, p. 39; *otī*, stay, wait, 431, 1624; *otīō*, *utīō*, remain, p. 39.

3rd pers. sing. *otīlā*, *utīlā*, let him remain, p. 39.

1st pers. plur. *otimmá*, *utimmá*, let us remain, p. 39.

2nd pers. plur. *otīlā̃r*, *utīlā̃r*, remain ye, p. 39.

3rd pers. plur. *otīlā*, *utīlā*, let them remain, p. 39.

Causal verb, infinitive, *wotasth*, to place, to pitch; *jilamá wotasth*, for pitching tents, 321.

Verbal noun, *uten*, place, put; *jilamá uten na band*, they cannot place, pitch, their tents, 1664.

Past, *utēa*, caused to stand, caused to rise; *tū utēash*, I have awoke thee, 1180; cf. base **OSHT**.

Imperative, *utē*, cause to remain, keep, 733; place, put, 1094; *viär n'ūtē*, do not place down, do not throw down, 225; *watē*, put, 233; *iā ushp b'bhīm piltisth dugā n'otē*, do not put my horse to fall on the ground, don't let my horse roll on the ground, 1190; *pshuikan n'ūtan*, do not keep me sleeping, don't let me sleep, 881; *otēō*, stop, 1592; *otīō*, stop, 1412.

Some of these forms are perhaps derived from other bases.

otēā, otiō, stop, see **OTI.**

UT, to use :—

Present 3rd pers. plur. *n'utend*, they do not use, 1656; cf. **ōt.**

ūtē, keep, see **OTI.**

otich, risest, see **OTI.**

utāh, subst., a chief priest, 1069, 1070, p. 3, footnote (here treated as the name of a man in an example taken from Sir G. Robertson).

athalon, in *vott athalon*, there is a bog ahead of you, 171. The translation is probably wrong and should be 'stones are falling'; see **ATL.**

atkhi, adv., near; *ạtkhī n'iyē*, do not go near, 261; *attkhi*, near, p. 60; *attkī attē kshī chārwēlī n'vṛēlā*, hide me near, do not let the Chārwēlo see me, 652.

utkor, adj., profit-making, of use; *bhīm n'utkor ess*, the land is useless, 761, cf. **ōt** and **KR.**

ATL, to fall :—

Verbal noun, *atlon*, falling, dropping; *atlon-gai*, having been dropped, having fallen, 1237; *atlon gwā*, it was dropped, it fell, 1233.

Present 3rd pers. plur. *athalon*, fall; *vott athalon*, stones are falling, 171 (translated 'there is a bog ahead of you').

Perfect 3rd pers. sing. *atteliss*, it fell, 1164.

Causal verb imperative *wē attalāo*, throw down, 1508; cf. **WATL.**

otilā, will remain, let him, them, remain, see **OTI.**

utilī, adj., quarrelsome, boastful, vain; *bilugh utilī manchī ess,* he is very vain, 1596; *tū utilī wār bēs kshī,* make an end to that boastful speech, cease that vaunting, 1602; *tū kai dugā̃ iā̃ tā̃ utilī buch ō̃ tū tā̃ utilī n'buttam,* why art thou quarrelsome against me, I do not wish to quarrel with thee, 1101; *Bilian biluk utilī buttett,* the Chitrālīs are much quarrelsome, oppress them much, 966; *utilī bul manchī,* quarrelsome being man, an oppressor, 967. The word is probably a participle.

otilom, I shall remain, see **OTI.**

otilammâ, we shall remain, see **OTI.**

otilār, remain ye, see **OTI.**

otilr, you will remain, see **OTI.**

otilosh, wilt remain, see **OTI.**

aietam, I eat, see **YŨ.**

aietam, aiētum, I go, see 1 **I.**

otim, I shall remain, see **OTI.**

otimmâ, we shall remain, let us remain, see **OTI.**

otimmish, we remain, see **OTI.**

ATAMSH, to bite, to sting:—

Past 3rd pers. sing. *babust iā̃ brâ kūr tā̃ atamshi,* a snake bit my brother in the leg, 1342; *bāmo iā̃st naskor tā̃ attamshī,* the hornet did sting my cheek, 1403.

Perfect 3rd pers. sing. *ūshpik iā̃ dusht atamshish* (i.e. *atamshiss*), the wasp stung my hand, 1637; *bubust iā̃ kūr tā̃ atamshiss,* a snake has bitten me in the leg, 1501 (wrongly translated 'a thorn has run into my foot'); cf. **ATURSH.**

ētimish, we go, we shall go, see 1 **I.**

otin, utin, remaining; **utan,** let; **uten,** to put up, see **OTI.**

otind, utind, they remain, see **OTI.**

utend, they use, see **UT.**

otinj, remainest, see **OTI.**

otinam, I remain, see **OTI.**

otinamizhbâ, utinamizhbâ, if we remain, see **OTI.**

otinn, utinn, remains, see **OTI.**

otinosh, thou art dead beat, see **OTI.**

utinshess, risest, see **OTI.**

otinassam, utinassam, etc., I had remained, see **OTI.**

otinazzam, utinazzam, etc., I was remaining, see **OTI.**

atĕr, atŭr, adv., inside; *inā basnā shu atĕr assā,* the hairs (wool) of this cloth are inside, this is the wrong side of the cloth, 1731; very commonly used as a postposition, the governed noun being followed by the postposition *tā*; thus, *adrē tā atĕr*, inside the box, 713; *nasur tā atĕr*, inside my nose, 931; *kālo tā atūr*, inside the fort, 637; *kunī tā atūr*, in the jar, 722; also *aturēnī*; thus, *iāst tapkiĕ ashī tā aturēnī,* inside the muzzle of my gun, 902; and *attĕr*, inside, p. 60. Cf. **attā.**

atŏr, atŭr, subst., hill country. Probably identical with the preceding, the hill country being the interior country; *atŏr manchī*, a hillman, 658; *atūr manchī*, a hillman, 888; *atūr*, in the hills, 898; *atūr*, in the hills, 1173; *atŏrē*, up hill, 656, p. 61 (*atŏre*).

atūr, subst., the lungs; *atūr bradzott,* my lungs ache, 838; probably my 'intestines'.

āotre, subst., a ford, crossing of a river, 518; *p'āotre patrem,* let us ford the river, 519; once written *ātr*, 332; cf. **āo.**

otăr, you remain, **otĕr,** you remained, see **OTI.**

āotrmir, subst., an inflated skin for crossing a river, 1452, 1702, 1704; *āotarmir*, 1321; cf. **āotre.**

aturēnī, inside, see **atĕr.**

ATURSH, to attack, to bite.

Past tense 3rd pers. sing. *krūi iā tā atursiā,* the dog attacked me, 89.

Future 3rd pers. sing. *krūī aturshilon,* the dog will bite you, 152, 154.

3rd pers. plur. *māchrik aturshilā,* bees will sting, 137; cf. **ATAMSH.**

uterestā, interjection, alas, wonderful, 1144, 1716 (*uterestā*), p. 63.

ATS, to come; the following forms of this base occur in the sentences :—

Verbal noun, *ats*, to come; *wāw-ats n'battam*, I cannot come down, I cannot dismount, 665; *badō yūs atsan-dā̃* (*tā̃* ?), from hill down coming in, in going downhill, 1535.

Present participle, *atsilī*, coming, becoming; *tū tā̃ ē tang atsilī assā*, to thee one rupee is becoming, thy due is one rupee, 1175.

Conjunctive participle, *atsitī*, having come, 308, 602; *ushp tā̃ wāwo etsatī emá*, let us go having come down from the horses, let us dismount, 340.

Indefinite present 1st pers. plur. *atsomā*, we are coming, we will come, p. 58.

Present 2nd pers. sing. *atsanjī*, art coming, 1672; *atsanjībá* (written *ats anjībá*), if thou comest back, 106.

3rd pers. plur. *atsand*, they are coming, 531, 1470, 1547.

Second present 1st pers. sing. *ushp tā̃ wāo atsatam piltiosam*, I am coming down from my horse, I fell; at the time of my dismounting I fell, 360. This form is perhaps a participle.

Past 3rd pers. sing. *adsā*, 379 (an ass has come), p. 58 (he came); *odsi* in *tapak bar odsī*, the gun went off, 3.

Future 1st pers. sing. *atsalam*, 1161 (*pilingītī atsalam*, I shall return); *atsalọm*, I am coming, 1065; I shall return, 1162; *atsolam*, I shall come; *wāo atsolam*, I shall come down, I shall descend, 775; *ptiwar atsolam*, I shall come behind, I shall follow, 776.

3rd pers. sing. *atsolā*, he will come, 506, 1091, 1189 (*badō pagiōr atsalā*, on-hill down will-come, it will come down from the hill); *atsēlī* in *noi mōs atsēlī*, new moon will come, 877.

1st pers. plur. *atsomā*, we shall come, p. 58; *ptior atsomā*, we shall come behind, we shall follow, 777.

Imperative 2nd pers. sing. *ats*, come, 14, 15, 17, 59, 105, 191 (*chillā̃ ats*, come slowly, go slow), 649, 666, 703, 784, 792, p. 58; *aets*, come, 415.

īts, subst., a bear; plur. *īts*, 129, 1123; *īts nasur wāksheṣs*, a bear tore off his hose, 930.

ots, ōts, õts, ō̃ts, I, see 2 Ī.

atiōsh, pour out, see **ATI.**

ētish, goest, see 1 **I.**

utēash, I wakened, see **OTI.**

utushtī in *palol utushtī para kshī*, fill it up with earth, 400; lit. perhaps 'having lifted clay make it full'.

atsalā, atsilī, will come, see **ATS.**

atsilī, coming, due, 1175; see **ATS.**

etasal, etsal, are, is, see **AS.**

atsalam, atsalom, atsolam, I shall come, see **ATS.**

atsomā, we shall come, see **ATS.**

Utsam, subst., name of a place, 1737.

atsand, they come; **atsanjī,** comest, see **ATS.**

atsir, atsiṛ, come back, return; *iā kuī atsir wīk*, until I return, 1143; *tū atsiṛ wīk*, until thou returnest, 1586. Probably from the base **ATS.**

utseṛ, subst., a calf, 220.

etassal, he goes, see 1 **I.**

atsitī, etsatī, having come, see **ATS.**

otisth, utisth, to remain, see **OTI.**

atsatam, am coming, see **ATS.**

attā, adv. and postposition, inside; *p'amu attā*, in, into the house, 420, 423, 706. Other forms are *atto* and *attu*; *atto en n'battam*, I cannot go inside, 674; *jallai nilē tā attu prēlā*, the ducks will go into, alight on, the pond, 1042. *Attā* is often combined with *busth*, to become, to be, in the sense of getting within, hiding; thus, *anī attā bamā*, let us hide here, 651; *bugdrē p'mish attā bistai*, they are hidden in the hollow, 667; *ikyē pāṛ attā bistai*, they are hidden in that ravine, 1126; *ikīā p'mish attā bistai*, they are hidden among them, 1137. Similarly also *attē kshī*, hide me, 652. Cf. **atēr.**

ått, subst., hunger; *iā gul tā bilugh ått ess*, in my country much hunger is, in my country is a famine, 445.

åttā, adj., hungry, starving; *iāst brā åttā mṛā*, my brother is starved to death, 1393; commonly used as a predicate with *busth*, to be hungry, 86, 693, 735, 855 (*áttā*), 916, 955 (*átta*), 1075, 1274, 1393.

1 **attī,** subst., seed; *attī mēsh*, from seed, 577.

2 **attī,** having come, see 1 **Ā**.

aiett, ett, goes, see 1 **I.**

otiti, utitī, uttī, having remained, see **OTI.**

uttā, that which remains, leavings, see **OTI.**

attkī, in *ī attkī attē kshī chārwēlī n'vṛēlā*, hide me in such a place that the Chārwēlo shall not see me, 652; the literal translation is probably 'hide me near (thee), let not the Chārwēlo see me'; see **atkhī.**

attkhi, near, see **atkhī.**

attalāō, throw, see **ATL.**

atteliss, it fell, see **ATL.**

ettam, I go, see 1 **I.**

attamshi, stung, see **ATAMSH.**

attēr, inside, see **atēr.**

attrī, adv., (1) the day after to-morrow, 562, 1030, 1530, 1531, p. 60.

(2) The day before yesterday, 1738; cf. **nottrē.**

(3) Tuesday (?), p. 65. In *spāhī barwai dalkiē attrī wasnāo*, collect the sepoys and coolies to-morrow at dawn, 276, *attrī* has been translated 'at dawn'. The translation is, perhaps, wrong, and should be 'to-morrow or the day after'. If the translation Tuesday on p. 65 is right, that would presuppose a week beginning with Sunday.

ATTUSH, to load a gun; past tense, *iā tapik tū kai soss tā attushiss?* why have you loaded my gun? 816.

ettishī, goest, **ettessal,** they go, see 1 **I.**

attiss, i.e. probably *attī ess*, in *krūī p'ashī attiss*, there is a bone in my dog's mouth, 174; cf. 1 **attī** and Sanskrit *asthi*, a bone.

ATTOTI, to shut up, to imprison; cf. **ATTĀ** and **OTI.**

Past tense, *pachan warī p'amu attā attotiss*, the enemy shut me in a house, 423.

Perf. pass. 1st pers. sing. *attotinissam*, I am bound, 424.

utetti, probably conjunctive participle of *OTI*, having arisen, having departed ; *tu barē lē assiā iā barē utettī ess*, your luck is good, mine has departed, is little, 836.

attett, they come, see 1 **Ā.**

ettett, they go, see 1 **I.**

AWĒ, to bring, to take. The following forms occur :—

Infinitive, *awēsth*, to bring, to take, p. 46.

Verbal noun, *kuī shū awēn na bāchī*, you will never be able to bring information, 1311.

Present participle, *awēl*, bringing, p. 46 ; *shū awēl*, news bringing, a spy, 1383, pp. 14, 15.

Conjunctive participle, *awētī*, having fetched, 1230 ; *awītī*, having fetched, p. 46.

Indefinite present 1st pers. sing. *awēm*, I shall bring, 80, p. 46 ; *awaṛambá*, if I bring, p. 47.

2nd pers. sing. *awaṛijbá*, if thou bringest, p. 47 ; *s̲h̲talē awaṛbá*, if thou bringest, 1222.

3rd pers. sing. *awaṛabá*, if he brings, p. 47.

1st pers. plur. *awēmá*, we shall bring, p. 46 ; *n'awēmá*, we cannot carry, 339 ; *awēmis̲h̲*, we bring, p. 46 ; *awaṛamis̲h̲bá*, if we bring, p. 47.

2nd pers. plur. *awēr*, you bring, p. 46 ; *awaṛērbá* (?), if you bring, p. 47.

3rd pers. plur. *awaṛabá*, if they bring, p. 47.

Present 1st pers. sing. *awēnom*, I bring, p. 46.

2nd pers. sing. *awēnj*, thou bringest, p. 46 ; *kōr stē awenjībá*, wherever thou canst fetch, 1354.

3rd pers. sing. *awēnn*, he brings, p. 46.

3rd pers. plur. *awend*, they are bringing, 1473 ; *awēnd*, they are bringing, p. 46.

Second present 1st pers. sing. *awētum*, I carry, I bring, 229, p. 46.

3rd pers. sing. *awett*, is bringing, 207; *awētt*, is bringing, p. 46.

3rd pers. plur. *awēttett*, they bring, p. 46; they will bring, p. 46.

Imperfect 1st pers. sing. *awēnazzam*, I was bringing, p. 46.

2nd pers. sing. *awēnazzish*, wast bringing, p. 46.

3rd pers. sing. *awēnazzī*, was bringing, p. 46.

1st pers. plur. *awēnazzamish*, we were bringing, p. 46.

2nd pers. plur. *awenazzār*, you were bringing, p. 46.

3rd pers. plur. *awēnazzī*, they were bringing, p. 46.

Past 1st pers. sing. *shtowa manchī awārā*, I have fetched four men, 466; *bōr awārā*, I have brought a load, 205; *prusht awārā*, I have brought a bed, 135; *sharr awārā*, I have brought a cloth, 1725; *host susnī awarī*, I have brought a handkerchief, p. 3; *ē bōr awērā*, I have brought a load, 956; *awērā'm*, *arwarā'm*, I brought, p. 46.

2nd pers. sing. *awērā'sh*, *arwarāsh*, broughtest, p. 46.

3rd pers. sing. *utah ano awrā*, the priest brought ghi, p. 3 (from Sir G. Robertson's papers); *basná awarā*, he has brought clothes, 1066; *bōr awārā*, he has brought a load, 205, 206, 815; *shū awerā*, he has brought news, 1383; *awērā*, he brought, p. 46; *arwarā*, he brought, 584, p. 46; *jugūr awrī*, he has brought a woman, p. 3 (from Sir G. Robertson's papers); he has married, 850, pp. 2, 3.

1st pers. plur. *awērāmish* (?), *arwarāmish* (?), we brought, p. 46.

2nd pers. plur. *awērār* (?), *arwarār*, you brought, p. 46.

3rd pers. plur. *dū sai dāo awārā*, two men have brought wood, 1714; *sai wōtt awārā*, the men have brought stones, 207; *awērā*, they have brought, 1233, p. 46; *arwarā*, they brought, p. 46.

Perfect and pluperfect 1st pers. sing. *gas dōm awarissī*, I have taken a herd of goats (to the hills), 827; *dū hōst susnī awarissī*, I have brought two handkerchiefs, 614; *awarissam*, *arwarissam*, I had brought, p. 46.

2nd pers. sing. *tū dār awēshtai*, thou hast brought wood, 384; *awaṛissish, arwaṛissish*, hast brought, p. 46.

3rd pers. sing. *kachwach awaṛiss īlā awaṛiss*, he has brought fruit and milk, 1362; *patī awaṛiss*, he has brought a letter, 798; *shtrī awaṛiss*, he has taken a wife, 742, p. 3; *awaṛissī, arwaṛissī*, he had taken, p. 46; *awaṛisthai*, he took, p. 46.

1st pers. plur. *awaṛissamish, arwaṛissamish*, we had brought, p. 46.

2nd pers. plur. *awaṛissār, arwaṛissār*, you had brought, p. 46; *dao aveṛestai*, you have brought wood, p. 4.

3rd pers. plur. *awaṛissī, arwaṛissī*, they had brought, p. 46; *lattrī aṛwristai*, they have brought my luggage, 112; *awaṛisthai*, they brought, p. 46.

Future 1st pers. sing. *awēlom*, I shall bring, 688, p. 46.

2nd pers. sing. *awēlosh*, wilt bring, p. 46; *tū awēloshbā*, if you bring, 1164.

3rd pers. sing. *awēlā*, will carry, bring, 229, p. 46.

1st pers. plur. *awēmā*, we shall bring; see indefinite present.

2nd pers. plur. *awēlṛ*, you will bring, p. 46.

3rd pers. plur. *awēlā*, they will bring, p. 46.

Imperative 2nd pers. sing., formed from the conjunctive participle of *gaiesth*, to take, to seize, and *ats*, come; cf. Hindōstānī *lē āō*; thus, *gaiets*, fetch, bring, get, 134, 160, 384, 465, 1098; *gaits*, fetch, bring, get, 597, 1225; *gats*, fetch, bring, get, 110, 156, 200, 264, 505, 558, 578, 581, 613, 782, 909, 1138, 1216, 1267, 1278, 1286, 1301, 1364, 1481, 1536, 1556, 1593, 1696, 1710, 1735, p. 47; *gia'ts*, fetch, bring, get, 1376; *giats*, fetch, bring, get, 72, 79, 157 (put), 184, 199, 219, 241, 265, 283, 313, 314, 320, 367, 422, 480, 501, 512, 638, 746, 753, 765, 775, 778, 796, 860, 867, 961, 1008, 1010, 1031, 1035, 1043, 1076, 1082, 1146, 1218, 1222, 1256, 1294, 1320, 1376, 1400, 1424, 1447, 1453, 1484, 1504, 1714, pp. 15, 47; *gīąts*, get, 195; *gyats*, fetch, bring, get, 535, 679, 796, 1106.

3rd pers. sing. *awēlā*, let him bring, 610, p. 47; *Imrā n'awēlōnn*, may God not bring, 1244.

1st pers. plur. *awēmá*, let us bring, p. 47.

2nd pers. plur. *gatsār*, bring ye, p. 47.

3rd pers. plur. *awēlā*, let them bring, p. 47.

AWI, UWE, to go up, to climb; *starak sē inzaṛin bilugh digar ess awī na bam*, the glacier is very bad this year, we cannot climb it (cross it), 557; *ashtrē tā ūwē n'balem*, we shall not be able to climb the hill, 436; cf. **Ū.**

AWEGU, to ask for, to obey.

Indefinite present 2nd pers. sing. *n'awēguch*, doest not obey, 940; *iā tā paisa awēguchī*, dost thou ask me for money? 933.

Second present 3rd pers. sing. *kai awegutā*, what does he beg for? 139; see **WAG.**

iwraki, subst., a fox; *iwrakī ayūr*, fox-like, cunning, 312; see **wrikī.**

AWITĀR, to keep back. Past tense, *awitārā*, kept; *achok bor kyā na awitārā?* why have you not kept some bread? 734; *biliugh āttā bissī giaktī n'awitārā*, being very hungry I kept none, 735.

awizh, subst., want, necessity; *iāst dapil awizhess pashku awizh n'ess*, I want a metal plate, not a wooden platter, 1025.

āyā, āyo, âyū, aiyo, came, see 1 **Ā.**

āyū, iyā, ate, see **YŪ.**

iyē, pronoun, he, that, pp. 10, 11. Probably means 'this', cf. **ī,** this; also written *iyī*; *iyī manchī bilugh shtār ess iyē p'amu stē nuksāo*, this man is a great thief, eject him out of the house, 410; *iyē pamu stē tōṛ kṛā*, I turned him out of the house, 1568; *iyē bado bilugh opigná ess*, this mountain is very lofty, 818.

iyī, pronoun, this, see **iyē.**

ayūr, like to; *iwrakī ayūr*, fox-like, cunning, 312, p. 9 (*wrikī*). Cf. **agūr, agyūr, yōr.**

iyasht, to eat, see **YŪ.**

āyosam, aiyōsam, I have come, see 1 **Ā.**

ayasar, they have come see 1 **Ā.**

az, aza, azia, ezā, see **AS.**

izē, pronoun, he, that, pp. 10, 11; nom. *izē*, he, 1661; cf. **akī,** he.

oz, came, see 1 **Ā.**

a<u>zh</u>ā, subst., an egg, 9; acc. plur. *azio*, 754; *a<u>zh</u>ao*, 409.

a<u>zh</u>e, subst., a bull; *a<u>zh</u>ē n'kaṛolam*, I will not work the bullock, I will not plough, 1586; cf. **a<u>sh</u>u.**

A<u>ZH</u>I, to throw, to sow, see **A<u>SH</u>.**

azhī, mouth, see **a<u>sh</u>ī.**

1 **a<u>zh</u>ō,** throw, see **A<u>SH</u>.**

2 **a<u>zh</u>ō,** be, see **AS.**

i<u>zh</u>ā, is, see **AS.**

u<u>zh</u>a, subst., medicine, 1480; *u<u>zh</u>ā*, medicine, 1593; *a<u>zh</u>ur*, medicine, 703; *u<u>zh</u>ur*, medicine, p. 3 (from Sir G. Robertson's papers); see **u<u>sh</u>ā.**

a<u>zh</u>ībā, if there be, see **AS.**

i<u>zh</u>ībā, you may go, see 1 **I.**

a<u>zh</u>ichi, thou art, see **AS.**

a<u>zh</u>ik, so much, see **ajik.**

a<u>zh</u>alā, may it be, see **AS.**

O<u>ZH</u>AM, to rest; infinitive, *o<u>zh</u>amesth*, to rest, 1158, 1159.

o<u>zh</u>umā, subst., a hospital; *o<u>zh</u>umā tā*, to the hospital, 703; cf. **u<u>sh</u>ā,** medicine.

a<u>zh</u>ir, subst., a violent shower, hail, 604; *a<u>zh</u>iṛ*, 1414.

a<u>zh</u>ur, u<u>zh</u>ur, medicine, see **u<u>sh</u>ā.**

a<u>zh</u>isto, so much, see **ajik.**

azinj in *baron azinj*, art vomiting, see **A<u>SH</u>.**

azār, numeral, four hundred (or, sometimes, thousand), p. 63.

azãr, you are, you were, see **AS.**

azēṛbā, if you are, see **AS.**

azs, azz, azzā, azziā, ezz, ezzā, was, see **AS.**

āzittā, when he came, **ozz,** came, see 1 **Ā.**

azzum, am, see **AS.**

UZZAM, to yawn; present 2nd pers. sing. *uzzamanj*, yawnest, 1733.

azzamish, azzumish, we are, we were, see **AS.**
azzirā, are you ? see **AS.**
azzish, azzush, art, wast, see **AS.**

B

b, ba, bi, preposition, in, on, towards, see **p.**
bā, became, see **BŪ.**
bá, bā, and (once) **wā,** a particle added to verbal forms, with a hypothetical force or denoting uncertainty; thus, *kōr ettabá,* they go somewhere or other, 1244; *izhībā,* (when thou hast rested) thou mayest go, 1157; *ão pa chuk wīk bibā,* (when the snow melts) the water may reach to the chest, 1183; *iã barē assabā,* to me hope may be, I hope, 589; *bibidī bibā,* in my mind may be, I hope, 424; *kai mãrnazushba,* thou saidest something, p. 4; *pochētr ngūsthabá kai faidā butt,* what use is there to keep fast ? 1141.

bá, bā, is very often used in subordinate sentences containing an interrogative pronoun. The following examples occur :—

With *chuk,* how much ? *ikīā kudūm chuk dī karbá kā paidā na ess,* that work how much even doest any result not is, however you do that work, it will be in vain, 1597.

With *kai,* what ? *tū kai manumbá,* whatever you order me, 968; *kaikotī wilāmbá,* what-having-said I tell, as I tell, 1594.

With *kuī, koī, kai,* when ? *kuī agal yũr onzībá,* when water down comes, when it rains, 1166; *kuī tū tã tapī onzībá,* when thee to fever comes, if you ever have fever, 1466; *kuī ossabū,* when he came, 1252; *koī ão pig bibā,* when one is thirsty, 1041; *kuī shillā bilugh bibá,* when it is very cold, 1431; *kuī stē ão chok biss-bā,* since the water became low, 1227; *kuī gujbá,* when you go, 1202, 1411; *koī purū kolaibā,* when you give me leave, 1003; *kuī pibá,* when you have drunk, 1480; *kai Chandrāl parizhbá,* when you reach Chitral, 1563; *kuī putarijbá,* when you cross, 1331; *koī samarijbá,* when you start, 1067; *kuī zīm vilnabā,* when the snow melts, 1183; *koī warībá*, when they appear, 822; *kuī waṛimbá*, when you see me, 1671; *kui waṛinbá*, when you see, 1308; note *kuī iāst shai tā wōtt praptawā*, when the stone hit me on the head, 1260, where *bá* seems to have been replaced by *wā*.

With *kōr*, where? *kōr hinju bundabá*, where tamarisks grow, 1465; *kōr stē awenjībá*, from wherever you can fetch, 1354; *tīnch n'ess korē endabá*, one does not know where they can go, 1125; *tīch n'bunn kōr asselabā*, I do not know where they may be, 1417; *korār assabá tīch n'ess*, I do not know where it may be, 1357.

If there is no interrogative pronoun such forms may be considered as a kind of conditional, and *bá*, *bā*, when added to the present, past, or future of a verb can be translated 'if', 'when'; see pp. 17 and 29. Most such forms occur in the paradigms of verbs. They are—

From *Ā*, to come: *anjībá*, if thou comest, 106, p. 58.

From *I*, to go: *enjībá*, if thou goest, 702, 1582, p. 17.

From *ACHŪN*, to run, in the paradigm on p. 37—

Sing. 1.	*achūnambá*.	Plur. 1.	*achūnamishbá*.
2.	*achūnashbá*.	2.	*achūrbá*.
3.	*achūnabá*.	3.	*achūnabá*.

From *AMJI*, to put on, in paradigm on p. 49—

Sing. 1.	*amjilambá*.	Plur. 1.	*amjimmabá*.
2.	*amjiloshbá*.	2.	*amjīlrbá*.
3.	*amjilabá*.	3.	*amjilabá*.

From *AS*, to be, in paradigm on p. 19—

Sing. 1.	*ashimbá*.	Plur. 1.	*azumishá*.
2.	*ashībá*.	2.	*azēṛbá*.
3.	*azhībá*.	3.	*azzabá*.

The following occur in the sentences: *ashībá*, if thou art, 617; *oshībá*, if thou art, 617; *azhībá*, if there is, 1381; *shtalē n'azilabá*, if there perhaps is not, 436.

From *OTI*, to remain, in paradigm on p. 39—

Sing. 1.	*otinambá.*	Plur. 1.	*otinamizhbā.*
2.	*otinazhbá.*	2.	*otịrbá.*
3.	*otinabá.*	3.	*otinabá.*

From *AWĒ*, to bring, in paradigm on p. 47—

Sing. 1.	*awaṛambá.*	Plur. 1.	*awaṛamishbá.*
2.	*awaṛijbá.*	2.	*awarīrbá* (?).
3.	*awaṛabá.*	3.	*awa ·bá.*

Other forms, occurring in the sentences, are: *awēloshbá*, if thou findest, 1164; *awaṛbá*, if you bring, 1222.

From *BŪ*, to become, in paradigm on p. 21—

Sing. 1.	*bulazzambá.*	Plur. 1.	*bomazzībá.*
2.	*bulazzishbá.*	2.	*bulāzrbá.*
3.	*bulazzībá bulazhbá.*	3.	*bulazzībá.*

Other forms, occurring in the sentences, are: *bimbá*, if I become, 952; *agal bibá*, if rain falls, 1119, 1120; *epor bibā*, when the rutting season comes, 1214; *namāj bibá*, when prayer-time comes, at the time for prayer, 101; *ē panishar bibá ē ptior bibá*, if one goes first and one behind, 907; *ruch bibá*, at daylight, 329 (*ruzh*), 785; *sū tsāwen bibā*, at sunset, p. 65; *bulozhbá*, if thou wilt stay, 1395.

From *GŪ*, to go, in paradigm on p. 23—

Sing. 1.	*gūmba.*	Plur. 1.	*gūmishbá.*
2.	*gūjbá.*	2.	*gūrbá.*
3.	*gūbá, gaiebá.*	3.	*gūbá.*

Of these the following occur in the specimens: *gujbá*, if thou goest, 46; *be gūbá* (written *begū bá*), when he goes out, 964; *gaiebá*, when it has gone, 922, 923.

From *JĀR*, to kill: *jāṛabá*, if you kill, 1564; *jārībá*, if one kills, 967.

From *KṚ*, to do, in paradigm on p. 25—

Sing. 1.	*kaṛbá* (also p. 17), *kulaibá*.	Plur. 1.	*kummabá* (?).
2.	*kulojbá, kunjībá, kshonjībá*.	2.	*kuṛbá* (?).
3.	*kaṛbá*.	3.	*kulabá*.

The following forms occur in the sentences: *kaṛbá*, if thou doest, 554, 577, 729; *kulaibá*, if thou makest, 1487; *shtār kulājbá*, if thou doest theft, 1396; *ptul kudūm kaṛbo manchī lesta balā*, if he does agriculture work, a man will be well, 22.

From *MUK*, to flee: *mukinjebá*, if I flee away from thee, 495.

From *MṚ*, to die, in paradigm on p. 27—

Sing. 1.	*mṛambá*.	Plur. 1.	*mṛamizhbá*.
2.	*mṛojbá*.	2.	*mṛēbá*.
3.	*mṛabá*.	3.	*mṛubá*.

From *NGĀ*, to take, in paradigm on p. 43—

Sing. 1.	*ngūtambá* (?).	Plur. 1.	*ngāmabá* (?).
2.	*ngūlazzībá* (?).	2.	*ngā'ṛbá* (?).
3.	*ngūtabá*.	3.	*ngūtabá*.

From *NISH*, to sit, in paradigm on p. 43—

Sing. 1.	*nizhēlambá*.	Plur. 1.	*nizhēlamishbá*.
2.	*nizhēlazhbá*.	2.	*nizhēlrbá*.
3.	*nizhēlabá*.	3.	*nizhēlabá*.

From *NIZHŌ*, to set, in paradigm on p. 55—

Sing. 1.	*nizhālezambá*.	Plur. 1.	*nizhālazamishbá*.
2.	*nizhālezishbá*.	2.	*nizhālezṛbá*.
3.	*nizhālezībá*.	3.	*nizhālezībá*.

From *POI*, to finish: *poishabá*, when you have finished, 479; *pūshabá*, when you have finished, 415.

From *PILT*, to fall: *piltabá*, if it falls, 1118, 1120, and perhaps *sū pinjebā*, at sunset, 672, 1437.

From *PILTŌ*, to fell, in paradigm on p. 57—

Sing. 1.	*piltōmbá.*	Plur. 1.	*piltōmabá* (?).
2.	*piltōshbá.*	2.	*piltôrbá* (?).
3.	*piltōbá.*	3.	*piltōlabá* (?).

From *PRĒ*, to give, in paradigm on p. 45—

Sing. 1.	*prēlombá.*	Plur. 1.	*prēlomishbá.*
2.	*prēloshbá.*	2.	*prēlõrbá.*
3.	*prēlābá.*	3.	*prēlābá.*

Further, *prēnjībá*, if thou givest, 555; *n'prenjībá*, if thou doest not give, 185.

From *PEṚ*, to break: *peṛinjībá*, if thou breakest, 187.

From *PSHĪ*, to grind, in paradigm on p. 51—

Sing. 1.	*pshīnambá.*	Plur. 1.	*pshīmishbá.*
2.	*pshīshbá* (?).	2.	*pshīrbá.*
3.	*pshībá.*	3.	*'pshībá.*

From *SHOTIN*, satisfied: *n'shotinestabá*, if (any man) is dissatisfied, 841.

From *SAMAR*, to start: *samrī bá*, when you start, 786.

From *WI*, to beat, in paradigm on p. 53—

Sing. 1.	*winambá.*	Plur. 1.	*winamishbá.*
2.	*winoshbá.*	2.	*wīrbá* (?).
3.	*winabá.*	3.	*winabá.*

Further, *vichībá*, if thou pushest, 1093.

From *WAṚ*, to see: *waṛinbá*, if thou seest, 1347.

From *YŪ*, to eat, in paradigm on p. 41—

Sing. 1.	*yūnambá.*	Plur. 1.	*yūmishbá.*
2.	*yūnjbá.*	2.	*yūrbá.*
3.	*yūnabá.*	3.	*yūndabá.*

Further, *iārabá*, if eaten, if one eats, 999, 1372, 1431.

From *ZĀṚ*, to know: *le zānchībá*, if I know thee as good, if thou pleasest me, 1029.

be, **bē**, adv., out; *do be afzia*, water comes out, leaks out, 412; *pamu be gūbá* (written *begū bá*), when he goes out of the house, 964; *pamu bē ī*, go out of the house, 974; *bē*, *begū*, outside of, p. 62 (*begū* literally means 'gone out'); *ikīā manchī duī tā luī bekshá*, that man's forearm from blood out make, bleed his forearm, 161.

bēo, subst., a wooden spade, 1364 (acc.); *chimbio*, an iron spade, 1364.

bī, subst., seed; *bī bhīm tā azhisth*, to throw seeds into the earth, to sow seeds, 835, 1253, 1363, 1516; *ba biā azhind*, they throw into seed, they winnow (the rice), 1697.

BŪ, to become, to be. The following forms occur in the sentences:—

Infinitive, *busth*, to become, pp. 20, 29, footnote.

Verbal noun, *boh*, to become; *mashikr boh less noh*, to be angry is not good, 43; *trāchī bō dugā*, in order to guard, 597.

Present participle, *bul*, becoming, 20; *utilī bul manchī*, oppressing being man, an oppressor, 967; *bom* in *bom-azzībá*, if we become, p. 21.

Past participle passive, *bist*, *bista*, *bistai*, become; *kapā bist waṛon ess*, angry become looking is, he seems vexed, 1607; *osht sē bist juk*, eight years become girl, a girl of eight years, 1709; *dots sē bista mariṛ*, boys of ten years, 1097; *uttā bistai sōn giats*, bring me the remains of the cloth, 1146; and perhaps also *ikīā ano uttā bistai ngātī gyē*, of that meat remaining become taking go, take away the remains of that meat, 1145. In the last example, however, *bistai* can also be past tense.

Conjunctive participle, *bissī*, having become, p. 20; *bitī*, having become, 335, 467, 973, 1260, 1394, p. 20; *bītī*, having become, 470, 569, 712, 907 (*yāmna bītī*, in pairs), p. 20; *mōs pichis oss bitī dū oss dī biss*, moon fifteen days having-become two days also have-become, it is two days after full moon, 879; *tinj bitī*, intentionally, 3, 951 (*bītī*); *dūr bitī ass*, bent having-become is, he has got cramp, 297; *kapā bitī*, having become angry, he is angry, 409 (in the last example *ass* has been dropped); *botī*, having become; *malal botī*, having become late, 770; *bot-asalā*, becoming-is? does it become? p. 20; *āṛu attī mē<u>sh</u> botasalā giṭu karbá botasalā*, peaches seed from coming-are, grafting make-if coming-are? do peaches come from seed or from grafting? 577; *butī*, having become, 134, 981 (*yamnā butī*, in pairs), p. 20; *būtī*, having become, p. 20.

Indefinite present 1st pers. sing. *bim*, I become, I may become; *eila bim-bá*, if I become going (upon the hill), if I climb, 952; *bimtā*, if I become, p. 21.

2nd pers. sing. *buch*, becomest, p. 20; *kāwo gul tā buch*, in which nullah dost thou live? 813; *utilī buch*, art thou quarrelling? 1101; *bi<u>sh</u>tā*, if thou becomest, p. 21.

3rd pers. sing. *bibá*, *bibā*, if it becomes; *agal bibá*, if rain falls, 119, 1120; *epor bibā*, when the rutting season comes, 1214; *ē pani<u>sh</u>ar bibá ē ptior bibá*, if one goes first and one follows, 907; *namāj bibá*, when prayer-time comes, at the time for prayer, 101; *ruch bibá*, at daylight, 329 (*ru<u>zh</u>*), 785; *sū tsāwen bibā*, sunset, p. 65; *koī áo pig bibá*, when one gets thirty, 1041; *kuī <u>sh</u>illā bibá*, when it is cold, 1431; *pa chuk wīk biḅā*, it may get up to the chest, 1183; *bibidī bibā*, it may be in my mind, I hope, 424.

1st pers. plur. *bumi<u>sh</u>*, *būmi<u>sh</u>*, we become, p. 20; *bimistá*, if we become, p. 21.

2nd pers. plur. *būr*, you become, p. 20; *bīr-dá*, if you become, p. 21.

Present 1st pers. sing. *bunam*, *būnam*, I become, p. 20.

2nd pers. sing. *būnjī*, thou becomest, p. 20.

3rd. pers. sing. *bonā*, it becomes, it is, 654, p. 20; *bunn*, it becomes, it is, 1187, 1191, 1328, 1372, 1417, 1433, 1465, 1466, 1468, 1472, 1569, 1595, 1715; *būnn*, it becomes, it is, p. 20.

3rd pers. plur. *bund*, they become, they are, 1371, 1602, 1678, p. 20; *ai<u>sh</u> k<u>sh</u>ī chil būnd*, take care they are soft, 1083; *kōr bundabá*, where they may be, 1465.

2nd present 1st pers. sing. *utilī n'buttam,* I do not wish to quarrel, 1101.

3rd pers. sing. *bittā* (?), if it becomes, p. 21; *ē par bitta tā,* when there becomes one direction, at the junction, 728; *bitto,* becomes, p. 20; *iā chitt bitto,* I have a mind to, 739; *butt,* becomes, is, 128, 254, 348, 387, 637, 865, 945, 1041, 1141, 1183, 1193, 1195, 1268, 1431, 1516, 1695, 1723; *būtt,* becomes, p. 21; *buttā,* becomes, 654; *būttā,* becomes, p. 20; *buttett,* becomes, is, 606, 1129, p. 20.

buttaser, becomes, p. 20; *buttosal,* there is, 759, are formed by adding tenses of *AS* to this present.

3rd pers. plur. *bittā,* if they become, p. 21; *shtowa bitta kshī,* make that four may become, divide into four, 1049 (very uncertain form); *troi wōs butt,* three days become, for three days, 349; *charra buttā,* (I fear) they will become idiotic, 1695; *buttet,* they are, 1082; *buttett,* they become, they are, 872, 883, 966, 1046, 1083.

Present definite, 1st pers. sing. *bulazzambá,* if I become, p. 21.

2nd pers. sing. *bulazzishbá,* if thou becomest, p. 21.

3rd pers. sing. *bulazhbá,* if he becomes, p. 21; *bulazzibá,* if he becomes, p. 21.

1st pers. plur. *bomazzībá,* if we become, p. 21.

2nd pers. plur. *bulāzrbá,* if you become, p. 21.

3rd pers. plur. *bulazzībá,* if they become, p. 21.

Past tense; the base is *bā,* or, sometimes, *biā* or *bo,* to which personal suffixes can be added.

1st pers. sing. *bā,* I became; *áo pik bā,* I have become, I am thirsty, 1496; *átta bā,* I am hungry, 955; *átta bá,* I am hungry, 855; *bā'm,* I became, p. 20.

2nd pers. sing. *bā'sh,* becamest, p. 20; *kai kotī shuā bāsh,* what doing alert becamest? how didst thou escape, 1716; *bōsh,* becamest, p. 20; *tū kā kapā bosh,* why didst thou get angry? why art thou angry? 234; *bozhā,* becamest, p. 20.

3rd pers. sing. *bā*, became, p. 20; can often be translated 'is' and is consequently also given as a present on p. 20; *álla bā*, (my stomach) has become big, is swelled, 857; *kai ōd bā*, what use has become? what is the advantage? 10; *digar bā*, has gone bad, is bad, 118 (*digara*), 302, 303, 604 (*digr*); *bilugh drē bā*, it is a long time, 1517; *deṛh bā*, he was surprised, taken by surprise, 1440; *gatrā bā*, he has got tired, 1545; *lē bā*, it has become plentiful, 1064; *lesta bā*, it has become good, 118; *pōnduk bā*, there has become a boil, there is a boil, 67, 68; *ruch bā*, light became, daylight, p. 64; *tū shū bā*, to thee knowledge became? didst thou feel? 1510; *shillā bā*, it has become cool, it is cool, 18, 26 (*shil*), 274; *shāra bā katī erwemá*, autumn has come, let us reap the wheat, autumn is the time for reaping wheat, 94; *shotik n'bā*, it is not fit, 242; *tinch n'bā*, certainty not became, I have no proof, 1078; *wosut bā*, spring has come, 587; *emá zur bā*, to us oppression became, we are oppressed, 1430; *biā*, became, *pār lang biā*, (the sun) has set, 274; *piz biā*, became lost, 114, 381; *wasut biā*, spring has come, 165.

1st pers. plur. *bamish*, we became; *gatrabamish*, we got tired, I got tired, 1060; *bámish*, we became, p. 20.

2nd pers. plur. *bōr*, you became, p. 20.

3rd pers. plur. *bā*, they became, p. 20; *chinai bā*, (the apricots) have become sour, 65; *pkhula bā*, they have become rotten, they are rotten, 1254; *poṛ bā*, they have become green, 587; *piz bā*, they have been lost, 1417; *pizh bā*, (of the trees) blossoms have become, 165; *pōj sē bā*, five years have become, five years ago, 406; *trē sa bā*, three years ago, 452; *shets sē bā*, for sixteen years, 1581; *latta wōs bā*, for many days, 350; *shto wōs bā*, for four days, 469; *sutt wōs bā*, for seven days, 1346.

Imperfect 1st pers. sing. *būnazzam*, *bunazzam*, I was becoming, p. 20.

2nd pers. sing. *būnazzish*, wast becoming, p. 20.

3rd pers. sing. *būnazzī*, was becoming, p. 20.

1st pers. plur. *būnazzamish*, we were becoming, p. 20.

2nd pers. plur. *būnazār*, you were becoming, p. 20.

3rd pers. plur. *būnazzī*, they were becoming, p. 20.

Perfect and pluperfect 1st pers. sing. *iā̆ ā̆o pig biss*, I have become thirsty, I am thirsty, 866; *ā̆ttā bissī*, I had become hungry, I was hungry, 86, 735; *bissam*, I have become, I am; *muzalmān bissam*, I have turned Musalmān, 452; *ā̆ttā bissam*, I have got hungry, 693; *ā̆o tā̆ p'mich bissam*, I have sunk into the water, 1316; *bissium*, I had become, p. 20; *bissum*, I had become, p. 20; *gatra bissum*, I have become tired, 229; *kapā bissum*, I have become annoyed, angry, 1063, 1361, 1606; *bosam*, I had become, p. 20, footnote; *gatrā bosam*, I have got tired, 644.

2nd pers. plur. *tū ā̆ttā biss*, thou hast become hungry, 1274; *tū ks͟hul bistā̆*, if thou hadst been wise, 1700; *bosis͟h*, hadst become, p. 20, footnote; *bissis͟h*, hadst become, p. 20; *chaṛṛā bissis͟h*, thou hast become idiotic, 701, 843 (*chaṭṭā*); *gatrā bissis͟h*, hast become tired, 107, 1157, 1503, 1523; *gatrā bissis͟hā*, hast thou become tired? 1307; *kapā bissis͟h*, thou art annoyed, angry, 543, 1217, 1667; *kai dugā s͟htār bissis͟h*, why have you become a thief? 985.

3rd pers. sing. *basa*, has become, is; *kāchī ngāla basa*, who is taking? who takes? 1458; *bosel*, has become, has happened, 830; has become, is, p. 20; *iā̆ purugul bosellā*, has there become leave to me? have I leave to depart? 36; *biss*, has become, is, 9, 103, 121, 147, 164, 169, 188, 223, 230, 237, 239, 252, 258, 301, 325, 326, 331, 377, 412, 521, 522, 553, 592, 595, 629, 634, 664, 712, 804, 826, 872, 902, 916, 937, 983, 1047, 1075, 1084, 1116, 1165, 1203, 1220, 1237, 1243, 1248, 1281, 1289, 1317, 1320, 1330, 1385, 1401, 1408, 1415, 1432, 1445, 1454, 1455, 1461, 1462, 1489, 1552, 1554, 1561, 1575, 1607, 1611, 1634, 1643, 1653, 1708, p. 59; *kuī stē ā̆o chok biss bā̆*, since the water fell, 1227; *iā̆ bilug͟h ūd bissam*, to me much use has-become to me, (your service) is very advantageous to me, 1264; *bissa*, has become; *mulc͟hun bissa*, she has become dirty, p. 8 (Abdul Hakīm K͟hān); *kaz͟hīrā bissā*, it has grown white, 131; *bissā*, has there become? 1290; *bissī*, had become, p. 20; *kilā bissī*, a quarrel had become, there was a quarrel, 354; *bissiā*, had it become? 1335; *tū kai bissish*, what has become to thee? 853; *kaī prōr bissish, tarwoch prōr bissizhā, tapkiē pondrik prōr bissishā*, what wound has become to thee? has a sword wound become to thee or has a bullet wound become to thee? 1724; *bistai*, had become, p. 20; *ushī bistai*, (my cloth) has become torn, 859; *uttā bistai*, has been left, 789, 1145; *digar bistai*, has grown bad, has been destroyed, 842, 1133; *kazhīra bistai*, has become white, 605; *siūm bistai*, has grown old, 943.

1st pers. plur. *bosamish*, we had become, p. 20, footnote; *gatrā bosamish*, we have become tired, we are tired, 608; *bissiumish*, we had become, p. 20.

2nd pers. plur. *bosār*, you had become, p. 20, footnote; *bissār*, you had become, p. 20; *gatrā bissār*, you have become tired, you are tired, 1315.

3rd pers. plur. *biss*, have become; *uttā biss*, they are left, 1365; *dū oss biss*, two days have passed, 879; *dū mōs biss*, two months have passed, two months ago, 884; *trē mōs biss*, three months have passed, for three months, 629; *dū sē biss*, two years have passed, for two years, 393; *chi sē biss*, how many years have passed? how long? 569; *troi sē biss*, for three years, 383; *emá tott wāo inā bagrām shtowa alo biss*, my forefathers have lived in this village for four generations, 549; *mehrkruē dits sē biss*, to the prince twelve years have become, the prince's age is twelve years, 1072; *kunzā jūs dots sē biss*, the princess's age is ten years, 1073; *bissā*, have become; *chok sē bissā*, how many years have gone? how old is he? 19; *nāru bissā*, there are clouds, 1002; *bissī*, they had become, p. 20; *bistā*, have become, 727; *bistai*, they had become, p. 20; *attā bistai*, they have got within, they are hidden, 667, 1126, 1137; *daḍar bistai*, (the cows) have grown thin, 972; *gū bistai*, (the pears) have become sour, 997; *kaṛtī bistai*, (the veins) stand out, 1604; *mol bistai*, they have become dirty, they are dirty, 267, 357; *mātā bistai*, they have become late, they are delaying, 1130; *parmenstuk bistai,* (the crops) have got stunted, 1428; *puz bistai,* (the goats) have been lost, 1217; *shangūr bistai,* (my fingers) have become numb, are numb, 936; *yagi bistai,* they have turned rebels, 1135.

Future 1st pers. sing. *balom,* I shall become; *kabā balom,* I will be angry, 187; *kujhēl balom,* I shall be happy, 555; *panishr balom,* I will go ahead, 1143; *bolam,* I shall become; *burùbiz bolam,* I will be angry, 46; *bulom,* I shall become, I shall stay, 1413, p. 20; *būlom,* I shall become, p. 20.

2nd pers. sing. *būlosh,* wilt become, p. 20; *digar būlosh,* wilt become wretched, wilt come to grief, 1080; *chārwēlī n'būlosh,* wilt not become Chārwēlī, 1160; *bulozhbá,* if thou stay, 1395; *bulass,* wilt become, p. 20; *bradzowo bolass,* wilt get ill, 475.

3rd pers. sing. *balā,* will become; *lessta balā,* it will be good, it is right, all right, 341, 907, 1222, pp. 20 note, 63; *bolā,* will become; *má bilugh paidā bolā,* much rice will be produced (the translation 'has been produced' is not correct), 1170; *tāp bolā,* it will be hot, 699; *bulā, būloh,* will become, p. 20; *bolan,* will become, may become; *ingol kā agol bolan,* perhaps rain will come, 268.

1st pers. plur. *būmmá,* we shall become, p. 20.

2nd pers. plur. *būlōr,* you will become, p. 20.

3rd pers. plur. *bulā, būloh,* they will become, p. 20.

Imperative 2nd pers. sing. *bō,* become, be, p. 21; *odh bō,* be merciful, 863; *kabā na bō,* do not be angry, 44; *kapā n'bō,* do not be angry, 1148; *nashtarwai bō,* get in front, go ahead, 138, 506; *panoi bo,* lead thou, 776; *tarāchī bo,* be on your guard, take care, beware, 127, 152 (*taraīchī*), 225, 439 (*trāchī*), 666 (*taraīchī*), 1108 (*tarāchī*), 1330 (*trāchī*), p. 63.

3rd pers. sing. *bā, bá, billie,* let him be, p. 21; *bilā,* let him be; *piz bilā,* let it be lost, leave it alone, 797; *n'gatri-bōla,* let there not be weariness, don't be tired, 182.

1st pers. plur. *bammá,* let us become, p. 21; *anī attā bamá,* let us get within here, let us hide here, 651.

2nd pers. plur. *bŭr*, become ye, p. 21; *panoi bŏr*, become ahead, lead ye, 777; *trăchī bŭr*, be careful, 1439.

3rd pers. plur. *bulā*, let them become, p. 21.

bābū, subst., a babu, 306, 566, 590, 868, 1655.

bibā, bibâ, it may be, when it becomes, see **BŪ.**

babdī, bibdī, bibidī, in the mind, see **bidī.**

b'bhīm, b'bhiom, in the ground, see **bhīm.**

bābakar, subst., a kind of bird, monāl, 1007.

bibimst, subst., a snake; *bibimst mēsh mishishth*, to show kindness to a snake, 741. Other forms of the same word are *babust*, 1342, and *bubust*, 1501 (wrongly translated 'a thorn').

bachā, bachī, thou canst, see **BAN.**

buch, thou becomest, see **BŪ.**

b'doī, b'duī, to hand, see **doī.**

b'dū, at the door, see 1 **dū.**

badi pāsha, subst., the fifth month of the year, p. 65.

badō, badu, on the hill, on the pass, see 1 **dō.**

bidī, subst., mind; *iăst bidī assā*, my mind is, I am sure, 899; *tū kai bidī ess*, what is thy mind? what is thy intention? 714; *tū bidī kā'st azz*, what is thy wish? 1701; *tōst bidī tā*, in thy mind, according to thy wish, 1369; *bidīo*, of heart, p. 5; *āl bidī*, high mind, noble disposition; *āl bidi-o*, of noble disposition, generous, 927; *āl bidīwā*, of noble disposition, generous, 361, 550 (*bidiwā*), 1055, p. 5; *digar bidī*, bad mind; *digar bidī-o*, of a bad heart, hard, 619; *less bidī*, good mind, manliness, 843; *le bidī-wā*, of good intention, kindhearted, 740, p. 5; *bidī* is often preceded by the preposition *pa*, and it is then generally abbreviated to *bdī* or, occasionally, *pdī*; the following instances occur: *babdī ess*, it is in the mind, (I) think, consider, 962, 1324; *bapdī ess*, I hope, 672; *iā babdī n'azziā*, it has not been in my mind, I have not remembered, 1148; *Imrā bapdī azhalā*, may it be in God's mind, may God bear it in mind (and give punishment), 526; *bibidī bibā*, it comes in my mind, I hope, 424; *bibdī kshām*, I make in my mind, I think, 810; *tū bibidī n'kshonjī tū* *kăktī zaronlosh*, thou in-mind not-makest thou what-having-done wilt-learn? you don't make an effort, how can you learn? 408; *babdī kashītī gijjī kshī*, in-mind having-made speech make, think before you speak, 1494; *babdī kshātam*, I put in my mind, I think, I suspect, I fear, 1042, 1179, 1441 (*kshâtam*).

Badakshān, subst., name of a country. The final *n* of this word can be dropped, and the preceding *ā* may then be nasalized. The following forms occur: *Badakshān*, in Badakshān, 1124; *Badakshān bakhta muzharla*, of the Badakshāni sheep, 1715; *Badakshā̃ mē*, to Badakshān, 458; *Badakshā̃ Shdral stē p'mich*, between Badakshān and Chitral, 540; *Badakshān'st ushp-bradzī*, Badakshānī horse-whips, 1678.

bedina-wā, adj., silly; *tū bilugh bedina-wā assish*, you are very silly, 1311.

badrai, subst., a kind of vegetable, 1168.

badūr, badur, badūṛ, bidūr, far, see **dūr.**

badere, badeore, badūrē, in the plains, see **diwar.**

b'darstā̃, bdristān, b'durestān, in the garden, see **darestān.**

b'dosh, b'dush, b'dusht, in the hand, see **dusht.**

badisnâ, subst., cloth; *badisnâ dugā̃*, for the cloth, 1068; see **basnâ.**

badist, subst., heaven, the sky; *dsudsuk ojē bàdiste n'zā̃ṛtett*, they do not know Hell and Heaven, 643; *badist azhir*, the hail of the heavens, 604; *badist tā̃ wō*, down from the sky, 758; *badistē*, from the sky, 396. It is possible that *badistē* and *badist* in some of these examples should be considered as a compound *ba di stē*, from in the sky; cf. 1 **dī.**

bdiwerr, on the sandbaṇks, see **diwar.**

budzun, subst., a cloak, 264; cf. **basnâ.**

begū, preposition, gone out, outside of, p. 62. In 964 *begū* should be changed to *be gū*, see **be** and **GŪ.**

bugdrē, subst., a hollow; *bugdrē p'mish*, in the hollow, 667. Perhaps *bu-kadr*, hole in the ground.

bāghrē, subst., an owl; *bāghrē lē afziā*, many owls come, 976.

baglao, baglo, b'gol, b'gul, in the river, in the valley, see **gol, gul.**

bogmā bradzai, subst., plague; *bogmā bradzai dugā mṛittett,* (our cattle) are dying of plague, 1020.

b'garak, to the neck, see **garak.**

bgrām, bagrām, bagrom, in the village, see **grām.**

boh, to become, see **BŪ.**

bhīm, subst., soil, ground, 321, 594, 760, 761, 762, 1019, 1034, 1269 (*kano-wā bhīm,* wooded ground, a shady place), 1330, 1447, 1632 (here the ground is hot, this is a warm place), 1664, p. 8; *bhīm tā,* in the ground, on the ground, 1253, 1363, 1516, 1591; *bhīma tā,* on the ground, 213; *bhīmā,* on the ground, 803; *b'bhīm,* on the ground, in the ground, 1190, p. 62; *b'bhiom,* into the ground, 1230.

bihishte, subst., heaven, 643; cf. **badist.**

būjē, subst., a sack; *būjē gats,* get me a sack, 1216; *būjē tā,* in the sack, 1216.

bējaṛ, adv., unknowingly, accidentally, 3.

bajit, in *boṛī na bajit jarand,* the food is not digested in my body, I have dyspepsia, 393; see **jitt.**

bakhta-muzharla, a kind of fat-tailed sheep (*lit.* ram-sheep), in *Badakshān bakhta-muzharla waruk,* the wool of the Badakshānī sheep, 1715.

BAKSH, to forgive. Imperative, *bakshio,* forgive; *iā varī bakshiō,* forgive my word, my crime, 300.

bekshā, in *luī bekshā,* blood out make, bleed, 161; see **be** and **KṚ.**

bekshī, cease, 236; see **bēs.**

bektsā, awaken, 881; see **BETS.**

balā, bolā, bulā, will be; **bilā,** let it be; **bul,** becoming; see **BŪ.**

balē, he can, see **BAN.**

bilugh, adj., great, much, many, p. 17. Commonly used as an attribute with nouns; thus, *bilugh gawā,* much cattle, 1172;

bilugh manchī, many men, 214, 467, 849, 1265. The following instances of this use occur: 214, 275, 302, 356, 370, 377, 378, 394, 410, 441, 442, 443, 445, 467, 582, 592, 634, 710, 713, 721, 768, 839, 849, 862, 872, 893, 928, 935, 959, 1068, 1168, 1172, 1178, 1232, 1264, 1265, 1379, 1401, 1408, 1433, 1485, 1517, 1569, 1571, 1633, 1712. Note *bilugh shtār*, a great thief, 410, 862; *bilugh shartrī*, a great hunter, 959. *Bilugh* is also used as a predicate; thus, *wutr bilugh asht*, fairies are plentiful, abound, 437; *damu bilugh ushtett*, wind much blows, there is much wind, 1228. The following instances occur: 386, 387, 437, 481, 861, 887, 1167, 1170, 1182, 1196, 1224, 1226, 1228, 1266, 1371, 1392, 1431, 1434, 1548, 1668. *Bilugh* is also used alone; thus, *bilugh iāro*, I have eaten much, too much, 394; cf. 405, 857, 880, 1616.

Bilugh is very commonly used as an adverb, much, very, 18, 20, 45, 48, 86, 87, 97, 162, 170, 183, 212, 223, 226, 238, 250, 260, 271, 280, 290, 292, 295, 305, 306, 311, 331, 333, 343, 344, 345, 357, 365, 377, 401, 426, 446, 451, 464, 468, 477, 486, 490, 508, 518, 525, 547, 548, 550, 557, 559, 594, 618, 630, 641, 655, 671, 687, 690, 707, 724, 725, 740, 764, 772, 801, 818, 838, 856, 882, 886, 917, 954, 972, 1004, 1026, 1027, 1044, 1045, 1050, 1062, 1089, 1103, 1113, 1123, 1124, 1141, 1155, 1165, 1187, 1191, 1199, 1217, 1218, 1228, 1231, 1240, 1247, 1263, 1264, 1272, 1291, 1292, 1296, 1311, 1315, 1320, 1324, 1334, 1344, 1348, 1390, 1397, 1398, 1406, 1408, 1414, 1415, 1448, 1454, 1472, 1475, 1478, 1489, 1490, 1496, 1500, 1503, 1520, 1545, 1572, 1585, 1587, 1590, 1596, 1598, 1601, 1604, 1606, 1612, 1621, 1632, 1645, 1658, 1663, 1664, 1678, 1689, 1692, 1719, 1743. Note *sundī tā bilugh ála*, all than much large, largest, 1334; *stā manchī tā bilugh damtōl lē*, that man than much clever good, more famous than that man, 446; *manchī todī bilugh kshul*, male than much clever, more clever than the male, 464.

Instead of *bilugh* we also find *bilugh*, very, much, 4, 8, 29, 303, 368, 568, 571, 586, 632, 657, 568, 765, 800, 1059, 1070, 1163, 1330, 1374, 1727, p. 61; and *bilūgh*, very, much, 20, p. 61; *bilūgh boṛ*, much bread, 85; further, *biliugh*, very, 735.

Other forms of the word are: *biliuk*, great, much, many, p. 14; it is used as an attribute, 699, 817, 844, 1108, 1414, 1547; as a predicate, 1032, and as an adverb, very, much, 1, 685, 695, 701, 708, 875, 927, 988, 1000, 1005, 1028, 1060, 1066, 1071, 1491, 1493, 1534, 1537, 1559, 1580, 1711, p. 8; *bīliuk*, much, very; *bīliuk aṛaṛ*, very tight, too tight, 1513; *biluk*, many, p. 14; used as an attribute, 901, 1430; as an adverb, much, very, 206, 693, 703, 712, 720, 732, 781, 820, 823, 966, 970, 998, 1418, 1650, 1687, 1732; *biluzh*, much; *biluzh rāṛā kutt*, (the horse) does much neighing, 916.

būloh, they will become, see **BŪ.**

Bulkhān, subst., name of a man, Bul khān, 630.

billiē, let it be, see **BŪ.**

balam, I shall be able, I can, see **BAN.**

balom, bulom, būlom, I shall become, I shall be, see **BŪ.**

Bilan, Bilian, subst., (1) the Bashgalī name for Chitrāl; *ba Bilan*, to Chitrāl, 1525; *ba Bilian puttan* (i.e. *putt tâ*), on the road to Chitral, 947; (2) belonging to Chitrāl, Chitrālī, 150, 253, 334, 437, 572, 750, 781, 825, 1027; a Chitrālī, 627, 800, 966; see also **bilankochī** and **biliankor.**

bōlan, it will become, see **BAN.**

bilankochī, subst., a small spoon (literally, perhaps, 'a Chitrālī spoon,' cf. **kochī**), 1376.

biliankor, subst., a magpie (literally, perhaps, 'a Chitrālī crow,' cf. **koṛṛ**), 840.

būlōr, you will become, see **BŪ.**

balas, is able, can, see **BAN.**

balosh, bilosh, wilt be able, canst, see **BAN.**

bulosh, būlosh, wilt become, see **BŪ.**

baless, he is able, he can, see **BAN.**

bolass, bulass, wilt become, see **BŪ.**

biluzh, much, see **bilugh.**

bulazhbâ, bulozhbâ, if he become, if thou becomest, see **BŪ.**

bulāzrbâ, if you become; **bulazzibâ,** if he, they, become;

bulazzishbâ, if thou becomest; **bulazzambâ,** if we become; see **BŪ.**

bam, I can; **bamâ,** we can; see **BAN.**

bā'm, I became, see **BŪ.**

bamâ, we shall become, see **BŪ.**

bamo, subst., a hornet, 674; *bamo attamshi,* the hornet stung, 1403.

bimbâ, if I become, see **BŪ.**

bammâ, we can, see **BAN.**

bummâ, let us become, we shall become, see **BŪ.**

bmrisht, of a corpse, corpse-like, see **mrisht.**

1 **bamish,** we can, see **BAN.**

2 **bamish,** we became, see **BŪ.**

bumish, we become, see **BŪ.**

bimtā, if I become; **bimistâ,** if we become, see **BŪ.**

bomazzibâ, if we become, see **BŪ.**

BAN, to be made. This verb is added to the base, or, when it is preceded by the negative particle, also to the base followed by *n*, of another verb, and it then means 'can', 'be able'. The following forms occur in the sentences—

Infinitive, *busth,* to be able, p. 58.

Indefinite present 2nd pers. sing. *jār bachā,* thou canst kill, 1214, p. 58; *kuī shū awēn na bachī,* thou canst not bring any information, thou wilt not do as a spy, 1311.

1st pers. plur. *ē na bam,* we cannot go, 639; *awī na bam,* we cannot cross, 557; *ē na bamâ,* we cannot go, 1483; *kaikote putr bamâ,* how can we cross? 1345; *putrē n'bamâ,* we cannot get across, 1147; *wār n'bamâ,* we cannot see, 657; *wār n'bammâ,* we cannot see, p. 58; *ngā n'bamish,* we cannot carry, 1349; *patren na bamish,* we cannot cross, 332.

Present 1st pers. sing. *banam,* I can, I am able; *ē na banam,* I cannot go, 1321, 1704 (*n'banam*); *n'ai iam banam,* I cannot go, 263, p. 58 (*n'iam*); *achūn na banam,* I cannot run, 1208; *amjī na banam,* I cannot wear, 1513; *uttī na banam,* I cannot stand up, 1328; *noshē n'banam*, I cannot swim, 1452; *nōsh ko banam*, I can swim, 1452; *nosh kun na banam*, I cannot swim, 1451; *petṛn* (i.e. *petṛ n'*) *banam*, I cannot cross, 1321; *strān na banam*, I cannot write, 1729; *yū n'banam*, I cannot eat, 1574; *n'pā banom*, I cannot go, 4; *nuksā n'bannam*, I cannot open, 1303.

2nd pers. sing. *achūn na banch*, thou canst not run, 1534; *achūn na banj*, thou canst not run, p. 58; *kyā 'ē banjī*, why canst thou not go? 1054.

3rd pers. sing. *badō ū n'bann*, he cannot climb on the hill, 1397; *pē botten na bann*, she cannot walk on, 1708; *n'pā bann*, (the horse) cannot go on, 223, 1545 (*na pā*).

3rd pers. plur. *band*, can; *uten na band*, they cannot raise (pitch tents), 1664; *ngā n'band*, they cannot carry, 1650; *wran na band*, they cannot see, 1536.

Second present 1st pers. sing. *battam*, I can; *n'battam*, I cannot, 644 (*ngā*, lift), 660 (*damen*, clutch), 664 (*en*, go), 665 (*wāvats*, dismount), 781 (*pilangon*, learn), 882 (*pshōn*, sleep), 1013 (*pshuik*, sleep), 1095 (*amji*, put on), 1297 (*ngā*, carry), p. 58 (*en na battam*, I cannot enter; *kshon na battam*, I cannot pull).

3rd pers. sing. *batt*, can; *ushp na batt*, a horse cannot [go], 296; *ē na batt*, he cannot go, 1174; *otī na batt*, he cannot, does not, stand still, 665; *pā n'batt*, he cannot go, 454; *buru palangen na batt*, he cannot go down hill, 307; *pilingen na batt*, he cannot go, p. 58; *ngā n'batt*, he cannot take, carry, 1187, 1296; *butt*, can; *dōr na butt*, one cannot bear it, 130; *buttett*, can; *kon n'buttett*, he cannot make, p. 58.

1st pers. plur. *damē n'battamish*, we cannot catch, 1099; *kshon n'battamish*, we cannot drag, 819.

3rd pers. plur. *kōn na battet*, they cannot make, 551; *ē n'battett*, they cannot go, 907; *waṛantan n'buttett*, they cannot be seen, 872.

Present definite 1st pers. sing. *ngā n'balam*, I cannot take, I cannot lift, 330, 656; *Dryus-ā na balam*, I cannot go to Drosh, 1118; *ūwē n'balem*, I cannot climb, 436.

2nd pers. sing. *pē n'balosh*, thou canst not cross, 1062; *n'pā balosh*, thou canṣt not go, thou wilt not be able to go, p. 58; *n'pā bilosh*, thou wilt not be able to go, 378.

3rd pers. sing. *ushp na balē*, a horse is not able (to traverse it), 1548; *n'pā balas*, he cannot go, 451; *n'pā baless*, he cannot go, 773; some of these forms should perhaps be classed as future tenses.

ben, subst., a forest; *ba ben*, in the forest, 129; *bannē tā*, in the forest, 1712.

bōn, subst., a chair, a seat, 271, p. 15.

bonā, becomes, is, see **BŪ**.

banch, canst, see **BAN**.

1 **band,** they can, see **BAN**.

2 **band,** confined, imprisoned; *mehr band kṛissā*, the chief imprisoned him, 1407, p. 3; *pachanwarī band kusth dugē*, for stopping the enemy, 574; *bāndī*, imprisoned; *Amir bāndī kṛiss*, the Emir imprisoned him, 1394.

bund, they become, see **BŪ**.

bangut, subst., a sangar, a breastwork, 1229, 1384.

banj, banjī, canst, see **BAN**.

bunjī, becomest, see **BŪ**.

banam, banom, bannam, I can, see **BAN**.

bunam, būnam, I become, see **BŪ**.

bann, can, see **BAN**.

bannē tā, in the forest, see **ben**.

bunn, becomes, is, see **BŪ**.

banūr, see **p'banūr**.

būnazār, you were becoming, etc., see **BŪ**.

bapdī, in the mind, see **bidī**.

bāpsā, subst., harm, loss; *kai bāpsā n'kṛissiā*, they have done no loss (harm), 832.

BṚ, to carry off, to take away. All the examples belong to the past tense and the 3rd person; they are—

Past indefinite 3rd pers. sing. *brā*, *bṛā*, *brī*, *bṛī*, he took away;

iā bōr kū brā, who took away my load? 1459; *ī basnā brā*, (a gust of wind) took away my clothes, 602; *iāst gash brā*, (the wolf) took off my goat, 1706; *kakkak brā*, he took off my fowl, 396, 532; *ī kaltacha brā*, (the thief) carried off my purse, 1090; *pashtug brā*, he took away my bag, 111; *iāst ptul brā*, (a mud stream) carried off (destroyed) my crops, 895; *iāst shugā brā*, he carried off my coat, 1251; *iāst digṛī bṛā*, did he steal my shirt? 1471; *dashta pṛētī bṛā*, he took the sleeves away having cut them, he cut off the sleeves, 1329; *duts gum koṛ bṛā*, he carried off ten stalks of corn, 1389; *lattri bṛā*, he carried off our property, 1209; *uṛṛ bṛī*, (a kite) took off my chickor, 744, p. 3; *ushp brī*, he took away the horse, 1460; *ushp bṛī*, he took a horse, pp. 2, 3. In one place *baro* is used instead of *brā*; thus, *kā shosh n'ai Karak sharṛ barokti* (i.e. *baro ktī*), there is no witness, Karak took the goats, having said, there is no witness that Karak took the goats, 1705.

3rd pers. plur. *brā*, they took; *shtowa juk brā*, they carried away four girls, 552; *tapak brā*, they took away the guns, 600.

Perfect 3rd pers. sing. *bṛiss*, he has taken away, 1087, 1322.

brâ, subst., a brother. The following instances of its use occur in the sentences:—

Singular, as subject, *brá*, 25, 38, 48, 50, 203, 204, 288, 351, 361, 383, 411, 428, 446, 461, 508, 703, 726, 973, 1028, 1393, 1451, 1489, p. 8. As agent, *brá*, 205, 849, 850, pp. 2, 3; *bra*, p. 4 (taken down by Abdul Hakīm Khāṇ).

Acc. *brá*, 984 1342.

Gen. *brá*, 245, 354, 473, 624, 687; *bráo*, 289, 432, 433, 588 (*brá-o*); *brozhī*, your brother's, 294.

Plural, as subject, *brá*, 808, 1114. As object, *bráson*, 1102.

tott brá, father and brother, blood relatives, a clan, 256, 421, 631, 1139, p. 7.

chir brá, foster-brother; *tū chok chir brá hōst*, how many foster-brothers have you, 528.

brē, subst., flour, food, 364, 501, 1278, 1279, 1353, 1655 (acc.).

Also written *bṛe*, 955 (nom.), and *bṛē*, 812 (acc.). Probably connected with *boṛ*, *bọṛī*, *buṛi*, food, bread (which see).

BṚĒ, (?) to shear. Imperative, *bṛē*; *inā muzharala bṛē*, shear this sheep, 1283.

bru, in *bilūgh buṭṭ iāsht, bru afziā*, I have eaten much rice and it is not being digested, 356. Perhaps 'indigestion'.

bar, adverb, out, outside, p. 60; preposition, outside of, p. 62. The following examples of the adverb, which is also written *baṛ*, occur in the sentences:—

bar odsī, (the gun) came out, went off, 3; *baṛ osth*, they came out, they appeared, 1429; *iā ushpē bilugh ashpā baranziss*, for my horse much sweat has come out, my horse has sweated much, 1446; *baṛ kshī*, put out (your tongue), 1532; *ē paṛmiṛ dī baṛ na lazar*, let not even a boy get out, escape, 1439.

baṛē, outer; *inā basnā shu atēr assā, ikīā baṛē assā*, the wool of this cloth is inside, that is the outer (right side), 1731. It is probable that *baron* in *baron azinj*, thou art throwing out, thou art vomiting, 1616, and *bar* in *tapka barkstaṛa*, he fired a gun, p. 4, belong to this word; cf. also *tapk barūten*, to fire a gun, 1293.

bara, subst., share, division; *bara-kshī*, shares-make, divide, 1279; *baraktī*, having made shares, having divided, 1278; also written *bata*; thus, *bata kshēr*, make shares, divide, 364.

baṛā, subst., a plough; *ashu baṛā*, a bullock plough, 1033; *ashu baṛā n'aischitt*, it is no good to plough, 1034.

barē, subst., fate, hope, luck, p. 98, footnote; *iā barē assabā*, to me is hope, 589; *to barē lē assiā iā barē utettī ess*, thy luck is good, my luck is small, 836; *ushp ailī wanamdī barēbā* (?), a horse will go, having led it there will be luck (?), a horse will go, but it must be led, 788.

baṛē, outer, see **baṛ**.

barī, subst., a blacksmith, 610; also *baṛī*, 719.

beṛ, bēṛ, bē̃ṛ, adj., foolish, idiotic; *beṛ ass*, he is foolish, idiotic, 837; *bē̃ṛ ass*, he is foolish, idiotic, 178, 228; *bēṛ assish*, thou art a fool, 974.

beṛān, nonsense, foolish talk, 839.

bēṛā, adj., insensible; *bēṛā biss*, he has grown insensible, 712. Probably connected with *beṛ*.

beṛu, bēṛī, adj., lazy; *ushp beṛu ass*, (my) horse is lazy, 559; *pshīash bēṛī biss*, the cat has grown lazy, 230. Cf. **beṛ**.

beṛū, adv., outside, p. 60; *beṛu*, postposition, outside of; *amu beṛu*, outside the house, 1091; *beṛū*, outside, p. 62. Cf. **baṛ**.

bōr, subst., a load. The same form is used in the singular and the plural, as subject and as object. The following instances occur:—

Singular: subject, 769, 797, 828; object, 205, 225, 229, 330, 370, 375, 501, 644, 656, 768, 815, 846, 898, 913, 956, 1194, 1296, 1298, 1333, 1397, 1423, 1459, 1567, 1732; once *bōra*, 1458.

Plural: subject, 639, 1478; once *bor*, 805; object, 206, 339, 513, 888, 907, 1349, 1458, 1650.

bŏr, bŭr, become ye, see **BŪ**.

boṛ, subst., bread, food. This noun corresponds to Hindōstānī *rōṭī*, and occurs in several slightly different forms, viz.:—

boṛ, bread, used as an object, 85, 185, 200, 555, 734.

boṛī, bread, food; *boṛī na bajit jarand*, the food is not digested in my body, I have dyspepsia, 393; *bilugh boṛī iăr*, I have eaten much food, 275.

buṛi, bread, food; case of the object, 44, 283.

buṛī, food, chupatti, 1127; case of the object, 388, 586, 1232, 1393, 1444.

buṛi churz, food distributor, henchman, 647.

buṛī kutan amu, food-maker house, kitchen, 743.

buṭi, food, p. 3.

Perhaps connected with *bṛē*, flour, food; *buṭṭ*, rice (which see).

buru, adv., downhill, 307, p. 60; *brūlē*, downhill, 656, p. 60.

barēbā, in *ushp ailī wanamdī barēbā*, a horse will go, but must be led, 788. *barēbā* is perhaps *barē bā*, there is luck, see **barē**; or = *brābar*, all right.

brābar, brobar, brōbar, barbor, barbōr, (1) like, equal. There is no difference between the various forms of this word; it is used as an adjective and adverb meaning 'like'; thus, *barbor n'aieṣht*, they are not alike, 891; *ē brobar ess*, they are one like, of the same value, 1282; *duī tā brobar āl*, big like the hand, 996; *tarwaçh brobar tsiā*, sharp as my sword, 1280; *Bastī brōbar damtōl*, as clever as Bastī, 1188.

(2) Respectable, all right; *brōbar manchī*, respectable people, 1155.

(3) All together, exactly; *brobar aḍr rang*, all together yellow coloured, yellow all over, 1378; *rador barbōr*, just at midnight, 865; *radhar brābar*, just at midnight, p. 64.

burubiz, adj., angry; *burubiz kutt*, he makes angry, he is angry, 48; *burubiz n'kṣhī*, do not be angry, 47; *iā burubiz bolam*, I will be angry, 46.

bīrdā, if you become, see **BŪ.**

bradsi, subst., a leather band; *iā uṣhp aṣhī bradsī*, the leather of the mouth of my horse, the reins, 1138; *uṣhp bradzī*, horse-whip, 1678; *prampor bradzī*, a crupper, 307.

1 **BRADSO,** to ache, to pain. *Ds* and *dz* are apparently used promiscuously in this base. The following forms occur:—

Present 3rd pers. sing. *bradsonn*, aches, 469; *bradzon*, aches, 952; *bradzonn*, aches, 952, 1350.

Second present 3rd pers. sing. *bradzot*, aches, pains, 593; *bradzōt*, aches, pains, 52; *bradzott*, aches, pains, 4, 5, 104, 130, 145, 248, 397, 432, 630, 671 (*bradzott*), 791, 836, 913, 980, 1048, 1095, 1298, 1344, 1534; *brazott*, aches, 1306.

Causal verb, present 3rd pers. sing. *bradzāott*, he hurts, 695.

2 **bradso,** subst., aching, illness, 664; oblique, *bradzai*; *bogmā bradzai dugā*, from plague, 1020; *bradso*, *bradzo*, is often also used as an adjective, *bradso* (*bradzo*) *esth*, to be ill. The following examples occur: *bradso*, 99, 703; *bradzo*, 23, 24, 250, 314, 331, 468, 790. The suffix *wā* is often added to *bradso*, *bradzo*, when used as a predicate in this way; thus, *bradso-wā*, ill, 632, 983, 1502; *bradsowā*, ill, 1359, 1720; *bradzo wā*, ill,

1104; *bradzo-wā*, ill, 1307; *bradzowā*, ill, 767; *bradzowo*, ill, 475. This form can also be combined with a copula and written in one word; thus, *bradzowai*, he is ill, 589; *bradswaio*, he is ill, 1236.

bragom, in a village, see **grām.**

Bragamatal, subst., name of a place, 846, 1139, 1531; *Bragamatal stē*, from Bragamatal, 1547; *Bragamatal pōr*, Bragamatal direction, towards Bragamatal, 1566.

barakshi, divide; **baraktī,** having divided, see **bara.**

barkstaṛa, he fired; *aske du tapka barkstaṛa*, he fired two guns, p. 4 (noted down by Abdul Hakīm Khān). Perhaps a compound; cf. **bar.**

barokti, took away, see **BR** and **KR.**

barēla, postposition (?), around; *inā p'amu barēla palgā*, walk up and down around my house, 70. Perhaps *bar ēl*, going out, outside.

brūlē, adv., downhill, 656, p. 60; see **buru.**

barm, adj., shut; *dū barm kshī*, make the door shut, shut the door, 1302.

bramishten, subst., the girth of a saddle, 1514.

brun, polo ground, see **brunz.**

baron, in *baron azinj*, thou art vomiting, 1616; see **baṛ.**

beṛān, subst., nonsense, foolish talk; *bilugh beṛān walett*, he talks much nonsense, 839; cf. **beṛ.**

brunz, subst., a lawn, a polo ground, 772, pp. 1, 7; *b'brunz-o pagūro*, on the polo ground, 1074; *brunz yūs*, lawn grass, turf, 1562.

brun, polo ground; *ē dī brun n'aiesht*, there is no polo ground, 1040.

baranziss, came out, exuded, see **baṛ** and **1 Ā.**

barpachargo (?), in *iāst sharr ikīā kāna tsá tā barpachargo psā* (?), hang my pagri on the branch of that tree, 616.

baristã, in the garden, 896; see **darestān.**

barūten, to fire, to shoot; *tapk barūten na zãrētam*, I do not know (how) to shoot, 1293; see **baṛ** and **TE.**

Bruts, subst., name of a place, Broz; *Bruts gūssam,* I went to Broz, 766; *Bruts tā̃,* to Broz, 1524; *Bruts torē̃,* near Broz, 1690; see **Broz.**

barwai, subst., a carrier, a coolie; singular, nominative, *barwai,* 227, 284, 395, 712, 828, 837, 934, 1144, 1296, 1397, 1423, 1432, 1567; agent, *barwai,* 815; dative, *barwai,* 712, 846, 1049.

Plural, nominative, *barwai,* 74, 75, 277, 279, 339, 374, 639, 805, 819, 822, 832, 928, 932, 1055, 1130, 1650; agent, *barwai,* 112; accusative, *barwai,* 276, 291, 953, 1018, 1131, 1566; genitive, *barwai,* 905; oblique base before postpositions, *barwai,* 184 (*b. dugē̃*), 1185 (*b. dugā̃*).

Broz, subst., name of a village, Broz; *Broz enda,* they will go to Broz, 563; *Broz stē,* from Broz, 1496; *Broz tā̃,* from Broz, 730; *Brōza tā̃ chĩr,* above Broz, 2; *Brōz-wārī,* an inhabitant of Broz, 709; *Bruz,* Broz, 146, 151, 1200, 1202; *Bruts,* Broz, 766, 1524, 1690.

brozhi, of thy brother, see **brâ.**

brazott, it aches, see 1 **BRADSO.**

bās, subst., flame, 491.

basa, is (?), in *kāchī ngālabasa,* who takes (is taking)? 1458; cf. **BŪ.**

bēs, adv., enough; *bēs iārā,* I have eaten enough, 419; *utilī-wār bēs kshī,* make enough of boasting, cease boasting, 1602; *inā kudūma bekshī* (i.e. *bēs kshī*), cease that work, 236.

bā'sh, bosh, bōsh, becamest, becomest, see **BŪ.**

bishtâ, if thou becomest, see **BŪ.**

buasht, adverb, verily, certainly, 56, p. 61.

bosel, becomes, see **BŪ.**

bosam, bosamish, I have become, we have become, see **BŪ.**

basnâ, subst., cloth, stuff, 1225, 1243, 1350, 1351; dress, skirt, clothes; nominative, 357, 1341, p. 7; accusative, 512, 602, 1014, 1066, 1095, 1267, 1461, 1504, 1636; genitive, *basnâ,* of the cloth, 1731; *basnâ tā̃,* in the clothes, 883, 1412; *basnâ shul,* clothes sewing, a tailor, 1243, 1289.

basenâ, cloth, p. 3.

basnâgor, cloth, in *inā basnâgor kaltachā kusth dugã lesst na ass*, this cloth is not good for making a waistcoat, 1623, is perhaps a miswriting; *kaltacha* means 'purse', 1090, and perhaps *gorkaltachā* is = waistcoat; connected or identical with *basnâ* are:

badisnâ, cloth; *ikīē badisnâ dugã*, for that cloth, 1068.

bazisnâ, cloth, clothes; used as a nominative, 267, 859, 943, 1199, 1468; as an accusative, 476, 1076, 1257; note *iã jūī noi bazisnâ prēlom*, I shall give new clothes to my girl, my girl is a bride, 194; *zīn p'tsir bazisnâ*, saddle on cloth, saddle cloth, 1220.

boshā, becamest, see **BŪ.**

biss, has become, see **BŪ.**

bosish, hast become, see **BŪ.**

Basti, subst., name of a man; nominative, *Bastī*, 3, 891, 899, 906, 1299, 1441, 1572, 1630, p. 9; accusative, *Bastī*, 3, 1356, 1422, 1549, 1579; *Bastī-ē*, 899; dative of possession, *Bastī-e ashī parmenstuk ess*, Bastī has a small mouth, 892; *Bastī-è guchī n'asht*, Bastī has no moustachios, 891; *Bastī brōbar*, like Bastī, 1188; *Bastī tã*, to Bastī, on Bastī, 3; *Bastī tā drgr*, taller than Bastī, 1464.

bist, bista, become, see **BŪ.**

bistâ, if you had been; **bistai,** has, have, become; see **BŪ.**

bosut, subst., spring; *bosut wokt tã*, in springtime, 831; see **wosut.**

1 **busth,** to become, see **BŪ.**

2 **busth,** to be able, see **BAN.**

bata, subst., share, division; *bata kshēr*, make division, divide, 364; see **bara.**

bāti, in *pachan warī p'amu attā attottiss: bātī mikiosam*, the enemy shut me in a house but I escaped, 423; *bātī* is perhaps *be-ātī*, having come out.

bitā, subst., meat, 156; cf. **biṭṭā.**

biti, buti, having become, see **BŪ.**

boot, subst., a boot (English loan-word), 1082.

būt, adj., thick; *nāru būt ess*, the clouds are thick, 268; *zap būt ess*, the cloth is thick, 266.

bātachol, subst., a pheasant, 1006, 1007 (nom. plur.).

bitil, subst., a plank, 371.

BETS, to awaken; imperative, *betsō*, awaken, 101, 102; *bektsâ*, awaken, 881.

bitish, botasalā, becomest, does it become, see **BŪ.**

batt, can, see **BAN.**

bitta, bitto, becomes, is, see **BŪ.**

biṭṭā, subst., meat; *ano biṭṭā iā n'iâr*, I have not eaten flesh or meat, I have not eaten any meat, 855; cf. **bitā.**

1 **buṭt, būtt,** becomes, see **BŪ.**

2 **butt,** can, see **BAN.**

buṭṭ, subst., rice, 356; cf. **boṛ.**

battam, I can, see **BAN**

botten, in *pē botten na bann*, she cannot walk further, 1708. Perhaps wrong for *p'pott en na bann*, she cannot go on the road.

buttaser, becomes, see **BŪ.**

battet, buttett, can, becomes, see **BŪ** and **BAN.**

bizul, in the jungle, see **zul.**

biznor, in *biznor ūm*, we will climb the hill, 262.

bzār, bazār, bāzār, subst., bazaar; *b'bzār stē*, from the bazaar, 558; *bāzār stē*, from the bazaar, 1294; *bazār stē*, from the bazaar, 1376.

bazira, in *bazira padrē ū prētt*, I have diarrhœa, 349; literally perhaps 'in my body the bowels go out'.

bazisnâ, subst., a cloth, clothes; used in the nominative, 267, 859, 943, 1199, 1468; in the accusative, 476, 1076, 1257. Note *noi bazisnâ prēlom*, I will give her new clothes, she is a bride, 194; *zīn p'tsir bazisnâ*, saddle on cloth, saddle-cloth, 1220; see **basnâ.**

C

ch, chī, suffix of the personal pronoun of the 2nd person, see **sh.**

1 **chå,** subst., a wall, 440, 1024, 1627.

2 **chå,** subst., noise, see 3 **cho.**

chai, subst., tea, 1466, 1642; *chaī*, tea, 173; *chaĭ*, tea, 1448.

chē, chī, how many? p. 13; *chī*, how much? p. 61; *chē amo*, how many rooms? 1192; *chē manchī*, how many men? 291, 1150; *chē wōs*, how many days? 1150.

chi sē, how many years? 570; *chī palā*, how many watchmen? 1639; *chī wōr*, how many times? 1519; *chī wōs pott*, how many days' march? 1387.

chī, adv., up; *indrōn chī ptess*, a rainbow is up, there is a rainbow, 1121; *sū chī presth wokt tå*, at the time of the getting up of the sun, at sunrise, 1436; cf. **chīr.**

1 **cho,** how many? see **chok.**

2 **cho,** in *n'cho*, leave it, 797, see **NACH.**

3 **cho, chō,** subst., clamour, noise (?); *cho witī*, having struck a clamour, loudly, 1463; *chō witī*, shouting, 1299; *chå witt*, he is howling, 681; he makes a noise, 721. Perhaps identical with Hindōstānī *shōr*.

chū, subst., leg, thigh, 1488; *chū tå*, in my leg, 1166; cf. **chōn.**

chuī, subst., a switch (for making a horse go), 1453.

chadrā, subst., a turban, pagri, 164.

CHAGŌ, to bite; *zawōr gū n'chagōtitt, wizdōr chagōtitt*, in winter ants do not bite, in spring they bite, 54, 55; *n'chagōtett*, they do not bite, 56.

chāgh, adj., scarce, rare. Also written *chogh, chak, chāk*, and *chok; gologh chāgh ess*, the water of the river is scarce, is low, 518; *kishu chāgh asht*, sandflies are few, 1228; *kachwach chāgh ess*, fruit is scarce, p. 9; *marach chogh asht*, mulberries are scarce, 1240; *zīm chak ptā*, there is little snow, 399; *īts chāk asht*, bears are rare, 1123; *do chok biss*, the water became low, 1227.

chaku, subst., a knife, 169.

chik subst., a ladder, 753, 1249.

chok, chuk, pronoun. (1) Interrogative, how many? how much? pp. 13, 61: both forms are used as attributes; thus, *chok,* how many? 19, 62 (*cho*), 528, 686; *chok,* how much? 688; *chuk,* how many? 1377, 1646, 1652; *chuk,* how much? 80; *ikīā kudūm chuk dī kaṛbá,* how much even you do this work, 1597.

(2) Indefinite, some, any, p. 14; *chok brē,* some flour, 1353; *inā barwai yo chok prē,* give some to each of the coolies, give one portion to each coolie, 1049; cf. **achok.**

chuk, subst., the chest; *pa chuk wīk,* up to the chest, 1183.

chkri, subst., a polo ball, 114.

chakūr, adj., gently sloping; *ikīā ashṭar chakūr assā,* is the hill a gentle slope? 1331.

chikūr, adj., dangerous; *ikīā ushtiwā chikūr assā,* that precipice (built up pari) is dangerous, 1062. The meaning is perhaps sloping, slippery, and *chikūr* identical with *chakūr.*

chukru, subst., rib; *pachukru,* on the ribs, 1169; cf. **chuk.**

chaktá, subst., a basket, 1259.

Chālū, subst., name of a man, 212 (*Chālu*), 906, 963, 1151, 1174, 1197, 1607, 1640; case of the agent *Chālū,* 1186, 1549; *Chālū-ē,* to Chālū, 975; *Chālū tā,* to Chālū, p. 4; *Chālū tā drgr,* taller than Chālū, p. 9.

1 **chil,** adj., soft; used as a predicate, 1083, 1341; *chilla basná,* a soft cloth, 1350; translated 'rough' in *iā bazisná chil asht,* my clothes are rough, 1199; there must be some mistake.

2 **chil,** subst., the back, 1350.

chili, subst., an outlaw; *chilī bitī gūs,* outlaw having become went, he is an outlaw, 973.

chillai, subst., a quarter, a fourth, p. 64; a half (?), 607.

chillē, adv., slowly, by stealth, p. 61; the form varies slightly; thus, *chillā,* slowly, 191; *chillē,* slowly, 1235; *chillē,* slowly, 282, 1332; secretly, 1251.

cham, subst., the skin, 641; accusative, *chamo,* 1320.

chemu, subst., iron, 570; also *chimr,* 718; in compounds *chim*;

thus, *chimã*, an iron chain, 240; *chimbio*, an iron spade, 1364 (see *bēo*, spade); *chimchich*, a needle, 914, 915, 1138, 1267; *chimētku*, an iron nail, 904.

chīm, in *shott chīm*, I take an oath, 939; the word is Khōwār.

chiom, subst., leather, 782; cf. **cham.**

chumbō, imperative, lie down, 1523. The final *bō* is the imperative of the base **BŪ.**

chamol, adj., knowing, acknowledging; *ko kai n'chamol manchī*, a man who knows no one, a proud man, 1080.

chimr, iron; see **chemu.**

cheno, adj., acid, sour (of fruit); *cheno asht*, is sour, 6; also written *chenai*, *chinai*, and *chin*; thus, *chenai kachwach*, sour fruit, 1362; *chinai bã*, is sour, 65; *chin-ai*, they are sour, 472; *chin-osht*, they are sour, 247.

chōn, subst., leg, 791; see **chū.**

chindor, subst., a saucepan, 1233.

Chandrāl, subst., Chitrāl, name of a district, 1530, 1563; *Chandrāl pōr*, Chitrāl way, towards Chitrāl, 1538; cf. **Shdrāl.**

CHANGR, to rub, to scratch; *changrōt*, (the horse) rubs (its mane), 842; *changrott*, (the horse) rubs (its mane), 1203.

chinosht, they are sour, see **cheno.**

chunzlī, adj., going up, rising; *sū chunzlī*, sunrise, p. 65; *sū chunzlī pōr*, sunrise way, east, 402, 403, p. 65; cf. **chī.**

CHAR, to plaster; *chá charesth dugã*, in order to plaster the wall, 1024.

chir, a Khōwār word, foster; *chir brá*, a foster-brother, 528; *chir piṭr*, a foster-child, 529; *chir sūs*, a foster-sister, 530.

chīr, high up, up stream; *chīr Maroī*, Upper Maroī, 1590; *chīr ess*, is higher up, 834; *chīr ēmá*, shall we go up stream? 1588; *Brōza tã chīr*, higher up than Brōz, above Brōz, 2.

chor, chur, subst., way, custom; *chor n'ess*, it is not the custom, 366, 603, 1086; *chur n'ess*, it is not the custom, 315, 576; can be added to a noun in order to form a kind of adjective; thus, *krūī chor*, dog way, like a dog, 298, p. 9 (*chōr*).

chur, subst., (1) a branch, 179; (2) the point of a sword, 1036; (3) the edge of a precipice; *ushtī pachur pazhē n'ai*, do not go near to the edge of the built-up pari, 407; *pachūrē ēlosh*, if thou goest to its edge, 1181.

churī, subst., a sickle, 1304; cf. Hindōstānī *chhurī*.

charagh, foolish, see **charra.**

chirāgh, subst., a lamp, a light, 168.

charra, adj., idiotic, foolish, mad; *charrā manchīān warī*, the talk of foolish men, 1585; commonly used as a predicate with *busth* or *esth*, 701, 1176, 1695; *charrā bitī piltiām*, I fell having become senseless, 1260; in *tū bilugh charagh ess*, thou art very foolish, 87, the final *gh* is perhaps due to the preceding *bilugh*.

Another form of the word is *chatta, chattā*; *chatta* is used as a predicate, 611, 839; *chattā* as an attribute, 508, and as a predicate, 843. In *chattā ess*, he is an impudent fellow, 705, the translation is somewhat free.

charrē, chattē, subst., nonsense; *charrē* (*chattē*) *walētish*, thou art talking nonsense, 929.

chārwēlī, subst., name of an official, 5, 192, 208, 280, 351, 409, 426, 652, 1131, 1150, 1160, 1236, 1571; case of the agent, *chārwēlī*, 318; accusative, *chārwēlī*, 319, 1160; genitive, *chārwēlī-o*, of the chārwēlī, 1497; oblique, *charwēlī dugā*, for a chārwēlī, 1220; *chārwēlī-ē dugā*, for the chārwēlī, in praise of the chārwēlī, 1055.

churz, subst., a distributor; *buri churz*, a food distributor, a khānsāmā, 647.

CHASH, to eat; present 3rd pers. plur. *n'chashand*, they do not eat, 620.

chusht, chūsht, adj., silent, quiet; used as predicate with the verb *esth*, to be; *chusht*, 1108, 1308, 1309, 1366; *chūsht*, 25, p. 63; note *chusht eshtinājē*, keep quiet, hide, 650.

chashton, num., four and four; *yō chashton*, four by four, p. 64; cf. **shto.**

chut, subst., sound, noise; *kūr chut*, foot-sound, footfall, 511;

varī chut, word-sound, voice, 1615; *wodaranchut*, thunder-sound, thundering, 1510.

chaṭṭa, chaṭṭā, foolish, see **charrā.**

chaṭṭē, nonsense, see **charrē.**

chitt, subst., mind, intention; *iā chitt bitto*, it is my intention, 739; *iā chitt n'ess*, it is not my intention, 716; *tū chitt kā'st azz*, what is thy intention, wish? 1701; *to chitt*, thy mind, as you please, 715, 1030 (*tō*); *to chitt tā manjī*, (thou art) a man in thy own intention, a wilful, independent fellow, 707, 1692 (*mōch*).

chatwāts, numeral, sixty, p. 63 footnote (from the collection of the Rev. Worthington Jukes).

chiwōl, postposition, near to, p. 62; *pō chiwol tā*, near the river, 1226.

D

dā, subst., wood, 894; see **dār.**

dâ, dā̃, another form of the postposition *tā*. *Dâ* occurs after a verbal form in the so-called conditional and after the verbal noun ending in *n*; thus, *bīr-dâ*, if you become, p. 21; *ien-dâ*, when going, at the time of going, 1057.

dā̃ occurs as a postposition with nouns; thus, *ushpā dā̃*, from the horses, p. 8 (noted down by Abdul Hakīm Khān). Further, in the so-called conditional; thus, *parim-dā̃*, when I arrived, p. 4; *piltim-dā̃n*, if I fall; *piltīr-dā̃*, if you fall, p. 55. Finally, after the verbal noun ending in *n*; thus, *ī en dā̃*, at the time of my going, p. 17; *atsan-dā̃*, when coming, 1535; *shū n'azzī tan dā̃* (?), news not being in, suddenly, 1429.

1 **dā̃,** in, see **dâ.**

2 **dā̃,** subst., gift, loan; *ē tang dā̃ kulom*, I will lend thee one rupee, 793; *ē tang dā̃ karsi'sh*, I have lent thee one rupee, 794, p. 11; cf. **dām.**

DAI, to cook; *inā burī zhillī ess; tū kai dugā n'daiess? zapp daiō*, this chupatti is raw; why hast thou not cooked it? Cook it immediately, 1127.

dāo, subst., (1) wood, 729, p. 1; accusative, *dao*, p. 4; *dāo*, 1710, 1714, p. 4; *dāo siu*, wooden bridges, 197; *dāo sell*, a carpenter, 238; *dāo sella*, a carpenter, 227; accusative, *dāo sellē*, 860. (2) A wooden stick, 1499; see **dār.**

1 **dī,** subst., the sky, 1324. Perhaps also contained in *badistē*, from the sky, 396; *badist*, from heaven, 604; *badist tā*, from the sky, 758; cf. **badist.**

2 **dī,** adv., even, also, pp. 61, 62; very frequent after nouns and other words; thus, 5, 38, 39, 272, 330, 347, 351, 541, 617, 702, 703, 772, 879, 900, 945, 971, 1067, 1086, 1149, 1150, 1155, 1195, 1212, 1218, 1234, 1239, 1244, 1249, 1336, 1364, 1376, 1400, 1414, 1415, 1462, 1582, 1635 (*di*), 1655; note especially *ē dī*, one even, 645, 875, 914, 1040, 1112, 1183, 1184, 1187, 1253, 1309, 1439, 1482, 1551, 1657, 1690; *eo dī*, 427, 538, 719, 823, 1133.

dī is often added to interrogative pronouns in order to make them indefinite; thus, *chuk dī*, how much even, however, 1597; *kā dī*, anything, with a negative nothing, 1209, 1252, 1297; *kuī dī*, sometimes, some day, 1189; with a negative never, 1162, 1179, 1312, p. 11; *koī dī*, 919.

Added after *to*, the particle of comparison, *dī* strengthens the meaning; thus, *jugur manchī todī bilugh kshul ess*, the female is much clever even than the male, the female is cleverer than the male, 464.

3 **dī,** adv., again, back again, p. 60; *tū dī ats anjībá*, if thou comest back, 106; *dī oz ess*, he has come back, 1568; *dī shtār n'kulā*, he will not steal again, 1087.

4 **dī,** suffix of the conjunctive participle, used after nasals and perhaps after *z*; *ublindī enn*, (flames) go high, 491; *achūndī*, having run, p. 36; *pilingdī*, having returned, 1624; *wanamdī*, having caught, 396, 788; *zhun duzdī zhundī*, she weeps crying weeping, she is weeping, 1654.

diu, two, see 2 **dū.**

1 **do, dō, du,** subst., hill, mountain, pass. Nominative, *do*, hill, 548; *dō*, hill, 653, 655. Genitive, *dō*, of the hill; *dō shai*, the top

of the hill, 657. Oblique, *dō*; *dō tā̃*, to the hills, 697. The word is very often preceded by the preposition *pa*, *ba*; cf. *ba-do*, on the hill, 124, 125, 263, 648, 818; in the pass, 155, 542, 1345, 1619; *ba-dō*, on the hill, 952, 1167, 1397; in the pass, 1436, 1520; *ba-du*, on the pass, 509; *ba-do pagur*, at the foot of the hill, on the pass, 502; *ba-dō pagūrā*, at the foot of the pass, 991; *ba-dō pagiōr*, to the foot of the hill, 1189; *ba-dō pagior yā̃r*, down to the foot of the hill, downhill, 1208; *ba-do ptiwar esth*, to go behind the hill, to cross the pass, 1023; *ba-do shai*, on the top of the hill, 795, 1147; *ba-dō shai*, on the top of the hill, 827, 920, 955, 1331, 1589, 1671; *ba-do shaiē stē*, from the crest of the hill, 299; *ba-do shai tā̃*, on the crest of the hill, on crossing the pass, 303; *ba-dō stē*, from on the hill, 848, 1169; *ba-dō yā̃r*, downhill, 1535.

2 **do,** in *kaido*, why? 309; see 3 **dū.**

doi, subst., the fore-arm, the arm, 980, 1095, also *duī*, p. 59; and *dūī*, 66; *duī tā̃*, from the fore-arm, 161; often translated hand; thus, *doī*, hand, 258; *duī*, hand, 318, 612; *iā̃ b'doī giats*, bring to my hand, produce, 1076; *toch baduī goī*, a bullet went to hand, I found a bullet, 213; *iā̃ duī tā̃ brobar*, like my hand, 996; cf. **dusht.**

1 **dū,** subst., a door, 1302, 1303; genitive, *dū*, of the door; *dū bitil*, a plank of the door, 371; oblique, *dū tā̃*, in the door, 240; *b'dū tā̃ torē̃*, near to the door, 1399; *duak-dū*, a window, 1694.

2 **dū,** numeral, two, p. 63; also *du do diu*, and *duī* (p. 63); *dū* is used before nouns, 160, 205, 229, 255, 265, 353, 362, 393, 480, 531, 547, 558, 614, 662, 793, 808, 846, 864, 879, 884, 907, 925, 965, 975, 1024, 1102, 1114, 1175, 1193, 1207, 1245, 1365 (*du*), 1395, 1714, pp. 4 (*du*), 12, 58; note, *dū achiē̃*, the two eyes, both eyes, 980; *dū troi wōs*, two three days, a few days, 1157; *dū wōr*, two times, twice, 1570, pp. 11, 60; *do mansia* (?), the seventeenth month of the year, p. 66.

diu azār je duts witsī, two fourhundred and ten twenties,

one thousand, p. 63; *du witsī*, two twenties, forty, p. 63; *dū witsī duts*, two twenties ten, fifty, p. 63; *dū vissī duts*, fifty, 1211.

dodun, two two; *yō dodun*, two and two, p. 64.

3 **dū, do,** in *kaidū*, why? p. 61; *kaidò*, why? 309; cf. **dugā.**

dibī, in *shutt dibī*, I take an oath, 939. The word is given within parentheses and is perhaps not Bashgalī but borrowed; it looks like a *b*-future of the base *DE*, to give.

debilāla, subst., the chanting priest, a kind of priest, 1071.

dudiēm, subst., a hollow (in the ground), 400.

dodmōss, subst., the gum of the mouth, 599.

dodun, two two, see 2 **dū.**

daḍr, adj., emaciated, thin, lean, used as a predicate with *busth* or *esth*, 693; usually written *daḍar*, 629, 972, 1489, 1490, 1492; also with the meaning emaciated, weak, 1650.

dugā, postposition, for the sake of, p. 62; occurs in various forms, viz.: *dugā, dugā̆, dugã, dugē, dugē̆, dugẽ*, and, according to p. 62, also as *tikā̆, kā, and gā*. The postposition is used in the following meanings:—

(1) For, for the sake of, for the benefit of; thus, *iā̆ dugā̆ gats*, bring for me, 200; *manchiān dugā̆ kudūm kshī less*, it is good for men to do labour, 752; *iā̆ dugā̆ digar*, unpleasant to me, 987; *tapik dugā̆ dorī*, the powder for my gun, 1053; *inā ushp dugā̆ shtowa vissī zamānī ngānam*, I will take eighty rupees for this horse, 1211; *emā̆ b'guì dugā̆ zhuk*, the salt for our valley, 1223; *tū dugā̆ lesst na bunn*, it is not good for thee, 1569; *iāst dugā̆ ōch karsam*, didst thou look out for me? 1669; *iā̆ dugā̆ paṛhī strasth dugā̆*, in order to write a letter for me, 1729; in this way *dugā̆* is added to nouns or pronouns in the following places, 200, 578, 581, 613, 684, 733, 752, 760, 769, 856, 924, 956, 987, 1043, 1053, 1061, 1075, 1081, 1082, 1167, 1185, 1211, 1216, 1220, 1222, 1223, 1259, 1286, 1395, 1447, 1473, 1484, 1511, 1536, 1569, 1593, 1605, 1613, 1636, 1669, 1694, 1695, 1696, 1729, 1735, p. 11.

dugā is used instead in 200, 743, 798, 1129, 1320, p. 3 footnote.

dugā̃ is used in 211, 214, 265, 290, 314, 316, 320, 359, 422.

dugē occurs in the same way in 149, 156, 184, 505, 512, 514, 545, 558, 568, 575.

dugē̃ is used in the same way in 160, 193.

gā̃ occurs in *tū gā̃ lesta kulom*, I will do good for thee, I will give thee a present, 84; and, in the form *gē̃*, in *ī-gē̃*, for me, p. 3 (noted down by Abdul Hakīm K͟hān).

In some few cases the postposition is used almost as an ordinary dative; thus, *iā̃ dugā̃ trē tanga mājib prēttett*, they give me (for my sake) three rupees wages, 995; *manchī dugā lesst kul*, doing good to people, respectful, 1156; *to gē̃ ku ptesesh*, who has given to thee? p. 4 (noted down by Abdul Hakīm K͟hān); in *aoghānī mullā katō̃ kē (?) mish ess*, to the Bashgalis there is hate of the Afghan priests, the Bashgalis hate the Afghan priests, 625, *kē* seems to have the same meaning as *dugā̃*, *gē̃*.

The postposition *dugā̃*, for the sake of, is very commonly added to the infinitive so as to form an infinitive of purpose; thus, *wōtt ukshosth dugā̃*, (get a pick) to pick out stones, 1008; *lālu kusth dugā̃ kuzhān*, good for making music, fond of making music, 1027. The infinitive usually ends in *sth*; in the following examples, however, it ends in *sthai*: *kūṛ jāristhai dugā̃ samariss*, he has started for shooting pigeons, 1011; *parchev mishisthai dugā̃*, (there is no place) for playing polo, 1040. The infinitive ends in *sthē* in the following instances: *shusthē dugā̃*, (get a needle) to sew them, 1138; *yusthē dugā̃ lesst ass*, it is good for eating, to eat, 1167; *purik kusthē dugā*, in order to make bullets, 778. The following instances of this use occur:—

With *dugā̃*, 584, 694, 717, 718, 770, 782, 860, 888, 893, 898, 942, 946, 961, 963, 1008, 1011, 1023, 1024, 1027, 1031, 1040, 1047, 1085, 1091, 1092, 1096, 1099, 1116, 1129, 1138, 1143, 1159, 1167, 1177, 1225, 1229, 1245, 1249, 1250, 1265, 1267,

1382, 1383, 1393, 1409, 1419, 1453, 1467, 1504, 1516, 1518, 1542, 1543, 1549, 1557, 1560, 1566, 1567, 1584, 1592, 1623, 1629, 1641, 1642, 1656, 1710, 1725, 1729; with *dugā*, 778, 1098, 1133, 1715; with *dugã*, 257, 264, 285, 566; with *dugē̃*, 537; with *dugē̃*, 471, 480, 488, 518, 574, 606.

Note *iā ushp b'bhīm piltisth dugã n'otē*, do not leave my horse to roll on the ground, 1190; *wischio dugã namāj kusth dugã pochētr ngusth dugã zarur n'ess*, to travellers there is no necessity for making prayers or keeping a fast, 1061; *manchīon dugā paṛhī ōsh kusth dugã lesst n'buttett*, for (ordinary) men it is no good to read books, 1129; *manchīēn shāron dugã yusthē dugã lesst ass*, (the rhubarb) is good for eating for men and goats, 1167.

(2) On account of, about; *chārwēlī-ē dugã warī kuttett*, they talk about the chārwēlī, they praise him, 1055; *mullā dugã widhertī*, for fear of the priests, 1139; *shtār dugã widarett*, she is in fear of thieves, 1247; *Bastī dugã kapā bissum*, I am angry with Bastī, 1606; *shtār dugē̃ vidraitī*, from fear of thieves, 460.

More especially, on account of, owing to, in a few cases after nouns; thus, *ushp ashpē dugã girī wishtangess*, owing to the sweat of the horse my girths have become stiff, 1402; *bogmā bradzai dugã mṛittett*, they die from plague, 1020; *zīm dugã achiē̃ lushtiā*, my eyes have become blind owing to the snow, 1346.

In this meaning the postposition is very common after pronouns; thus, *iā dugã*, therefore, 307, 849 (*iā*); *iā dugā*, therefore, 399; *ikiā dugã*, therefore, 1154; *ikīā dugā*, for the following reason, 1178; *ikīā dugā*, therefore, 1238; *ikīē dugã*, therefore, 1179, 1228 (*ikiyē̃*), 1440, 1608, 1616, p. 61 (*ikiē̃*); *ikīē dugā*, therefore, 1435; *ikīā dugã*, therefore, 380; *askē dugã*, therefore, 701; *kā dugã*, why? 589; *kā dugā*, wherefore? 420; *kai dugã*, wherefore? 689, 771, 790, 933 (*kāi*), 1093, 1127, 1130, 1131, 1134, 1175, 1203, 1232, 1288, 1366, 1463, 1552, 1607, 1654, 1684, p. 61; *kai dugā*, why? 737, 985, 1180; *kai dugē̃, kai dugē*, why? 573.

dugă, owing to, is sometimes also added to an infinitive; thus, *chillam bilugh kshaiesth dugă iă tă shai bradzott*, my head aches owing to pulling a hookah too much, 671; *sū garo yaristhē dugă*, owing to an eclipse eating the sun, owing to an eclipse of the sun, 325; cf. further 693, 913, 1344, 1401 (*agul osthē dugă*, owing to the falling of rain), 1489, 1604 (*achūnisthē dugă*, owing to running).

In one instance *dugă*, owing to, is added to the conjunctive participle; thus, *badist azhir attī dugă*, owing to hails having come from the heavens, 604.

digr, adj., bad. The usual form of this word is *digar*; other forms are *dagar*, 426, 618, 710, 1584; *digr*, 607, p. 7; *digara*, 118, 322; *digarī*, 1213 (*tarwach digarī kṛiss*, it has spoilt my sword); *digrī*, 237 (*argru*), 239 (*tūs*), 678 (*ushp*), 889, p. 7 (*putt*); *dīgrī*, 1200 (*putt*). There is no difference in the word according to whether it is used as an attribute or as a predicate; the meaning differs slightly; thus:—

(1) Bad, wretched, wicked; *spāhī digar-ā*, the soldiers are bad, 63, p. 19; *digar manchī assish*, thou art a bad lot, 224, 919, 940; in this way *digar* is used as an attribute in 105, 222, 224, 619, 724, 840, 900, 919, 940, 1163; and as a predicate in 63, 64, 108, 140, 253, 421, pp. 7, 19; *dagar manchī*, an evil man, 426; *digr manchī*, an evil man, p. 7; note *krūī digar ai*, the dogs are bad, fierce, 368.

(2) Bad, unpleasant, nasty; *dumī digar bā*, the wind was bad, 303; *iă dugă digar ess*, is unpleasant to me, I dislike, 359, 575 (*dugē*), 987 (*dugă*); *amnīo tă digar assish*, they dislike thee, 1018; *digar gun*, nasty smell, 1336, 1338, 1404, p. 14; *digar koṛ manchī*, a bad colour man, an ugly man, 1572; *digar pilingī*, a bad procedure, injury, p. 3; *dagar pilingī*, injury, 710.

(3) Bad, hard, difficult, dangerous; used as a predicate, 261, 324, 355, 404, 557, 908, 988, 989, 1043; *inā pashu bilugh dagar ess*, this hill is very hard, 618; *putt digrī ess*, the road is bad, 889, 1200 (*dīgrī*); *digrī putt*, a bad road, p. 7 (but cf. 355, 404, 908, 1043).

(4) Bad, useless, unfit, unskilful; *jilamā wotasth digar ess*, (the ground) is unfit for pitching tents, 321; *shōch kusth dugē digar ai*, they are useless for fighting, 471; *digar shodr assish*, thou art a bad servant, 1262; cf. further 1723, 1730, 1744; note *nōt digara kuttett*, they dance badly, 322; *krūī digar ess*, the dog is useless (lazy), 774; *digrī ushp*, a bad (lazy) horse, 678, p. 11.

(5) Bad, unlucky; *iāst miuk digar ess*, my fate is bad, 455; *inā mōs dagar ess*, this month is unlucky (for contracting marriages), 1584.

(6) Bad, deteriorated, spoiled; *ptul digar bā*, my crop is spoiled, 302, 870 (*ess*), 1133 (*bistai*); *dro digar bistai*, the hair (of the mane) has got bad, 842; *katī digar ess*, the harvest is bad, 1032; *emā kudūm digar kariss*, thou hast spoilt our business, 1375; *ptul digr bā*, my crop is damaged, 604; *gum digara bā* the wheat is bad, 118; *tsamaṛ iā tarwach digarī kṛiss*, rust has destroyed my sword, 1213; *argru digrī biss*, the ceiling is bad, 237; *tụs digrī biss*, the chaff has gone bad, 239. Note *tū digar kalom*, I will ruin thee, do thee harm, 941; *digar kuttett*, they harm, oppress, 1045; *digar bulosh*, thou wilt come to grief, 1080.

digri, subst., a shirt, 1289, 1469, 1471; *ē tang digṛī*, a shirt (cloth) for one rupee, 219; plural, *digṛī*, shirts, 1651.

duk, see **âo-duk,** a well, 1657.

diktī, in *epos diktī*, presently, in a short time, 1065; see **epos.**

dal, adj., worn out; *daliss*, it is worn out, 1289.

DUL, to milk.

Indefinite past 1st pers. sing. *gdo dulē*, I have milked the cow, 867.

Imperative, *dolamāo*, milk it, 867 (literally, perhaps, 'milking come').

dalkiĕ, dalkīa, adv., to-morrow, p. 60. The following slightly different forms of this word occur in the sentences: *dalkiā*, 1625, 1648; *dalkiĕ*, 132, 276, 329, 398, 402, 403, 661, 663, 714, 1030, 1048, 1118, 1121, 1132, 1134, 1147, 1305, 1324, 1370, 1383, 1436, 1530, 1588, 1629; *dalkiē*, 560, 785, 792, 877.

dilkār, subst., Sunday, p. 65.

DAM, to catch, to seize. The following forms occur in the sentences :—

Infinitive, *damīsth*, to catch, p. 58.

Verbal noun, *damē, damen*, to catch ; *damē n'battamish*, we cannot catch, 1099 ; *damen n'battam*, I cannot catch, 660, p. 58 (*na battam*).

Conjunctive participle, *damētī*, having seized, having taken, 829 ; *damītī gwā*, having seized, went, carried away, 758, p. 3.

Present 3rd pers. sing. *damitt*, catches, 230 ; *tupik damitt*, he seizes his gun, he is aiming, 25 ; *manchīē varī damitt*, he catches the word of the man, he allows it, 35 (wrongly translated 'he allowed it').

Past tense 3rd pers. sing. *damiā*, he was caught, 1631.

Imperative, *damē*, catch, 231.

dām, adj., owing ; *dām assum*, I owe, 975 ; cf. **dā.**

damu, subst., air, wind, 162, 1178, 1228, 1414, 1612, 1663, 1697 ; *damu tā kāno ranzann*, the tree shakes with the wind, 1271 ; another form of the same word is *dumī* ; thus, *dumishtatt*, there is wind, 26 (cf. 387) ; *dumī n'ishtatt*, there is no wind, 27 ; *bilugh dumī yuds*, the wind is very cold, 271 ; cf. 167, 303, 387, 542, 602, 637 ; in one place we find *duma* instead ; *yazh duma ozz*, in the morning a wind came, 1679 (translated 'a whirlwind came').

dōm, subst., a flock, herd, 827 ; with *tisth*, to herd ; *dizho dom tittī afzia*, goats herding came, goats are herding, 499 ; *e dom dom tiness*, a herd was herding, 648.

dūm, subst., smoke ; *dūm parē*, full of smoke, 1339.

dumā, adj., dry ; *dumā sē*, a dry year, a draught, 380 (*duma*), 1428 ; *ptul dumā parmenstuk bistai*, the crops have become dry and small ; the crops are stunted, 1428.

dumi, wind, see **damu.**

damkolwā, adj., dry; *inā sē damkol wā*, this is a dry year, 286.

dumrī, subst., the tail (of a horse), 1457.

damtōl, adj., alert, sharp, energetic, able; used as an attribute, 1, 344, 446, 571, 597, 1054, 1188, 1325, 1348; and as a predicate 8, 29, 417, p. 9; note *damtōl lē manchī ess,* he is able good, he is famous, 446; *damtōl manchī ashī,* thou art an able man, a powerful man, 1054; *amost damtōl mochis widarthī mugis,* the slave has run away from fear of his cruel (sharp) master, 1325; *pachanwarī tā damtōl asht,* they are braver (lit. more energetic, see 417) than the enemy, p. 9; *Bastī sundī manchīōn tā damtōl azz,* Basti is the most powerful (able) of all men, p. 9.

Dān Malik, subst., name of a man; the same form is used as a subject, 900, 906; as an object, 939; and as an agent, 1356.

dīn, subst., religion, faith; *Muzzulmān dīn,* the Mussalmān religion, 1141.

dōn, subst., the handle (of an axe), 615.

dang, adj., tight, tough, hard; *tūr dār dang ess,* the mountain-ash wood is strong, 77; *ikīā manchī dang ess,* that man is tight, avaricious, 97; *iā tōtt dang manchī ess,* my father is a stringent, a stern, man, 1398; *dangu,* unyielding; *boot dangu buttet silkiottett,* boots are too unyielding and slip, 1082.

dangar, adj., lazy; *shtarī ushp dangar ess,* the female horse is lazy, 681; *shodr dangar ess,* the servant is lazy, 1263; *dangariwak assā,* he is a lazy lam. (?), 1424 (not translated); cf. **digar.**

dunyā, subst., the world; *dunya tā,* in the world, 1721.

dapil, subst., a metal plate, 1025.

drē, adv., late, p. 60; *gompōk drē āya,* the harvest came late, 623; *drē aiyosh,* thou hast come late, 769; *drē kusth,* to make late, to make delay, 337, 1130; *bilugh drē bā,* a long time has passed, it is very long since, 1517.

dri, dry, see **dari.**

dro, subst., hair; *maroik tā dro,* the hair in the mane, 842; *maroik dro,* the hair of the mane, 1203; *īsta dru kazhera assa,* my hair is white, p. 8 (noted down by Abdul Hākīm Khān); cf. **zho.**

dru, hair, see **dro.**

dār, subst., wood, perhaps of the feminine gender, p. 1 ; several instances occur in the accusative, 13, 187, 384, 484, 784 ; *kāo dār*, the wood of the olive, 946 ; *romēn dār*, the wood of the aspen tree, 81 ; *tūr dār*, the mountain-ash wood, 77 ; *watesth dār*, fire-wood, 485 ; *z͟hila dār*, wet (green) wood, p. 8. In one place we find *dā* instead ; thus, *anī dā lē ai*, here is much wood, 894 ; more common is the form *dāo*, wood, 729, 1710, 1714, pp. 1, 4 ; *dāo*, a wooden stick, 1499 ; *dāo siu*, wooden bridges, 197.

dār-sell, a carpenter ; *dār-sellē tā peḍṛī assā*, to the carpenter is an axe, the carpenter has an axe, 1234 ; *dāo sell*, a carpenter, 238 ; *dāo sella*, a carpenter, 227 ; *dāo sellē*, a carpenter, 860.

daṛ, subst., a troop ; *psūr daṛ*, relations by marriage (literally father-in-law troop, i.e. father-in-law, etc.), 1139.

dara, subst., brass, 180.

darā, subst., endurance, patience ; *darā ks͟hī*, have patience, 994.

daṛē, adj., weak ; *stā barwai daṛē n'ess*, that coolie is not weak, 837.

ḍarī, adj., dry ; *ḍarī yūs*, dry grass, hay, 581, 629 ; *ḍariss*, (the fruit) is dried, 1388 ; *yūs ḍaristai*, the turf is dried up, 1562 ; also written *ḍrī* ; *ḍrī dār*, dry wood, 384.

dāṛi, subst., a beard, 131 ; also written *dāṛī*, 392, pp. 1, 7 ; *daṛi*, p. 8 ; the word is said to be feminine, note *kaz͟hīrī dāṛī*, a white beard, p. 7 ; but *daṛi kaz͟hera assa*, the beard is white, p. 8 (noted down by Abdul Hakīm K͟hān) ; *dāṛi kaz͟hīra bissā*, the beard is become white, 131

dāru, subst., gunpowder, 601 ; see **dorē.**

dārū, subst., medicine, 1442 (*dāru*), p. 12 ; also written *dāriu* ; thus, *to gē dāriu ku ptesesh*, who has given thee medicine ? p. 4 (noted down by Abdul Hakīm K͟hān).

derē, deorē, lowlands, plains, see **diwar.**

DIR, to clean ; perfect, *kai dugā dus͟h n'dariss*, why hast thou not washed thy hands ? 1232 ; imperative, *dirē*, make it clean, 258, 522.

Dīr, subst., Dīr, name of a place; *Dīr Khān,* the Khān of Dīr, 864; *Dīr pōr,* Dīr way, towards Dīr, 1539; *Dīr stē,* from Dīr, 1387; *Dīr wīk,* to Dīr, 1557.

DŌR, to endure, to venture; verbal noun, *dōr na butt*; it is not to bear, it cannot be borne, 130.

Present 3rd pers. sing. *putrēn n'dronn* (?), he does not venture to cross, 1520.

dorē, subst., gunpowder, 1550; also written *dorī,* 1053; probably identical with *dāru,* gunpowder, 601.

1 **dūr,** adj., far, distant; *badūr,* far, p. 60; *badūr asth,* they are (equally) far, 447; *Dryus badūr ess,* Drosh is far, 449; *badūr n'nishī,* don't sit far off, 448; also written *duṛ*; thus, *baduṛ samiritsam,* I am starting to far off, I am off on a journey, 733.

2 **dūr,** adj., bent crooked; *poi tā shillē dūr bītī ass,* in the water from cold crooked having become is, he got cramp in the water owing to the cold, 297; also written *dūṛ*; thus, *dūṛ biss,* (my stick) is become bent, 147.

duṛa, duṛu, dūṛu, adj., blunt; *pets duṛa biss,* the axe has become blunt, 103; *chaku duṛu biss,* the knife has become blunt, 169; *trūtsan salī duṛu biss,* the scissors have become blunt, 1243; *tarwach dūṛu biss,* the sword has become blunt, 1454.

derbūn, adj., wonderful; *derbūn varī ess,* it is a wonderful tale, 1717.

drich, adj., torn; *drich bunn,* (the cloth) tears, 1468; *digṛī drich kṛiss,* he has torn my shirt, 1469.

drgr, adj., long; used as an attribute, 1472, p. 7, and as a predicate, 1193; *drgr kusth,* to make long, to lengthen, 1405 (*drgṛ*), 1532. Also used of human beings, tall, long; as an attribute, p. 9, and as a predicate, 1464, p. 9. A feminine (?) form, *drgrī,* occurs in *drgrī argrū,* as long log, p. 7; *drgrī ushp,* a long horse, p. 7; and in the form *drigrī,* in *argru drigrī ass,* the log is long, 820; *drigrī yūs,* long grass, reeds, 1137.

dargrin, adj., high; *in dō dargrin assiā,* this hill is high, 653.

deṛh, adj., surprised, taken by surprise; *derh bā,* he was taken by surprise, 1440.

drīn, subst., the fifteenth month of a year, p. 66.

drōn, subst., a bow, 175, 1293, p. 59; acc. *drōn,* 72; cf. **inḍrōn,** a rainbow, 1121.

drun, in *drun tapē,* pistol, 1016 (acc.); perhaps 'bow-gun'.

drangai, adj., long; *ikīā drangai shtan lushē,* burn that long stick, 215; cf. **drgr.**

dronn, he ventures, see **DOR.**

dorinōt, subst., a pouch, 1051.

dros, subst., grapes, 580; *chaktā dros parē ktī,* having filled a basket with grapes, 1259; also written *drosh,* in *drosh grīts,* vine-trees, 1610.

Drushp, subst., name of a place; *Drushp gosāosh,* thou wentest to Drushp, 1660.

drisht, subst., a span, p. 64.

drushtī-wā, adj., having poverty, poor, destitute, humble, p. 5; used as an attribute, 823, and as a predicate, 343, 690.

Drāsan, subst., name of a place; *Drāsan tā,* to Drāsan, 1498; *Drāsan wīk,* up to Drāsan, 1458.

1 **dariss,** washedest, see **DIR.**

2 **dariss, daristai,** is dried up, see **darī.**

darestān, subst., a garden; *shingīra darestān,* a pretty garden, p. 7 (said to be feminine); also written *durestān, dristān, darestā,* and *daristā.* The following forms occur in the sentences: nom. *darestā,* garden, 831; loc. *daristā,* in the garden, 1551; *dristān,* in the garden, 584; oblique, *b'darestā,* in the garden, 976; *bdristān,* in the garden, 580; *b'durestān,* in the garden, 547, 896; *baristā,* in the garden, 896.

duṛwa, subst., a musician; case of the agent plur. *duṛwa,* the musicians, 901.

Dryus, subst., Drōsh, name of a place, 449; with verbs of motion, to Drōsh, 922, 1118 (read *Dryus ā na balam,* I shall not be able to come to Drōsh); loc. *Dryus nishīlom,* I shall remain at Drōsh, 990; oblique, *Dryus p'mīsh*, in Drōsh, 897; *Dryus* *ar*, beyond Drōsh, 153; *Dryus stē*, from Drōsh, 1184, 1200, 1473, 1546, 1619; *Dryus wīk*, as far as Drōsh, 1496. Other forms are *Dryūs*, 299 (nom.), 1178 (in Drösh), and *Dryos* (*gāsam*), (I went) to Drōsh, 1660.

1 **dus,** adverb, yesterday, 45, 85, 159, 352, 354, 404, 673, 745, 795, 827, 930, 1017, 1058, 1060, 1063, 1076, 1149, 1164, 1298, 1306, 1403, 1449, 1655, 1660, 1669, 1700, 1728, 1737, pp. 4, 60; also *dūs*, 509, 641, 1148, 1237, 1342, 1670, p. 60; *dus p'tramjuk*, last night, 532; *dus radar*, last night, 371, 901; *dus radur*, last night, 1090, 1385, 1386; *dus rador*, last night, 766, 1627, 1733; *dus radōr*, last night, 1691, 1706; *dūs rador*, last night, 1615; *dus radhar*, last night, 1510.

2 **dus,** hand, see **dusht.**

3 **dus,** ten, see **dots, duts.**

dsudsuk, subst., Hell, 642, 643.

1 **dush,** subst., blame, fault; *dush n'wásam*, there is no fault to me, I am innocent, not to blame, 711, 731, p. 58.

2 **dush, dosh,** hand, see **dusht.**

dushān, of goats, see **dizhā.**

deshpilsal, subst., lightning, 807.

dashpaṛ, handback, see **dusht.**

dashta, subst., sleeve; *dashta pṛētī bṛā*, he cut off the sleeves, 1329; probably same word as the following.

dusht, subst., hand, arm; this noun occurs in several slightly different forms, viz. *dusht*, *dush*, *dosh*, *dus*, *dash*, and perhaps *dazh*.

dusht, hand, acc., 611, 1308, 1537, 1637; gen. *dusht*, of the hand, 1509; oblique, *dusht-ā*, on the hand, p. 5; *dusht tā̃*, on the hand, 1634; *b'dusht tā̃*, from the hand, 1343.

dusht, arm, 202; *dusht p'tsir*, around the arm, 1725; *dusht tā̃*, in the arm, 1166; *ē dusht*, one arm, the length from the elbow to the end of the middle finger, p. 64; *maro dusht*, the length from the elbow to the end of the clenched fist, p. 64.

dush, hand; acc., 1176, 1232; *b'dush*, on his hand, 1239; *b'dush gwā*, he fell into (the enemy's) hands, 1440.

dosh, hand; *b'dosh*, in his hand, 829.

dus, hand; *pachûtr dus pōr ī*, go right hand way, turn to the right, 1563.

dashpar, the back of the hand (?); *dashpar purstha diwar*, flat like the back of the hand, 492.

dusht sachī, the wrist, 1728.

This word is perhaps also contained in *dazh-nojī*, swimming with the hand, swimming, 1616; *dazh-noshē n'banam*, I cannot swim with the hand, I cannot swim, 1452.

dsul, subst., manure, 844.

dsulī, subst., a bush; *dsulī tā*, in the bush, 217.

daiess, hast cooked, see **DAI.**

dust, numeral, forty, p. 63 footnote (from the collection of the Rev. Worthington Jukes).

dut, teeth, see **dutt.**

dâtik, subst., a wager; *dâtik kusth*, to make a wager, 1619, 1620 (said to be a Khōwār idiom).

DITKIT, to shiver, to tremble; *kai dugā ditkichī*, why are you shivering? 1290; *tū jidd kai dugā ditkiochī*, why is thy body shivering? 1552. The word is probably onomatopoetic; the final *chī* contains the pronominal suffix of the 2nd pers. sing.; cf. **sh, shī.**

1 **dits,** subst., tongue, 1532 (accusative).

2 **dits,** numeral, twelve, 1072, p. 63.

ditus. numeral, in *twā ditus*, fifty, p. 63 footnote (from the collection of the Rev. Worthington Jukes).

dots, duts, numeral, ten, p. 63; *dots* occurs 1073, 1085, 1097; *duts*, 17, 249, 478, 530, 1389, 1473, p. 59; a third form *dus* occurs in *dus katō manchī nom*, ten Kafir names, 906; *dotsam*, ten, in *dotsam amu*, ten houses, 609, must, if correct, owe its final *am* to the following *amu*.

duts ē pōr, ten one way, tenfold, p. 64.

duts wōr, ten times, p. 60.

duts witsī, ten score, two hundred, p. 63.

dū vissī duts, two score ten, fifty, 1211, p. 63 (*du witsī duts*).

dutt, subst., a tooth, 599, 1535; nom. plur. *dut*, teeth, 945.

datziē, adj., right; *datziē achiē bradzott*, the right eye aches, 432.

dawōk, subst., a chimney, 251.

diwānbegī, subst., a certain official, 494, 771.

1 **diwar,** subst., plain, lowland, 728; also written *divarā*; thus, *inā divarā Morī divarā prishta wishtar ess*, this plain is as broad as the Morī plain, 1022. After the preposition *pa, ba* the word is changed in various ways; thus, *bdiwerr*, in the lowland, on the sandbanks, 1227; *badeore manchī*, the men of the plains, 658; *badūrē*, in the lowlands, 654.

2 **diwar, diwarī,** adj., level, flat; *dashpaṛ purstha diwar*, flat like the handback, 492; *pott diwarī ess*, the road is level, 885.

DUZ, to cry, to weep; *zhun duzdī zhundī*, she weeps crying weeping, 1654 (the translation is uncertain).

dazh, with the hand (?), in *dazhnoshē*, to swim, 1452; *dazhnojī*, swimming, 1616, see **dusht.**

dizhā, subst., goat; nom. plur. *ḍizhā*, 1217; *dizhē*, 1172; *dizho*, 499; gen. plur. *dushān pott*, a goats' track, 993

dozako, subst., Hell; *dozako tā ēlosh*, thou wilt go to Hell, 863; cf. **dsudsuk.**

F

This letter does not belong to the language and only occurs in loan-words.

faidā, subst., advantage, use; *kai faidā butt*, what is the use (of keeping a fast)? 1141; see **paidā.**

frāk, adj., wide, loose; *frāk zapp n'amjind*, they do not wear loose clothes. 824.

G

gā, gâ, cow, cattle, see **gâo.**

gã, gẽ, postposition, for; *gã*, for the sake of, p. 62; *tugã*, thee (dative), 84; *ĩgẽ*, for me, p. 3; *to gẽ*, thee (dative), p. 4; see **dugã.**

GAI, to seize, to carry off. The following forms of this base occur in the sentences.—

Infinitive, *gaiesth*, to seize; *shtalē juṭ askīē gaiesth dugã atsalā*, perhaps a leopard will come to seize him, 1091.

Verbal noun, *gaiet*, to seize, to bring, 969.

Conjunctive participle, *gaitī*, having seized; *Mehr salām gaitī*, having paid my respects to the chief, 37.

Imperative, *gaiē*, take away, 78; take, choose, 255; *giē*, take away, 912; *gyē*, take away, 1145, 1146. Very common is the compound *gaiets*, *gaits*, etc., formed from a conjunctive participle *gaī*, having seized, and *ats*, come. This form is used as an imperative to *AWĒ*, to bring; cf. *gaiets*, fetch, bring, get, 134, 160, 384, 465, 1098; *gaits*, fetch, bring, get, 597, 1225; *gats*, fetch, bring, get, 110, 156, 200, 264, 505, 558, 578, 581, 613, 782, 909, 1138, 1216, 1267, 1278, 1286, 1301, 1364, 1481, 1536, 1556, 1593, 1696, 1710, 1735, p. 47; *gia'ts*, get, 1376; *giats*, fetch, bring, get, 72, 79, 157 (put), 184, 199, 219, 241, 265, 283, 313, 314, 320, 367, 422, 480, 501, 512, 638, 746, 753, 765, 775, 778, 796, 860, 867, 961, 1008, 1010, 1031, 1035, 1043, 1076, 1082, 1146, 1218, 1222, 1256, 1294, 1320, 1376, 1400, 1424, 1447, 1453, 1484, 1504, 1714, pp. 15, 47; *gīats*, get, 195; *gyats*, fetch, bring, get, 535, 679, 796, 1106.

2nd pers. plur. *gatsăr*, bring ye, p. 47.

gâo, subst., a cow; also occurs in slightly varying forms such as *gâ*, 833; *gawā*, 1172, and *gā*, p. 8 (Abdul Hakīm K͟hān); the word is stated to be of the feminine gender, p. 1; cf. *kaz͟hīrī gâo*, the white cow, 1681, p. 7; *kas͟hīrī gâo*, the white cow's, 220; *gâo kaz͟hīrī assā*, is the cow white? 294; *gā kacheri assa*, the cow is white, p. 8; but *gâo mṛā*, the cow, the cows, died, 232, p. 2; the following forms occur in the sentences:—

Nom. sing. *gáo,* cow, 294, 381, 629, 1681, 1741, 1742, pp. 1, 2, 7; *gā,* cow, p. 8 (Abdul Hakīm Khān).

Acc. sing. *gáo,* the cow, 867.

Gen. sing. *gáo,* the cow's, 220.

Oblique, *gáo dugĕ,* for the cow, 505; *gáo dugā̆,* for the cow, 1222; *gáo tā̆,* than the cow, 1742.

Nom. plur. *gáo,* cows, cattle, 232, 363, 972, 1020, 1172, 1284; *gá,* cattle, 833; *gawā,* cattle, 1172.

gáo patsā, a cowherd, 295.

zūgh gáo, the yak, 1732.

giā̃, adverb, (1) otherwise, 1321, 1452, p. 61; also written *gyān,* 1704; and *giyān* (*azzā,* it is) otherwise, 1713; (2) for nothing, gratis, p. 61; other words which probably belong to the same base are *giān,* only, 1432; *giaktī,* therefore, 494, 735; thus, 1594; *gitā,* thus, 1347; *gittā,* thus, 1600; cf. **gijj.**

giē, take away, see **GAI.**

1 **GŪ,** to go; a defective base; other forms are derived from *I.* Like this latter base *GŪ* is used as an auxiliary with other verbs, especially in the so-called passive; cf. *atlongai,* falling went, fell, 1237; *atlon gwā,* fell, 1233; *gittangus,* has got knotted, 748; *jā̆ra gwā,* was killed, p. 59; *ktol kaṛungo,* belly made, belly full, 1365; *lushingwā,* it is dried up, 286; *luzhengam,* etc., I, etc., was frostbitten, p. 30; *luzhengossam,* etc., I, etc., had been frostbitten, p. 30; *maṛelgō,* dead, 1358; *mṛalogom,* dead, 461; *mizhongai oss,* lying having gone is, he played a trick, 1553; *pēṭe-gā,* go and cut, 318; *peṛingā* (1488), *peṛongā* (202, 1194), *peṭangā* (633), *peṭangwā* (641, 723, 809, p. 59); *peṭangawā* (66), *paṛengī* (201), *peṛongī* (pp. 2, 59), was broken; the corresponding perfect 'has been broken' is *peṛingess,* 869, 1535; *peṭangess,* 196, 198, 307, 615, 860, 1033, p. 59; *prēṭangess,* 49; *peṭangus,* p. 59; *peṭanguss,* 240; *peṭṭangus,* 175; in the future we find *peṛengēlā* (written *peṛeng*

ēlā), will break, 1190; *peṭangellā* (written *peṭang ellā*), will break, p. 59; cf. further *tapā gwā*, they were killed, p. 59.

The following forms of this base occur in the sentences :—

Infinitive, *gūsth*, to go, p. 22; *gūsthā*, to go, 10.

Conjunctive participle, *gītī*, having gone, 1202, 1301, p. 22; another form *gai* occurs in *mizhongai iā tā oss*, lying having gone me to is, he has played a trick on me, p. 22.

Past participle, *go*, gone, in *ktol kaṛun-go pul ār*, the horse has eaten his belly done (full) of grain, 1365; *maṛelgō*, dead, 1358; *mṛalogom*, dead, 461; *gust*, *giest*, in *uchangust*, steeply sloping, steep, 1331; *uchangiest*, steep, 1397.

Indefinite present 1st pers. sing. *gūmbá*, if I go, p. 23.

2nd pers. sing. *gujbá*, if goest, when goest, 46, 1202, 1411; *gūjbá*, if goest, p. 23.

3rd pers. sing. *gūbá*, if he goes, when he goes, 964, p. 23.

1st pers. plur. *gūmishbá*, if we go, p. 23.

2nd pers. plur. *gūṛbá*, if you go, p. 23.

3rd pers. plur. *gūbá*, if they go, p. 23.

Past 1st pers. sing. *gā'm*, I went, 1301, p. 22; *luzhengam*, I got frostbitten, p. 30.

2nd pers. sing. *gā'sh*, wentest, p. 22; *gā-osh*, (why) didst thou go? 783; *luzhengash*, wast frostbitten, p. 30.

3rd pers. sing. *gā*, went, in *luzhengā*, was frostbitten, p. 30; *peṛingā*, was broken, 1488; *peṛon gā*, was broken, 202, 1194; *peṭangā*, was broken, 633; *gai*, *gaie*, went, gone; *gaiebá*, when it has gone, if it went, 922, 923, p. 23; *atlongai*, falling went, fell, 1237.

gī, went, in (*māṛī*) *paṛengī*, (my stick) is broken, 201; (*māṛī*) *peṛongī*, (my stick) is broken, pp. 2, 59.

goī, went; *toch baduī goī*, a bullet went to hand, I found a bullet, 213.

gwā, went, 758, 1538, p. 3, footnote; *pachanwarī b'dush gwā*, he fell into the enemy's hands, 1440; *p'kōr gwā*, went to ear, was heard, 635, 830, 871, 1104, 1510; *gwā* often has the meaning of a perfect, has gone; thus, 48, 787, 979; *poī gwā* has fallen into the river, 444, 797 (*po-ē*); note *atlongwā*, falling went, dropped, 1233; *jāra gwā*, killed went, was killed, p. 59; *lu<u>sh</u>ingwā*, (the corn) is dried up, 286; *peṭangwā*, is broken, 641, 723, 809, p. 59.

gawā, went, p. 22; *p'kōr gawā*, went to ear, was heard, 511, 1615; *peṭangawā*, got broken, is broken, 66.

1st pers. plur. *gāmi<u>sh</u>*, we went, 403, p. 22; *lu<u>zh</u>engāmi<u>sh</u>*, we got frostbitten, p. 30.

2nd pers. plur. *gār*, you went, p. 22; *lu<u>zh</u>engār*, you got frostbitten, p. 30.

3rd pers. plur. *gā*, they went, in *lu<u>zh</u>engā*, they got frostbitten, p. 30.

gyē, they went, 1738, p. 22.

gwā, they have gone, 697; *tapā gwā*, they were killed, p. 59; *gawā*, they have gone, 33; they went, p. 22.

Perfect and pluperfect 1st pers. sing. *gāsam*, I have gone, I went, 1660; *gossam*, I had gone, in *lu<u>zh</u>engossam*, I had got frostbitten, p. 30; *gūssam*, I went, 766, 1177, 1316 (*yūr gūssam*, I went down, I sank); I have gone, 1482; I had gone, p. 22.

2nd pers. sing. *gāsa<u>sh</u>*, hast gone, 420; *gosāo<u>sh</u>*, wentest, 1660; *gossi<u>sh</u>*, hadst gone, in *lu<u>zh</u>engossi<u>sh</u>*, hadst got frostbitten, p. 30; *gūssi<u>sh</u>*, hast gone, 1519; hadst gone, p. 22.

3rd pers. sing. *gosā*, has gone; *p'kōr n'gosā*, it has not gone to (their) ears, they have not heard of, 642.

gosī, has gone; *kaikotē gosī*, why has he gone, 1685.

gūs, has gone; *chilī bitī gūs*, outlaw having become has gone, he has become an outlaw, 973; *<u>sh</u>tār katī gūs*, theft having made has gone, he has stolen away, 1261; *gūs*, went, 1661, 1677, p. 22; *gittangus*, (my rope) has got knotted, 748; *peṭṭangus*, is broken, 175; *peṭangūs*, is broken, p. 59.

gess, has gone; *na pū-gess*, (the sun) has not gone down, 1266; *peṛingess*, has got broken, is broken, 869, 1535; *peṭangess*, has got broken, is broken, 196, 198, 307, 615, 860, 1033, p. 59; *prēṭangess*, is broken, 49.

giess, has gone; *putt kōr-ā giess*, where has the road gone? where is the road? 1300.

guss, has gone, in *peṭanguss*, is broken, 240.

gossā, had gone; *luzhengossā*, had got frostbitten, p. 30.

gussā, had gone; *pshutti gussā*, had gone to sleep, 1261.

gūssā, has gone; *Ashrett pōr gūssā*, has he gone towards Ashrett? 1538; *zīm gūssā*, has the snow gone? 1589; *gūssā*, had gone, p. 22.

1st pers. plur. *gossamish*, we had gone, in *luzhengossamish*, we had got frostbitten, p. 30; *gūssamish*, we went, 1737; we had gone, p. 22.

2nd pers. plur. *gussār*, you had gone, in *luzhengussār*, you had got frostbitten, p. 30; *gussēr*, you went, 1737; *gūssēr*, you had gone, p. 22.

3rd pers. plur. *gostai*, they have gone, 1284; *gūstai*, they had gone, p. 22; *gusthai*, they had gone, in *luzhengusthai*, they had got frostbitten, p. 30.

Future 3rd pers. sing. *gēlā*, *gellā*, will go, in *peṛengēlā* (written *peṛeng ēlā*), will be broken, 1190; *peṭangellā* (written *peṭang ellā*), will be broken, p. 59.

Imperative, *gā*, go (?), *pēṭegā*, go and cut, cut, 318.

2 **gū**, subst., an ant; nom. plur. *gū*, ants, 53, 54, 55, 56.

3 **gū**, subst., a worm; agent plural, *gū*, worms, 1722; probably identical with the foregoing.

4 **gū**, adj., sour, *gū bistai*, (the pears) have become sour, 997.

guchi, subst., mustachios, 891.

giḍr, subst., a sheaf (of corn), 1282.

Gāgrawott, subst., name of a pass, Gangalwott; *Gāgra wott bado pagur*, under, on, the Gāgra wott (Gāgra stone) pass, 502; also written *Gāgrī-wott*, 989, 991.

gijj, pronoun, what? *gijj pitshun*, in what war? 1630; to the same base belong *gijjī*, some one, p. 14; case of the agent, *gizhē manchīē*, some man, 1038; and probably also *gijjā̃*, for nothing, gratis, 513, 933; *gijā̃*, for nothing, gratis, p. 61; cf. **giā̃**.

1 **gijjī,** subst., word, speech; is used as an object with *kusth,* to do; *gijjī kusth,* to make words, to say, to speak, 537, 696, 805, 828, 868, 869, 906, 930, 1081, 1129, 1177, 1257, 1353, 1356, 1422, 1423, 1483, 1494, 1522, 1567, 1570, 1644, 1682, 1723, pp. 11, 14.

2 **gijji,** some one, see **gijj.**

gujr, gujar, gajr, gajar, subst., a day; *sutt gujr,* seven days, 1346; *trē gujr,* three days, 990; *iā amu biliuk gujr ess,* my house is many days (sc. distant), my house is very far, 185; *ē gujr pott,* one day's march, 846; *dū, trai, gajr pott,* two, three days' march, 846; *sang gujr,* all days, daily, 320, p. 60; *gujr,* by day, 328; *gajr,* by day, 650; *ē gujar,* in one day, 1619; *ē gujar p'mīsh,* in one day, 1214; *starak gujr,* to-day, 271, 327, 351 (*shtarak*), 404, 756 (*strak*), 959, 1063, 1104, 1121, 1497; *starak gujar,* to-day, 443; *starak gajar,* to-day, 879; loc. sing. *gujrẽ, gujarẽ,* in a day; *eo gujrẽ ē wōs pott kalom,* in one day one day's march shall do, every day I shall do a march, 327; *eo gujrẽ,* every day, daily, p. 60; *eo gujarẽ,* every day, daily, 1056, 1061, p. 5.

giakti, adverb, therefore, 494, 735; thus, 1594; cf. **giā.**

gol, gul, subst., a nullah, a valley, often translated country; thus, 197, 292, 348, 445, 570, 573, 576, 691, 1123, 1282, 1657; this translation is not, however, strictly correct; *gol, gul* can often be translated river, stream; thus, 518, 534, 1182, 1183, 1418, 1698; see below. The word is stated to be feminine, p. 1; cf. *arūṇī gol,* a narrow valley, a defile, a gorge, 336; *aruṇī gol,* 574, 728; but *gōl ariṇ assā,* the valley is narrow, 1598.

The following forms occur in the sentences:—

Nom. sing. *gol,* valley, 292, 336, 574, 1723; *gōl,* valley, 1598; *Parish lesst gul assā,* Asmār is a good valley (a good place), 1153.

Gen. sing. *gol do,* the water of the valley, the river, 500, 728; *gol ūgh,* the river, 1182.

Nom. plur. *gul,* nullahs, 935.

Oblique, *b'gol,* in the nullah, 363, 365, 1599; *emā b'gol manchī*, a man of our valley, 520; *Asrett b'gol manchī*, a man of the Ashrett valley, 471; *b'gul*, in the nullah, 27, 871, 1168, 1515 (on the river bank), 1646; *inā b'gul ắo*, the water in this nullah, 1418, 1698; *emắ b'gul dugắ*, for (the people) in our valley, 1223; *iắ b'gul tắ*, in my valley, 1196; *inā b'gul tắ*, in this nullah, 1183, 1224; *gol tắ*, in the nullah, 348, 534; *kōr gol tắ*, in which nullah? where? 389; *gul tắ*, in the nullah (in the country), 197, 445, 570, 573, 576, 691, 871, 1123, 1168, 1657; note *inā gula tắ*, in this valley, 304; *emắ gul tắr*, in our nullah (country), 1282.

aruṇī gol, a narrow nullah, a defile, gorge, 336 (*arūṇī*), 574, 728.

gol ắo, the water of the nullah, the river, 500, 728.

golo, the water of the nullah, the river; *golo āo*, the water of the river, 518; *b'gol-o*, into the river, 463; *golo tắ petrēmắ*, we will cross (by wading) in the river, 1618.

gul-o, the river; *b'gul-o*, in the river, 1421.

glao, the river; *baglao*, in the river, 1421.

glo, the river; *baglo*, into the river, 463.

gologh, the river, 518, 1182.

golūgh, the river, 1182.

gilos, subst., cherry; *sang gilos chinosht*, all the cherries are sour, 247.

gā'm, I went, see 1 **GŪ**.

giāmi, in *giāmī prushkarē*, easily (?), 1456; cf. **giā**.

gum, subst., wheat; nom. *gum*, 118, 286, 870, 1282; acc. *gum*, 501, 1029, 1133, 1216, 1294, 1304, 1505; gen. *gum*, 1049, 1389; *gum pul*, the grain of the wheat, 1668; *gum purstha*, wheat-like, rosy-faced, 1197; cf. **zhum**.

gumbắ, if I go, see 1 **GŪ**.

gómpōk, subst., wheat ripening, harvest, 623.

Gumāra, subst., Gumāra, name of a man, 631, 1682.

gāmish, we went; **gūmishbắ**, if we go, see 1 **GŪ**.

1 **gāno**, subst., charity, alms, bakshish, 224; probably identical with **giān**, reward, 1164.

2 **gāno,** adj., heavy; *ēmá bōr gāno ai,* our loads are heavy loads, 639; *gānowā,* heavy; *zīn gānowā assā,* the saddle is heavy, 1218; *gāwā,* heavy; *emá bor gāwā asht,* our loads are heavy, 805; *gānowaktī,* heavy having done, violent; *gānowaktī damu ushtiā,* violently a wind arose, a violent storm came, 1414.

1 **giān,** subst., reward, bakshish; *ē tang giān prēlom,* I will give you a reward of a rupee, 1164; probably identical with 1 **gāno.**

2 **giān,** adv., only, 1432; see **giā.**

gun, subst., smell, scent; nom. *gun,* 1001, 1195, 1242, 1336, 1338; *digar gun,* a bad smell, a stink, 1336, 1338, 1404, p. 14; acc. *gun; kā gun kunn,* what does (the dog) smell? 1327.

gunā, adj., open; *iā aḍr gunā n'ess,* my box is not open, 960; *gunā kusth dugā pets giats,* bring an axe to open it, 961.

gaṛ, subst., jewel; *gaṛ lē prētt,* he gives many jewels, 726.

gāṛ, subst., a log; *gāṛ utinā,* logs are stranded, 1227; *gāṛa,* log, 1515; *gārā mēsh band krissā,* he has bound him in the stocks, 1407; cf. **argru.**

garo, subst., eclipser, an eclipse (translated 'shadow'); *pōj sē bā sū garo n'yāriss,* five years have gone, an eclipse has not eaten the sun, 406; *sū garo garisthē dugā,* owing to an eclipse eating the sun, 325; cf. Sanskrit *graha.*

GĪR, to count; imperative, *gīrē,* count, 291.

GĪṚ, GIR, to fasten, to tie.

Infinitive, *giristh dugā,* for fastening, 285.

Imperative, *gīṛo,* tie, 1511; cf. **giṛangusth** and **gittangus.**

giṛi, subst., saddle-girth, 1402.

1 **gor, gōr,** subst., a handful; acc. sing. *gōr,* 613 (*gor*), 1222, 1294; nom. plur. *gor,* 1365.

2 **gor,** in *Rāolī-gor,* the Rawali Pass, 988, 989; perhaps 'gorge'.

1 **gur,** subst., sugar, 1431.

2 **gur,** adj., goitred; *tū chī sē biss gur bītī,* how many years have you had goitre? 569.

guṛu, adj., deep; *ātr guṛu ess,* the ford is deep, 332.

garib, adj., poor; *garib assum,* I am poor, 300, 391 (*garīb*); *garib manchī assumish,* we are poor people, 1044.

gūṛbā, if you go, see 1 **GŪ.**

grik, subst., ankle, 49, p. 59.

1 **garak,** subst., neck; *b'garak,* up to the neck, 1183; *garak tā,* on my neck (throat), 1507; *girēk,* neck, 1487 (acc.).

2 **Garak,** subst., Garak, name of a man, 906, 917.

grām, subst., a village; nom. sing. *grām,* 151, 991, 1206, 1435, 1500, 1590; gen. *grām*; *sundī grām ē utāh ess,* to each village is a chief priest, each village has a chief priest, 1069; *sundī grām ē pshar ezz,* each village has a maternity hospital, 683; oblique, *grām pabunor,* round the village, 1439.

grām is very often preceded by the preposition *pa* in the forms *b, ba, bi,* and in that case *grām* may be changed to *grom*; *r* is occasionally transposed before *g.* The following instances occur:—

bugrām, in the village, 62, 343, 358, 425, 545, 546, 609, 1092, 1155, 1156, 1163, 1433, 1581, 1650, p. 11; *bgrām,* in the village, 1521; *bigrām,* in the village, 1609: *bagrom,* in the village, 227, 289, 368, 427, 450 549, 609, 686, 823, 845, 914, 1050, 1256; *bargām,* in the village, p. xii; *bragom,* in the village, 232, 322; *Kām-bragām,* to the Kām village, to Kamdēsh, 1519; postpositions can be added; thus, *inā bugrām mī,* in this village, 1159; *b'grām p'mich,* in the village, 1249; *ema bagrom p'mich,* in our village, 428; *bgrom stē,* from the village, 552.

gūrūm, subst., cock-crow, dawn; *gūrūm ettā,* dawn coming, dawn, p. 64.

grammā, see *krām-grammā,* a threshing-floor, 1506.

giṛangusth, subst., the knot (of a rope); acc. *giṛangusthē,* 1578; lit. knotted gone, knotted; cf. **GĪṚ** and **gittangus.**

grish, subst., the hot part of the day, noon, 865; also the time about three o'clock p.m., 262; *garish-bā,* noon (and the time immediately after noon), p. 65; *grishbō,* the time from noon to three o'clock p.m., 18; *grish painjī,* the time from 3 p.m. to evening, 18, p. 64.

grosam, in *purū grosam,* I have got leave to depart, 37; *grussish* in *iā pur n'grussish,* I have not given thee leave to depart, 783; see **purū** and **NGĀ.**

Gairath, subst., Gairath, name of a place, 447; *Gairath esth,* to go to Gairath, 561, 1530; *Dryus stī Gairath p'mich,* between Drōsh and Gairath, 1184.

grīts, subst., a creeper, a tree; *drosh grīts peṛia,* he has cut down our vine-trees, 1610.

gosā, gosi, gus, went; **gā'sh, gaosh,** wentest, see 1 **GŪ.**

gash, subst., a goat; nom. sing. *gash,* 1017; acc. sing. *gash,* 1706; gen. sing. *gash,* 606; nom. plur. *gash,* 566, 588, 1417, 1705; acc. plur. *gash,* 566, 1396, 1705; gen. plur. *gash,* 827.

Gish, subst., the war god, 568.

gushrogu, subst., a locust; agent plur. *gushrogu,* 817.

gāsam, I went; **gess, giess, guss, gussā,** went; **gosāosh,** wentest; **gūssam,** I went; **gūssamish,** we went; **gūssêr,** you had gone; **gūssish,** hast gone; **gostai, gūstai,** they went; **gūsth,** to go, see 1 **GŪ.**

gaiet, to bring; **gaiti,** having taken; see **GAI.**

gitā, adv., thus, 1347; *gittā,* thus, 1600.

gitī, having gone, see **GŪ.**

giṭu, subst., grafting; *giṭu kosth,* to do grafting, to graft, 576; *giṭu kaṛbā,* when you do grafting, by grafting, 577.

gatrā, adj., tired, weary; used as a predicate, 107, 134, 608, 644, 1157, 1307, 1315, 1432, 1503, 1523, 1545, 1611, 1708; *gatrā bitī,* having got tired, defeated, 335; *iā gatrā kunjī,* thou makest me tired, vexest me, 1608.

gatra, tired, weary, 229, 1060; *gatri,* weariness; *n'gatribōla,* let there not be weariness, don't be tired, 182.

gatrabā, tired, weary, 457.

gotr, subst., the upper arm; *iāst gotr tā,* on my upper arm, 1449; *iāst gotrā tā,* on my upper arm, 67.

gaiets, gaits, gats, giats, bring; **gatsār,** bring ye, see **GAI** and **AWĒ.**

giṭṭā, thus, 1600; see **gitā.**

goṭṭ, subst., a stack (of grass), 1386 (acc.).

gittan, adj., knotted; *gittangus,* (the rope) has got knotted, 748; cf. **GĪṚ** and **giṛangusth.**

gawā, gwā, went, see 1 **GŪ.**

gãwā, heavy, 805; see **gāno, gānowā.**

gyē, take away, see **GAI.**

gyān, adv., otherwise, 1704; *giyān azzā,* it is otherwise, 1713; see **giā.**

gyats, bring, fetch, see **GAI** and **AWĒ.**

gizhē, pronoun, some one; *gizhē manchīē ptess,* some man gave, 1038; see **gijj.**

guzz, subst., bug; nom. plur. *guzz,* bugs, 210.

H

This consonant is apparently foreign to the language. It occurs as an initial in some loan-words, and is sometimes, cockney-way, added before an initial vowel.

hai hai, interjection, alas! 28, p. 63.

hāu, camest, p. 58; see 1 **Ā.**

hē, interjection, O! pp. 5, 6.

hukm, subst., order, command; acc. *hukm,* 318, 420, 969, 1148, 1205, 1221, 1245.

Hindustān, subst., Hindōstān; *Hindustān-o manchī,* the people of Hindōstān, 998.

hinju, subst., the tamarisk, 1465.

haiss, has come, 537; see 1 **Ā.**

1 **host,** subst., hand; *host susnī,* a handkerchief, p. 3; *hōst susnī,* a handkerchief, 614.

2 **hōst,** they are, 528; **hosth,** they are, p. 19; see **AS.**

hatt, adv., there, 58, p. 61.

huzhuts, numeral, hundred, p. 63 footnote (from the collection of the Rev. Worthington Jukes).

J

je, conjunction, and, 576, 1293, 1310, 1640; *jē*, and, p. 62; *ajē*, and, 1277; *ojē*, and, 643, 647, 1464, p. 62.

jū, subst., a daughter, 326, 1709, p. 8; agent sing. *jū*, p. 4; dat. sing. (with pronominal suffix of 1st person) *iā jūī noi bazisnā prēlom*, I will give my daughter new clothes (translated 'my girl is a bride'), 194.

ju-s, his daughter, p. 4 (acc.); *iā nawōs jus*, my nephew's daughter (acc.), 918; *kunzā jūs*, the queen's daughter, the princess, 1073; cf. **juk.**

jidd, subst., body, 469, 1552; see **jitt.**

jaga, jagā, subst., a place; nom. sing. *jaga*, 893; acc. sing. *jagā*, 893; oblique *tū jilamā jagā torē*, near the place of thy tents near thy camping-ground, 1639; *jaga tā*, in the place (for pitching tents), 1713.

jigor, subst., maize, 840 (acc.); see **jawār.**

jugūr, subst., a woman; nom. sing. *jugur*, 464; *jugūr*, 207, 696, 1688; *jugūr*, 1707; acc. sing. *jugūr awṛī*, he took a woman, he married, 850, pp. 2, 3; gen. sing. *jugūr*, 803; nom. plur. *jugūr*, 573, 915, 1406; cf. **jū** and **juk.**

jijil, adj., loose; *jijil biss*, (my horse's girth) has become loose, 826; *s̲h̲irr jijil ks̲h̲ī*, loosen the loin cloth, 821; *jinjil biss*, has got loose, 553.

juk, subst., a girl, 1709, p. 8; acc. plur. *juk*, 552; see **jū** and **jugūr.**

jil, subst., a girl, 1009 (acc.), 1078 (nom.); acc. plur. *jil*, 160.

jallai, subst., a duck; nom. plur. *jallai*, ducks, 30, 385, 1042.

jilamā, subst., a canvas house, a tent; acc. sing. *jilamā*, 1679; gen. *jilamā*, of (my) tent, 1261; oblique, *jilamā dugā*, for the tent, 1447; *jilamā* [*sic*] *tā*, at (my) tent, 1638; nom. plur. *jilamā*, 1473; gen. plur. *jilamā jagā*, camping-ground, 1639; acc. plur. *jilamā uchasth*, to raise, to pitch, tents, 893, 1019,

1713.; *jilamá uchaiesth*, to erect tents, 594; *jilamá uten na band*, they cannot pitch their tents, 1664; *jilamá wotasth*, to pitch tents, 321; oblique plural, *jilamá dugã*, for the tents, 684.

jion, subst., life; *jion* (?) *nuksálam*, I will take his life, 1090; cf. **shion.**

jiōn, killed, see **JĀ̃R.**

jinjil, adj., loose, 553; see **jijil.**

JAR, to be digested; *borī na bajit jarand*, the loaves are not digested in my body, I have dyspepsia, 393.

JĀ̃R, to kill; the following forms occur in the sentences:—

Infinitive, *jãristh*, to kill, 598, 1549 (*j. dugã*); *jãristhai dugã*, in order to kill, to shoot, 1011,

Verbal noun, *jãr bachā*, thou canst kill, 1214, p. 58.

Present participle, *jãrl*, killing; *manchī jãrl assā*, he is a man-slayer, a murderer, 900.

Past participle, *jãra*, killed; *jãra elār*, you will go killed, you will be killed, p. 59; *jãra gwā*, he went killed, he was killed, p. 59; *jãronn* (?), was killed, 673 (translated 'I killed').

Conjunctive participle, *jãrītī*, having killed, 959, 973.

Indefinite present 2nd pers. sing. *jãrabā*, if thou killest, 1564; 3rd pers. sing. *jãrībá*, if one kills, 967.

Present 3rd pers. sing. *jãrana*, he is killing, p. 4 (noted down by Abdul Hakīm K͟hān).

Past 1st pers. sing. *jãronn* (?), I killed, 673; probably, 'was killed'; see past participle.

2nd pers. sing. *jãriã*, thou hast killed, p. 4 (Abdul Hakīm K͟hān).

3rd pers. sing. *jiōn* (?), he killed him, 319; *jãriā*, he killed, 3, 319; *jãriã*, he killed, p. 4 (Abdul Hakīm K͟hān).

Perfect and pluperfect 1st pers. sing. *n'jãriss*, I have not killed, 711

2nd pers. sing. *jãriss*, killedest, 984.

3rd pers. sing. *jãriss*, has killed, 270, 899, 1356, 1512;

killed, 795, 1573, 1579; *jārissī,* he had killed (his daughter), p. 4 (Abdul Hakīm Khān); *jāristai,* he has killed (the prisoners), 1074.

3rd pers. plur. *jāristai,* they have killed (some), 1135.

Future 1st pers. sing. *jārlam,* I shall kill, 106, 939, 1093, 1396, 1558; *jārlom,* I shall kill, 739.

2nd pers. sing. *jārlosh,* wilt kill, 1160.

3rd pers. sing. *jārlā,* will kill, 459, 1189, 1326, 1441.

1st pers. plur. *jārlmā,* we will kill, 779.

3rd pers. plur. *jārlā,* they will kill, 1144.

Imperative, *jār,* kill, 964.

JĀṚ, to know, see **ZĀṚ.**

jarob, subst., stockings, 1406 (acc.).

jerik, jirik, subst., shame, modesty; *tū kai jirik n'ess,* thou hast no shame, 670; *tū jerik n'ass,* thou hast no shame, 1273; *jerik n'zāṛ,* do not know shame, do not be ashamed, 1274; *jerik-na-wā,* a not shame man, shameless; *jerik na wā shtār assish,* thou art a shameless thief, 1275.

jus, subst., his daughter, p. 4; *iā nawōs jus,* my nephew his daughter, 918; *kunzā jūs,* the queen her daughter, the princess, 1073; see **jū.**

jasht, jisht, jast, jash, adj., eldest, principal; *jisht brā,* elder brother, 411; *jash tōtt,* the elder father, a paternal uncle, 1573; *jisthā,* uncle, 331; *jasht angur,* the principal finger, the thumb, 1509, 1634; as a noun *jasht* means principal, headman, leader; in this meaning it is used in the nominative, 632, 780, 969; in the accusative, 779; and, in the form *jast,* before postpositions. thus, *jast panishr,* before the headman, 1373.

juṭ, subst., a leopard, 1091 (nom.), 795, 1543 (acc.); a tiger, 1512 (acc.).

jitt, subst., the body, 4, 52, 999; also written *jidd,* 469, 1552; *bajit,* in the body, 393.

jawār, subst., maize, Indian corn, 1408, p. 3; *jowār tā,* (more) than corn, 1170; also written *jigor,* 840.

K

1 **ka,** pronoun, the base of the interrogative pronoun, who? what? Many forms of this base are also used in subordinate interrogatory clauses, often followed by the particle *bá*, which see. The various forms of the base *ka* are also used as indefinite pronouns. The following forms of the pronoun occur in the sentences:—

(1) As an interrogative—

Nom. sing. who? *kū*, p. 13; *kāchī*, 1458, 1682, p. 13; *kett*, 1702, p. 13.

What? *kā*; used as a noun in *kā—kā*, what—what, either—or, p. 14; *kā rits kā gum būjē tā parē kshī*, fill either barley or wheat in the sack, 1216; *kā* is commonly used as an adjective, 1554, 1724.

kyā; *tā kyā nām ess*, what is thy name? 749.

kai, used as a noun, 80, 126, 177 (predicate), 521, 714, 853, 1141; used as an adjective, 10, 342, 749, 799, 830, 847, 915, 1014, 1160; *kai wōkt*, what time? when? p. 60; *kāchī*, p. 13.

kett; *kett tū mārоī assā*, which is thy stick? 1676.

Acc. sing. whom? *kū*, p. 13.

What? *kā*; *kā-ktī*, what having done? how? 408, 485, p. 61; used as an attribute, *kā gun kunn*, what smell does he make? what does he smell? 1337; *kā varī karosh*, what word did he make to thee? what did he say to thee? 1665.

kyā; *kyā gijjī karā'sh*, what word did he make to thee? p. 12.

kai, 139, 747, 854, 1033, 1149, 1194, 1235; *kaiko*, what having done? why? 460; *kaikotē*, why? 1130, 1176, 1685, p. 61; how? 1194, 1304, 1345 (*kaikote*), p. 61; *kaikotē̃*, why? 1667; *kaikotī*, why? 759; how? 1122, 1423, 1645, 1716.

Agent sing. who? *ko*, 1016, p. 17; *ku*, pp. 3, 4; *kū*, 270, 1459, pp. 12, 13; *kāchī*, p. 13.

Gen. sing. whose? of what? *kū*, *kā'st*, *ku'st*, *kāwo*, p. 13; *kust ushp*, whose horse? 1683.

Oblique sing. (*a*) as a noun, who? *kā mē͟sh*, from whom? p. 13; *kū tā*, to whom? p. 13.

What? *kā dugā*, what for? why? 420; *kā dugā*, why? 589; *kai do*, why? 309; *kai dū*, why? p. 61; *kai dugā*, why? 737, 985, 1180; *kai dugā*, why? 689, 771, 790, 1093, 1101, 1127, 1130, 1131, 1134, 1175, 1203, 1232, 1288, 1290, 1307, 1340, 1366, 1463, 1552, 1607, 1654, 1684, 1733, p. 61; *kāi dugā*, why? 933; *kai dugē, kai dugē*, why? 573.

(*b*) As an attribute, *kai soss tā*, in what thought? for what purpose? why? 816; *kāwo gul tā*, in what nullah, where? 813.

Nom. plur. *kāchī*, who? p. 13.

Acc. plur. *kāchī*, whom? p. 13.

Agent plur. *kāchī*, who? p. 13.

Gen. plur. *kā'st, ku'st*, whose? p. 13.

Oblique plur. *kett mē͟sh*, from whom? p. 13; *kett tā*, to whom? p. 13.

(2) As an interrogative in subordinate sentences, *kai*, whoever, whatever, p. 14; *tū kai manumbā*, whatever thou orderest me, 968; *ōts kaikotī wilāmbā*, what doing I tell thee, as I tell thee, 1594; *kettā manchī*, what man, the man who, p. 14.

(3) As an indefinite pronoun we find *kai, ko, kū, kāch, kāchī*, anybody; *kā, kai*, anything; *kā, ko, kai, kuī*, some; *kā, kai, kuī, kāchī*, any; thus—

Anybody—*kai n'aie͟sht*, anybody not is, there is nobody, 1301, 1393 (*kai na a͟sht*); *ko kai n'chamol*, anybody not knowing, acknowledging nobody, proud, 1080; *kō*, anybody, p. 14; *ko warī*, anybody's word, 940; *kū winozhā*, has anyone hit thee? 1470; *kāch n'ess*, anybody not is, there is nobody, 148; *kāchī na*, anybody not, nobody, 1581, p. 14.

Anything—*kā paidā na butt*, anything produced not becomes, nothing grows, 1723; *kā paidā na bunn*, nothing comes of it, 1595, 1597 (*na ess*); *wārē kā n'iār*, I ate nothing else, 955; *kā dī*, anything even, with a negative, nothing; *wārā kā dī n'aie͟sht*, there is nothing else, 1209; *kā dī n'wāṛiām*, I saw nothing, 1252; *kā dī ngā n'battam*, I cannot carry anything, 1297; *kai n'asht*, anything not is, there is nothing, 933; *kai na prēlom*, I will not give anything, 1063, 1149; *koi dī kai n'prēlom*, I will never give (thee) anything, I will never forgive, 919; *kai widerasth n'ess*, there is nothing to fear, 1181; *kai n'amniō*, anything not attack, do not attack him in any way, 90.

Note *kā no, kai no*, nothing, with the adjective suffix *wā*; thus, *kā-no-wā*, having nothing, being nothing, useless, unfortunate, poor, used as a predicate, 1155, 1580, 1590, 1649; *kai-no-wā*, of no account, poor, used as a predicate, 966, 1109, 1171, 1172; *kai nowā manchī*, a poor man, 875.

Some—*kā*, p. 14; *kā mōch*, some man, somebody, 1353; *ko manchūān jārlā*, it will kill some men, somebody, 1189; *kai lattrī*, something, 1149; *kai mār*, some word, p. 4; *kuī wōs tā̃*, some day, 1198, p. 60.

Any—*kā widegh na ess*, any fear not is, there is no fear, 458; other examples of *kā*, any, 711, 912, 1215, 1444, 1705; *kai bradzo nēss*, any ailment not is, there is no ailment, 24; *kai ūd n'ess*, there is no use for, 81, 1111; *kai wōs tā̃*, at any time, p. 60; other examples of *kai*, any, 430, 664, 670, 832, 843, 921; *kuī wōs tā̃*, at any time, p. 60; *kāchī manchī*, any man, 841, 1102, 1675; *kāchī zōtr*, any relation, 1140.

Other words formed from the same base are *kā, kyā, kyē, kyē̃, kyū̃*, why? *kai, koī, kuī*, when? *kāchī*, sometimes; *kōr, kōrā, korār*, where? *kā'st*, of what kind? how great? *kett*, whereabouts?

2 **kā, kyā, kyē, kyē̃, kyū̃**, wherefore? why?

kā, why? 234, 362, 678, 783.

kyā, why? 87, 734, 952, 1054.

kyē, why? 1470, 1605.

kyē̃, why? p. 61.

kyū̃, why? 64, p. 61.

3 **ka**, conjunction, if, p. 62; *ka-na*, if not, otherwise, p. 62.

4 **kā**, conjunction, that; *ingol kā*, it is possible that, perhaps,

268, p. 61; also written *ki*; thus, *waṛan wīk ki Sāhib pilingdī ann*, until thou seest that 'the Sahib comes back', until thou seest that I am returning, 1624.

1 **kai,** what? some, any, see 1 **ka.**

2 **kai,** when? see **koī, kuī.**

kāo, subst., the olive-tree; *kāo dār*, the wood of the olive, 946.

kē, postposition, to; *aoghānī mullā katō kē* (?) *mish ess*, there is hate of the Afghan priests to the Bashgalis, the Bashgalis hate the Afghan priests, 625; cf. **dugā.**

1 **kō,** adj., left; *kō dusht*, the left hand, 611; see **kōwar.**

2 **kō,** who? anybody, see 1 **ka.**

3 **ko,** doing, to do, see **KṚ.**

kō̃, subst., mosquito; *kō̃ bilugh yūttett*, mosquitos bite much, 882.

koī, kuī, interrogative adverb, when? as in the case of the interrogative pronoun *ka*, this adverb is also used in subordinate clauses and as an indefinite adverb.

(1) As an interrogative adverb—

koī, when? at what time? p. 60.

kuī, when? *kuī samarlosh*, when wilt thou start? 1546; *kuī wīk*, up till when? 1669.

(2) In subordinate sentences, when; in such clauses the verb is often followed by the particle *bå, bā*, instead of which we once find *wā*; the following examples occur—*koī å̊o pig bibā*, when one is thirsty, 1041; *koī purū kolaibå*, when you give me leave, 1003; *koī kudūm pūshabå*, when thou hast ended thy work, 415, 479 (*poishabå*); *koī samarijbå*, when thou startest, 1067; *koī barwai waṛībå*, when the coolies appear, 822; *kuī torē̃ assium*, when I approached, 1327; *kuī parmenstuk azzī*, when thou wast young, 1335; *kuī wigiā izhībā*, when thou art rested, thou canst go, 1157; *kuī tū ī shodr kaṛūsh*, since I made thee my servant, 1312, p. 11; *kuī agal yūr onzībå*, when rain comes down, 1166; *kuī tū tå ṭapī onzībå*, when fever comes over thee, 1466; *kuī ossabā*, when he came, 1252; *kuī shillā bibå*, when it gets cold, 1431; *kuī gujbå*, when thou goest, 1202, 1411; *kuī pibå*, when

thou hast drunk, 1480 ; *kuī putarijbá*, when thou crossest, 1331 ; *kuī zīm vilnabá*, when the snow melts, 1183 ; *kuī waṛimbá*, when thou seest me, 1671 ; *kuī waṛinbá*, when thou seest, 1308 ; note *kuī iãst shai tã wōtt praptawā*, when the stone hit me on the head, 1260, where the particle appended to the verb is *wā* and not *bá* ; *kuī stē ão chok biss bā*, from when, since, the water became low, 1227 ; *kuī atsir wīk*, till I return, **1143** ; *kuī wīk pochētr na peṭlon enna*, till the fast has not been broken, till the end of the fast, 1413 ; cf. Hindī *jab tak na*.

kai, when, is only used once in this way, *kai Chandrāl parizhbá*, when thou reachest Chitrāl, 1583.

(3) As an indefinite adverb—

koī dī, ever, 919.

kuī, some time, 1183, 1326 ; *kuī dī*, some time, 1189.

kuī kuī, sometimes, 1698 ; *kuī wōs tã*, some day, 1198, p. 60 ; see 1 **ka** (3).

kuī, ever, at any time, 346, 1312, p. 60 ; *kuī wōs tã*, at any time, p. 60, see 1 **ka** (3) ; *kuī na*, at any time not, never, 1311 ; *kuī—na*, never, 1234 ; *kūī—na*, never, p. 60 ; *kuī dī—na*, never, 1162, 1179, 1312, p. 11.

1 **kū,** subst., hump ; *ashē kū n'aiesht*, to the bulls are no humps, the bulls have no hump, 691.

2 **kū,** who ? any, see 1 **ka.**

kuī, when ? when, ever, see **koī.**

kuiã, adv., in the early morning, p. 60 ; *kuiyã*, early ; *ushpo sir manchī tã kūro manchī kuiyã prāl*, a footman will arrive early from (earlier than) a mounted man, 889 ; *kuiyẽ*, early (in the morning), 398 ; early (in the year), 623.

kabā, adj., angry ; used as a predicate, 44, 187 ; see **kapā.**

Kābul, subst., Kābul ; *Kābul waṛiān*, hast thou seen Kābul ? 1255 ; *Kābul gosī*, (why) did he go to Kābul ? 1685 ; *Kābul amīr*, the Amīr of Kābul, 600.

kach, adj., shut ; *dū kach ess*, the door is shut, 1303.

kachai, subst., a wart, 1634 (nom.).

1 **kāchī, kāch,** who? some, any, see 1 **ka.**

2 **kāchī,** adv., sometimes, 1356, p. 60.

kochī, subst., a spoon, 1376 (acc.); *bilankochī,* a Chitrālī (?) spoon, a small spoon, 1376 (acc.).

kuch, doest, makest, see **KṚ.**

kachkarā, subst., an arm-pit; *iāst kachkarā pōnduk bā,* in my arm-pit is a boil, 68; oblique, *kachkruī wīk,* up to the arm-pits, 1345.

kchāl in *ano kchāl,* a cook, 647; literally perhaps meat making; cf. the forms beginning with *ksh* of the base **KṚ.**

kachor, subst., a mule, 898 (nom.); nom. plur. *kachar,* 897, 907.

kachwach, subst., a fruit, 1178, 1270, 1435, 1448, 1668, p. 9 (nom.); 1343, 1362 (acc.); *pagī kachwach,* unripe grapes (fruit), 1700 (acc.); *kachwach kāno,* fruit-tree, 772, 1551, 1722; *kachwech,* a fruit; *īsta jū kachwech yāṛissi,* my daughter had eaten the fruit, p. 4 (noted down by Abdul Hakīm Khān); *kajwaj,* a fruit, 910, 1250, 1388; *kazhwaj,* a fruit, 6; *kazhwajh,* a fruit, 535; *kazhwazh,* a fruit, 162.

KUD, to ask; infinitive, *shū kudosth dugā,* in order to ask for news, in order to scout, 1245; indefinite present 2nd pers. sing. *kudoch,* askest, questionest, 1105.

Second present 3rd pers. sing. *kuḍāt,* asks, inquires, 1150.

kudūm, subst., work, job, act, action, proceeding; affair, business; nom. *kudūm,* 41, 489, 741, 1373, 1587, 1595, 1719, 1730, p. 5; acc. *kudūm,* 342, 366, 415, 479, 524, 554, 752, 951, 963, 1065, 1215, 1231, 1375, 1597, 1658, p. 12; *kuduma,* 224; *kudūma,* 336, p. 5; oblique, *inā kudūm p'mīsh,* in this business, 1160, 1701 (*p'mish*).

ushp kudūm, horse work, grooming, 591 (acc.), p. 4; *ptul kudūm,* crop work, agriculture, 22; *kudūm kul,* work doing; *kudūm kul manchī,* working people, 1720; *biliuk kudūm kul,* much work doing, industrious, 708; *lē kudūm kul,* good work doing, industrious, p. 15; *less kudūm kul,* good work doing, industrious, p. 9.

kadr, subst., a hole; *tū p'nishr kadr ess,* there is a hole in front of thee, 666; perhaps same as the following; cf. **kandr.**

kaḍṛ, subst., a quicksand; *tū panishr kaḍṛ ess,* there is a quicksand in front of thee, 1107.

kāgrē, adv., loud, aloud, 1235, p. 61.

khel, subst., sport, prancing; *zin tokūm ushp khel tā zhilā biṣs,* my saddle-cloth has got wet from the horse's prancing (translated 'with the horse's sweat'), 937. If the translation 'sweat' is correct, *khel* must be a loan-word; cf. 592, 1402, 1445, where 'sweat' is *ashpa.*

khān, subst., a khān; *Dīr khān,* to the khān of Dīr, 864; used as a surname, *Mir khān,* Mir khān, 647 (nom.); *Pir khān,* Pir khan, 647 (genitive).

khunzā, subst., a queen, a princess, pp. 1, 2, see **kunzā.**

khur in *p'khur,* on the top of; *inā bado p'khur,* on the top of this hill, 648.

khozla, subst., a certain vegetable, 1168.

khāzonn, subst., treasure; *spāhī khazonn nganda,* are the Sepoys taking treasure? 1550.

kujhī, subst., cultivation, 153; see **kruzhī.**

kujhēl, adj., happy; *kujhēl balom,* I shall be happy, 555; see **kuzhāl.**

kajwaj, subst., fruit, 910, 1250, 1388; see **kachwach.**

kakok, kakkak, kakkok, subst., a fowl; acc. sing. *kakkak,* 396; *kakkok,* a cock, 758; acc. plur. *kakkak,* fowls, 531, 532.

nai kakkak, a cock, 305, 645 (nom.); 270 (acc.); cf. *kakkok,* cock, 758; *ishtrī kakkak,* hen, 645 (nom. plur.), 754 (agent plur.); *istrī kakok duts kuṛ asht,* the hen has ten chickens, 249.

kāktī, kaikotē, kaikoti, what having done? why? how? see 1 **ka** (1) and **KṚ.**

kalā, kilā, subst., a quarrel, a difference; nom. *kilā,* a difference, 354; *kilā kuttett,* they are quarrelling, disputing, 362; *kalā kund,* they are quarrelling, fighting, 1726; *kellē kaṛīyā,* he has caused them to quarrel, 1102; *kil-warī,* a matter of quarrel, a difference;

amnī dū manchī kilwarīān a͟sht, there are differences between these two men, 353.

kālo, subst., a fort, 834 (nom.); *S͟hdrāl noi kālo siūmē kālo tā lesst ass*, the Chitral new fort is stronger than the old fort, 527; *kālo tā aṭūr*, inside the fort, 637; oblique also *kālē*; thus, *siūmē kālē tā*, in an old fort, p. 7.

kul, doing, making; **kulā,** will do; **kulājbā, kulojbā,** if doest; **kullā,** will do; **kalom,** etc., shall do; see **KṚ.**

kēlik, subst., mulberry, 896 (nom. plur.).

kallā, subst., tin; *kallā tuch*, tin lead, tin, 1521; *kallā tuch kaṛ*, a tin-smith, 1522.

kellē, subst., a quarrel; *kellē kaṛīyā*, he has caused them to make a quarrel, 1102; see **kalā.**

ḳalin, subst., a rug, 1204 (nom.).

kalon, will make; **kolann,** makes; **kulonn,** will make; see **KṚ.**

kalandarē, subst., a mendicant, a beggar, 861 (nom. plur.).

kalor, subst., a certain vegetable, 1168 (nom.).

kilār, subst., cheese, 246 (acc.).

kūlr, you will make; **kulosh,** wilt make; see **KṚ.**

kaltacha, subst., (1) a purse, 1090 (acc.); (2) a waistcoat; *kaltachā kusth dugā*, for making a waistcoat, 1623.

Kām, subst., name of a village in Kāmdē͟sh; *Kām-bra-gām*, to the Kām village, to Kāmdē͟sh, 1519.

Kāmdē͟sh, the Kām country, Kāmde͟sh; *pō Kāmdē͟sh assium*, last year I dwelt in Kāmdē͟sh, 390; *Kāmdē͟sh sundī manchī*, all the men of Kāmdē͟sh, 1135.

kom, I do, see **KṚ.**

kumo, subst., neck; *kumo bradzott*, my neck aches, 913.

komlik, subst., in *komlik pgoluk*, a certain bird, the golden oriole, 970.

KAN, to laugh; *kai dugā kanich*, why art thou laughing? 771.

kāna, subst., a burial, a funeral; *kāna satē*, bury, 216; oblique, *kānai dugā*, for the burial, 214; *kānē dugē*, for the burial, 545.

kāno, subst., a tree, 1271 (nom. sing.), 1270 (acc. sing.); *kāno* *kuṛu*, the trunk of a tree, 1556; *kāno lū*, the root of a tree, 1193; *kāna tsá tā*, on the branch of a tree, 616; plural, *kāno*, trees, 668, 958, 1485, 1712 (nom.); *iamru kāno*, a walnut-tree, 1628 (dat. of possession); *kachwach kāno*, fruit-tree, 772 (nom. plur.), 1551 (nom. sing.), 1722 (gen. plur.); *romo kāno*, willow-tree, 1690 (nom. plur.); *tarak kāno*, poplar, 1046 (nom. plur.); *wanzī kāno* holly-tree, 688 (nom. plur.); *kāno-wā*, full of trees, shady, 1269 1713, p. 5.

1 **kon**, subst., an arrow; *kon vītī*, arrow striking, with an arrow, 1579.

2 **kōn**, subst., a mine; *tuch kōn*, a mine of lead, 871.

3 **kōn, kun**, to do, see **KṚ**.

kunā, subst., a table; *kunā ptsir*, on my table, 948.

kuni, subst., a jar, a lotah; acc. *kuniyā*, 829; oblique, *kunī ti* in the jar, 722.

kund, they make; **kunji**, makest, see **KR**.

kandr, adj., hollow; *kandr kshi*, hollow it out, 1556; cf. **kadr**.

kanjik, subst., a sapling, 1230 (acc. plur.).

kanik, subst., a rope, 285, 748, 1194 (nom.), 1511, 1529 (acc.) *kanikī*, of my rope, 1578.

kaṛtā kanik, a thick rope, 1423.

lamṛ kanik, a thin rope, a string, 1423.

kunam, I do; **kunn**, does; **kunazzam**, I was doing, etc., see **KṚ**.

Konisht, subst., name of a place, Ranbūr, 390 (in Ranbūr), 523 (oblique), 996 (gen.), 1003 (to Ranbūr), 1283 (oblique).

kuníyā, subst., a lotah, 829; see **kunī**.

kunzā, subst., (1) a queen, 1104; *kunzā jūs*, queen's daughter, princess, 1073; (2) a princess, p. 1.

khunzā, (1) a queen; *khunzā mṛlī*, the queen will die, p. 2; (2) a princess, p. 1.

kapā, adj., angry; used as a predicate, 234, 409, 543 (sulky), 617, 1063, 1148, 1667; sad, sorrowful, annoyed, 1217, 1360, 1361, 1602.

kabā, angry, 44, 187.

kappā, angry, 1606 (*Bastī dugā*, with Bastī), 1607, 1608.

KṚ, to do, to make; this base occurs in a great many different forms; the past and tenses formed from the past contain the *ṛ* throughout, in other tenses there are three sets of forms, one (base I) without the *ṛ*, another (base II) with the *ṛ*, and a third (base III) with an *sh* after *k*; thus, *kunam* and *kaṛōnam*, I do; *kunjī* and *kshonjī*, dost. Forms such as *kaṛōnām*, I do, are probably originally causals; similarly, in Māhārāshṭrī Prākṛit we find both *kuṇaï* and *karēï*, does; the base *kṛ* is used in numerous idioms, of which the most important ones are:—

ão k., to make water, 1592; *ū k.*, to lift, 1308; *achu k.*, to give a back, 107, 457; *uchar k.*, to empty out, 413, 414; *adap k.*, to respect, 1154; *ulēr k.*, to pick up, 1009; *aluts k.*, to play quoits, 1113; *ãr k.*, to inflate, or, perhaps, to turn downwards, 498; *ush k.*, to look, 88, 344, 822, 851, 964, 1113; to look out, take care, 1083; to look out for, to expect, await, 100, 431; to look after, to take care of, 1018; to look after, to cure, 314; to ask for, 388, 510; to ascertain, 74, 75, 76; *ōsh k.*, to see, to inspect, 1092, 1126, 1231, 1532, 1540, 1541, 1547, 1714; *paṛhī ōsh k.*, to inspect a book, to read, 1129; *ōsh k.*, to consider, to think, 1273; to look for, to want, to search, 718, 963, 1143, 1249, 1412, 1467, 1542, 1669; *ushp k.*, to give a foal, 503; *attē k.*, to hide, 652; *azhē k.*, to plough, 1586; *be k.*, to bleed, 161; *bibdī k.*, to think, 408, 810, 1042, 1179, 1441, 1494; *band k.*, to stop, 574; *baṛ k.*, to put out, 1522; *bara k.*, to divide, 1278, 1279 (cf. *bata k.*); *burubiz k.*, to be angry, 47, 48; *barm k.*, to shut, 1302; *bēs k.*, to cease, 236, 1602; *bata k.*, to divide, 364 (cf. *bara k.*); *dā k.*, to lend, 793, 794, p. 11; *drē k.*, to delay, 337, 338, 1130; *darā k.*, to have patience, 994; *dâtik k.*, to make a wager, 1619, 1620 (Khōwār idiom); *gijjī k.*, to make word, to say, 537, 696, 805, 819, 828, 868, 869, 906, 930, 1081, 1129, 1177, 1234, 1257, 1353, 1356, 1422, 1423, 1494, 1522, 1567, 1570, 1644, 1682, 1723, p. 11; *gun k.*, to smell, 1337; *giṭu k.*, to graft, 576, 577; *kalā*, *kilā k.*, to fight, to dispute, 362, 1726; *kōr k.*, to hear, to listen,

183, 770, 810, 906; *kish k.*, to cultivate, 1603; *kushulwā k.*, to be careful, 225; *ktol k.*, to eat one's fill, 1232, 1274, 1365; *kutt k.*, to make done, to carry out, 91, 92; *lālu k.*, to sing, 1027, 1071, 1315, p. 9; *less katī*, well, entirely, severely, 1087, 1274; *lessl katī*, clearly, 1235; *lestā k.*, to avoid, 98, 99; to assist, 83, 84; *marmarī k.*, to destroy, 515; to graze, 584; to rub, 1213; *mash k.*, to be merciless, 863; *mashu k.*, to be angry, 771; *mishī k.*, to play, 546; *mata k.*, to decide, 1031; *mātā k.*, to have patience, to forgive, 1065, 1148; *namáj k.*, to say prayers, 1056–61; *nmēlā k.*, to change, 242, 429; *nōsh k.*, to swim, 498, 1451, 1452; *nōt k.*, to dance, 322, 323; *nazor k.*, to take snuff, 315, 1015; *pubī k.*, to scream, 1247, 1281; *paidā k.*, to produce, 1075; *palā k.*, to effect guarding, to guard, 1638, 1639; *para* (*parē*, *parī*) *k.*, to fill, 400, 474, 1052, 1216, 1259; *puru k.*, to give leave, 1003; *pshuikbut k.*, to belch, 142; *pitzen k.*, to break, 186; *rāṛā k.*, to neigh, 916; *rāṛṛa k.*, to bray, 183; *shū k.*, to sigh, 1307; *shuch* (*shōch*, *shuj*, *shush*) *k.*, to fight, 122, 336, 471, 1600; *shamash k.*, to thank, to be grateful, 582, 1474; *shuṛṭṛ k.*, to make sport, to hunt, 694; *shus k.*, to take breath, 191; *shtār k.*, to make theft, to steal, 1087, 1186, 1261, 1322, 1389, 1396, 1487; *shtarī k.*, to marry, 918, 1584; *shott k.*, to swear, 1444; *suntrō k.*, to mix, 874; *sōs k.*, to seize the opportunity, 964; *sots k.*, to ache, 980; *tabal k.*, to use, 1594; *tīch k.*, to make it even, to equal, 965; *tamkio k.*, to smoke tobacco, 315, 603, 1015, 1340, 1526; *taṛā k.*, to leave behind, 786; *tōṛ k.*, to eject, to turn out, 1568; *wā k.*, to unload, to take down, 375, 1583, p. 8; *welī k.*, to ask, to demand, 1085; *varī k.*, to make word, to speak, to say, 1131, 1494, 1665, 1718; *vrī k.*, to say, 1299, 1471, 1680; *warī k.*, to say, 639, 1000, 1055, 1163, 1235, 1299, 1308, 1309, 1315, 1366, 1416, 1558; *vrich k.*, to spend, 1369; *wrēch k.*, to sell, 1257; *wā-wā-wā k.*, to mumble, 945; *zār k.*, to dye, 392; *zōr* (*zur*) *k.*, to do violence, to oppress, 1430, 1571, 1611.

The base *kṛ* alone is often used instead of *gijjī k.*, *warī k.*, to say; thus, 5, 314, 488, 515, 516, 642, 1077, 1150, 1198, 1236

1705, p. 11; note especially the use of *ktī*, having said, 1705; of *katī*, having said, 642, 1150, 1198; of *kutt*, says, 868, 1081, 1177, 1422, 1423, 1483, 1522; of *kuttā*, says, 696; and of *kuttett*, say, 1055, after a direct quotation. Such forms are used almost like the Sanskrit *iti*; the following forms of the base occur in the sentences:—

Infinitive: Base I—*kuṣth*, to do, to make, 315, 1056, pp. 24, 29 footnote; *kusth dugā*, for making, 1715; *kusth dugā*, for making, 257, 264; *kusth dugȁ*, for making, 584, 694, 770, 860, 946, 961, 1027, 1061, 1129, 1143, 1225, 1229, 1249, 1265, 1409, 1419, 1542, 1544, 1584, 1592, 1623, 1642, 1710; *kusth dugē*, for making, 471, 574, 606; *nā kusth kudūm*, a not to do work, an unworkable business, 1587; *kusthā*, for making, 336; *kusthē dugā*, for making, 778; *giṭu kosth*, to do grafting, to graft, 576.

Base II—*korusth*, to do, to make, p. 24; *padrī kaṛosth dugȁ*, for making an axe, 718.

Base III—*chillam bilugh kshaiesth dugȁ*, from much pulling at a hookah, 671; cf. *tamkio kusth*, to smoke tobacco; it is, however, doubtful whether this form belongs to our base.

Verbal noun: Base I—*kō, ko, ku*, to make; *ko banam*, I can do, 1452; more commonly found before the negative particle, with an *n* added; *kōn na battet*, they cannot do, 551; *kon n'buttett*, he cannot do, p. 58; *kun na banam*, I cannot do, 1451.

Base II—*koṛ*, to make (a fire), 484, 1714; *kurik* (?) in *āsh kurik*, to cook, 283.

Base III—*kshī*, to do, 173, 752.

Present participle: Base I—*kul*, making doing, pp. 15, 24; *kudūm kul*, work doing; *kudūm kul manchī*, working-men, 1720; *biliuk kudūm kul*, much work doing, industrious, 708; *lē kudūm kul*, good work doing, industrious, p. 15; *less kudūm kul*, industrious, p. 9; *lālu kul*, singing doing, singing, 1071, p. 9; a singer, 1315; *lesst kul*, good doing, respectful, 1156.

Base II—*kaṛ*, making; *kallā tuch kaṛ*, tin making, a tinsmith, 1522; *pach kaṛ*, a weaver, 1652; *kaṛōl*, making, p. 24; *ziān kuṛōl*, loss making, destructive, malicious, harmful, p. 9; spiteful, 1374 (*kaṛol*).

Base III—*kchāl*, making (?); *ano kchāl*, a cook, 647.

Second present participle, *kutan*, making; *ano kutan amu*, food making house, kitchen, 743.

Past participle: Base I—*kutt*, *kuttā*, made, accomplished; *inā warī nai kutt koshī*, thou dost not make this matter accomplished, dost not make an attempt to follow this up, 92; *inā warī kuttā kshē*, make an attempt to follow up this intention, 91; this participle perhaps occurs in *inā kuttā-to-m*, this said-in-to-me, when he asked me, 51.

Base II—*kaṛungo*, made, done; *ktol kaṛungo pul iā̃r* (the horse) has eaten his belly done (full) of grain, 1365.

Conjunctive participle: Base I—*ko*, having made; *kai-kō*, what having made? why? 460; *kusth* (?), having made, p. 24; *dâtik kusth*, having made a wager, 1620; *dâtik kustham*, I made a wager, 1619 (the last two idioms are said to be Khōwār); *ktī*, having made, 1259, 1322, 1532, p. 24; *ktī*, having said (used like Sanskrit *iti* after a direct quotation); *kā shosh n'ai Karak shaṛī baro-ktī*, there is no witness having said 'Karak took the goat', 1705; *ktī*, having made, is common in compounds, thus, *ā̃rktī*, having inflated, or, perhaps, having turned downwards, 498; *baraktī*, having divided, 1278; *giaktī*, thus having done, therefore, thus, 494, 735, 1594; *gānowaktī*, violent having done, violently, 1414; *kāktī*, what having done? how? 408, 485, p. 61; *shtāraktī*, theft having done, stealing, 1087.

katī, having done, 874, 964, 965, 1261, 1389, p. 24; having said (used like Sanskrit *iti* after direct quotations); *Katō tā p'kōr n'gosā dsudsuk assā katī*, it has not come to the ears of the Kāfirs saying (that) 'there is a hell', 642; *widernam kuī wōs tā vitlelī katī*, I fear having said (that) 'some day it will fall', 1198; *chē wōs dī katī ragat*, how many days also having said (for how long) does he want? 1150; cf. *katī*, up to, p. 61; note *less katī*, well having done, severely, 1087; entirely, 1274;

lesst katī, clearly, 1235; *ī purstha katī*, doing like me, like me, 1174.

keti, having made (?), having said (?); *sang keti psiā*, all having said (cf. Sanskrit *iti*) are lost, I have lost them all, 827; *puruketi*, truly, 1110.

kotē, having done; *kaikotē*, what having done? why? 1130, 1176, 1685, p. 61; how? 1194, 1304, 1345 (*kaikote*), p. 61; *kaikotē̃*, why? 1667; *kōtē̃*, having done, violently, p. 61; *kotē̃*, loudly, violently, 166, 830, p. 61; *kotī*, having done; *kaikotī*, why? 759; how? 1122, 1423, 1645, 1716.

Base II—*koṛ*, having made; *koṛ awaṛā*, having made brought, he has made and brought, 1066.

Base III—*kshī*, having made (?), 236, 1009, 1049, 1442; *kashītī*, having made; *babdī kashītī*, having made in the mind, having thought, 1494.

Indefinite present: Base I—1st pers. sing. *kom*, I do, I make, p. 24; *kāktī angā kom*, how shall I make fire? 485; *aish kshī kom*, I will say 'cure me', 314.

2nd pers. sing. *kuch*, makest, 80, 224, 1000; *kuchā, kuchiā*, makest? 510; *tū iā parmenstuk kuchī*, if thou makest me small, offendest me, 941.

1st pers. plur. *kummā́*, we do, we shall do, p. 24; *kummubā́*, if we do, p. 25; cf. future.

2nd pers. plur. *kūr*, you do, p. 24; *kuṛbā́* (?), if you do, p. 25.

Base II—1st pers. sing. *kaṛbā́*, if I make, p. 25.

2nd pers. sing. *kaṛbā́*, if makest, 554, 577, 1597.

3rd pers. sing. *kōr*, he does, he makes, p. 24; *nōsh kōṛ*, he swims, 498, 1451; *kaṛbā́*, if one makes, 729; *kaṛbo*, if one makes, 22.

Base III—1st pers. sing. *kshām*, I do, p. 24; *bibdī kshām*, I think, 810.

2nd pers. sing. *kashī*, thou dost, makest, p. 24; *koshī*, makest, 92; *shū kshā́chī*, (why) art thou making sighs? 1307.

tamkio n'kusoch, dost thou not smoke tobacco? 1340.

Present: Base I—1st pers. sing. *kunam*, I make, I do, 1015, 1257, p. 24.

2nd pers. sing. *kunjī*, makest, dost, 1605, 1608, p. 24; *kunjībá*, if makest, 1558, p. 25.

3rd pers. sing. *kunn*, makes, does, 1177, 1246, 1337, 1353, 1356, 1422, 1432, 1522, 1633, 1682, p. 24.

3rd pers. plur. *kund*, they make, they do, 805, 819, 1129, 1130, 1154, 1603, 1694, 1726, p. 24.

Base II—1st pers. sing. *kaṛōnam*, I make, I do, p. 24.

3rd pers. sing. *kaṛonn*, he does, 1571.

3rd pers. plur. *kaṛond*, they do, 1430.

Base III—2nd pers. sing. *kshonjī*, makest, dost, 408, p. 24; *kshonjībá*, if thou makest, dost, p. 25.

3rd pers. plur. *tamkio n'kshond*, they do not smoke tobacco, 1526.

2nd present: Base I—1st pers. sing. *kotam*, I do, I make, p. 24; *ōsh kotam*, I want, 718; *kuttam*, I do, I make, 100, 582, 1257.

2nd pers. sing. (*mash*) *kotish*, dost (mercy), 863; *aīsh n'kutish*, dost not look after, show pity, 1018.

3rd pers. sing. *kett*, does, in *shūskett*, (the horse) is gasping, 548.

kott, does, in *supkott*, stammers, 1390.

kutt, makes, does, 48, 183, 323, 388, 916, 945, 963, 1113, 1154, 1247, 1281, p. 24; *gijjī kutt*, makes word, says, 828, 868, 869, 906, 930, 1081, 1234, 1257, 1423, 1567, 1644, 1723; *kutt*, he says, 5; note also the instances in which *kutt*, says, is used in the same way as Sanskrit *iti* after a direct quotation; thus, *bābū gijjī kutt rits pshiō kutt*, the Bābū makes word, 'grind the barley' says, the Bābū says, 'grind the barley,' 868; further examples, 1081, 1177, 1422, 1423, 1522.

kuttā, he does, he says; *gijjī kuttā iāst mōsh mṛiss kuttā*, she makes word, 'my husband is dead,' she says, she says her husband is dead, 696; *kuttā's*, he says about him, 1236.

kuttett, makes, 1163; *kuttētt*, makes, p. 24.

3rd pers. plur. *kutt*, they say; *gijjī kund emá ē na bamá kutt*, they make word, 'we cannot go,' they say, they say that they cannot go, 1483.

kuttett, they make, 183, 322, 362, 515, 546, 601, 639, 743, 928, 980; *kuttētt*, they make, p. 24; *digar kuttētt*, they oppress, 1045; *kuttett*, they say, 488; *warī kuttett bilugh ál bidī-wā manchī ess kuttett*, they make word, 'he is a high-hearted man,' they say, they say that he is a high-hearted man, 1055.

Base III—1st pers. sing. *babdī kshātam*, I make in mind, I think, 1042, 1179; *babdī kshátam*, I make in mind, I think, 1441; *tamkio n'kshátam*, I do not smoke tobacco, 1015.

Present definite (Base I) 1st pers. sing. *ōsh kulom*, seeing doing-am, I see, 1540, 1541; *ōts kalom*, I see, 1547; *nazor kolum*, I take snuff, 315; *shamash kulom*, I thank you, 1474; *shott kulom*, I swear, 1444.

3rd pers. sing. *shuj kulai*, fight doing is, he fights, 122; *kolann*, he does, p. 24; *mashu kolann*, he is angry, 771.

Base III—1st pers. sing. *tamkio n'ksholam*, I do not smoke tobacco, 603.

Imperfect: Base I—1st pers. sing. *kuṇazzam*, I was doing, p. 24.

2nd pers. sing. *kunazzish*, wast doing, p. 24.

3rd pers. sing. *kunazzī*, was doing, p. 24.

1st pers. plur. *kunazzamish*, we were doing, p. 24.

2nd pers. plur. *kunazzār*, you were doing, p. 24.

3rd pers. plur. *kunazzī*, they were doing, p. 24.

Indefinite past, *karā*, *kaṛo*, made, did, p. 24; to these forms and to the more common *kṛā* suffixes can be added; the following forms occur:—

1st pers. sing. *áo uchar kṛā*, I emptied the water out, 414: *ātsh kṛā*, I have ascertained, 75; *ōsh kṛā*, I have seen, 1126; *namáj kṛā*, I said my prayers, 1058; *tōṛ kṛā*, I turned him out, 1568; *kṛā*, I said; *n'kshīr kṛā*, I said 'do not do it', I forbade them, 516; *namáj n'kaṛā*, I did not say prayers, 1060; *karā'sh*, I made thee, 1312 (*kaṛāsh*), p. 11; I made for thee, p. 11.

ōsh karo-sh, I thought about thee, 1273.

gijjī kāro-sh, I have told thee, 1570.

2nd pers. sing. *krā*, hast made, p. 3; *karā*, hast made, 1023.

3rd pers. sing. *krā*, made, did, 1414, p. 13; *karā*, has made, p. 3; *karā'sh*, he made to thee, p. 12; *kā varī karo-sh*, what word did he make to thee? what did he tell thee? 1665.

3rd pers. plur. *shuch krā*, they made fighting, they fought, 1600.

Perfect and pluperfect, *krissā*, *krissī*, I, we, had made; *krissā*, *krishtai*, thou, you, he, they, had made, p. 24; the following forms occur in the sentences:—

1st pers. sing. *ōsh karsā*, I have inspected, 1231; *gijjī karsī*, I said, 537; *karsish*, I made for thee, to thee, 794, 1063, p. 11.

2nd pers. sing. *karsā*, hast thou made? 544, 951; *ktol n'karsā*, hast thou not made thy belly? hast thou not eaten thy fill? 1232; *karsam*, hast done for me, 582, 1669, p. 11; *iā tā krās'm*, hast said, promised, to me, 1077, p. 11.

pa ptī bōr kress, hast made, put, a load on (the donkey's) back, 370; *kriss*, hast made, 543; *kariss*, hast made, 1375; *ots vina vina karessam*, hast made me beaten, I am beaten, 132 (*karesam*), p. 59.

kristai, hast made, 1658.

3rd pers. sing. *ushp karats*, (the mare) gave a foal, 503.

kriss, has made, 918 (he has married), 1213, 1394, 1469; (*band*) *krissā*, has made (him bound, has bound him), 1407, p. 3.

kristai, has made, 1186; *krishtai*, has made, 982; *lader krishtai*, has made messengers, has sent as messengers, 864; *korishtai*, has made, 392.

3rd pers. plur. *kars*, they have done, 710; *kress*, they have done, p. 3; *kriss*, they have done, 817; they made, 901; they had made, 1358; *krissiā*, they have done, 832; *azio karistā*, (my hens) have made (laid) eggs, 754.

Future: Base I—1st pers. sing. *kulaibá*, if I make, p. 25; *kalom*, I shall do, make, 107, 327, 941, 1023, 1033, 1215, 1395, p. 24; *kulom*, I shall do, make, 84, 457, 485, 793, 968, 1194, 1444, 1532, 1693, 1740, p. 24.

2nd pers. sing. *purū kolaibá*, when thou givest me leave, 1003; *s͟htār kulaibá*, if thou wilt do theft, 1487.

kulojbá, if thou wilt make, p. 25; *s͟htār kulájbá*, if thou stealest, 1396.

kulos͟h, wilt make, p. 24.

3rd pers. sing. *kulā*, he will do, make, 1087, 1315, p. 24.

1st pers. plur. *kummá*, we shall make, 1059, p. 24; see indefinite present.

2nd pers. plur. *kūlr*, you will make, do, p. 24.

3rd pers. plur. *kulā*, they will make, do, p. 24; *kulabá* (?), if they make, do, p. 25; *kullā*, they will do, 1640.

Base II—1st pers. sing. *kaṛolam*, I shall do, 1586; *kaṛōlam*, I shall do, p. 24; *chī palā kṛolam*, how much guard shall I make? how many watchmen shall I put on? 1639.

Imperative: Base I—1st pers. plur. *kummá*, let us do, make, p. 25.

2nd pers. sing. *kōr ktē*, make ear, listen, 906; *kōr ktī*, listen, 183, 810.

3rd pers. sing. and plur. *kulā*, let him, them, make, p. 25; *us͟hp s͟hus kalon*, let the horse take breath, 191; *lālu kulonn*, let him sing, 1315.

Base II—2nd pers. sing. *kṛō*, make, do; *palā kṛō*, make guard, do sentry duty, 1638; *wasankṛō*, collect, 276.

Base III—2nd pers. sing. *ks͟hē*, do, make, 91, 119, 186; *ks͟hī*, do, make, 47, 74, 76, 83, 88, 98, 99, 125, 142, 193, 211, 225, 242, 269, 314, 337, 338, 342, 344, 366 (*kshī*), 400, 413, 429, 431, 474 (*ks͟hi*), 481, 482, 507, 515, 644, 652, 731, 786, 804, 805, 821, 822, 851, 859, 929, 964, 986, 994, 1031, 1052, 1057, 1065, 1075, 1083, 1085, 1092, 1113, 1131, 1146, 1148, 1213, 1216, 1235, 1241, 1249, 1274, 1279, 1299, 1302, 1308,

1309, 1315, 1347, 1354, 1366, 1369, 1405, 1412, 1416, 1454, 1455, 1467, 1471, 1494, 1532, 1556 (*kshi*), 1558, 1594, 1602, 1611, 1680, 1714, 1718, p. 25.

kshá, in *bekshá*, take out, bleed, 161; *wakshá*, take off, take down, p. 8; *ksho*, in *wākshο*, take down, unload, 1583; *waokshō*, take down, 375.

2nd pers. plur. *kshēr*, do ye, 364; *kshīr*, do ye, 515, 516, 640, 1384, 1543, p. 25; in 1221 we must read and translate *mehar hukm ptāsamish ikyē lesst kshīr*, the Mehtar gave order to us: 'set this right'; *chusht azhō kshīr, ē dī warī n'kshīr*, make 'be silent', do not make even one word, 1309.

Causal verb, past tense 3rd pers. sing. *kellē kaṛīyā*, he has caused them to make a quarrel, 1102.

kra, subst., *see kra*, the eleventh month of a year, p. 66.

kṛā, made, did, see **KṚ,** past.

kṛō, do, in *palā kṛō*, do watching, 1638; *wasan kṛō*, collect, 276; see **KṚ,** imperative.

kruē, subst., son (?), *mehrkruē dits sē biss*, to the prince (the Mehtar's son) have become twelve years, 1072.

krūi, subst., a dog, 71, 117, 152, 154, 235, 444, 774, 1152, 1337, 1378, p. 9 (nom. sing.); 786, 964, 1091 (acc. sing.); 174, 1336, 1377, 1404, p. 14 (gen. sing.); oblique, *krūī chor*, dog-like, like a dog, 298, p. 9; nom. plur. *krūī*, 368.

krūi, dog, 89 (agent sing.).

krūi, dog, 1038 (dat. sing.).

nah krūī, a he dog, 369.

shtarī (ishtri) krūī, a bitch, 369; instead of *krūī* we find *kūrī*, dog, 7.

kar, subst., ear; *kar tēnum*, I hear, p. 4 (Abdul Hakīm Khān), see 1 **kōr.**

kār, subst., work, need; *p'kār ess*, it is in need, is wanted, 1204; *p'kār assā*, it is in need, is wanted, 1557.

1 **kār,** adj., blind, 163, 539, 1252 (predicate).

2 **kār,** adj., empty; *tol kār biss*, the cauldron is empty, 412.

kaṛ, making; *kallā tuch kaṛ,* tin-making, tinsmith, 1522; *pach kaṛ,* weaver, 1652; see **KṚ,** present participle.

kaṛā, kaṛo, made, see **KṚ,** past.

kaṛo, subst., a knife; *kaṛo mish,* with a knife, 1314; see **kato.**

kaṛu, subst., the trunk of a tree, 1556.

kiṛā, subst., a shield, 1288 (acc. plur.).

Kiār, subst., name of a place; *Kiār gyē,* they went to Kiār, 1738.

1 **kor, kōr,** subst., an ear; nom. *kōr,* 397, 542; acc. *kar tēnum,* I hear, p. 4 (noted down by Abdul Hakīm Khān).

kōr kusth, to hear, 770; *kōr ktē,* listen, 906; *kōr ktī,* listen, 810; *kor ktī,* listen, 183; oblique, *p'kōr,* into the ear, 649, 1680; *p'kōr n'gosā,* it did not go to ear, it was not heard of, 642; *p'kōr gwā,* went to ear, was heard, 511, 635, 830, 871, 911, 1104, 1510, 1615.

2 **kor,** subst., animal; *shtur digar kor ess,* the camel is a bad animal, 222.

3 **kōr,** adverb, (1) interrogative, where? 389, 1673; *kōr stē,* whence? 1672, p. 61.

(2) Relative, where, *kor asht wāṛō,* show me where they are, 1037; *tīch n'bunn kōr asselabā,* I do not know where they may be, 1417; *kōr hinju bundabá,* where tamarisks grow, 1465; *kōr stē awenjībá,* from wherever you can fetch, 1354.

(3) Indefinite, somewhere, 890, p. 60; anywhere, p. 60; *kōr-na,* nowhere, 698.

kōr-ā, where; *wāṛō putt kōr-ā giess,* show me where the road has gone, 1300.

korē, where; *tinch n'ess korē endabá,* one does not know where they may go, 1125.

korār, where? which way? 1647, pp. 14, 61; *kurār,* where? 1677; *emá p'amu korār zhī shugā assabá tīch n'ess,* I do not know where in my house the dark cloak may be, 1357.

1 **koṛ,** subst., colour, 278; *digar koṛ manchī,* a bad-coloured, ugly, man, 1572; *zhī koṛ manchī,* a dark-coloured man, 1197.

2 **koṛ,** subst., stalk (of corn), 1389 (acc. plur.).

3 **koṛ,** to make, see **KṚ,** verbal noun and conjunctive participle.

kō̃ṛ, does, see **KṚ,** indefinite present.

koru, subst., a mud-stream, 1420; *kūri,* a mud-stream, 895.

kur, subst., (1) an ass, 82, 183, 379, p. 9; *kurē tā̃,* than an ass, 898, p. 9; nom. plur. *kur,* asses, 279.

(2) A donkey, 330, 585, 1184; *igē kurē pa ptī,* on the back of this donkey, 370; *kurē tā̃,* than the donkey, 585; nom. plur. *kur,* donkeys, 547.

kür, adj., alone, solitary, 456, 1140 (predicate); *kūr kūr,* one by one, separately, 905, p. 61; *kūr kūr,* one by one, separately, p. 61; *kūrē kūrē,* one by one, separately, 1277, p. 60; *kūrẽ kūrẽ,* separately, p. 60; *kū̃rē kū̃rē,* separately, 282; *yo kūrē,* one by one, pp. 14, 64; *yu kūrē,* one by one, 953.

kūr, kūir, subst., foot, leg; nom. *kūr,* foot, 130, 509; leg, 172, 189; acc. *kūr,* leg, 308, 317, 1703; nom. plur. *kūr,* feet, 273; oblique, *kūr tā̃,* in the leg, 1342, 1501; *kūr wrā̃,* with, by means of, the feet, 952; *kūir warē,* with the feet, on foot, 1625; note *s͟hto-kuro-ett,* he marches on four feet, he creeps, 298.

kuīr angur, foot fingers, toes, 1528.

kūr chut, foot-sound, footfall, 511.

kurk, a heel, 641.

kūro manchī, a footman, a pedestrian, 510, 889.

kūr nūng, the sinew of the leg, 1314.

kūir tūr tā̃, by the foot ford, by wading, 1618; it is possible that *kūr,* foot, is also contained in the postposition *pagiōr, pagiur, pagur, pagūro,* under, originally 'at the foot of'; cf. *wetsa tār pagur palāno lesst buttett,* tauchins are better than pubboos for snow, 1083; the literal translation is perhaps: pubboos than on-the-feet (below) tauchins good are; the postposition is used as follows:—

Preceded by a noun unaccompanied by any other postposition or preposition, *anī pagur,* under it, 1350; *ktol pagiur,* under the belly, 1445.

The governed noun is preceded by the preposition *p*, *b*; *b'brunzo pagūro*, on the polo ground, 1074; *bado pagiōr*, to the foot of the hill, down the hill, 1189; *bado pagior*-*yūr*, down to the foot of the hill, downhill, 1208; *bado pagur*, at the foot of the hills, on the pass, 502; *badō pagūrā*, at the foot of the pass, 991; *pkūsh pgūro*, under the willow-tree, 1035.

The governed noun is followed by the postposition *tā*; thus, *prusht tā pagūr*, underneath my bed, 1576.

pagūr is also used as an adverb; *ptul pagūr tāristai*, it beat down my crops, 1420; cf. *pagiōr*, *pagūr*, under, p. 62; *pagâr*, upon, p. 62.

kuṛ, subst., a chicken, 249 (nom. plur.).

kūṛ, subst., a pigeon, 1011 (acc. plur.).

kūrē, kūrē, alone; see **kūr.**

kūri, subst., a dog, 7; see **krūi.**

kūri, subst., a mud-stream, 895; see **koru.**

kaṛbâ, if do, see **KṚ,** indefinite present.

kaṛbo, in *ptul kudūm kaṛbo manchī lestabulā*, agriculture is good for man, 22; probably the indefinite present of the base *KṚ* with the particle *bo* = *bâ*; the literal translation would then be, if he does agriculture work a man will be well.

kuṛbâ, if you do, see **KṚ,** indefinite present.

karbosh, subst., a cotton crop, 289 (nom.).

karbiza, subst., a melon, 857 (acc.).

karch, adj., cooked; *inā ano nā karch ess*, this meat is not cooked, is underdone (raw), 1128.

kaṛoh, postposition (?), in (?); *patel kaṛoh*, in that cave, 235.

krujā, subst., cultivation, field; *krujā shisthā* (i.e. probably *krujā* or *kruzhī ashisthā*), for sowing the fields, for cultivation, 310; see **kruzhī.**

Karuk, subst., name of a man, 906; agent, *Karak*, 1705; gen. *Karuk*, 1634.

kurk, subst., a heel; *iāst kurk-tā*, on my heel, 641; cf. **kūr.**

kūrik, in *āsh kūrik*, to cook (infinitive of purpose), 283, perhaps a verbal noun of the base **KṚ.**

kaṛol, making; **kaṛolam,** I shall make; see **KṚ.**

1 **KRĀM,** to thresh; imperative 2nd pers. sing. *krāmō*, thresh, 1505.

2 **krām,** subst., threshing; *krām-grammā*, a threshing-floor; *krām-grammā tā*, on the threshing-floor, 1506.

krūm, subst., a roof; *p'krūm*, to the roof, 753; *p'krum*, in the roof, 1191, 1198.

karīna, subst., the sixth month of a year, p. 65.

kaṛond, they make; **kaṛōnam,** I make; **kaṛonn,** he makes, see **KṚ,** present.

kaṛungo, perfect participle passive of **KṚ,** to do; *ushap ktol kaṛungo pul iār*, the horse has eaten his belly done (i.e. filled) with grain, 1365; cf. *ktol kusth*, to eat one's fill.

kraīru, subst., a quail, 1099 (nom. plur.).

kaṛṛū, subst., the root (of a tree), 1722 (acc.); perhaps connected or identical with *kaṛu*, the trunk (of a tree), 1556.

korār, kurār, where? somewhere, see 3 **kōr.**

koṛṛ, subst., a crow, 304 (nom. plur.); *bilian-kor*, a Chitrālī crow, a magpie, 840.

kurr, adj., bald; *kurr ess*, he is bald, 113.

kaṛs, kaṛaīs, kaṛsā, kaṛsī, kṛishtai, kṛistai, kṛess, kṛiss, made, have made, see **KṚ,** perfect.

karosth, korusth, to make, see **KṚ,** infinitive.

kaṛt, kaṛtā, kaṛtī, kaṛtab, adj., (1) fat; used as a predicate, *kaṛt*, 212, 1263; *kaṛta*, p. 8; *kaṛtā*, 223, 1534; *kaṛtab*, 454; used as an attribute, *kaṛtā kanik*, a thick rope, 1423.

(2) Swelled, big, strong; *kaṛtī ālī ushp*, a strong tall horse, 1424, p. 7 (*āllī*); *luikon kaṛtī bistai*, the veins have got swelled, are standing out, 1604.

(3) Strong, hard, cruel, 306 (predicate); *kaṛtē*, forcibly, violently, 517, p. 61.

kartē, adverb, violently, 517, p. 61; cf. **kaṛt.**

kaṛtawōr, subst., a big matter, a fuss; *kaṛtawōr kunn,* he is making a fuss, he is grumbling, 1432; cf. **kaṛt** and **katrawōr.**

kaṛwā, adj., strong; *kaṛwā asht,* they are strong, powerful, 658; *kaṛwa manchī,* a strong man, 206; *kaṛwā damu,* a strong wind, 1612.

kruzhi, subst., cultivation; *Katō kruzhī bilugh lesst ess,* the Kāfirs' cultivation is very good, 311; other forms of the same base or the same word are:—

kujhī, cultivation; *Dryus pār kujhī n'aieshta,* beyond Drōsh there is no cultivation, 153; *krujā,* cultivation, field; *krujā shisthā* (i.e. *krujī* or *kruzhī ashisthā*) *wosut less,* the spring is good for sowing the fields, spring is the good time to cultivate, 310.

kish, cultivation; *kish kund,* they cultivate, 1603.

KAS, to cough, to crow; 2nd present 1st pers. sing. *kassetum,* I am coughing, 838.

3rd pers. sing. *kasett,* coughs, 856; *kasitt,* coughs, 290; *kakkak bilugh kasitt,* the cock crows much, 305.

KÂS, to complain; 2nd present 3rd pers. plur. *kâsettett* (the Sepoys) are complaining, 280.

kusoch, smokest, see **KṚ.**

KSH, to rub, to groom; *kshē mīsh kshē,* groom (the horse) with a wisp, 592.

kshâ, ksho, in *wakshâ,* take down, p. 4; *wāksho,* unload, 1583; *waokshō,* take down, 375; see **KSHO.**

1 **kshē,** subst., a wisp (for grooming); *kshē mīsh kshē,* groom (the horse) with a wisp, 592.

2 **kshē, kshi,** do, see **KṚ.**

KSHO, to drag, to pull; infinitive, *kshosth dugā,* in order to pull (the beam), 1085; *u-kshosth dugā,* for pulling out, 1008, 1098; *chillam bilugh kshaiesth dugā,* owing to much pulling at a hookah, 671; the form *kshaiesth* is, however, doubtful and may perhaps belong to the base **KṚ,** which is regularly used with words such as *tamkio,* tobacco; *nazur,* snuff.

Verbal noun, *ks̲h̲on na battam*, I cannot pull, p. 58; *ks̲h̲on n'battamis̲h̲*, we cannot drag (so large a load), 819.

Imperative 2nd pers. sing. *kz̲h̲á, ks̲h̲o*, pull; *waks̲h̲á*, take down (the saddle off the horse), p. 4; *wāks̲h̲ō*, drag down, unload, 1583; *wao-ks̲h̲ō*, drag down, unload, 375; these forms perhaps belong to the base *KṚ*.

2nd pers. plur. *ks̲h̲ôr*, pull (the rope), 1529.

3rd pers. plur. *argru wa-ks̲h̲ol*, let them drag the beam out, 376.

kas̲h̲ī, kos̲h̲i, makest, see **KṚ.**

kis̲h̲, subst., cultivation; *kis̲h̲ kund*, they cultivate, 1603; see **kruz̲h̲ī.**

kūs̲h̲, subst., a willow-tree; *pkūs̲h̲ pgūro*, under the willow-tree, 1035.

ks̲h̲âchi, art making, see **KṚ.**

kas̲h̲k, in *kas̲h̲k wetzá*, shoes, 1292 (nom. plur.).

ks̲h̲ūl, ks̲h̲ul, kas̲h̲ul, adj., skilful, clever, wise; *tū ks̲h̲ul as̲h̲ī*, if thou art skilful (wrongly translated 'willing'), 1693; *tū ks̲h̲ul bistá*, if thou hadst been wise, 1700; *kas̲h̲ul ess*, is clever, 260, 464; *ks̲h̲ūl manchī*, a clever, wideawake man, 1187; *ks̲h̲ul manchī*, a skilful, brave, man, 1743; *kus̲h̲ulwā*, skilful, careful; *kus̲h̲ulwā ks̲h̲ī*, have a care, 225.

ks̲h̲ām, I make, see **KṚ.**

ks̲h̲on, to drag, see **KSHO.**

kus̲h̲ān, adj., contented; *kus̲h̲ān n'aiesht*, they are discontented, 358; see **kuz̲h̲ān.**

ks̲h̲ond, they do (they smoke tobacco); **ks̲h̲onjī,** doest, see **KṚ.**

ks̲h̲ēr, ks̲h̲īr, do ye, see **KṚ.**

kshōr, pull ye, see **KSHO.**

kashīr, adj., white, 490, 756 (attribute); *kas̲h̲īrī gáo*, a white cow, 220; *gáo kas̲h̲īrī iz̲h̲ā*, is the cow white? 294; see **kaz̲h̲īr.**

ks̲h̲aiesth, to pull; *chillam bilug̲h̲ ks̲h̲aiesth dugā*, owing to much pulling at a hookah, 671; see **KṚ (?)** or **KSHO (?).**

ks̲h̲osth, to pull, see **KSHO.**

kas͟hītī, having made; **ks͟hâtam, ks͟hâtam,** I do, see **KṚ.**

kus͟htun, subst., a hammer, 1234 (nom.).

kasmat, subst., distribution, arrangement; *tū dugā lesst kasmat kalom,* I shall make a good arrangement for thee, I will make thee comfortable, 1395.

kassetum, am coughing, see **KAS.**

1 **kāst,** adj., of what kind? what like? *akī pōr kāst azzā,* what is the other side like? 1331; *kā'st bītī assā,* what like having become 's he? what is his condition? 1394; *tū chitt kā'st azz,* what is thy mind like? what is thy mind? 1701; *kā'st us͟hpa,* what sort of horse? 1666; also written *kāsth*; thus, *koṛ kāsth ezz,* how is the colour? 278; *kāstē tā,* at what kind of time? when? 1670, p. 60 (*tār*).

2 **kā'st, ku'st,** whose? see 1 **ka** (1).

kosth, kusth, to do, doing, see **KṚ.**

kustham, I made; *dâtik kustham,* I made a wager, 1619; see **KṚ,** conjunctive participle.

kasett, kasitt, coughs, crows, see **KAS.**

ktâ, a knife, see **kato.**

ktē, ktī, make, see **KṚ.**

ktī, kati, kotē, kotī, having done, see **KṚ.**

Katā, subst., a Bas͟hgalī Kāfir; nom. plur. *Katā,* 246, 409, 628, 643, 966; *Katā manchī,* Kāfirs, 1039, 1129, 1526, 1603, 1651 (*manchi*); gen. plur. *Katō,* 311, 683, 991, 1069, 1609; *Katō parmēr,* the boys of the Kāfirs, 1026; *Katō warī,* the language of the Kāfirs, 732, 1000, 1467 (*varī*), 1518; *Katō warī,* the language of the Kāfirs, 764; *Katōst tapak,* the guns of the Kāfirs, 600; *Katō manchī,* of the Kāfirs, 906; oblique, *Katō kē* (?), to the Kāfirs, 625; *Kātō tā,* to the Kāfirs, 642; *Katō manchī dugā,* for the Kāfirs.

katâ, a knife, see **kato.**

1 **katī,** subst., harvest, 94 (acc., translated 'wheat'), 621, 622, 1032 (nom.).

2 **katī,** subst., a beam, 195 (acc. plur.).

3 **katī,** adverb, up to, p. 61; see also **KṚ,** conjunctive participle.

kato, subst., a knife, a dagger; nom. *katá,* 1280; *ktá, kato,* 948; acc. *kato,* 746; oblique, *kaṛo mish, katā mis͟h,* with a knife, 1314; *kato mēs͟h,* with a knife, 316; *katō vītī,* striking with a dagger, with a dagger, 319.

keti, having done, having said; *sang keti psiā,* all having said (cf. the use of Sanskrit *iti*) are lost, I have lost them all, 827; *puruketī,* having made complete, completely, truly, 1110; see **KṚ,** conjunctive participle.

kōt, subst., faculty of work, power, strength; *inā us͟hp tā köt n'aies͟ht,* there is no strength in this horse, 1424; *putrē n'bamá, kōt n'ess,* we cannot cross, there is no possibility (it cannot be helped), 1147.

kotē, adverb, actingly, energetically, violently, strongly, loudly, p. 61; *angā kotē parchiō,* blow the fire strongly, 166; *kotē warī iā p'kōr gwā,* loudly a sound came to my ear, I heard a loud sound, 830; *kötē,* violently, p. 61; cf. **KṚ,** conjunctive participle.

KUT, to be lame, see **KUTT.**

KUTO, to say; *kutoss,* he says, 969.

ktol, subst., stomach, belly, 145, 275, 593, 857, 1048, 1408 (nom.); *ktol ārktī,* having inflated his belly, or, perhaps, having turned his belly downwards, 498; *us͟hp ktol pagiur,* under the horse's belly, 1445; *ktol kusth,* to do one's belly, to fill one's belly; *ktol n'kaṛsā,* hast thou not eaten enough? 1232; *ktol ks͟hī,* eat your belly full, 1274; *ktol kaṛungo pul iār,* (the horse) has eaten grain, his belly filled, 1365; *ál ktol,* a big belly; *ál ktol oss,* he is a big belly, he is corpulent, 288; *ál ktol manchī,* a big-belly man, a fat man, 190; *ál ktol-wā,* big-bellied, stout, portly, 1049, 1415 (predicate); *ál ktol-wā assis͟h,* thou art big-bellied, greedy, 586.

ktelik, subst., a lid; *achē-ktelik,* eyelid, 434 (acc.).

kotam, I do, see **KṚ.**

kutan, making, doing; *buṛī kutan amu,* food-making house, kitchen, 743.

katrawōr, adj., disrespectful; *katrawōr kudūm essā*, it is a disrespectful deed, 1373; according to p. xii identical with *kaṛtawōr*, which occurs in *kaṛtawōr kunn*, he is making a fuss, he is grumbling, 1432.

katsā, subst., millet, 870 (nom.).

kotish, kutish, doest, see **KR.**

1 **kett,** (1) who? see 1 **ka** (1); (2) whereabouts? 1674, p. 61.

2 **kett,** in *shūskett*, (the horse) is gasping, lit. does hissing, panting, 548; see **KṚ.**

KUTT, KUT, to be lame, to limp; present, *kutann*, (the cow) is lame, 1681; *kutass*, (the horse) is lame, 661.

Second present, *kutātt*, is lame, 661, 663; *kuttātt*, is lame, 756, 757, 1707; *kuttātt*, he limps (is bandy-legged?), 115.

3rd pers. plur. *kuttāttett*, they are lame, 757.

kutt, kuttā, kuttett, does, says, see **KṚ.**

kuttātom, in *inā kuttātom tū kā walach*, when he asked me, what answer gavest thou? 51; cf. **KṚ,** past participle.

kawa, subst., a basket, 120 (nom.); 119, 207 (acc.).

kāwo, what? whose? see 1 **ka** (1).

kōwar, kūwar, kō, adj., left; *kō dusht*, the left hand, 611; *kōwar*, 791, 1208; *kūwar*, 1166, 1176 (all examples predicates).

kiwitt, subst., a fig, 472 (nom. plur.).

kyā, kyē, kyẽ, kyū, why? see 2 **kā.**

kuiyā, adv., early; *ushpo sir manchī tā kuiyā*, early from a horseman, earlier (quicker) than a horseman, 889; *kuiyẽ*, early, 398, 623; see **kuiā.**

KAZ, to sneeze; infinitive, *bilugh kazisth* (?) *dugā*, owing to much sneezing, 1344; compare **KAS.**

kāzī, subst., the Kāzi; *kāzī tār*, before the Kāzi, 1103.

kazhē, subst., a weight, fifteen seers (30 lb.), p. 64; *shto kazhē*, four kazhē, sixty seers, p. 64.

kuzhāl, kuzhān, adj., happy, contented; *sundī kuzhāl kulom*, I shall make you all contented, 1740; *kuzhān assum*, I am satisfied, 1231; *tū kuzhān ashībā ō dī kuzhān assum*, if thou art contented, I am contented, 617; *tū kuzhān kālom*, I shall make thee happy, 1023; *lālu kusth dugā kuzhān asth*, they are happy at singing, fond of singing, 1027; other forms of the same word are:—

kujhēl balom, I shall be happy, 555.

kushān n'aiesht, they are not contented, 358.

kazhīr, kashīr, adj., white; translated 'grey', 588, 605, 1219; *kazhīr* is used as an attribute, 662, 1084, 1189, 1377, p. 7; *kashīr* is used in the same way, 490, 756; *kazhīr*, is used as a predicate; *gash kazhīr ess*, my goats are grey, 588; *ǵo kazhīr assā*, the water is white (clear), 1418. A fuller form *kazhīra* is also used; thus, *kazhīra ushp*, a white horse, p. 7; *dāṛi kazhīra bissā*, the beard has become white, 131; *zhū kazhīra bistai*, the hair has become grey, 605; Abdul Hakīm Khān writes *kazhera* instead; thus, *azhē kazhera assa*, the bull is white, p. 8; *ushpa kazhera assa (ashta)*, the horse (the horses) is (are) white, p. 8; *daṛi kazhera assa*, the beard is white, p. 8; *dru kazhera assa*, the hair is white, p. 8; *kazhera ushpā dā*, from the white horses, p. 8. A third form *kazhīrī* (Abdul Hakīm *kazheri*) or *kashīrī* is perhaps feminine; thus, *kazhīrī ushp*, the grey horse, 1219; *kazhīrī dāṛī*, white beard, p. 7; *kazhīrī gáo*, white cow, 1681, p. 7; *kazhīrī pit*, a white hillock, 659; *kazhīrī zhū*, white hair, p. 7; *gā kazheri assa*, the cow is white, p. 7; *ishtri ushpa kazheri assa*, the mare is white, p. 7; *kashīrī gáo*, a white cow, 220; *gáo kashīrī izhā*, is the cow white? 294.

kazhish, subst., saltpetre, 1224.

kazhwaj, fruit, 6; *kazhwajh*, fruit, 535; *kazhwazh*, fruit, 162; see **kachwach.**

L

le, lē, adj., (1) good; used as an attribute the form *le* occurs in *le manchī*, a good man, 12; another form *leo* in *leo ūgh*, good water, 909; *lē* is the most common form; see 238, 418, 477, 554, 926, 1000, 1071, 1379, 1475, pp. 4, 15; *lē bidīwā*, of good intention, kind-hearted, 740, p. 5; *damtōl lē manchī*, a clever good man, 446 (translated 'famous'); *lē damtōl manchī*, a good clever man, 1348 (translated 'brave'); *lē varī*, a good matter, an amazing business, 41; *lē*, good, is also occasionally used as a predicate, 568, 836; *tū ī lē zānchībā*, if I think thee good, if thou pleasest me, 1029; *lē ess*, is good, is usually written *less*; see below; as an adverb *lē* means 'well', very well, 414, 704, 906, 1000, 1113, p. 61.

(2) Much; plentiful, numerous; *pul lē n'ētē*, do not give much grain, 811; *lē iāsth*, to eat much (from this), to eat more, 419; *le iaṛō*, I have eaten (too) much, 145; *le, lē*, plentiful, numerous, is very commonly followed by the verb substantive or some similar verb; thus, *koṛṛ le asht*, crows are numerous, there are many crows, 304; *bābakar le asht*, there are lots of monāls, 1007; *tāb le butt*, there is much heat, 637; instances of *lē* used in this way are 53, 95, 96, 116, 136, 210, 256, 416, 570, 636, 845, 894, 896, 938, 976, 1064, 1100; note *dumī lē ishtett*, wind plentiful blows, the wind blows fast, 167; *gaṛ lē prētt*, jewels plentiful gives, he gives a lot of jewels, 726.

less occurs as another spelling of *lē ess*; thus, *āo less*, the water is plentiful, 1421; *less*, is good, 12, 154, 310, 336, 404, 514, 752, 924, 967, 1056, 1099; *tā tōtt warī less*, thy father's speech is good (clear), 259; often, however, *less* is an adjective, being good, good; it is sometimes used as an attribute; thus, *less kazhwajh*, good (fresh) fruit, 535; *less bidī*, a good mind, manliness, 843; *less wokt*, a good season, 1516; more commonly it occurs as a predicate, 11, 43, 82, 127, 243, 405, 419, 429, 489, 514, 594, 598, 621 (read *lesst-uiā*?), 622, 680, 725, 760, 888, 893, 946, 1019, 1158, 1220, 1372, 1388, 1468, 1641, 1643; *less* is also used as an adverb, well; thus, *less kudūm kul*, well work doing, industrious, p. 9; *less katī*, having done well, thoroughly; *less katī wī*, beat him severely, 1087; *less katī ktol kshī*, fill your stomach thoroughly (to your heart's content), 1274; *less tarwochē wil*, well with sword striking, a good swordsman, 1456; note *less kusth*, to make good, to repair, 860; *lest, lesst,* good, is used in the same way as *less*; *lest* occurs as an attribute, 741; and as a predicate, 150, 572, 574; the common form is *lesst,* which is used as an attribute, 597 (*lesst dumtōl manchī,* a good clever man, a sharp man), 1153, 1273, 1315, 1395, 1406; as a predicate, 311, 455, 527, 621 (read *lesst-uiā* instead of *less tuiā*), 791, 898, 1041, 1083, 1096, 1129, 1167, 1170, 1184, 1191, 1195, 1221, 1242, 1264, 1269, 1313, 1382, 1431, 1466, 1569, 1613, 1623, 1678, 1695, 1715; note *lesst kshī,* make good, clean, 269; *lesst* is also used as an adverb, well, 945, 970, 1174, 1180, 1348, 1615, 1658; *manchī dugā lesst kul,* doing well to men, respectful, 1156; *lesst kaṛā,* thou hast made well, a good arrangement, 1023; *lesst katī walō,* well having made speak, speak clearly, 1235; the fuller form *lesta, lessta,* good, is never used as an attribute; as a predicate we find *lesta,* 118, and *lessta,* 606; quite common is *lesta balā,* will be good, is good, is well, 21, 22, 341, 856, p. 20 footnote; also *lessta balā,* 907, 1222, p. 63 (*lesstā*); as an adverb we find *lesta,* well, 122, 323; *lessta,* well, 729; *lesta kulom,* I shall do well, I shall reward, 84; *iā lesta kshī,* set me right, help me, 83; *lesta kshī,* set it right, mend it, 859; *lesstakā,* well, 876; *lesstaka,* well, p. 61.

loī, blood, see **lui.**

lū, subst., root, 1193, p. 7.

luī, subst., blood; nom. *luī,* 164, 1411; *loī,* 521; acc. *luī,* 161.

lui-kon, blood-vessel, vein, 1604.

ldel, participle, lying; *ladēl ess,* he is lying, he lies, 862; *n'ldel assā,* he is not lying, he does not lie, 1021; cf. **LAR.**

laḍer, subst., a messenger, 864.

laga, participle, applied (?); *yūs yūti laga biss,* grass having eaten applied became, grass is eaten up, p. 59; probably borrowed from Hindōstanī.

lugā, adj., light; *lugā kshī,* make (our loads) light, 805.

lālu, subst., song, singing; *lālu kusth,* to make singing, to play music, 1027; *lālu kul,* song-making, a singer, 1071, pp. 9, 15;

lālu kulonn, bilugh lesst lālu kul assā, let him sing (make song), he is a very good singer, 1315.

lillik, adj., young, 1741, 1742 (of a cow; used as a predicate).

liliwak, subst., a boy, 297.

lambar, subst., a certain measure, the length from shoulder to end of middle finger, p. 64.

lamṛ, adj., thin; *lamṛ kanik*, a thin rope, a string, 1423; *lamṛ pachen*, a thin thread, 1138; *lamaṛ assā*, (my waist) is small, 1621; *limṛai*, thin, narrow; *limṛai pott*, a narrow path, 992.

lonī, subst., a slave, 1325.

LUN, to fall; the following forms occur:—

Infinitive, *lunishti mish*, by falling, 723; *lunishtī mēsh*, by falling, p. 15.

Conjunctive participle, *lunētī*, having fallen, 438.

Past tense 3rd pers. sing. *ushp lunī*, the horse fell, 159; *gâo poē lunī*, the cow fell into the river, 381.

Perfect and pluperfect 1st pers. sing. *luniosam*, I fell, 360; *lunissā*, I have fallen, 83; *lunissam*, I fell, 252, 954.

3rd pers. sing. *lunis*, he has fallen, 228; *luniss*, he has fallen, 284; fell, 1017.

Future 2nd pers. sing. *lunelosh*, wilt fall, 190.

lang, in *sū pār lang biā*, the sun has set, 274; *pār lang* perhaps means 'gone beyond', cf. Sanskrit *laṅgh* and **PALANG.**

LAR, to lie; the following forms occur:—

Present participle, see **ldel.**

Indefinite present 2nd pers. sing. *laraichī*, thou tellest lies, 144; *larēchī*, thou tellest lies, 430; *larich*, thou tellest lies, 52.

Perfect, *larissā*, I have told a lie, I have made a mistake, 873

LAṚ, to demur; 2nd present 3rd pers. plur. *laṛettett*, they demur, 339.

LAS, to come out, to flow out; 2nd present 3rd pers. sing. *shur lāsett*, mud (?) flows out, I have dysentery, 394.

Causal, *laz*; imperative 2nd pers. plur. *ē parmiṛ dī baṛ na lazar*, let not even a boy come out (escape), 1439; it is doubtful whether this form belongs to the base **LAS.**

LUSHT or **LUZH,** to burn, p. 15; passive, to be frostbitten, p. 30; the following forms occur:—

Infinitive, *lushtisth*, to burn, p. 15.

Past tense, *lushtiā*; *zīm dugā achiē lushtiā*, my eyes were burnt on account of the snow, got snow-blind, 1346; *kūr lushtia*, (the cold) burned my foot, my foot was frostbitten, 509; *pachanwarīē iāst sang lattrī lushtiā*, the enemies burned all my property, 1079; it will be seen that the meaning of this form is, as in the case of all transitive verbs, passive.

Perfect, *kuīr angur lushtistai*, my toes are frostbitten, 1528.

Imperative, *lushē*, burn, 215.

A passive conjugation is formed by adding forms of the bases *I* and *GŪ*, to go; according to the paradigm on pp. 30 and f., several uncompound forms are also used as passives; the following forms occur, almost all of them only in the paradigm on pp. 30, 31:—

Infinitive, *lushtisth*, to be frostbitten, p. 30.

Present participle, *lushtil* (?), being frostbitten, p. 30.

Conjunctive participle, *lushtītī*, having been frostbitten, p. 30.

Indefinite present 1st pers. sing. *lushtimtān*, if I am frostbitten, p. 31.

2nd pers. sing. *lushtichtān*, if thou art frostbitten, p. 31.

1st pers. plur. *luzhēmish*, we are frostbitten, p. 30; *lushtemishtān* (?), if we are frostbitten, p. 31.

2nd pers. plur. *luzhēr*, you are frostbitten, p. 30; *lushtērtān* (?), if you are frostbitten, p. 31.

Present 1st pers. sing. *luzhēnam*, I am frostbitten, p. 30.

2nd pers. sing. *luzhenj*, art frostbitten, p. 30.

3rd pers. sing. *luzhēnn*, is frostbitten, p. 30; *lushtinntān*, if he is frostbitten, p. 31.

3rd pers. plur. *luzhēnd*, they are frostbitten, p. 30; *lushtinntān* (?), if they are frostbitten, p. 31.

Past 1st pers sing. *lužhengam*, I got frostbitten, p. 30.

2nd pers. sing. *lužhengaṣh*, gottest frostbitten, p. 30.

3rd pers. sing. *lužhengā*, got frostbitten, p. 30; *gum luṣhingwā*, the corn has got burned, dried up, 286.

1st pers. plur. *lužhengāmiṣh*, we got frostbitten, p. 30.

2nd pers. plur. *lužhengār*, you got frostbitten, p. 30.

3rd pers. plur. *lužhengā*, they got frostbitten, p. 30.

Imperfect 1st pers. sing. *lužhēnazzam*, I was frostbitten, p. 30.

2nd pers. sing. *lužhēnazziṣh*, wast frostbitten, p. 30.

3rd pers. sing. *lužhēnazzī*, was frostbitten, p. 30.

1st pers. plur. *lužhēnazzamiṣh*, we were frostbitten, p. 30.

2nd pers. plur. *lužhēnazzār*, you were frostbitten, p. 30.

3rd pers. plur. *lužhēnazzī*, they were frostbitten, p. 30.

Perfect and pluperfect 1st pers. sing. *lužhengossam*, I had been frostbitten, p. 30.

2nd pers. sing. *lužhengossiṣh*, hadst been frostbitten, p. 30.

3rd pers. sing. *lužhengossā*, had been frostbitten, p. 30; *luṣhingostai*, (his eyebrow) got burnt, 433.

1st pers. plur. *lužhengossamiṣh*, we had been frostbitten, p. 30.

2nd pers. plur. *lužhengussār*, you had been frostbitten, p. 30.

3rd pers. plur. *lužhengusthai*, they had been frostbitten, p. 30.

Future 1st pers. sing. *lužhēnēlom*, I shall be frostbitten, p. 30.

2nd pers. sing. *lužhēnēloṣh*, wilt be frostbitten, p. 30.

3rd pers. sing. *lužhēnellā*, will be frostbitten, p. 30; *luṣhtilā*, will be frostbitten, 542.

1st pers. plur. *lužhēlemá*, we shall be frostbitten, p. 30.

2nd pers. plur. *lužhēlr*, you will be frostbitten, p. 30.

3rd pers. plur. *lužhēnellā*, they will be frostbitten. p. 30.

Imperative 2nd pers. sing. *luṣhē*, be frostbitten, p. 31 (I do not think that this form can be correct; see *luṣhē*, burn, above); the remaining forms of the imperative on p. 31 are simply the future forms. None of them would be likely to occur.

less, lesst, lessta, lest, lesta, good, see **le, lē.**

lesta, a prohibitive particle; *lesta kṣhī*, do not do, avoid, 98, 99.

lāsett, flows out, see **LAS.**

Lutkui, subst., name of a nullah, Luttkhū; *Lutkui gol ȧo,* the water of the Luttkhū nullah, 728.

latrī, thing, property, see **lattrī.**

litrā, subst., help, assistance; *tū iȧ litrā prēchī,* thou art giving me assistance, 84.

latta, adj., many; *latta wōs bā,* many days became, for many days, 350; cf. **le.**

lattrī, subst., a thing; *kai lattrī ess,* what sort of thing it is, 915; *kai lattrī,* something, 1149 (acc.); *sundī lattrī,* all things, everything, 1233; *bzul lattrī,* a thing of the jungle, wild, 1689; *lattrī* nas been translated 'cloth', 109, 242 (probably wrong); also one's things, luggage, 112, 1031 (*lattrī giats,* bring the luggage); commonly = property, goods; nom. *lattrī,* 1172; acc. *latrī,* p. 2; *lattrī,* 1079, 1209, p. 9; *p'putt lattrī ngalā,* on road property taking, a highway robber, 1188, p. 9 (*rangal* instead of *ngalā*); *trasu lattrī,* household property, household goods, 573; *tūrsūn lattrī,* household property, household goods, 1079.

lattrī-wā, possessing property, rich, p. 5; used as an attribute, 1171, and as a predicate, 1070, 1155, 1415.

Another form, *lettrī,* occurs in *wāṛā lettrī,* additional things, bribes, 192.

lazhom, subst., a bridle, a bit, 157, 198, 231.

lazar, let him escape, 1439, see **LAS.**

M

1 **m,** pronominal suffix of the 1st pers. sing.; used to denote various cases.

It denotes a direct object in *ōts vina vina kaṛessam,* hast made me beaten beaten, I am beaten, 132, p. 59; *tū kai manu-m-bȧ,* whatever thou mayest order me, 968; *vinā'm,* you, they, beat me, p. 12; *vinās'm,* he beat me, p. 12; *vinoss'm,* he beat me, p. 12; *vinossa'm,* you, they, beat me, p. 12; *kuī waṛi-m-bȧ,* when thou seest me, 1671; it denotes an indirect object, thus, *inā kuttā-to-m*, this-said-in-to-me, when he said this to me, when he asked me, 51; *kṛās'm*, hast promised me, 1077, p. 11; *ptā'm*, gavest to me, hast given to me, 794, 1148, 1474, p. 11; he gave to me, p. 12; you gave to me, p. 12; they gave to me, p. 12; *tū ushp kā ptās'm*, why hast thou given me the horse? 678; *ushp ptās'm*, he gave me a horse, 677; *hukm ptās'm*, he gave me an order, 318; *askā kudūm iā tā wiliāsi-m*, he ordered me that work, gave me that order, 524, p. 12 (*wiliās'm*); it is further used as a dative of possession and interest or as a genitive; thus, *tū ōsh karsā-m*, hast made outlook for me, hast looked out for me, 1669, p. 11; *tū mihrbānī karsam*, thou hast done me kindness, 582; *iāst anī winā'm*, he beat my side for me, he beat me on my side, 1306; *iāst shai winā'm*, he beat me on my head, p. 12; similarly also in *tū wariā-m* (?) *iāst digrī Mirak bṛā*, didst thou see for me (in the matter concerning me), Mirak took my shirt? did you see Mirak stealing my shirt? 1471, if this form is correct; note *mṛalogom* (?) *vizhom* (?), dead for me, feigning for me, feigning dead, 461; *waranṭam*, can he be seen by me? 60; *ngattam*, takest from me, 784.

Usually *m* denotes a subject of the 1st pers. sing.; thus, *ayāsum*, I came, 134; *aiyōsam*, I came, p. 58; *āyosam*, I have come, I came, 1053; *ossam*, I came, 1488; *ossum*, I have come, I came, 1111; *alossam*, I shall dwell, 390; *ēlom*, am coming, 704; *ēllom*, shall come, 1734; *n'aim*, I won't go, 1119; *anam*, I shall go, p. 22; *n'annam*, I cannot go, 1301; *ennam*, I go, I will go, 1524, 1582, 1625, 1704, p. 22; *ennom*, I go, 1162; *aietam*, I go, p. 22; *aiētum*, I go, 180; *aīetum*, I go, 327; *ettam*, am going, will go, 922, p. 22; *ēlam*, shall go, p. 22; *ēlom*, shall go, 37, 40, 47, 329, 560, 702, 753, 923, 1003, 1120, 1278, 1619, p. 22; *ēnazzam*, I was going, p. 22; *enazzam*, I was going, 1208; *achūnam*, I run, pp. 18, 36; *achūnambā*, if I run, pp. 18, 37; *achūniā'm* (?), I ran, p. 36; *achūnazzam*, I was running, pp. 18, 36; *achūnissam*, I have run, 1496; *achūnissum*, I had run, pp. 18, 36; *achūnlom*, I shall run, pp. 18, 36; *ajholam*,

I will whisper, 649; *amjinam*, I put on, p. 48; *amjiā'm*, I did put on, p. 48; *amjinazzam*, I was putting on, p. 48; *amjissim*, I had put on, p. 48; *amjilom*, I shall put on, p. 48; *amjilambá*, if I put on, p. 49; *edsam*, I am, 456; *adzum*, I am, p. 19; *assum* I am, 300, 314, 391, 539, 617, 690, 709, 767, 852, 875, 975, 1061, 1105, 1109, 1140, 1171, 1172, 1231, 1252, 1486, 1608, 1736, pp. 17, 19; *issam*, I am, 814; *azzum*, I am, 617 pp. 19, 26; *dush n'wásam*, fault not having am, I am innocent, 711, 731, p. 58; *tarwaj wásam tapik na wásam*, sword having am gun not having am, I have a sword, I have not a gun, 626; *ashimbá*, if I be, p. 19; *assium*, I was, 390, 767, 1327, p. 19; *otim*, will stay, 1120; *otinam, utinam*, I remain, p. 39; *utinam*, I am done, 1332; *wotinam*, I am done, 1276; *otinambá, utinambá*, if I remain, p. 39; *otiniā'm, utiniā'm*, I remained, p. 38; *otinazzam, utinazzam*, I was remaining, p. 38; *otinassam, utinassam*, I had remained, p. 38; *otilom, utilom*, I shall remain, p. 38; *atsatam*, am coming, 360; *atsalam*, shall come, 1161; *atsalom*, shall come, 1065, 1162; *atsolam*, shall come, 775, 776; *awēm*, I bring, I shall bring, 80, p. 46; *awēnom*, I bring, p. 46; *awētum*, I bring, 229, p. 46; *awērā'm, arwarā'm*, I brought, p. 46; *awarambá*, if I bring, p. 47; *awēnazzam*, I was bringing, p. 46; *awarissam, arwarissam*, I had brought, p. 46; *awēlom*, I shall bring, 688, p. 46; *oshinam*, I am knitting, 747; *azhēlam*, I shall throw, 1205; *azhēlom*, I shall throw, 1262, 1375; *bulazzambá*, if I am becoming, p. 21; *bimbá*, if I become, 952; *bimtā*, if I become, p. 21; *bunam, būnam*, I become, p. 20; *buttam*, I become, 1101; *bā'm*, I became, p. 20; *bunazzam, būnazzam*, I was becoming, p. 20; *bissam*, have become, had become, became, 452, 693, 1316; *bissium*, had become, p. 20; *bissum*, have become, had become, 229, 1063, 1361, 1606, p. 20; *bosam*, have become, had become, 644, p. 20; *balom*, shall become, 187, 555, 1143; *bolam*, shall become, 46; *bulom*, shall become, 1413, p. 20; *būlom*; shall become, p. 20; *banam*, I can, 263, 1208, 1321, 1328, 1451, 1452, 1513, 1574, 1704, 1729, p. 58; *banom*, I can, 4;

bannam, I can, 1303 ; *battam*, I can, 665, 781, 882, 1013, 1095, 1297, p. 58 ; *balam*, I will be able, I can, 656, 1118 ; *gūmbá*, if I go, p. 23 ; *gā'm*, I went, 1301, p. 22 ; *gāsam*, I went, 1660 ; *gūssam*, I have gone, I had gone, I went, 766, 1177, 1316, 1482, p. 22 ; *purū grosam*, I have got leave, 37 ; *jārlam*, I shall kill, 106, 939, 1093, 1396, 1558 ; *jārlom*, I shall kill, 739 ; *kalom*, I am doing, 1547 ; *kolum*, I am doing, 315 ; *kulom*, I am doing, 1444, 1474, 1540, 1541 ; *ksholam*, I am doing, 603 ; *kom*, I do, shall do, 314, 485, p. 24 ; *kshām*, I do, shall do, 810, p. 24 ; *kunam*, I do, 1015, 1257, p. 24 ; *kaṛōnam*, I do, p. 24 ; *kotam*, I do, 718, p. 24 ; *kuttam*, I do, 100, 582, 1257 ; *kustham*, I made, 1619 ; *kunazzam*, I was making, p. 24 ; *kalom*, I shall make, 107, 327, 941, 1023, 1033, 1215, 1395, p. 24 ; *kulom*, I shall make, 84, 457, 485, 793, 968, 1194, 1444, 1532, 1693, 1740, p. 24 ; *kaṛolam*, I shall make, 1586 ; *kaṛōlam*, I shall make, p. 24 ; *kṛolam*, I shall make, 1639 ; *luniosam* I fell, 360 ; *lunissam*, I fell, 252, 954 ; *lushtimtān*, if I am frostbitten, p. 31 ; *luzhēnam*, I am frostbitten, p. 30 ; *luzhengam*, I was frostbitten, p. 30 ; *luzhēnazzam*, I was being frostbitten, p. 30 ; *luzhengossam*, I had been frostbitten, p. 30 ; *luzhēnēlom*, I shall be frostbitten, p. 30 ; *mukonam*, I am fleeing, 494 ; *mikiosam*, I escaped, 423 ; *mikalom*, I shall escape, 424 ; *mṛambá*, if I die, p. 27 ; *mṛēnam*, I die, p. 26 ; *mṛētam*, I die, 1106, p. 26 ; *mṛethum*, I die, 367, p. 26 ; *mṛā'm*, I died, p. 26 ; *mṛēnazzam*, I was dying, p. 26 ; *mṛissam*, I had died, p. 26 ; *mṛlom*, I shall die, 185, p. 26 ; *mizhōnam*, I lie, p. 28 ; *mizhiā'm*, I lied, p. 28 ; *mizhōnazzam*, I was lying, p. 28 ; *mizhessiam*, I had lied, p. 28 ; *mizhhōlam*, I shall lie, p. 28 ; *ngānam*, I take, 1211, p. 42 ; *ngūtā'm*, I took, p. 42 ; *ngūtambá* (?), if I took, p. 43 ; *ngūnazzam*, I was taking, p. 42 ; *ngūtūssam*, I had taken, p. 42 ; *ngālam*, I shall take, 1103, 1194, 1423 ; *ngālom*, I shall take, 661, p. 42 ; *nuksálam*, I will take, 1090 ; *nizhēnam*, I sit, p. 32 ; *nishiā'm*, I sat, p. 32 ; *nizhinazzam*, I was sitting, p. 32 ; *nishinissam*, I have sat down, I live, 814 ; *nizhēnassim*, I had sat, p. 32 ; *nishīlom*, I shall sit.

990, p. 32; *nizhēlom*, I shall sit, p. 32; *nizhēlambá*, if I sit, p. 33; *nizhōnam*, I set, p. 54; *nishēā'm*, I did set, p. 54; *nizhōnazzam*, I was setting, p. 54; *nizhōnassam*, I had set, p. 54; *nizhōlom*, I shall set, p. 54; *nizhālezambá*, if I set, p. 55; *áo pīnam*, I am drinking water, I am thirsty, 313; *piltimdán*, if I fall, p. 35; *piltēnam*, I fall, p. 34; *piltam*, I fell, 201; *piltiām*, I fell, 1208, 1260, 1555, p. 34; *piltinassam*, I was falling, p. 34; *paltiosam*, I fell, 828; *piltiosam*, I fell, 360; *piltissam*, I fell, 1728; I had fallen, p. 34; *piltilom*, I shall fall, p. 34; *piltōmbá*, if I cause to fall, p. 57; *piltōnam*, I cause to fall, p. 56; *piltēā'm*, I caused to fall, p. 54; *piltōnassam*, I was causing to fall, p. 54; *piltōssum*, I had caused to fall, p. 54; *piltōlom*, I shall cause to fall, p. 54; *p'mishtalom*, I shall forget, 526; *pmishtēlam*, I shall forget, 984; *parimdā*, when I arrived, p. 4; *prom*, I may give, will give, 607; *prōm*, I will give, p. 44; *prēnam*, I give, p. 44; *ptā'm*, I gave, p. 44; *prēnazzam*, I was giving, p. 44; *ptāssiam*, I had given, p. 44; *prēlom*, I shall give, 44, 194, 479, 554, 703, 919, 933, 1029, 1063, 1077, 1149, 1161, 1164, 1210, 1477, pp. 11, 44; *prēlombá*, if I give, p. 45; *purjanam*, I understand, I think, 531, 593, 1121, 1246, 1313, 1326, 1335, 1523, 1615; *purjinam*, I understand, I think, 1254, 1437; *purjonam*, I understand, I think, 1122, 1137, 1203, 1281, 1425, 1495; *purzhanam*, I expect, 1323; *purzanam*, I think, 983; *purjitam*, I understand, I think, 916, 1235; *purjitom*, I think, 839; *purjittam*, I suppose, 1212; *purjōsam*, I understand, 854; *pshīnam*, I grind, p. 50; *pshīnambá*, if I grind, p. 51; *pshā'm*, I ground, p. 50; *pshīnazzam*, I was grinding, p. 50; *pshīssam*, I had ground, p. 50; *pshīlom*, I shall grind, p. 50; *peṭalam*, I shall cut, 1487; *pituraisalam*, I shall come behind, 138; *patītom*, I believe, 143, 144; *ragattam*, I want, 1257; *ragalam*, I will ask, 1211; *samīlam*, I will give leave, 784; *samiritsam*, I am off, 733; *kar tēnum*, I give ear, I hear, p. 4; *telam*, I will give, 244; *tipām*, I may warm, 1645; *vinom*, I beat, p. 13; *winom*, I beat, p. 52; *winambá*, if I beat, p. 53; *winā'm*, I did beat, p. 52;

winazzam, I was beating, p. 52; *winossam*, I had beaten, p. 52; *vilom*, I shall beat, 132, 737, p. 13; *wilom*, I shall beat, 707, 738, 802, 1088, 1422, 1486, p. 52; *wiālōm*, I will cause to rest, 1219; *waiētum*, I want, 180; *wideram*, I fear, 1181; *vidarnom*, I fear, 619; *widarnam*, I fear, 459, 494; *widarnom*, I fear, 1233; *widernam*, I fear, 1144, 1198; *widharnam*, I fear, 1695; *widerthum*, I fear, 137, 367; *widarēttum*, I fear, 954; *widaram*, I was frightened, 401; *wagattam*, I want, 290; *wagalom*, I shall get, 663; *wilāmbá*, (as) I may say, 1594; *walatom*, *waliōsam*, I replied, 52; *wanomalom*, I shall catch, 1090; *wopsanasum*, I am done for, 644; *wopsanassum*, I was left behind, 955; *wṛantam*, I see, 646; *wṛantum*, I see, 539; *waṛentam*, I see, 1037; *waṛiām*, I saw, I have seen, I found, 287, 476, 667, 807, 930, 932, 1124, 1246, 1252, 1327, 1579, 1655; *wṛālom*, I shall show, 1301; *vrāghalam*, I shall receive, 1136; *wisilom*, I shall stay, 1370; *washitam*, I think, 1002; *washītam*, I think, 567; *wūshtātum*, I am anxious, 57; *woshtettum*, I think, 699; *wushtatāsum*, I considered, 281; *wezhanam*, I think, I apprehend, 1115; *wizhanam*, I am sure, 803; *yūnam*, I eat, p. 40; *yūnambá*, if I eat, p. 41; *aietam*, I eat, 987, p. 40; *yūlazzam*, *yūnazzam*, I was eating, p. 40; *iārissam*, I had eaten, p. 40; *yūlom*, I shall eat, p. 40; *zāṛlsam*, I know, 750; *jāṛlsam*, I know, 751; *zārtam*, I know, 591; *zārētam*, I know, 1293; *jānrētam*, I know, 1173.

2 **m**, a suffix forming participles and verbal nouns; thus, *achūnam*, running, quickly, 18, 36, 60, 337, 1107; *atsatam*, coming (?), 360; *bom-azzībá*, becoming-are-if, if we become, p. 21; *dām assum*, I am owing, 975; most of these instances are far from being certain; in *n'iam banam*, I cannot go, p. 58; *n'ai iam banam*, I cannot go, 263, the final *m* in *iam* is probably due to the following *bana-m*, and is perhaps simply the pronominal suffix of the 1st pers. sing.

1 **má**, subst., rice, 1170.

2 **má**, pronominal suffix of the 1st pers. plural; there is another suffix, *mish*, of this person, which see; *má* and *mish* are used in

the indefinite present and the 1st present; *má* is the regular form in the future and the imperative; it is sometimes shortened to *m*; the following instances occur:—*ūm*, let us go, 262, p. 23; *ēmá*, we shall go, 398, 403, 714, 785, 1092, 1324, 1370, 1498 (*emá*), 1530, 1588, 1618, 1648, 1702, p. 22; *ēmá*, let us go, p. 23; *achūnlammá*, we will run, let us run, pp. 36, 37; *amjimmá*, we shall put on, let us put on, pp. 48, 49; *amjimmabá*, if we put on, p. 49; *epamá*, let us make, 717; *erwemá*, let us reap, 94; *otimmá*, *utimmá*, we shall remain, let us remain, pp. 38, 39; *otilammá*, *utilammá*, we shall remain, p. 38; *atsomā*, we are coming, we will come, 777, p. 58; *awēmá*, we will bring, carry, 339, p. 46; let us bring, p. 47; *būmmá*, we shall become, p. 20; *bammá*, let us become, 651, p. 21; *na bam*, we cannot, 557, 639; *bamá*, we can, 1147, 1345, 1483; *bammá*, we can, p. 58; *jārlmá*, we will kill, 779; *kummá*, we do, we shall do, 1059, p. 24; let us do, p. 25; *kummabá*, if we do, p. 25; *luzhēlemá*, we will be frostbitten, let us be frostbitten, pp. 30, 31; *mṛēmá*, we die, let us die, pp. 26, 27; *mizhōmá*, we shall lie, p. 28; *mizhammá*, let us lie, p. 29; *ngāmá*, we will take, 513, p. 42; let us take, p. 43; *ngāmabá*, if we take, p. 43; *nizhēmá*, we will sit, 1159, p. 32; let us sit, 1268 (*nizhēmā*), 1438, p. 33; *nizhōlmá*, we will set, p. 54; *nizhāmmá*, let us set, p. 55; *piltēmá*, we fall, p. 34; *piltilēmá*, we shall fall, let us fall, pp. 34, 35; *piltōmá*, we cause to fall, p. 56; *piltōmabá*, if we cause to fall, p. 57; *piltōlemmá*, we shall cause to fall, p. 56; *piltōmmá*, let us cause to fall, p. 57; *prēmá*, we give, we shall give, let us give, pp. 44, 45; *promá*, we shall reach, 1437; *prezhamá*, let us take breath, 1332; *pshīmá*, we shall grind, let us grind, pp. 50, 51; *petremá*, we shall cross, 1618; *putremá*, we shall cross, 1436; *patrem*, let us cross, 519; *ruimá*, we shall cut, 1304; *tamu*, let us build, 195; *wimá*, we shall beat, let us beat, pp. 52, 53; *wasemá*, let us halt, 608; *yūmá*, we shall eat, let us eat, pp. 40, 41; cf. **mish.**

mē̃, mi, postposition, in, into; also written *mē*, *mẽ*; thus, *Badakshā̃ mē*, into Badakhshān, 458; *Mastīch mē*, into Mastuj,

1565; the governed word can be preceded by the preposition *ba*; thus, *inā bagrām mī*, in this village, 1159

mi, pronoun, self; *Mirak mī shtār ass,* Mirak himself is a robber, 1187; *Mirak mī kṛā,* Mirak himself made, p. 13.

machī, adj., sweet; *chaī machī ass,* the tea is sweet, 1448.

mich, mīch, in *p'mich, p'mīch,* in, see **pa,** in, and **mij.**

mōch, subst., a man, a person; nom. sing. *mōch,* 1353, 1692, p. 14; *mŏch,* 1000; agent sing. *patsa mochī,* the herding man, the shepherd, 1287; nom. plur. *mōch,* men, 573; acc. plur. *mŏch,* men, 1098; *mochī's,* his man, his master, 1326 (nom.); *mochis,* his man, his master, 1325 (acc.); cf. **manchī.**

mācherik, subst., a bee, 136, 137 (nom. plur.).

MAD, to cause to go, to drive on; *ushpē madasth dugā,* for making my horse go, 1453.

MUG, to run away, to flee, see **MUK.**

mĕh, subst., damp, mist, 872; dew, 348; hoar-frost, 541.

mehr, subst., a mehtar, a chief, a ruler; nom. *mehr,* 35, 730, 1391; *mehar,* 382, 694, 928, 1154, 1564; agent, *mehr,* 524, 677, 742, 789, 864, 1258, 1259, 1407; *mihrē,* p. 12; *mehar,* 982, 1221, 1565, p. 3; dat. *mehr shotik n'ess,* there is no leisure to the mehtar, 770; *mehr salām gaitī,* having paid my respects to the mehtar, 37; *mehrē leṣs,* fit for a mehtar, 489; gen. *mehr,* 438, 495, 647; *mehar,* 386, 1205; *mehr'st patī,* a letter from the mehtar, 798, p. 4; *mehar'st shodr,* the mehtar's subjects, 1154; *mehrkruē,* a prince, 1072 (gen.), 1074 (agent).

mihrbānī, subst., kindness, 582 (acc.); *ē tang mihrbānī kaṛsish,* I gave thee one rupee in charity, 1063.

mij, subst., the middle; occurs in several forms such as *mich, mīju, mijhū, minj, mish, mizhu*; is used as a noun in *p'mijhū,* in the middle, 820; more commonly, preceded by the preposition *p',* as a postposition.

p'mich, in the midst of, between, p. 61; *amnio p'mīch,* among them, 42; *Badakshā Shdrāl stē p'mich,* between Badakhshān and Chitral, 540; *yū p'mich,* between yourselves, 364; can often be translated 'in', 'into'; thus, *ão p'mich*, in the water, into the water, 284 (*p'mich*), 1227; the governed noun is often accompanied by another preposition or postposition; thus, *b'grām p'mich*, in a village, 1249; *bagrom p'mich*, in a village, 427, 428; *pson p'mich*, in the woods, 1122; *ptul p'mich*, in the field, into the field, 287, 379, 1241 (*p'mīch*); *ão tã p'mich*, into the water, 1316.

p'mij, in the midst of, 1653; *Shdrāl Brus p'mij*, between Chitrāl and Brōz, 151.

p'mīju, on; *p'shai p'mīju*, on my head, 949.

p'mijhū, in the middle, 820; in the midst of, p. 62; *Argich Konisht p'mijhu*, between Urgūch and Ranbūr, 523.

p'minj, between, p. 61.

p'mish, in the midst of, among, between, in; *ikīē p'mish*, within it, 1485; *ikīā p'mīsh*, among them, 1137; *amshiā p'mish*, amongst themselves, 901; *shto manjīān p'mish*, amongst the four men, 1279; *Dryus stē Gairath p'mīsh*, between Drōz and Gairath, 1184; *undsão p'mish*, in the spring, 1379; *bugdrē p'mish*, in the hollow, 667; *Dryus p'mīsh*, in Drōz, 897; *ē gujar p'mīsh*, in one day, 1214; *inā kudūm p'mish*, in this business, 1160 (*p'mīsh*), 1701; *poi p'mīsh*, into the river, 954.

p'mizhu, in *Dryus stē Bruz p'mizhu*, between Drōsh and Brōz, 1200.

MIJŌ, to lie, see **MIZHŌ.**

mājib, subst., pay, salary, 995, 1136 (acc.).

major, subst., age; *inā maṛiṛē major kai ess*, what is this boy's age? 177; in *bilūgh manjar ess*, much age is, he is very old, 20, 365, the word is written *manjar*.

miok, subst., (1) face, mouth; said to be feminine, p. 1; nom. *miok*, face, 983; forehead, 1727; acc. *miok andhṛ kunn*, he makes his face dark, he scowls, 1246; *miōk andṛ kṛiss*, thou hast made thy face dark, thou art frowning, 543; oblique, *p'miok*, on the face, 1239; *p'miōk*, before, p. 61; *miok-o, mugho*, on the face, 1335; *mukā tã*, on the face, 435; (2) fortune, luck; *tū kai* *miok ness*, there is no luck for thee, it is not desirable for thee, 342; *miuk*, fortune, fate, 455.

MUK, MUG, to run away, to flee, to escape; the following forms occur in the sentences:—

Conjunctive participle, *muktī*, having fled, 1139.

Present 1st pers. sing. *mukonam*, I am fleeing, 494; *mukin-jebá*, if I flee from thee, 495.

Second present 3rd pers. plur. *mukettett*, they are fleeing, 344.

Past 3rd pers. *mikiā*, fled, 335; has fled, 344, 496; had fled, 281; *mukiā*, they have run away, 460, 1092, 1207; he bolted, 1343; they ran away, 1600.

Perfect 1st pers. sing. *mikiosam*, I escaped, 423; 3rd pers. sing. *mugis*, he has run away, 1225; *mugiss*, he escaped, he fled, 1358, 1565; *mukiss*, he has fled, 780; *mikios*, he escaped, 461; 3rd pers. plur. *mugistai*, they have run away, they fled, 1209, 1647, 1662; *maikiyāsar*, they have run away, 460.

Future 1st pers. sing. *mikalom*, I will escape, 424; 3rd pers. plur. *mugulā*, they will fly, 1241; *mikēlā*, they will flee, 962; *mukelā*, they will flee, 486 (*mükelā*), 779.

Imperative, *mugō*, flee, 458, 650.

mālā, subst., the eighth month in a year, p. 65.

maulai, subst., Maulai, a certain Musalmān sect, 620 (nom. plur.).

mol, mul, adj., dirty; *mul basená*, a dirty cloth, p. 4; *tu basená mul kṛā*, thou hast made the cloth dirty, p. 3; commonly used as a predicate; thus, *mol*, 258, 267, 47 ; *mul*, 357, 687, 1084, 1272, 1351, 1561; *mulchun*, dirty, p. 8 (used of human beings in sentences noted down by Abdul Hakīm Khān).

muldār, subst., a thing unlawful to eat, an unclean thing, 488; cf. **mol.**

Malik, subst., name of a man; *Dān Malik*, Dān Malik, 900 (nom.), 939 (acc.); *Shēr Malik*, Shēr Malik, 1066 (agent).

mulkhen, subst., a violet; *mulkhen pīsh*, violet flower, 1614; *mulkhen rang*, violet colour, 1613.

malāl, adj., late; *tū malāl botī aiyosh,* thou late having become camest, hast come late (inopportunely), 770.

mullā, subst., a mullah, a priest, 692 (gen. sing.); plural, *mullā,* 625 (gen.), 1129 (nom.), 1135 (acc.); *mullā dugā,* on account of the priests, 1139.

Māmret, subst., name of a place; locative, *Māmret,* in Ranbūr, 497; in the Bamboreth valley, 1040; *Māmreth,* in Bumboreth, 136.

MAN, to mean, to intend; to order; indefinite present 2nd pers. sing. *kai manīchī,* what is thy meaning? 854; *tū kai manu-m-bá,* what thou intendest me (to do), what thou orderest me, 968.

mana, subst., a walnut; *iamru mana,* walnuts, 1628.

manē, adj., imprisoned; *manē manchī,* prisoners, 1074 (acc.).

manoī, subst., a stick, a walking-stick; nom. *manoī,* 301; *manuī,* 147; acc. *manoī,* 316, 1111; *manoi-ā,* with a stick, 738; *manoī mēsh,* with a stick, 630; acc. plur. *manoī,* sticks, 946; cf. **maroi.**

mino, subst., forehead; *tu p'mino,* on thy forehead, 521.

manchi, subst., a man, a human being; a male (464); people (998, 1155, 1602); the following forms occur in the sentences:—

Voc. sing. *manchī-ā,* O man, p. 6.

Nom. sing. *manchī,* man, 1, 12, 22, 50, 90, 97, 105, 113, 115, 139, 140, 170, 190, 206, 208, 224, 226, 295, 312, 333, 345, 359, 372, 388, 410, 411, 426, 446, 477, 487, 498, 508, 520, 525, 536, 550, 571, 619, 689, 705, 708, 720, 724, 740, 765, 829, 839, 841, 869, 875, 889, 919, 927, 940, 968, 994, 1001, 1005, 1014, 1021, 1054, 1055, 1080, 1089, 1103, 1133, 1163, 1171, 1187, 1197, 1261, 1273, 1333, 1368, 1374, 1383, 1390, 1398, 1472, 1475, 1520, 1557, 1559, 1572, 1596, 1675, 1687 (*manchi*), 1723, 1743, pp. 6, 7, 9, 15.

Acc. sing. *manchī,* man, 283, 510, 517, 518, 537, 806, 900, 930, 967, 973, 1246, 1258, 1412, 1467, 1542, 1564, 1566; *manchī-ē,* man, p. 6.

Dat. sing. *manchī-ē,* to a man, 176.

Agent sing. *manchī*, man, 392, 768, 798, 1002, 1251, pp. 3 footnote, 12; *manchi-ē*, 1038; *manchī-ē*, 1362, 1460, pp. 2, 3, 6.

Gen. sing. *manchī*, of the man, 11, 161, 287, 473, 1241; *manchīā*, of the man, 435; *manchī-ē*, of the man, 35, 1313, 1462; *manchī-s*, of the man, p. 6; *manchī-est*, of the man, pp. 4, 6.

Oblique sing. *manchī*, man; *manchī tā̆*, to a man, 131; than a man, 446, 889; *manchī todī*, than the male, 464; *manchī-ē* in *manchī-ē stē*, from a man; *manchī-ē tā̆*, to a man, p. 6.

Voc. plur. *manchī-ā*, O men, p. 6.

Nom. plur. *manchī*, men, 16, 33, 62, 69, 108, 214, 291, 322, 343, 344, 351, 353, 358, 362, 416, 417, 418, 425, 437, 467, 470, 471, 488, 490, 545, 551, 601, 658, 777, 779, 823, 825, 849, 873, 888, 900, 926, 965, 969, 985, 998, 1027, 1039, 1044, 1045, 1047, 1129, 1135, 1144, 1155, 1163, 1265, 1301, 1348, 1430, 1502, 1526, 1529, 1547, 1602, 1603, 1651 (*manchi*), 1697, 1720, pp. 6, 9, 19; *manchīān*, men, 1238, 1590, p. 6.

Acc. plur. *manchī*, men, 466, 710, 806, 864, 969, 1024, 1037, 1074, 1150, 1419; *manchīo*, men, 1229; *manchiān*, men, 376; *manchīān*, men, 465, 1189, 1245; *manchīon*, men, 1092; *manchīōn*, men, p. 6.

Dat. plur. *manchīān*, to the men, 1245.

Agent plur. *manchī*, men, 669; *manchiā̆*, men, p. 4 (Abdul Hakīm Khān); *manchīōn*, men, p. 6; *manchon*, men, 1600.

Gen. plur. *manchī*, of the men, 906; *manchīān*, of the men, 1585; *manchion*, of the men, 229; *manchīōn*, *manchīōn'st*, of the men, p. 6.

Oblique plur. *manchī*, in *manchī dugā̆*, to the men, for the men, towards people, 568 (*dugē*), 1156 (*dugā*), 1695; *manchiān*, in *manchiān dugā̆*, for men, 743 (*dugā*), 752; *manchīan*, in *manchīan mē̆sh*, with men, 1439; *manchīēn*, in *manchīēn dugā̆*, for men, 1167; *manchīon*, in *manchīon dugā*, for men, 1129; *dū manchīon pashē*, as two men, 1193; *sundī manchīon tā̆ damtol*, powerful among all men, more powerful than all, p. 9;

manchīōn, in *manchīōn stē*, from the men; *manchīōn tā̃*, to the men, p. 6.

apshīan manchī, a miller, 869.

ōr manchī, a dwarf, 388.

ushp sir manchī, a horseman, 1037; *ushpo sir manchī*, a horseman, 510, 889.

kūro manchī, a footman, 510, 889.

manē manchī, a prisoner, 1074.

shū ugal manchī, a spy, 1723; *shū awēl manchī*, a spy, 1383.

trāchī manchī, a sentry, 1261.

There are several other forms of this word, viz.:—*mōch*, *mōchī*, *manjī*, *mōsh*, and, according to p. xii, also *munshī*, thus—

mōch, a man; nom. sing. *mōch*, 1353, 1692, p. 14; *mōch*, 1000; agent sing. *patsa mochī*, the herding man, the shepherd, 1287; nom. plur. *mōch*, men, 573; acc. plur. *mōch*, men, 1098; *mochī-s*, his man, his master, 1326 (nom.); *mochis*, his man, his master, 1325 (acc.).

manjī, man: nom. sing. *manjī*, man, 707, 930, 1257; agent sing. *manjī*, man, 1087; oblique sing. *manjī tā̃*, to the man, 1309; nom. plur. *manjī*, men, 1483; oblique plur. *shto manjīān p'mish*, among the four men, 1279.

mosh, man, p. 7 (nom.); *mōsh*, man, husband, 696 (nom.); *mōsh*, men, 1085 (acc.).

manjar, subst., age; *bilūgh manjar ess*, much age is, he is a very old man, 20, 365; see **major.**

munshī, subst., a munshī, 1729 (acc.); *munshī tār*, to the munshī, 1085.

MṚ, to die; the following forms occur of this base:—

Infinitive, *mṛisth*, to die, p. 26.

Verbal noun, *maṛel*, *mṛal*, in the passive *maṛelgō vishti*, having feigned dead, 1358; *mṛalogom vizhom*, having feigned dead, 461.

Present participle, *mṛt* (?), dying, p. 26.

Past participle, *mṛiss*, dead; a corpse, 803; *mṛisht*, dead; *mṛisht azzum*, I am dead, p. 26; *mṛisht ushp*, a dead horse, 1617; *mṛisht krūī*, a dead dog, p. 14; *mṛisht*, a corpse; *manchī mṛisht*, a man's corpse, 287; *manchī bmṛisht nizhān*, likeness of the corpse of a man, a scarecrow, 1241; acc. *mṛishta*, a corpse, 216; gen. *mṛisht'est digur gun ann*, of a corpse a bad smell comes, 1338; *mṛist*, dead; *mṛist krūī*, a dead dog, 1404; *mṛisth*, dead, p. 26.

Indefinite present 1st pers. sing. *mṛambá*, if I die, p. 27.

2nd pers. sing. *mrojbá*, if diest, p. 27.

3rd pers. sing. *mṛabá*, if he dies, p. 27.

1st pers. plur. *mṛēmá*, we die, p. 26; *mṛamizhbá*, if we die, p. 27.

2nd pers. plur. *mṛēbá*, if you die, p. 27; *mṛēr*, you die, p. 26.

3rd pers. plur. *mṛabá*, if they die, p. 27.

Present 1st pers. sing. *mṛēnam*, I die, p. 26.

2nd pers. sing. *mṛēnjī*, diest, p. 26.

3rd pers. sing. *mṛenn*, dies, p. 26.

3rd pers. plur. *mṛend*, they die, p. 26.

2nd present 1st pers. sing. *mṛētam*, am dying, die, 1106, p. 26; *mṛethum*, am dying, die, 367, p. 26 (*mṛēthum*).

3rd pers. sing. *mṛētt*, he dies, p. 26; *maṛett*, he is dying, 57.

3rd pers. plur. *mṛett*, they die, p. 26; *mṛettett*, they are dying, 1020.

Past tense 1st pers. sing. *mṛā'm*, I died, p. 26.

2nd pers. sing. *mṛā'sh*, diedest, p. 26.

3rd pers. sing. *mṛā*, died, 351, 438, 1038, 1497, p. 2 (*ushp mṛā*, the horse died; *gáo mṛā*, the cow died), 26; has died, is dead, 204, 330, 890, 1393; *mṛā̃*, died, 1630; *maṛā*, died, 3; is dead, 28, 220; *ishtrī mṛī*, my wife died, 1691; *ishtrī mṛī*, a woman has died, p. 2; *ushp maṛiā*, the horse died, 352.

1st pers. plur. *mṛāmish*, we died, p. 26.

2nd pers. plur. *mṛār*, you died, p. 26.

3rd pers. plur. *mṛā,* they died, p. 26 ; they have died, 232, 456, 467, 566, 579 ; *maṛā,* died, 31.

Imperfect 1st pers. sing. *mṛēnazzam,* I was dying, p. 26.

2nd pers. sing. *mṛēnazzish,* wast dying, p. 26.

3rd pers. sing. *mṛēnazzī,* he was dying, p. 26.

1st pers. plur. *mṛēnazzamish,* we were dying, p. 26.

2nd pers. plur. *mṛēnazār,* you were dying, p. 26.

3rd pers. plur. *mṛēnazzī,* they were dying, p. 26.

Perfect and pluperfect, 1st pers. sing. *mṛissam,* I had died, p. 26.

2nd pers. sing. *mṛissish,* hadst died, p. 26.

3rd pers. sing. *mṛiss,* has died, 351, 696, 971, 1361 ; *mṛissā,* is dead, 330 ; had died, p. 26 ; *mṛissī,* (my mother) died, 884.

1st pers. plur. *mṛissamish,* we had died, p. 26.

2nd pers. plur. *mṛissār,* you had died, p. 26.

3rd pers. plur. *mṛsī,* they died, 470 ; *mṛistai,* they are dead, 538 ; they had died, p. 26 ; *mṛishtā,* have died, 212 ; had died, p. 26.

Future 1st pers. sing. *mṛlom,* I shall die, 185, p. 26.

2nd pers. sing. *mṛlosh,* wilt die, 73, 350, 439 ; *mṛlōsh,* wilt die, p. 26.

3rd pers. sing. *mṛlā,* will die, 244, 567 (*mrlā*), 632, 1122, 1323, 1359, 1495, p. 26 ; *mṛlī,* (the queen) will die, 1104, p. 2 ; *n'mṛlī,* (the horse) will not die, 589.

1st pers. plur. *mṛēmish,* we shall die, p. 26 (it seems as if this form is really a present, while the form we would expect in the future, *mṛēmá,* has been given as a present).

2nd pers. plur. *mṛḗr,* you will die, p. 26 (probably simply the present form).

3rd pers. plur. *mṛēlā,* they will die, p. 26.

Imperative 2nd pers. sing. *mṛē,* die, p. 26.

3rd pers. sing. *mṛēlā,* let him die, p. 26.

1st pers. plur. *mṛēmá,* let us die, p. 26.

2nd pers. plur. *mṛēr, mṛḗr,* die ye, p. 26.

3rd pers. plur. *mṛēlā,* let them die, p. 26.

mrai, subst., a brick, 193, 257 (acc. plur.).

mṛi, subst., earth, soil, 1381 (acc.).

MAR, to shampoo; imperative, *marō,* shampoo, 1276.

1 **MAR,** to say, to speak; indefinite present 2nd pers. sing. *kai mārechī,* what dost thou say? 1235.

Imperfect 2nd pers. sing. *mārnazush* (written *mār nazush*), thou wast speaking, p. 4 (noted down by Abdul Hakīm Khān).

2 **mār** in *mār wāṛa,* the fourteenth month in a year, p. 66.

marē, subst., a hawk, 628 (acc. plur.), 1543 (acc. sing.); *zhī marē,* the black hawk (agent), variously translated eagle, 396; kite, 744, p. 3 footnote, and lammergeier, 758.

maṛi, subst., money; *bilugh maṛī ptē,* thou hast given much money, paid too much, 1068; *maṛī prētī gats,* money having given bring, buy, 558; *maṛī prētī ngusth,* to buy, 566; also written *mārī,* 219; *maṛī-wā,* valuable, 1601 (predicate).

mārī, stick, see **māroī.**

maro in *maro dusht,* a certain measure, the length from the elbow to the end of the clenched fist, p. 64.

māroī, subst., a stick, a walking-stick; the word is said to be feminine, p. 1; cf. *kaṛtī māroī,* a thick stick, 1484 (acc.); the word occurs in the nom., 1295, 1676; in the acc., 1094, 1400, 1508; and oblique, *māroī mēsh,* with a stick, with sticks, 1306 (*mīsh*), 1422, 1479; the word is also written *mārī,* p. 59; *māṛī,* p. 2, and *māṛī,* 201; all these forms occur as nominatives combined with the verb *paṛengī, peṛongī,* is broken.

Another form of the word with a dental instead of a cerebral *n* is *manoī, manuī,* which occurs in the following places, nom. *manoī,* 301; *manuī,* 147; acc. *manoī,* 316, 1111; oblique, *manoi-ā,* with a stick, 738; *manoī mēsh,* with a stick, 630; acc. plur. *manoī,* sticks, 946.

Maroī, subst., name of two villages, *Chīr Maroī,* Upper Maroī, and *Nīrē Maroī,* Lower Maroī, 1590.

1 **mir,** subst., an inflated skin; *ḍo-tr-mir,* an inflated skin for crossing a river, 1321 (*ḍotarmir*), 1452, 1702, 1704.

2 **Mir,** subst., name of a man; *Mir Khān,* Mir Khān, 647, 711; *Miramza,* Mir Hamza, 598.

Morī, subst., Morī, name of a man; nom. *Morī,* 906, 1415, 1495, 1544, 1677; acc. *Morī,* 1456; gen. *Morī,* 1022; agent, *Morī,* 918.

marach, subst., mulberry, 1240 (nom. plur.).

mārchī, subst., honey, 669 (acc.).

morch, subst., pepper, 999 (acc.).

maroik, subst., neck; *maroik tā dro,* the hair in the neck (of a horse), a mane, 842; *maroik dro,* mane, 1203; also written *marengī,* 842.

māruk, subst., a frog, 538 (nom. plur.).

Mirak, subst., Mirak, name of a man; nom. *Mirak,* 891, 906, 959, 1151, 1187, 1188, 1197, 1252, 1422, 1464, 1520, 1553, 1559, 1596, 1640, 1673, 1739, pp. 4, 9; *Mīrak,* 229; acc. *Mirak,* 1299, 1441; agent, *Mirak,* 1322, 1356, 1471, 1579, 1620, p. 13; dat. of possession, *Mirak,* 891, 892; gen. *Mirak,* 851, 1277, 1439, 1490, 1540, p. 4; *Mīrak,* 3; oblique, *Mirak mēsh,* with Mirak, 1619; *Mirak pursthā,* like Mirak, 1721; *Mirak stē,* from Mirak, 1186; 1187; *Mirak tā,* to Mirak, 1315.

maṛelgō̃, passive participle of the base *mṛ,* dead-gone, dead; *maṛelgō̃ vishtī,* feigning (to be) dead, 1358; *mṛalogom* (?) *vizhom* (?), feigning for me (to be) dead, 461.

marmarī, adj., Arabic *marmarīs,* hard, bare, unproductive; *dristān marmarī kusth,* to make the garden bare (?), to graze in the garden, 584; *ptul marmurī kuttett,* they are damaging the crops, 515; *marmarī kshī,* rub (my rusty sword with sand), 1213.

Miramza, subst., 598, see 2 **Mir.**

marengī, subst., neck, 842, see **maroik.**

marangats, subst., a bird, 133, 217, 840, 903, 970; gen. *marangatsē,* 126, 1696; nom. plur. *marangats,* 155, 903, 1241.

komlik pgoluk marangats, the golden oriole, 970.

satr marangats, a maina, 903.

marapsawai, subst., a falconer, 438 (nom.); cf. **marē.**

maṛiṛ, subst., a boy; nom. *maṛiṛ*, boy, 260, 309, 583, 801, 971; *maṛiṛ*, child, 250; agent, *maṛiṛ*, the boy, 1389, 1408, 1469, p. 3; gen. *maṛiṛ*, the boy's, 357; *maṛiṛē*, the boy's, 177; oblique, *maṛiṛē dugē*, for a child, 512; nom. plur. *maṛiṛ*, boys, 546, 1097; oblique plur. *maṛiṛ mēsh*, for boys, 725; cf. **āṛi** and **paṛmiṛ**.

marish, mirish, subst., an ibex, or orial; acc. *mirish*, 673, 959; nom. plur. *mirishen*, 697; gen. plur. *marish*, 648 (a herd of ibex); *mareshin chiom*, ibex leather, 782.

mṛisht, subst., a corpse; nom. *mṛiss*, 803; acc. *mṛisht*, 287; *mṛishta*, 216; gen. *mṛisht'est*, of a corpse, 1338; *manchī bmrisht nizhān*, a likeness with the corpse of a man, a scarecrow, 1241; cf. **mṛiss, mṛisth, mṛisht,** dead, **MṚ,** past participle.

mōs, subst., (1) the moon, 876; *noi mōs atsēlī*, a new moon will come, 877; *mōs pichis oss*, the fifteenth day of the moon, the day of full moon, 879; (2) a month, 922, 1056, 1584; *ē mōs*, for one month, 1693; *pōē mōs*, last month, 767; *ē mōs ptiwar*, after one month, 1136; *mos tā*, for a month, per mensem, 995; *sōr mōsa tā*, next month, 922; nom. plur. *mōs*, months, 629, 884; *dū mōs tā*, for two months, 793.

mash, subst., cruelty, anger; *tū mash kotish*, (if) thou makest cruelty, art merciless, 863; *mashu*, (1) cruelty, anger; *mashu kolann*, he makes anger, is angry, 771; *mashu-wā*, brutal, 208 (predicate); (2) an enemy, 609 (nom.); *mashūbata*, an enemy, 60 (nom.); *mashu warī*, an enemy, 281, 496 (nom.); (3) cruel; *mashū oss*, he is cruel, 280.

mashoghott, he became angry, 45.

mashikr, anger-making, angry, 43 (predicate).

mēsh, mēsh, mish, mish, postposition, with; to; by means of; from; the most common form is *mēsh*, which occurs, 40, 316, 386, 630, 644, 703, 725, 875, 1372, 1422, 1439, 1479, 1611, 1619, 1702, 1704, pp. 15, 62; *mēsh* is used instead in 577, 658, 965, 978, 1407, p. 5; *mēsh* occurs 13, 1074, 1610, p. 62; *mesh*, 636; *mish*, 592, 1306, 1321, and *mish*, 723, 874, 1314, 1442, 1452, 1561, 1595, 1699, p. 62; the variety in form does not affect the meaning.

(1) with, together with, in company, *mĕ̄sh, mish*, p. 62; *ī mĕ̄sh*, with me, 703, 1702 (*iă*); *emă mĕ̄sh*, with us, 965; *Mirak mĕ̄sh*, (I made a wager) with Mirak, 1619; *ăo mish*, (mixed) with water, 874, 1442; *ano mĕ̄sh*, with meat, 1372; note *parmenstuk zira mĕ̄sh asth*, they are with small heart, they are small-hearted, 658.

(2) with, towards, to; *iă mĕ̄sh puru kshī*, give help to me, 644; *ikīo mĕ̄sh*, (do not use violence) with him, 1[illegible]1; *maṛiṛ mĕ̄sh less n'ess*, it is not good for boys, 725.

(3) with, in the possession of; *iă mĕ̄sh ē paiz dī n'aiesht*, there is not even a pice with me, 875; *wezō tū mĕ̄sh assē*, hast thou got an axe? 978.

(4) with, by means of, *mĕ̄sh, mēsh, mish*, p. 62; *ăo mish*, (wash it) with water, 1561; *ăotrmir mĕ̄sh*, by means of an inflated skin, 1702, 1704; *ăotrmir mīsh*, by means of an inflated skin, 1321, 1452; *gără mĕ̄sh*, (he has been bound) by means of the stocks, in the stocks, 1407; *kaṛo mish*, with a knife, 1314; *kato mĕ̄sh*, with a knife, 316; *kshē mīsh*, with a wisp, 592; *manoī mĕ̄sh*, with a stick, 630; *măroī mĕ̄sh*, with a stick, 1422, 1479; *măroī mīsh*, with a stick, 1306; *puch mish*, with a cloth, 1699; *skă mĕ̄sh*, with a broom, 386; *skă mesh*, with a broom, 636; *woshī (wanzo) mĕ̄sh*, with an axe, 13, 1610; *tarwochī mēsh*, with his sword, 1074; *ushpo mĕ̄sh ēlom*, I go by means of a horse, on horseback, 40; *manchīăn mĕ̄sh*, (surround it) with men, 1439.

(5) on account of, from; *mĕ̄sh, mēsh, mish*, by, in act of, p. 61; *attī mĕ̄sh*, from seeds, 577; *ikīă mish*, from it, 1595; *lunishtī mĕ̄sh*, by the falling, on account of the falling, p. 15; *lunishti mish*, by falling, 723.

1 **mish,** subst., hatred, enmity, 625; cf. **mash.**

2 **mish,** subst., middle; *p'mish*, in the midst of, among, between, in, 667, 901, 1279, 1379, 1485, 1701; *p'mīsh*, 897, 1137, 1184, 1214; *p'mĭsh*, 954, 1160; see **mij.**

3 **mish,** pronominal suffix of the 1st pers. plur. alternating with *mă*; *mish* is occasionally used to denote a direct or indirect

object or a dative of possession; thus, *winām'ish* (?), i.e. *winā-mish*, they attacked us, 1429; *mehar hukm ptasam-ish* (read *ptāsa-mish*), the Mehtar gave us order, 1221.

More commonly *mish* is used to denote the subject; thus, often in the present or indefinite present, and, as a rule, in the second present and in all tenses of the past. The following examples occur:—*ēmish*, we go, shall go, 16, 32, 562, 1305, p. 22; *ēnazzamish*, we were going, p. 22; *achūnamish*, we run, p. 36; *achūnamishbá*, if we run, p. 37; *achūniāmish*, we ran, p. 36; *achūnazzamish*, we were running, p. 36; *achūnissamish*, we had run, p. 36; *amjimish*, we put on, p. 48; *amjiāmish*, we did put on, p. 48; *amjinazzamish*, we were putting on, p. 48; *amjissimish*, we had put on, p. 48; *assumish*, we are, 1044; *azumish*, we are, p. 19; *azumishbá*, if we are, p. 19; *azzamish*, we are, 1580, 1649; *paisa n'wáttettamish*, money not having we are, we have no money, 1044; *azzumish*, we were, p. 19; *otimmish*, *utimmish*, we remain, p. 38, *otinamizhbá utinamizhbá*, if we remain, p. 39; *otiniāmish*, *utiniāmish*, we remained, p. 38; *otinazzamish*, *utinazzamish*, we were remaining, p. 38; *otinassamish utinassa-mish*, we had remained, p. 38; *awēmish*, we bring, p. 46; *awēṛāmish*, *arwaṛāmish*, we brought, p. 46; *awēnazzamish*, we were bringing, p. 46; *awaṛissamish*, *arwaṛissamish*, we had brought, p. 46; *bumish*, *būmish*, we become, p. 20; *bamish*, we became, 1060; *bámish*, we became, p. 20; *būnazzamish*, we were becoming, p. 20; *bosamish*, we have, had, become, 608, p. 20; *bissiumish*, we had, become, p. 20; *bamish*, we can, 332, 1349; *battamish*, we can, 819, 1099; *gūmishbá*, if we go, p. 23; *gāmish*, we went, 403, p. 22; *gūssamish*, we had gone, we went, 1737, p. 22; *kunazzamish*, we were doing, p. 24; *luzhēmish*, we are frostbitten, p. 30; *lushtemishtān*, if we become frostbitten, p. 31; *luzhengāmish*, we were frostbitten, p. 30; *luzhēnazzamish*, we were being frostbitten, p. 30; *luzhengossamish*, we had been frostbitten, p. 30; *mṛāmish*, we died, p. 26; *mṛamizhbá*, if we die, p. 27; *mṛēnazzamish*, we were dying, p. 26; *mṛissamish*, we had died, p. 26; *mṛēmish*, we shall die, p. 26; *mizhōmish*, we tell lies, p. 28; *mizhiāmish*, we lied, p. 28; *mizhōnazzamish*, we were lying, p. 28; *ngāmish*, we take, p. 42; *ngūtāmish*, we took, p. 42; *ngānazzamish*, we were taking, p. 42; *ngūtūssamish*, we had taken, p. 42; *nizhēmish*, we sit, p. 32; *nishiāmish*, we sat, p. 32; *nizhinazzamish*, we were sitting, p. 32; *nizhēnazzamish*, we had sat, p. 32; *nizhēlamishbá*, if we sit, p. 33; *nizhōmish*, we set, p. 54; *nīshēāmish* (?), we did set, p. 54; *nizhōnazzamish*, we were setting, p. 54; *nizhōnassamish*, we had set, p. 54; *nizhālazamishbá*, if we are setting, p. 55; *piliangsamish*, we have marched, 657; *piltiāmish*, we fell, p. 34: *piltinassamish*, we were falling, p. 34; *piltissamish*, we had fallen, p. 34; *piltimishtá*, if we fall, p. 35; *pilteāmish*, we felled, p. 56; *piltōnassamish*, we were felling, p. 56; *piltōssumish*, we had felled, p. 56; *ptāmish*, we gave, p. 44; *prēnazzamish*, we were giving, p. 44; *ptāssamish*, we had given, p. 44; *prēlomishbá*, if we give, p. 45; *pshīmish*, we grind, p. 50; *pshīmishbá*, if we grind, p. 51; *pshāmish*, we ground, p. 50; *pshīnazzamish*, we were grinding, p. 50; *pshīssamish*, we had ground, p. 50; *wimish*, we beat, p. 52; *wināmish*, we did beat, p. 52, *winamishbá* (?), if we beat, p. 53; *winazzamish*, we were beating, p. 52; *winossamish*, we had beaten, p. 52; *wichádzmish*, we shall travel, 1059; *yūmish*, we eat, 1086, p. 40; *yūmishbá*, if we eat, p. 41; *iāramish* (?), we ate, p. 40; *yūnazzamish*, *yūlazzamish*, we were eating, p. 40; *iārissamish*, we had eaten, p. 40; *jānṛamīsh*, we know, 1238.

MISHI, to play, to jest.

Infinitive, *mishishth*, to play, to jest, 725; *bibimst mēsh mishishth*, to play with a snake, to show kindness to a snake, 741; *parchev mishisthai dugā*, for playing polo, 1040.

2nd present 3rd pers. plur. *mishittett*, they play, 1026, 1039.

mishi, subst., a play, a game; *mishī kuttett*, they are playing, 546.

MISHŌ, to tell lies, see **MIZHŌ**.

mosh, subst., a man, p. 7; *mōsh,* a husband, 696; *mōsh,* men, 1085, see **manchī.**

mashūbata, subst., an enemy, 60; see **mash.**

mushich, subst., the lucerne plant, *mushich bī,* lucerne seeds, 835.

mashoghott, he became angry; see **mash.**

mashikr, adj., angry, 43 (predicate); see **mash.**

misht, subst., the hilt of a sword, 660.

mushtē, subst., the girth (of a horse), 553; cf. *bramishten,* the saddle girth, 1514.

mushtar in *wāo mushtar,* a hunchback, 692.

mussā, subst., a mouse, 890 (nom. plur.); acc. plur. *mussu,* mice. *āl muzzā,* big mice, rats, 1125 (nom.).

Missarmin, subst., Tirich Mir, a certain mountain; *Missarmin,* on Tirich Mir, 437.

mustā, adj. (?), clever; *stā mustā ness,* he is not clever, he has no brains, 178.

Mastīch, Mastīj, subst., Mastūj, name of a place; *Mastīchī putt,* the road to Mastūj, 1300; *Mastīj gol,* the Mastūj valley, the Mastūj nullah, 1723; *Mastīj gol āo,* the water of the Mastūj nullah, 728; *Mastīch mē,* to Mastūj, 1565.

mātā, uncertain word; *mātā bistai,* they are delaying, 1130; *mātā kshī,* have patience, forgive, 1065, 1148; *tū ēsth dugā starak matakshi,* please decide the day for starting, 1031.

matsa, subst., a fish; *āo matsa,* a water fish, a fish, 488; *āo matsī purstha,* like a fish in the water, 1451.

MIZH, to break; past 3rd pers. sing. *chimētku nāchē tā mizhē,* an iron nail has broken my finger-nail, 904.

MIZHŌ, to tell lies; the last consonant of this base also occurs as *j* and as *sh*; the following forms occur:—

Infinitive, *mizhosth,* to tell lies, 799; *mizhōsth, mijōsth,* to tell lies, p. 28.

Present participle, *mijōl,* lying, p. 28; *mishāl,* lying, 800 (used as a verb = lies); *bilugh mishāl mishott,* much lying lies, he is a great liar, 1163; *mizhāl*, lying, a liar, 1559; *mizhol*, a liar, 1313; *mizhona*, lying; *mizhona shtalē wulann*, lying perhaps speaks, maybe he is lying, 1472.

Conjunctive participle, *mijētī*, having lied, p. 28; *mizhētī*, having lied, by treachery, 1549; *mizhongai*, lying having gone, having cheated; *mizhongai iā tā oss*, having lied with me is, he has played a trick on me, 1553.

Indefinite present, *mizhē-tān* (?), if I, etc., lie, p. 29.

2nd pers. sing. *mishoch*, (if thou) liest, 802; *mishochī*, thou liest, 1175.

1st pers. plur. *mizhōmish*, we lie, p. 28.

2nd pers. plur. *mizhōr*, you lie, p. 28.

Present 1st pers. sing. *mizhōnam*, I lie, p. 28.

2nd pers. sing. *mizhōnjī*, thou liest, p. 28.

3rd pers. sing. *mizhōnn*, he lies, p. 28.

3rd pers. plur. *mizhend*, they lie, p. 28.

2nd present 3rd pers. sing. *mishott*, he lies, 801, 1089, 1163.

Past 1st pers. sing. *mizhiā'm*, I lied, p. 28.

2nd pers. sing. *mizhiā'sh* (?), thou liedst, p. 28.

3rd pers. sing. *mizhiā*, he lied, p. 28.

1st pers. plur. *mizhiāmish* (?), we lied, p. 28.

2nd pers. plur. *mizhiār*, you lied, p. 28.

3rd pers. plur. *mizhiā*, they lied, p. 28.

Imperfect 1st pers. sing. *mizhōnazzam*, I was lying, p. 28.

2nd pers. sing. *mizhōnazzish*, wast lying, p. 28.

3rd pers. sing. *mizhōnazzī*, he was lying, p. 28.

1st pers. plur. *mizhōnazzamish*, we were lying, p. 28.

2nd pers. plur. *mizhōnazzār*, you were lying, p. 28.

3rd pers. plur. *mizhōnazzī*, they were lying, p. 28.

Pluperfect 1st pers. sing. *mizhessiam*, I had lied, p. 28.

2nd pers. sing. *mizhessī*, thou hadst lied, p. 28.

3rd pers. sing. *mizhestai*, he had lied, p. 28.

1st pers. plur. *mizhessī*, we had lied, p. 28.

2nd pers. plur. *mizhessār*, you had lied, p. 28.

3rd pers. plur. *mizhestai*, they had lied, p. 28.

Future 1st pers. sing. *mizhōlam*, I shall lie, p. 28.

2nd pers. sing. *mizhōlash*, thou wilt lie, p. 28.

3rd pers. sing. *mizhōlā*, he will lie, p. 28.

1st pers. plur. *mizhōmā*, we shall lie, p. 28.

2nd pers. plur. *mizhōlr*, you will lie, p. 28.

3rd pers. plur. *mizhōlā*, they will lie, p. 28.

Imperative 2nd pers. sing. *mizhō*, lie, p. 29; *na mizhāō*, do not lie, 1416.

3rd pers. sing. *mizhōlā*, let him lie, p. 29.

1st pers. plur. *mizhammā*, let us lie, p. 29.

2nd pers. plur. *mizhōlār*, lie ye, p. 29.

3rd pers. plur. *mizhōlā*, let them lie, p. 29.

mizhim, adv., in the morning; *dalkiē mizhim*, to-morrow morning, 1324.

mazhūra, adj., mixed; *mazhūra kshī*, mix, 1442.

muzharala, subst., a ram, 1285; acc. sing. *muzharala*, the ram, the sheep, 1283; agent sing. *mazhurala*, the ram, 1122; gen. sing. *mazharlē ano*, ram's flesh, 1185; gen. plur. *muzharla waruk*, the wool of the sheep, 1715.

muzalmān, subst., a Musalmān, 452; *muzzulmān dīn*, the Musalmān religion, 1141.

muzzā, subst., a mouse; *āl muzzā*, big mice, rats, 1125; see **mussā**.

N

1 **na**, the negative particle, not, pp. 61, 62; the final vowel is often dropped; thus, *na banam*, I cannot, 1208, 1321, 1328, 1451, 1513, 1729; but *n'banam*, I cannot, 1452, 1574, 1704; in other cases it is lengthened or else changed in various ways; the following such forms occur:—

nā, 1128, 1173, 1587, 1657, pp. 61, 62.

nai, 92, 342, p. 62; *n'ai*, 263.

ne, 47; *nē*, 695, 1162.

no in *kā-no-wā*, nothing man, poor, 1580, 1590, 1649; *kai-no-wā*, poor, 875, 966, 1109, 1171, 1172.

noh, 43 (*mas͟hikr boh less noh*, to be angry is not good), 277 (*noh osth*, they have not come), pp. 61, 62; it is not possible to see that the difference in form affects the meaning.

(1) The negative particle is sometimes placed before adjectives and words used as adjectives; thus, *n'utkor*, not profit-making, useless, 761; *n'chamol*, not knowing, 1080; *nā karch*, not roasted, underdone, 1128; *na kusth*, not to do, unworkable, 1587; *na pagī*, not ripe, unripe, 1700; *n'zā̆ṛasth*, not to understand, unknowable, hard to learn, 732.

(2) The negative sometimes follows the word it qualifies; thus often after an indefinite pronoun, in which case it usually precedes the verb; cf. *kā—na*, any-not, none, 458, 1705; *kāī—na*, never, p. 60; *kuī dī nē*, never, 1162; cf. 1 **ka** (2); in some cases adjectives are formed from such indefinite pronouns followed by the negative by adding the suffix *wā*; thus *kā-no-wā*, nothing man, 1580, 1590, 1649; *kai-no-wā*, 875, 966, 1109, 1171, 1172; in the same way is formed *jerik-na-wā*, shame not man, shameless, 1275.

(3) In most cases the negative precedes the verb; if the verb is an auxiliary the negative often precedes the principal verb; cf. *pā n'batt*, he cannot go, 454; *n'pā bann*, he cannot go, 223; *pē n'balos͟h*, thou canst not cross, 1062; *n'pā balos͟h*, thou canst not go, p. 58; all such cases will be noted below, though the different position of the negative does not appear to make any difference in the meaning.

The negative particle is used in the following instances in the sentences:—

With *Ā*, to come; *n'aiyo*, he did not come, 50; *n'āyā*, they have not come, 848, 932, 1177; *n'ais*, has not come, 1144; *n'aisī*, did not come, 1635; was not, p. 19; *n'ozz*, did not come, 1615; *na ozz*, has not come, 1739; *noh osth*, they have not come, 277; *n'aosth*, they have not come, 873; *n'allon*, will not come, 1121.

With *AI*, to be; *n'ai*, is not, 253, 427, 428, 485, 529, 570, 622, 706, 845, 868, 1184, 1705, 1721, p. 19; *nā ai*, is not, 1657; *n'āio*, there are not, 969.

With *I*, to go; *n'aim*, I shall not go, 1119; *tū n'ai*, if thou dost not go, without thee, 1704; *n'annam*, I do not go, I cannot go, 1301; *n'ennam*, I cannot go, 1704; *na ennam*, I do not go, 1582, 1625; *na anjī*, dost not go, 952; *n'enjībd*, if thou dost not go, 702; *na enjībd*, if thou dost not go, 1582; *n'aietam*, I do not go, 40; *n'aiett* (read perhaps *nai ett*), it does not go, 911; *pshutī n'yett*, he does not go asleep, he cannot sleep, 928; *n'ēlom*, I will not go, 702; *ne ēlom*, I will not go, 47; *n'ēmd*, we shall not go, 714, 1618; *n'ai*, do not go, 158, 324, 407, 440, 542, 1107, 1137, 1410, 1462, 1476, 1525; *na ī*, do not go, 1410; *n'iyē*, do not go, 261, 355.

With *AFZ*, to come; *n'afziā*, they have not come, 75.

With *UMA*, to keep; *na umattett*, they do not keep, 628.

With *AMJI*, to wear; *n'amjind*, they do not wear, 824.

With *AMNI*, to attack; *n'amniō*, do not attack, 90.

With *AS*, to be; *n'assum*, am not, 23, 1486; *n'ass*, is not, 1156, 1183, 1188, 1273, 1293, 1388, 1559; *na ass*, is not, 1378, 1623, 1643; *na wō ass*, is not up, 1253; *n'ldel assā*, he is not lying, 1021; *n'assiā*, is not, 653; *n'ess*, is not, 11, 81, 82, 140, 148, 257, 272, 315, 366, 373, 430, 504, 520, 533, 536, 541, 576, 655, 670, 684, 716, 725, 760, 770, 792, 830, 837, 840, 893 (*ne'ss*), 912, 921, 930, 942, 950, 960, 991, 992, 1013, 1019, 1025, 1036, 1061, 1109, 1111, 1112, 1125, 1128, 1147, 1173, 1181, 1194, 1220, 1313, 1357, 1468, 1486, 1567, 1641, 1645; *ness*, is not, 127, 178, 342, 405, 419, 483, 489, 594, 598, 603, 637, 741, 749, 803, 843, 870, 993, 1086; *nēss*, is not, 24; *na ess*, is not, 272, 458, 1179, 1250, 1518, 1521, 1597, 1599; *n'oss*, is not, 790; *n'asht*, is not, are not, 197, 243, 251, 372, 538, 891, 903, 910, 933, 1155, 1367; *na asht*, is not, are not, 1393, 1690; *n'aesht*, is not, are not, 1130, 1133, 1482; *n'aiesht*, is not, are not, 135, 149, 151, 155, 285, 289, 358, 437, 497, 691, 719, 769, 823, 875, 891, 957, 958,

1007, 1040, 1116, 1140, 1196, 1209, 1301, 1304, 1423, 1424, 1551; *n'aieshta*, is not, 153; *n'aiest*, is not, 914; *n'aiasth*, is not, 450; *n'aiesth*, is not, 645, 668, 697, 1206; *n'aza*, is not, p. 8; *n'assī*, was not, 955; *n'azzī*, was not, 1429; *n'azziā*, was not, 1148; *n'azilābá*, if there is not, 436.

With *aischitt*, it is good; *n'aischitt*, it is no good, 1034.

With *USHT*, to rise; *n'otich*, risest not, 1180; *n'utinshess*, hast not risen, 1232; *dumī n'ishtatt*, there is no air, 27.

With *ētē*, give; *n'ētē*, do not give, 811.

With *OTI*, to remain; *n'otē*, do not allow, 1190; *n'ūtē*, do not throw down, 225; *n'ūtan*, do not let me, 881.

With *UT*, to use; *n'utend*, they do not use, 1656.

With *ATS*, to come; *kuī dī nē atsalom*, I will never return, 1162.

With *AWĒ*, to bring, to carry; *n'awēmá*, we cannot carry, 339; *n'awētum*, I do not carry, 229; *n'awērā*, they have not brought, 1233; *n'awēlonn*, may he not bring, 1244.

With *AWĒGU*, to obey; *n'awēguch*, dost not obey, 940.

With *AWITĀR*, to keep back; *n'awitārā*, I did not keep, 735; *na awitārā*, (why) didst thou not keep? 734.

With *BŪ*, to become, to be; *n'bā*, is not, 242, 1078; *n'bunn*, is not, 1417; *na bunn*, is not, 1187, 1472, 1569, 1595; *n'buttam*, am not, 1101; *n'butt*, is not, 348, 945, 1695; *na butt*, is not, 130, 1723; *n'buttett*, is not, 1129; they do not grow, become, 872, 1046; *n'buttosal*, does not become, 759; *na biss*, has not been, 664, 1432; *n'bistā*, they have not become, 727; *n'bulosh*, wilt not become, 1160; *n'bō*, do not become, 1148; *na bō*, do not become, 44; *n'gatri-bōla*, let there not be weariness, 182.

With *BAN*, to be able; *na balē*, he cannot, 1548; *n'pā balas*, he cannot go, 451; *n'pā baless*, he cannot go, 773; *na bachī*, canst not, 1311; *n'banam*, I cannot, 1452, 1574, 1704; *na banam*, I cannot, 1208, 1321, 1328, 1451, 1513, 1729; *n'iam banam*, I cannot go, p. 58; *n'ai iam banam*, I cannot go, 263; *n'pā banom*, I cannot go, 4; *n'bannam*, I cannot, 1303; *na banch*, canst not, 1534; *na banj,* canst not, p. 58; *n'ē banjī,* canst not go, 1054; *n'bann,* cannot, 1397; *na bann,* cannot, 1545, 1708; *n'pā bann,* he cannot go, 223; *na bam,* we cannot, 555, 639; *n'bamâ,* we cannot, 657, 1147; *na bamâ,* we cannot, 1483; *n'bammâ,* we cannot, p. 58; *n'bamish,* we cannot, 1349; *n'band,* they cannot, 1650; *na band,* they cannot, 1536, 1664; *n'battam,* I cannot, 644, 660, 665, 674, 781, 882, 1013, 1095, 1297; *na battam,* I cannot, p. 58; *n'batt,* he cannot, 454, 1187, 1296; *na batt,* he cannot, 296, 307, 665, 1174; *n'buttett,* he cannot, p. 58; *n'battamish,* we cannot, 819, 1099; *n'battett,* they cannot, 907; *na battet,* they cannot, 551; *n'balam,* I will not be able, I cannot, 330, 656; *n'balem,* I will not be able, 436; *na balam,* I cannot, 1118; *na bamish,* we will not be able, 332; *pē n'balosh,* thou canst not cross, 1062; *n'pā balosh,* thou wilt not be able to go, p. 58; *n'pā bilosh,* thou wilt not be able to go, 378.

With *BRADZO,* to pain; *ne brādzāott,* he will not hurt you, 695.

With *CHAGŌ,* to bite; *n'chagōtett,* they do not bite, 54 (*chagōtitt*), 56.

With *chamol,* knowing; *n'chamol,* not knowing, 1080.

With *CHASH,* to eat; *n'chashand,* they do not eat, 620.

With *DAI,* to cook; *n'daiess,* hast not cooked, 1127.

With *DAM,* to catch; *na damitt,* he does not catch, 230.

With *DIR,* to wash; *n'dariss,* hast not washed, 1232.

With *DŌR,* to venture; *n'dronn,* he does not venture, 1520.

With *GŪ,* to go; *n'gwā,* did not go, 635; *n'gosā,* has not gone, 642.

With *grussish,* tookest (leave); *n'grussish,* hast not got (leave), 783.

With *giats,* bring; *n'giats,* do not bring, 1043; *n'gyats,* do not bring, 679, 796.

With *JAR,* to be digested; *na jarand,* they are not digested, 393.

With *JĀR*, to kill; *n'jāriā*, he did not kill, 3; *n'jāriss*, I have not killed, 711.

With *KṚ*, to do; *n'kshholam*, I do not smoke, 603; *na kuch*, dost not do, 224; *nai kutt koshī*, dost not try to follow up, 92; *n'kusoch*, dost not smoke, 1340; *na kunam*, I do not do, 1257; *na kunjī*, dost not do, 1605; *na kunjībá*, if thou dost not do, 1558; *n'kshonjī*, dost not do, 408; *na kund*, they do not do, 1603, 1726; *n'kshond*, they do not smoke, 1526; *n'kutish*, dost not do, 1018; *n'kshdtam*, I do not smoke, 1015; *n'kaṛā*, I did not do, 1060; *n'kaṛsā*, hast not done. 1232; *n'kṛissiā*, they have not done, 832; *na kalom*, I will not do, 1215; *na kulom*, I will not do, 1444; *n'kaṛolam*, I will not do, 1586; *n'kummá*, we will not do, 1059; *n'kshī*, do not do, 47, 142, 338, 366, 929, 1611; *na kshī*, do not do, 1680; *nai kshī*, do not do, 342; *n'pitzen kshē*, do not make broken, do not break, 186; *n'kshīr*, do not ye do, 515, 516, 1309, 1384.

With *ldel*, lying; *n'ldel assā*, he is not lying, 1021.

With *LAS*, to go out; *baṛ na lazar*, let not (anybody) get out, 1439.

With *MUK*, to flee; *n'mukettett*, they do not flee, 344; *n'mukēlā*, they will not flee, 486; *na mugo*, do not flee, 458.

With *MṚ*, to die; *n'mṛlā*, he will not die, 244, 567; *n'mṛlī*, he will not die, 589.

With *MISHI*, to play; *n'mishittett*, they do not play, 1039.

With *MIZHŌ*, to lie; *na mizhāō*, do not lie, 1416.

With *NGĀ*, to take, to carry; *na ngattett*, they do not carry, 1288; *n'ngāmá*, we will not carry, 513; *n'ngā*, do not take, 1201; *n'ngattam*, I did not give thee leave, 784.

With *NUKSĀ*, to remove; *na nuksāo*, do not take off, 1461.

With *NIZHI*, to sit; *na nizhinistai*, have not lived, 1581; *n'nishī*, do not sit, 448.

With *PI*, to drink; *na pī*, do not drink, 378, 1067.

With *PAG*, to get ripe; *na pagann*, does not get ripe, 1179;

n'pagistai, has not got ripe, 1178; *n'piess*, is not ripe, 209; *na pagalā*, will not get ripe, 1179.

With *pā gū*, to do down; *na pūgess*, (the sun) has not set, 1266.

na pēkshē, do not touch, 1537.

With *PALANG*, to walk up and down; *n'palengā*, he does not walk up and down, 1626; *n'palangett*, he cannot walk, 288.

With *PMISHT*, to forget; *n'pmishtēlam*, I will not forgive, 984; *n'p'mishtal*, do not forget, 525.

With *PRĒ*, to give; *n'prenjībá*, if thou dost not give, 185; *n'prēnn*, he does not give, 590; *n'prend*, they do not give, 409; *na prētt*, he does not give, 1131; *na prēttett*, they do not give, 1163; *n'ptā*, I did not give, 420; *n'ptā'm*, didst not give me, 794, p. 11; *n'prēlom*, I will not give, 919, 1149; *na prēlom*, I will not give, 1063.

With *PRĒ*, to go, to come; *na prētt*, (snow) does not come, 1117; *n'ptā*, (snow) did not fall, 380, 443.

With *PEṚ*, to cut; *na peṭann*, does not cut, 1243; *na peṭlon ennā*, it is not broken, 1413; *n'pṛēliss*, it will not break, 946.

With *PARCH*, to burn; *na parchitt*, it does not burn, 243.

With *PURJ*, to understand; *n'purjosam*, I do not understand, 854; *n'purjitam*, I do not understand, 1235.

With *PSHU*, to sleep; *n'pshusiā*, didst not sleep? 1733.

With *PATĪ*, to believe; *n'patītom*, I do not believe, 143, 144.

With *RAG*, to ask for; *n'ragattā*, dost not obey, 1205.

With *ṚANZĒ*, to shake; *na ṛanzēī*, I have not shaken, 1271.

With *ṚAṬṬ*, to bark; *n'ṛaṭṭatt*, he does not bark, 774.

n'shotinestabá, if he is not contented, 841.

With *SANG*, to hear; *na sanganch*, hearest not, 1570; *n'sangāyā*, I did not hear, 807.

shē n'tilā, it will not freeze, 533.

With *WĒ*, to go; *na wēlī*, cannot go, 1184.

With *WĪ*, to beat, *n'vinōsash*, didst not beat, 1312; I did not beat thee, p. 11; *na wī*, do not beat, 1479.

With *WAG*, to obey; *n'wagattett*, they do not obey, 516.

With *WAL*, to speak; *na walett*, she does not speak, 945.

With *WAṚ*, to see; *n'wṛantam*, I will not see, 646; *n'wṛantum*, I will not see, 539; *n'waṛentaṃ*, I do not see, 1037; *n'waṛiām*, I did not see, I have not seen, 698, 1252; *n'waṛainsā*, I have not seen, 347; *n'waṛins*, I have not seen, 1234; *n'waṛīns*, I have not seen, 1255; *n'waṛīs*, I have not seen, 921; *n'waṛains*, he has not seen, 347; *na vṛēlā*, he will not see, 651, 652; *na wāṛo*, do not show, 1319; *n'waṛoins*, it does not come to sight, 657; *wāṛon na ett*, is not visible, 1434; *n'waṛion butt*, is not visible, 128; *n'waṛon prētt*, is not visible, 876; *na waṛon end*, they are not visible, 1392; *waṛantan n'buttett*, they are invisible, 872.

na vrāg͟huttus, I have not got, 1136.

With *-wás*, to be of, to possess; *n'wásam*, I have not, 711, 731, p. 58; *na wásam*, I have not, 626; *n'wáttettamis͟h*, we do not possess, 1044; *na wái*, he has not, 627; see 4 **wā**.

With *YŪ*, to eat; *n'yūlai*, they do not eat, 1086; *n'yūmis͟h*, we do not eat, 1086; *n'aietam*, I do not eat, 987; *n'yūtt*, he does not eat, 581, 840; *n'yūttett*, they do not bite, 493; *n'iār*, I have not eaten, 855, 955; *na yāressi*, I had not eaten, p. 4; *n'yāriss*, he has not eaten, 406; *na yulozis͟h*, wouldst not have eaten, 1700; *n'yūlom*, I will not eat, 1048; *n'yūlā*, they will not eat, 246; *n'yū*, do not eat, 880; *n'āyū*, do not eat, 586.

With *ZĀ̃Ṛ*, to know; *n'zāṛlsam*, I do not know, 750; *n'jāṛlsam*, I do not know, 751; *n'zāṛtam*, I do not know, 591; *n'zāṛētam*, I do not know, 1293; *na jānṛetam*, I do not know, 1173; *n'z͟hāṛtis͟h*, dost not know, 611; *na jānṛetis͟h*, dost not know, 1176; *na jānṛamis͟h*, we do not know, 1238; *n'zāṛtett*, they do not know, 643; *n'zātett*, they do not know, 915; *jerik n'zāṛ*, do not be ashamed, 1274.

na zass, is not produced, 1628.

2 **na, nai,** interrogative particle introducing the second part of disjunctive questions, *aoghān spāhī lest ai na Bilian lest ai*, is the Afg͟hān or Chitrālī soldier the better? 150; *sū chunzlī pōr*

ētimishā nai sū puēli pōr ētimisha, shall we go east (sunrise way) or shall we go west (sunset way)? 402; originally a negative interrogative, identical with 1 **na,** and meaning 'is it not?'

nai, male; *nai kakkak,* a male fowl, a cock, 270, 305, 645, p. 4 (*kakak*).

neo, male, p. 1; *neo ushp,* a male horse, 677, p. 1.

nah nāh, male, p. 1; *nah ashu,* male cattle, bull, 212; *nāh krūī,* a he dog, 369; *nāh ushp,* a male horse, 675, 680, 682.

noi, adj., new; used as an attribute, 527, 834, 877 (*noi mōs,* a new moon), 920, 982; *noi bazisná prēlom,* I will give her new clothes, she is a bride, 194.

NACH, to loose, to leave, to let go.

Conjunctive particle, *nachētī,* having left; *iā manoī nachētī ossum,* my stick having lost I have come, I quitted my stick, 1111.

2nd present 3rd pers. plur. *nachåttett,* they let (their horses) go, 825.

Perfect 1st pers. sing. *nachiess,* I left, 1091; *nachess,* I have left behind, 1622.

Imperative, *n'cho,* leave it, let it alone, 797.

nadziā, he spoilt, see **NAZH**.

NGĀ, to take, to carry; *pochētr ngusth,* to take the fast, to keep the fast, 693, 1056, 1061, 1141, 1489; the following forms occur in the sentences :—

Infinitive, *ngusth,* to take; *pochētr ngusth mōs,* the fast month, 1056; *ngusth dugā,* for carrying, 888, 898, 1557, 1567; *pochētr ngusth dugā zarur n'ess,* there is no necessity for fasting, 1061; *ngusth dugā,* from carrying, owing to carrying, 913; *pochētr ngusth dugā,* owing to fasting, 1489; *ngūsth,* to take, p. 42; *pochētr ngūstha-bá,* if one keeps fast, 1141; *ngūsth dugā,* in order to buy (to take), 566, 1116, 1177; *ngutesth,* to be taking; *pochētr ngutesth dugā,* owing to fasting, 693.

Verbal noun (used with the base *BAN,* to be able), *ngā,* to take, to carry, to lift, 330, 644, 656, 1187, 1296, 1297, 1349, 1650.

Present participle, *ngal*, taking, p. 42; *shū ngal*, information taking, a spy, 1665, 1723.

ngalā, taking; *p'putt lattrī ngalā*, on road property taking, a highway robber, 1188; *rangal*, taking; *p'putt lattri rangal*, a highway robber, p. 9; *ngāla-basa*, (who) is taking? (who) will take? 1458; *ngūllazzībā* (?), if thou art taking, p. 43.

gul (?), taking, in *puru-gul*, leave-taking, 36; see *pur*.

Conjunctive participle, *ngātī*, having taken, 474, 501, 638, 1369, 1505, 1555, 1594, p. 42; can often be translated 'having taken', 'with', 907, 1301, 1397; *ngāti*, having taken, 846; *ngatī*, having taken, 1258 (refers to the object of the sentence); *ngātī gyē*, having taken go, take away, 1145; also written *nātī*, 474; *ngātētī*, having been taking; *ngātētī giats*, taking bring, lead (my horse), 775.

Indefinite present 1st pers. plur. *ngāmabā* (?), if we take, p. 43; *ngāmish*, we take, p. 42.

2nd pers. plur. *ngār*, you take, p. 42.

Present 1st pers. sing. *ngānam*, I take, 1211, p. 42; *pochētr ngānam*, I keep the fast, 452.

2nd pers. sing. *nganj*, takest, p. 42.

3rd pers. sing. *ngann*, he carries, he takes, 1732, p. 42.

3rd pers. plur. *ngand*, they carry, they take, 573, p. 42; *nganda*, *ngandā*, are they taking? 1550.

2nd present 2nd pers. sing. *tū purū n'ngattam*, thou leave not takest from me (?), I have not given thee leave, 704.

3rd pers. sing. *ngatt*, he takes, p. 42.

3rd pers. plur. *na ngattett*, they do not carry, 1288.

Past tense 1st pers. sing. *ngūtā'm*, I took, p. 42; *ngūtambā*, if I took (?), p. 43.

2nd pers. sing. *ngūtā'sh*, thou tookest, p. 42.

3rd pers. sing. *ngūtā*, he took, 768, p. 42; *ngūtabā*, if he took, p. 43.

1st pers. plur. *ngūtāmish*, we took, p. 42.

2nd pers. plur. *ngūtār*, you took, p. 42.

3rd pers. plur. *ngūtā*, they took, p. 42; *ngūtabá*, if they took, p. 43.

Imperfect 1st pers. sing. *ngānazzam*, I was taking, p. 42.

2nd pers. sing. *ngānazzish*, thou wast taking, p. 42.

3rd pers. sing. *ngānazzī*, he was taking, p. 42.

1st pers. plur. *ngānazzamish*, we were taking, p. 42.

2nd pers. plur. *ngānazzār*, you were taking, p. 42.

3rd pers. plur. *ngānazzī*, they were taking, p. 24.

Perfect and pluperfect 1st pers. sing. *purū grosam*, I have taken leave, 37; *ngūtassī*, I have carried, 1298; *ngūtūssam*, I had taken, p. 42.

2nd pers. sing. *pur n'grussish*, hast not taken leave, 783; *ngūtūssish*, thou hadst taken, p. 42.

3rd pers. sing. *ngūtūssī*, *ngūtastai*, he had taken, p. 42; *ngutastai*, he has taken, 1163.

1st pers. plur. *ngūtūssamish*, we had taken, p. 42.

2nd pers. plur. *ngūtūssār*, you had taken, p. 42.

3rd pers. plur. *ngūtūssī*, *ngūtastai*, they had taken, p. 42.

Future 1st pers. sing. *ngālam*, I shall take, I shall bring, 1103, 1194, 1423; *ngālom*, I shall take, I shall hire, 661, p. 42.

2nd pers. sing. *ngālōsh*, thou wilt take, p. 42.

3rd pers. sing. *ngālā*, he will take, p. 42.

1st pers. plur. *ngāmá*, we shall take, p. 42; *n'ngāmá*, we will not carry, 513.

2nd pers. plur. *ngālr*, you will take, p. 42; *ngālrbá*, if you will take (?), p. 43.

3rd pers. plur. *ngālā*, they will take, p. 42.

Imperative 2nd pers. sing. *ngā*, take, carry, 1283, p. 43; used as a plural in 364; *tū nmēlī n'ngā*, don't take amiss, 1201.

3rd pers. sing. *ngālā*, let him take, p. 43.

1st pers. plur. *ngāmá*, let us take, p. 43.

2nd pers. plur. *ngār*, take ye, p. 43; *ngār*, take ye, 1458.

3rd pers. plur. *ngālā*, let them take, p. 43.

nigā, he has washed, p. 3; see **NINJ**.

nighōlā, he will set, p. 54, misprint for *nizhōlā*; see NIZHŌ.

nāh, adj., male, 675, 680, 682, p. 1; see **nai.**

noh, not, 43, 277, pp. 61, 62; see 1 **na.**

nijinistai, they are hiding, 1301; see NIZHI.

najiss, they have done damage, 541; see NAZH.

nakīrwa, subst., the seventh month of a year, p. 65.

NUKSĀ, to remove, to take away; the following forms occur in the sentences:—

Verbal noun, *nuksā n'bannam*, I cannot remove (the lock of the door, I cannot open it), 1303.

Past tense 3rd pers. sing. *nuksēyā*, he removed him, he turned him out, 1565.

Future 1st pers. sing. *nuksālam*, I will take away (his life), 1090.

3rd pers. sing. *nuksālā*, he will remove (you), turn (you) out, 1564.

Imperative 2nd pers. sing. *nuksā*, take away (the cloth), 1351; *na nuksāō*, don't take off (your clothes), 1461; *nuksāō*, remove, undo (the knot), 1578; cf. NACH.

nuksān, subst., damage; *biliuk nuksān krā*, (the wind) did much damage, 1414.

nāl, subst., a horseshoe, 1292 (nom. plur.).

nilē, nīlē, subst., lake, pond; *pa-nilē*, on the lake, on the water, 385; *inā p'nilē*, in this pond, 1272; *pa-nīlē*, in the lake, 755; *nilē tā*, on the pond, 1042.

noll, subst., a rush; *noll waron ettā*, rushes are visible, 1212; cf. **naruki.**

nilon, subst., the first month of a year, p. 65.

nalos, subst., trouble; *tū kā nalos biss*, what trouble has overtaken thee? 1554; *nālus-warī*, a man in trouble, a poor man; *nālus-warīān digar kuttett*, they oppress the poor, 1045; *naluz-wās*, trouble having is, he is a beggar, 140; *naluzo*, troubled, quiet, peaceful, 90.

nelus, subst., excuse; *tū kai nelus n'ess,* thou hast no excuse, 430; perhaps identical with *nalos,* 'thou hast no trouble.'

naluz, subst., trouble; *naluz wás,* he is troubled, a beggar, 140; see **nalos.**

naluzo, adj., troubled, quiet, peaceful, 90 (attribute); see **nalos.**

NAM, to send.

Past tense 3rd pers. sing. *namiā,* he has sent, 1258.

Imperative 2nd pers. sing. *namō,* send, 518, 1245, 1542, 1566.

nām, subst., name, 749 (nom.); *nom,* name, 1014; acc. *nom,* 905, 906 (plur.).

namāj, subst., prayer; *namāj kusth,* to say prayers, 1056, 1057, 1058, 1059, 1060, 1061; *namāj bibá,* when prayer comes, at the time for prayer, 101; *namāj biss,* prayer-time has come, the feast day after the fast month has come, 1047; *namāch wasā,* prayer day, Thursday, p. 65.

nmēlā, participle (?), changed, exchanged; *nmēlā kshī,* make it exchanged, exchange it, 242, 429 (*nmelā*); *nmēlī n'ngā,* do not take exchanged, do not take amiss, 1201.

non, numeral, nine, 478, p. 63.

nōn, subst., mother, 884, 985, 1086; *nūn,* mother, 456; *nōn's,* his mother, 971.

nanden, subst., the leg, 190, p. 59.

nang, adj., dirty, nasty; *inā ūgh nang ess,* this water is nasty, 909.

nūng, subst., a sinew; *iā kūr nūng,* the sinew of my leg, 1314.

NINJ, to wash.

Past tense 3rd pers. sing. *nigā,* he has washed, p. 3 (Abdul Hakīm Khān).

Imperative 2nd pers. sing. *ninjō,* wash, 1561, 1636; *nizhē,* wash, 267.

nanwṛī, subst., a headman, a governor, 575, 631.

napūṛ, subst., the half moon day, 878.

NAR, to weed; imperative 2nd pers. sing. *narē*, weed (the grass out), 1653.

narē in *yo narē*, one each, p. 14; cf. **narik.**

nāru, subst., cloud; nom. plur. *nāru*, 128, 268, 876, 1002, 1266, 1392, 1434.

nīr, adv., low down (in a valley), down stream, 1588, p. 60; *kālo nīr ess*, the fort is low down, 834; *S̲h̲trālo sta nīr ess*, it is down stream from Chitral, 146; *Nīrē Maroī*, Lower Maroi, 1590.

nuṛī, subst., butter, 218.

naṛgī, adv., separately, 1718; see **narik.**

nirgō, postposition, in front of, p. 60; *p'amu tā nirgo*, in front of the house, 386.

narik, adv., separately; *yō narik*, one by one, p. 64; *yo nirikē*, separate, p. 60; *yo niṛikē warī ks̲h̲ī*, make each word separately, speak one word at a time, speak distinctly, 1235; *eo naṛgī varī ks̲h̲ī*, speak one word at a time, 1718; *yo narē*, one each, p. 14.

naṛukī, subst., reed; *naṛukī drigrī yūs*, reeds and long grass, 1137; cf. **noll.**

nasib, subst., luck; *s̲h̲talē ī nasib n'azilabá*, perhaps to-me luck not-is-if, if my luck is bad, 436.

nis̲h̲ē, nis̲h̲ī, sit, see **NIZ̲H̲I.**

nis̲h̲ī, verbal noun from the base *NIZ̲H̲I*, sitting; *nis̲h̲ī amu*, a sitting house, a residence, a palace, 982.

nis̲h̲iā, sat, see **NIZ̲H̲I.**

nis̲h̲ēā, set, see **NIZ̲H̲Ō.**

NOS̲H̲, to swim; the following forms occur in the sentences:—

Verbal noun, *nos̲h̲, nōs̲h̲*, swimming; *nos̲h̲ kun na banam*, I cannot do swimming, I cannot swim, 1451; *nos̲h̲ kōṛ*, he swims, 498; *nōs̲h̲ kōṛ*, he swims, 1451; *nōs̲h̲ ko banam*, I can swim, 1452; *daz̲h̲-nos̲h̲ē n'banam*, I cannot swim with the hands, I cannot swim, 1452.

Conjunctive participle, (*daz̲h̲*)-*nojī*, swimming (with the hands), 1618.

nis̲h̲ēl, sitting; **nis̲h̲ilom,** I shall sit, see **NIZ̲H̲I.**

nishān, subst., a mark, 435; see **nizhān.**

nishīn, sitting, see **NIZHI.**

nishr, subst., front, priority; only used with the preposition *pa*; in this way is formed:—

(1) The ordinal number, *pa-nishr*, first, p. 64; *panishr stē ptibar*, first-from behind, second, p. 64.

(2) An adv., *panishr*, in front, previously; *koī samarij-bá panishr áo na pī*, when thou startest do not previously drink water, 1067; *panishar, panishār*, in front, ahead; *ē panishar bibá*, if one is ahead, goes first, 907; *panishār oss*, he came first, 487.

(3) A postposition, *p'nishr*, in front of, ahead of, 666; *p'nishar*, in front of, ahead of, p. 61; *panishr*, in front of, ahead of, 1107, 1143; in front of, in the presence of, 1373.

nashisth, to damage, to harm, see **NAZH.**

nishisth, to sit, see **NIZHI.**

noshpā, subst., a bird's beak; *marangatsē noshpā kai etsal*, what is in the bird's beak? 126.

nashtā, adj., stingy; *nashtā ass*, he is stingy, 917.

nashtontī, adv., surely, certainly, 350, p. 61.

nashtarwai, adv., in front, p. 60 (*nashtarwaí*); *nashtarwai bō*, be in front, go in front, 138, 506, 539; cf. **nishr.**

naskor, subst., the cheek, 245; *naskor tā*, in the cheek, 1403.

nasur, subst., nose, 930; *nasur tā atēr*, inside the nose, in the nostril, 931.

naswūr, subst., snuff; *naswūr kunam*, I take snuff, 1015; *nazor kolum*, I take snuff, 315.

nāti, having taken, 474; see **NGĀ.**

nōt, subst., dancing; *nōt kusth*, to do dancing, to dance, 322, 323.

n'utkor, not profit-making, useless, 761; see **utkor.**

nēits, numeral, nineteen, pp. 12, 63.

nottrē, adv., the day before yesterday, 1661, p. 60; cf. **attrī.**

nawōs, subst., a nephew, 918 (gen.).

NAZH, to spoil, to damage; the following forms occur in the sentences :—

Infinitive, *nashisth dugā̃*, in order to damage, for harming, 963.

Past participle, *nazhī*, spoilt; *tuch na zhī ett*, the tin spoilt goes, the tin is bad, 1522.

Past tense 3rd pers. sing. *nazhā*, (the water) has spoilt (my threshing floor), 1506; *nadziā*, (the wind) spoilt (the fruit), 162.

Perfect 3rd pers. plur. *najiss*, they have done damage, 547; cf. **NACH.**

nizhā, subst., an orchard, garden, 1711 (nom.); *nizhāo tā̃ chá*, the wall of the garden, 1627.

nizhē, wash, 267; see **NINJ.**

NIZHI, to sit; the following forms of this base occur :—

Infinitive, *nizhisth, nishisth*, to sit, p. 32; *ushp p'sir nizhisth*, to sit on horseback, to ride, 1173; *ushp sir nishisth dugā̃*, for riding, 1096; *nizhisthā*, (a seat) for sitting, 241, p. 15.

Verbal noun, *nishī*, sitting, residing; *nishī amu*, a residence, a palace, 982.

Present participle, *nishēl*, sitting, p. 32; *ushp p'tsir nishēl*, sitting on horseback, a rider, p. 9; *ushp p'sir nishel*, a rider, 1174; *nishīn*, sitting, 217, 235, p. 32; *nishīn azz*, he was sitting, he sat, p. 32; *nishin*, sitting, p. 15; *ushp p'tsir nizin ess*, (vultures) are seated on the horse, 1617.

Conjunctive participle, *nishītī*, having sat, p. 32.

Indefinite present 1st pers. plur. *nizhēmish*, we sit, p. 32.

2nd pers. plur. *nizhēr*, you sit, p. 32.

Present 1st pers. sing. *nizhēnam*, I sit, p. 32.

2nd pers. sing. *nizhenj*, thou sittest, p. 32.

3rd. pers. sing. *nizhēnn*, he sits, p. 32.

3rd pers. plur. *nizhēnd*, they sit, p. 32.

2nd present 3rd pers. plur. *nishittett*, (ducks) are sitting down, alight, 30.

Past tense 1st pers. sing. *nishiā'm*, I sat, p. 32.

2nd pers. sing. *nishiā'sh* (?), thou sattest, p. 32.

3rd pers. sing. *nishiā*, he sat, p. 32.

1st pers. plur. *nishiāmish*, we sat, p. 32.

2nd pers. plur. *nishiā*, you sat, p. 32.

3rd pers. plur. *nishiā*, they sat, p. 32.

Imperfect 1st pers. sing. *nizhinazzam*, I was sitting, p. 32.

2nd pers. sing. *nizhinazzish*, thou wast sitting, p. 32.

3rd pers. sing. *nizhinazzī*, he was sitting, p. 32.

1st pers. plur. *nizhinazamish*, we were sitting, p. 32.

2nd pers. plur. *nizhinazzār*, you were sitting, p. 32.

3rd pers. plur. *nizhinazzī*, they were sitting, p. 32.

Perfect and pluperfect 1st pers. sing. *nishinissam*, I have sat down, I have settled, I live, 814; *nizhēnassim*, I had sat, p. 32.

2nd pers. sing. *nizhēnassish*, thou hadst sat, p. 32.

3rd pers. sing. *nizhēnassī*, *nizhēnistai*, he had sat, p. 32.

1st pers. plur. *nizhēnassamish*, we had sat, p. 32.

2nd pers. plur. *nizhēnassār*, you had sat, p. 32.

3rd pers. plur. *nijinistai*, they have sat down, they are hiding, 1301; *nishīnistai*, (ducks) have alighted, 385; *kāchi na nizhīnistai*, nobody has settled, nobody has lived (there), 1581; *nizhēnazzī*, *nizhēnistai*, they had sat, p. 32.

Future 1st pers. sing. *nishīlom*, I shall sit, I shall stay, 990, p. 32; *nizhēlom*, I shall sit, p. 32; *nizhēlam-bá*, if I sit, p. 33.

2nd pers. sing. *nizhēlosh*, thou wilt sit, p. 32; *nizhēlazhbá*, if thou sittest, p. 33.

3rd pers. sing. *nizhēlā*, he will sit, p. 32; *nizhēlabá*, if he sits, p. 33.

1st pers. plur. *nizhēmá*, we shall sit, stay, 1159, p. 32; *nizhēlamishbá*, if we sit, p. 33.

2nd pers. plur. *nizhēlr*, you will sit, p. 32; *nizhēlrbá*, if you sit, p. 33.

3rd pers. plur. *nizhēlā*, they will sit, p. 32; *nizhēlabá*, if they sit, p. 33.

Imperative 2nd pers. sing. *nishē*, sit, stay, 17, 141, 236, 448,

507, 911; *ushp p'sir nishē*, sit on your horse, mount your horse, 885; *n'nishī*, do not sit, 448; *nizhē*, sit, remain, 1143, 1319, p. 33.

3rd pers. sing. *nizhá*, *nizhēlā*, let him sit, p. 33.

1st pers. plūr. *nizhēmá*, let us sit, 1438, p. 33; *nizhēmā*, let us sit, 1268.

2nd pers. plur. *nizhēlr*, sit ye, p. 33.

3rd pers. plur. *nizhēlā*, let them sit, they should remain, 1245, p. 33.

Causal verb, see **NIZHŌ.**

NIZHŌ, to cause to sit, to set; no forms of this verb occur outside the paradigm on pp. 54, 55. Those are:—

Infinitive, *nizhōsth*, to set, p. 54.

Present participle, *nizhōl* (?), setting, p. 54.

Conjunctive participle, *nizhōti* (?), having set, p. 54.

Indefinite present 1st pers. plur. *nizhōmish*, we set, p. 54.

2nd pers. plur. *nizhōr*, you set, p. 54.

Present 1st pers. sing. *nizhōnam*, I set, p. 54.

2nd pers. sing. *nizhōnj*, thou settest, p. 54.

3rd pers. sing. *nizhōnn*, he sets, p. 54.

3rd pers. plur. *nizhōnd*, they set, p. 54.

Present definite, *nizhāl-ezambá*, if I set; *nizhāl-ezishbá*, if thou settest; *nizhāl-ezībá*, if he sets, if they set; *nizhāl-azamish-bá*, if we set; *nizhāl-ezrbá*, if you set, p. 55.

Past tense 1st pers. sing. *nishēā'm*, I set, p. 54.

2nd pers. sing. *nishēā'sh*, thou settest, p. 54.

3rd pers. sing. *nishēā*, he set, p. 54.

1st pers. plur. *nishēāmish* (?), we set, p. 54.

2nd pers. plur. *nishēr*, you set, p. 54.

3rd pers. plur. *nishēā*, they set, p. 54.

Imperfect 1st pers. sing. *nizhōnazzam*, I was setting, p. 54.

2nd pers. sing. *nizhōnazzish*, thou wast setting, p. 54.

3rd pers. sing. *nizhōnazzī*, he was setting, p. 54.

1st pers. plur. *nizhōnazzamish*, we were setting, p. 54.

2nd pers. plur. *nizhōnazzăr*, you were setting, p. 54.

3rd pers. plur. *nizhonazzī*, they were setting, p. 54.

Pluperfect 1st pers. sing. *nizhōnassam*, I had set, p. 54.

2nd pers. sing. *nizhōnassish*, thou hadst set, p. 54.

3rd pers. sing. *nizhōnassī*, he had set, p. 54.

1st pers. plur. *nizhōnassamish*, we had set, p. 54.

2nd pers. plur. *nizhōnassăr*, you had set, p. 54.

3rd pers. plur. *nizhōnassī*, they had set, p. 54.

Future 1st pers. sing. *nizhōlom*, I shall set, p. 54.

2nd pers. sing. *nizhōlosh*, thou wilt set, p. 54.

3rd pers. sing. *nizhōlă* (wrongly printed *nighōlă*), he will set, p. 54.

1st pers. plur. *nizhōlmá*, we shall set, p. 54.

2nd pers. plur. *nizhŏlr*, you will set, p. 54.

3rd pers. plur. *nizhōlă*, they will set, p. 54.

Imperative 2nd pers. sing. *nizhăō*, set, p. 55.

3rd pers. sing. *nizhălă*, let him set, p. 55.

1st pers. plur. *nizhămmá*, let us set, p. 55.

2nd pers. plur. *nizhōr*, set ye, p. 55.

3rd pers. plur. *nizhălă*, let them set, p. 55.

nizhān, subst., a mark, 847; *pror nizhăn*, a wound mark, a scar, 1239 (nom.); *manchī bmṛisht nizhăn*, the mark of the corpse of a man, a scarecrow, 1241 (acc.); *tarja nizhăn na jănṛamīsh*, we do not understand the marks of the scales, 1238; *zhī nishăn*, a black mark, 435.

nazor, subst., snuff, 315; see **naswür.**

nazush in *măr nazush ba*, wrong instead of *mărn-azush-bá*, see **MĂR.**

P

pa, ba, bi, preposition, in, on, towards, p. 62. The initial consonants of this preposition interchange in such a way that *b* is used before words beginning with soft consonants, and *p* before words beginning with a vowel, a hard consonant, *w*, or a nasal. The vowel *a* is often dropped so that only the consonant remains, p. 62; *pa, ba*, is used alone or in connexion with postpositions, such as *stē, tā*, etc. Adjectives and other words qualifying the governed noun are placed before the preposition; thus, *ikya ba-grom*, in that village, 227; *inām ba grām*, in that village, 62; *parē Kato bi-grām*, in each Bashgali village, 1609; *Shāwalo ba-do*, on the Shāwal pass, 155. This preposition sometimes forms a kind of adjectives from nouns; thus *manchi bmrisht nizhān*, a mark, a figure, of the corpse of a man, a scarecrow, 1241; *p'pshu lattrī*, in-jungle thing, jungly thing, wild, 1689; *p'putt lattrī rangal*, on-road thing taking, a highway robber, p. 9; *zīn p'tsir bazisnâ*, saddle on-top cloth, saddle cloth, 1220, etc. The following examples occur in the sentences :—

(1) *ba, b'*—

ba biā azhind, they throw into seed, they winnow, 1697.

ba Bilan n'ai, do not go to Chitral, 1525; *ba Bilian puttan* (i.e. *putt-tā*), on the road to Chitral, 947.

ba ben, in the forest, 129.

ba bdī, in the mind; *babdī ess*, it is in the mind, (I) think, consider, 672 (*bapdī*), 962, 1324; *iā babdī n'azziā*, it has not been in my mind, I have not remembered, 1148; *Imrā bapdī azhalā*, let it be in God's mind, may God bear it in mind (and give me punishment), 526; *bibidī bibā*, it comes in my mind, I hope, 424; *bibdī kshām*, I make in my mind, I think, 810; *tū bibidī n'kshonjī tū kāktī zaronlosh?* thou in-mind not-makest, thou what-having-done wilt-learn? you don't make an effort, how can you learn? 408; *babdī kashītī gijjī kshī*, in-mind having-made speech make, think before you speak, 1494; *babdī kshātam*, I think, I suspect, I fear, 1042, 1179, 1441 (*kshâtam*).

b'bhīm, in the ground, on the ground, 1190, p. 62; into the ground, 1230.

b'brunz-o pagūro, on the polo ground, 1074.

b'bzār stē, from in the bazaar, from the bazaar, 558.

badistē, from the sky, 396; see **badist.**

bado, on the hill, in the pass, 124, 125, 155, 263 (*bado n'ai banam*, I cannot go upon, climb, the hill), 542, 648, 818 (*iyē bado bilugh opigná ess*, it is very lofty on this mountain), 1345 (*bado putr*, to cross the pass), 1619; *badō*, on the hill, in the pass, 952, 1167, 1397 (*inā badō bilugh uchangiest assā barwai bōr ngātī badō ū n'bann*, it is very steep on this hill, the coolies cannot go up on the hill having taken their loads), 1436, 1520; *badu*, on the pass, 509; *bado pagur*, at the foot of the hill, on the pass, 502; *badō pagūrā*, at the foot of the pass, 991; *badō pagiōr*, to the foot of the hill, 1189; *bado pagior yūr*, down to the foot of the hill, down hill, 1208; *bado ptiwar esth*, to go behind the hill, to cross the pass, 1023; *bado shai*, on the top of the mountain, 795, 1147 (*bado shai putrē*, to cross on the top of the hill, to cross the pass); *badō shai*, on the top of the mountain, of the pass, 827, 920, 955, 1331, 1589, 1671; *bado shaiē stē*, from the crest of the hill, 299; *bado shai tā dumī bilugh digar bā*, on the crest of the hill the wind was very bad, on crossing the pass the wind was very bad, 303; *badō stē*, from on the hill, from the hill, 848, 1169; *badō yūr*, down hill, 1535.

b'doi, baduī, to the arm, to hand; *toch baduī goī*, a bullet came to hand, I found a bullet, 213; *iā b'doī giats*, bring to my hand, produce, 1076.

b'dū tā torē̃, in front of the door, 1399.

badūr, at a distance, far off, p. 60; *badūr n'nishī*, do not sit far off, 448; *Dryus badūr ess*, Dryus is far off, 449; *Shogoi Gairath tīch badūr asth*, Shogoth and Gairath are equally far, 447; *badur samiritsam*, I am off on a journey, 733.

badūrē, down below, 654; *badeore manchī*, man of the plains, 658.

b'dristān, in the garden, 580; *b'darestā*, in the garden, 976; *b'durestān*, in the garden, into the garden, 547, 896; also abbreviated *baristā*, in the garden, 896.

b'dosh, in the hand, 829; *b'dush*, in the hand, 1239;

pachanwarī b'dus͟h gwā, he fell into the hands of the enemy, 1440; *ī b'dus͟ht tā*, from my hand, 1343.

b'diwerr, on the sandbanks, 1227.

b'gol, in a valley, 363 (in a district), 365, 471, 520 (*emá b'gol manchī*, a man of our valley), 1599.

b'gul, in a valley, 27, 871, 1168, 1196, 1418 and 1698 (*inā b'gul ḍo*, the water in this valley, of this river), 1515 (on the river bank); *b'gul dugā*, for the river, 1223; *b'gul tā*, in the valley, in the river, 1183, 1124.

baglao (i.e., *ba gul-ḍo*), in the water of the valley, in the stream, 1421; *b'gul-o*, in the stream, 1421; *baglo*, into the river, 463; *b'gol-o*, into the river, 463.

b'garak piu butt, the water reaches up to the neck, 1183.

bagrām, in a village, 62, 343, 358, 425, 545, 546, 609, 1092, 1155, 1156, 1163, 1433, 1581, 1650, p. 11; *bgrām*, in a village, 1521; *bigrām*, in a village, 1609; *bagrom*, in a village, 227, 289, 368, 427, 450, 549, 609, 686, 823, 845, 914, 1050, 1256 (to the village). The *r* of *grām*, *grom*, is sometimes transposed before the *g*; thus, *bargām*, p. xii; *bragom*, 232, 322; *Kām-bragām*, to the Kām village, to Kāmdēsh, 1519; postpositions are added in *inā bagrām mī*, in this village, 1159; *emá bagrom p'mich*, in our village, 428; *b'grām p'mich*, in the village, 1249; *bgrom stē*, from the village, 552.

bajit, in the body; *borī na bajit jarend*, the loaves are not digested in my body, I have dyspepsia, 393.

bizul, in the jungle, as an ambuscade, 1126; *b'zul stē*, from the jungle, 1429; *bzul tā*, in the jungle, 1485; *b'zul lattrī*, a thing of the jungle, wild, 1689.

biznor (?) *ūm*, we will climb on the hill, 262. This word does not perhaps contain the preposition at all.

bazira, in the chest, in the body; *iā bazira padrē ū prētt*, in my body the bowels (?) go out, I have diarrhœa, 349.

(2) *pa*, *p'*—

p'ochen ettett, they come to eyes, come to light, 890.

p'amu, pamu, in the house, 70, 71, 76 (*p'amū*), 237, 251, 493, 646, 674, 804, 925 (to the house), 1051, 1053, 1094, 1157, 1191, 1192, 1357, 1481, 1622, 1671 (to the house), 1720. Post-positions are often added; thus: *p'amu attā*, into the house, 420, 423; inside the house, 706; *pamu bē*, out of the house, 974; *pamu begū*, out of the house, 964; *p'amu barēla*, around the house, 70; *pamu pabanūr*, round the houses, 1202; *p'amu ptior*, behind, round, the house, 762, 772; *p'amu stē*, from in the house, out of the house, 410, 1568; *p'amu stē*, out of the house, 517; *pamu stha*, from the house, 160; *p'amu tā nirgo*, in front of the house, 386; *p'amu tār*, at the house, 1413; *p'amu torē*, near the house, 844; *pamu tawarē*, near the house, 958; *pamu torē tā*, near the house, 1562.

p'apshē, at the mill, 590.

p'ashī, in the mouth, 174.

piash, in the morning; *dalkiē piash*, to-morrow morning, 1048; *starak piash*, to-day in the morning, 1038.

poshtre, on the hill, 499.

p'dotre, at the ford; *p'dotre patrem*, let us ford the river, 519.

p'banūr, around; see separately.

pa chuk wīk, up to the chest, 1183.

pa chukru, on the ribs, 1169.

pachūr, around, p. 61; *pachūrē*, around, 640; see separately.

pachur, to the edge (of the precipice), 407; *pachūrē*, to the edge (of the precipice), 1181.

pagior, below; see separately.

p'khur, on the top of, postposition used with nouns preceded by *ba*, *pa*; thus, *bado p'khur*, on the top of the hill, 648.

p'kār, in the business; *p'kār ess*, it is wanted, 1204; *pkār assā*, it is wanted, 1557.

p'kōr, to the ear; with *gusth* or *ēsth*, to go, it means to come to the ear, to be heard, 511, 635, 642, 830, 871, 911, 1104, 1510, 1615; *p'kor ajholam*, I will whisper into your ear, 649; *p'kōr vrī kshī*, into-ear word make, whisper, 1680.

p'krūm, to the roof, 753; *pkrum*, on the roof, 1191, 1198.

pkūsh (*pgūro*), (under) the willow-tree, 1035.

p'mich, p'mij, p'mish, in the midst of, between, among, in. The vowel of *mich mij, mish*, is sometimes long and sometimes short, and sometimes also nasalized. The final consonant can also be *jh* or *zh*, and *j* or *jh* can be followed by a *ū*. The word is sometimes used alone; thus, *p'mijhū pēṭang*, cut it in the middle, cut it in two pieces, 820. Usually, however, it is a postposition, sometimes used alone, and sometimes in connexion with the preposition *ba, pa*, and the postposition *tā̃*. The following instances occur:—

p'mich, p'minj, between, p. 61; *p'mijhū*, in the midst of, p. 62; *p'mijhū*, in the middle, 820; *ikīē p'mish andhaṛ ess*, it is dark within it, 1485; *shiok p'mij*, in the midst of my vegetables, 1653; *ikīā p'mīsh*, among them, 1137; *amnio p'mīch*, among them, 42; *amshiā p'mish*, amongst themselves, 901; *shto manjīān p'mish*, amongst the four men, 1279; *yā p'mich*, between yourselves, 364; *Argich Konisht p'mijhu*, between Urgūch and Ranbār, 523; *Shdrāl Bruz p'mij*, between Chitrāl and Brōz, 151; *Badakshā Shdrāl stē p'mich sirtā̃*, the frontier in the midst of Chitrāl to Badakhshān, between Badakhshān and Chitrāl, 540; *Dryus stē Bruz p'mizhu*, between Drōsh and Bruz, 1200; *Dryus stē Gairath p'mīsh*, in the midst from Drōz to Gairath, between Drōz and Gairath, 1184. Most commonly this postposition can be translated in, into; thus, *ďo p'mich*, in the water, into the water, 284, 1227; *inā undsďo p'mish*, in this spring, 1379; *bugdrē p'mish*, in the hollow, 667; *Dryus p'mīsh*, in Drōz, 897; *ē gujar p'mīsh*, in one day, 1214; *inā kudūm p'mīsh*, in this business, 1160, 1701 (*p'mish*); *poi p'mīsh*, into the river, 954. The governed noun often takes the preposition *ba, pa*, or the postposition *tā̃*; thus, *bgrām p'mich*, in a village, 1249; *bagrom p'mich*, in a village, 427, 428; *p'shai p'mīju*, on my head, 949; *pson p'mich*, in the woods, 1122; *ptul p'mich*, in my field, into my field, 287, 379, 1241 (*p'mīch*); *ďō tā̃ p'mich*, into the water, 1316.

p'miok, on the face, 1239; *p'miōk*, before, p. 61.

p'mino, on the forehead, 521.

panoī (?), in front, p. 60; *panoi bō*, lead you, 776, 777.

panilē, on the water (or, probably, on the lake), 385; *panīlē*, in the lake, 755; *inā p'nilē*, in this pond, 1272.

p'nishr, in front of, ahead of, 666; *p'nishar*, in front of, p. 61; *panishr*, in front of, ahead, 1107, 1143; *panishr*, in front of, in the presence of, 1373; also used as an adverb, *panishăr oss*, he came in front, he came first, 487; *ē panishar bibá*, if one is ahead, if one goes first, 907; *koī samarijbá panishr âo na pī*, when you start do not previously drink water, don't drink water previously to starting, 1067; used as an adjective *panishr* is the ordinal number, first, p. 64; *panishr stē ptibar*, first from behind, second, p. 64.

p'pshu, in the hills, hilly; *p'pshu lattrī*, a thing of the hills, wild, 1689.

pa ptī, on the back, 370; from the back, 375; *p'ptī tā*, on the back, 1377; from the back, 1583.

p'pott, on the road, 1548; *p'putt*, on the road, 352, 1164, 1188, 1245, 1629, p. 9; *pa putt*, on the road, 1548; *p'putt tā*, on the road, 1233; *p'putt tār*, on the road, 1541.

p'sē, in the year; *starak p'sē*, this year, 441, 1668.

pshai, on the head, 630; *p'shai p'mīju*, on the head, 949; (*pshai*, head, accusative *pshaio*, p. 5, is probably incorrect).

p'shur tā, in the swamp, 1443.

pshtarak, in this day, to-day, p. 60; *pstarak*, to-day, 734, p. 60; *p'starak stē*, henceforth, 646; *pstarak wīk*, up to now, 657.

p'sōn, in a forest, 825; *pson p'mich*, in the woods, 1122.

p'sir, on the top of, on, 885, 887, 1173, 1174, 1319, 1625; *p'tsir*, on the top of, on, 948 (*ptsir*), 1220 (*zīn p'tsir bazisná*, saddle cloth), 1617, 1725 (*tū dusht p'tsir*, on, around, your arm), p. 9; *ushp p'tsir stē*, from on a horse, from a horse, 1488 *p'tsiru*, on, 233.

ptol tā, into the pot, 1052.

ptul, in the field; *ptul kudūm*, work in the field, agriculture, 22; *ptul pachūrē*, around the field, 640; *ptul p'mich*, in, into the field, 287, 379, 1241 (*p'mtch*); *ptul tã*, in the field, 596, 717.

ptul, what is in the field, crop, 302, 515, 604, 817, 870, 895, 1133, 1420, 1428.

patos, on the shoulder, 1297.

pitshun, in war, 1630, 1631.

pa wott, on a stone, 745.

1 **pā**, to go, 4, 223, 378, 451, 454, 773, 1545, p. 58; see 1 **PRE.**

2 **pā**, subst., a keg; *tin pā*, kegs of spirits, 1201 (nom. pl.).

pá, with the foot, 737, 738; see 4 **po.**

1 **pē**, to go, to walk, 1062, 1708; see 1 **PRE.**

2 **pē**, subst., charcoal, 243 (nom. sing.).

1 **PI**, to drink; the following forms occur in the sentences:—

Infinitive, *pisth*, to drink, 1041, 1466, 1643; *pisth dugã*, for drinking, 1641; *pits*, to drink, 1041.

Present participle, *pin* (?), drinking; *tin pin*, he (is) drinking spirits, he (is) a drunkard, 383, see present; *pig* in *do pig*, water-drinking, thirsty, 377, 866, 1041; *do pik*, thirsty, 1496.

Present 1st pers. sing. *do pīnam*, water drinking-am, I want to drink, 313.

3rd pers. sing. (?), *pin*, drinks; *tin pin*, he drinks wine, he is a drunkard, 383; see Present participle.

2nd present 3rd pers. sing. *pitt*, he drinks, 377.

Past tense 2nd pers. sing. *kui pibá*, when you have drunk, 1480.

Future 1st pers. sing. *pilom*, I will drink, 866.

Imperative, *pī*, drink, 378, 874, 1067, 1442.

Causal verb 2nd pers. imperative, *piāo*, make (the horses) drink, 1555.

2 **pi**, adj., ripe; *iã zhum n'piess*, my buckwheat is not ripe, 209; cf. **PAG.**

piu, river, see 3 **po.**

1 **PO,** to make, to finish; the following forms occur in the sentences:—

Infinitive, (*sūī*) *postho,* in order to make (a bridge), 465.

Future 1st pers. plur. *yō epamá,* we will make a water channel, 717.

2 **po, pō,** adj., last; *pō-ē mōs,* last month, 767; *po sē,* last year, p. 9; *pō sē,* last year, 503, 623, 648, 794, 850, 895, 1208, 1240, 1289, 1316, 1488, 1635, p. 60; *pō,* last year, 121, 390, 442, 470, p. 60; *poē,* last year, 331; cf. 2 **pū.**

3 **po, pō,** subst., river, water; nom. *piu,* river; *b'garak piu butt,* the river reaches to the neck, 1183; loc. *po-ē,* into the river, 284, 381, 797; *pō-ē,* into the river, 228; *poī,* into the river, 439, 444; *poiē,* on the river, 498; *poi-ē,* into the water, 438; oblique, *pō chiwol tā,* near the river, 1226; *pōē pār,* across the river, 992; *poi p'mīsh,* into the river, 954; *poi pēr,* on the opposite bank of the river, 965; *poi tā,* in the water, 297; *poh pēr,* across the river, 7.

4 **po, pū,** subst., foot, leg; nom. *pū,* leg, 1328; *kōwar po pūptā,* I broke my left leg, 1208; *pá visth,* to strike with the foot, to kick, 737, 738.

poh, foot, footprint; *poh ōsh kusth,* to trace one's footsteps, 1541, 1542.

1 **pū,** foot, see 4 **po.**

2 **pū, pu,** adv., behind (?), down; *sū pu-ēlī,* sun down-going, sunset, p. 65; *sū pu-ēlī pōr,* sunset way, west, 402 (*puēli*), 403, p. 65; *sū pū ettann pōr,* west, 1662, p. 65 (*puettan*); *sū pū esth pōr,* west, 1663, p. 65 (*puesth*); *sū na pū-gess,* the sun has not gone down, has not set, 1266; perhaps also contained in *sū pinjebā,* when the sun goes down, at sunset, 672, 1437.

3 **pū,** hurt, damaged (?), used with *PRE*; thus, *ushp wōtt tā pū prētī piltiss,* my horse fell, having become damaged against a stone, having stumbled by knocking against a stone, 1427; *po pū-ptā,* my leg was damaged, I broke my leg, 1208; *zān pa*

wott pū-pta, my knee was hurt on a stone, a stone hurt my knee, 745.

pubi, subst., screaming; *pubī kutt,* she is screaming, 1247, 1281.

p'banūr, adv., around, p. 60; postposition, around, p. 61; *emā pamu pabanūr,* (go) round by our house, 1202; *grām pabunor azhō,* surround the village, 1439.

pchu, subst., leg, 1276 (acc. plur.).

1 **PACH,** to cook, to roast; the following forms occur in the sentences:—

2nd present 3rd pers. sing. *pachitt,* he is cooking, 1001.

Imperative 2nd pers. sing. *pachō,* roast, 1185.

2 **pach,** cloth; *pach kaṛ,* cloth-making, a weaver, 1652 (nom. plur.); cf. **puch.**

pōch, numeral, five, 15, 554, 1056, 1061, 1158, 1186, 1191, 1214, pp. 12, 63; also written *puch,* 5, p. 63; *pōj,* 99, 406, p. 63; *pōnj,* 969, 1058.

pōch vissī, fivescore, hundred, 1419, 1439; *pōch wissī,* hundred, 1515; *pōch witsī,* hundred, p. 63; *pōnj watsa,* hundred, 69; *pōch witsī ptiwar* (?), hundredth, p. 64.

puch azār, five four-hundred (lit. thousand), two thousand, p. 63.

puch, subst., a duster, a cloth; *puch mish,* (wipe) with a cloth, 1699; cf. 2 **pach.**

pachuk, to the chest, 1183; see **chuk.**

pachukru, on the ribs, 1161; see **chukru.**

pachen, subst., a thread, 1138 (acc.); *pachēn,* a thread, 1504.

p'ochen, to the eyes, 890; see **achẽ.**

pachanwari, subst., an enemy; nom. *pachan warī,* 88, 459, 651, 938, 1092, 1209, 1386, 1647; *pachanwarī,* 344, 416, 667, 872, 962, 1126, 1137, 1309, 1383, 1600; *pachanwarī,* 1246, 1662; acc. *pachan warī,* 336, 1347; *pachanwarī,* 574, 1308; agent, *pachan warī,* 423, 1429, 1509; *pachanwarī,* 1358, 1610; *pachanwarīẽ,* 1079; gen. *pachan warī,* 490; *pachanwarī,* 780,

1037, 1143, 1440; *pachanwarī-ē*, 779; oblique, *pachan warī tā*, than the enemy, p. 9; *pachanwarī tā*, than the enemy, 417; *pachan warī tā*, to the enemy, 1319 (indirect object); *pachanwarīān tā*, to the enemy, 1367 (dative of possession); *pachanwarī manchī*, the enemy, 779, 1144.

pachur, pachūrē, to the edge, see **chur.**

pachūr, postposition, around, p. 61; *pachūrē*, around, 640.

pachūr, adj., right, 611, 1509; see **pachūtr.**

pichis, fifteen, see **pachits.**

pochētr, subst., the Musalman fast, 453 (acc.), 1047, 1413 (nom.); *pochētr ugusth*, to keep fast, 452, 693, 1056, 1061, 1141, 1489.

pachūtr, adj., right; used as an attribute, 1166, 1176, 1634; *pachūtr dus pōr ī*, go right-hand way, turn to the right, 1563; also written *pachūtr*, 1696; *pchūtar*, 791, and *puchūr*, 611, 1509.

pachits, numeral, fifteen, p. 63; also written *pichis* in *mōs pichis oss bitī dū oss dī biss*, moon fifteen days having become two days also have become, it is two days after full moon, 879.

pachwâts, numeral, seventy, p. 63 footnote (from the collection of the Rev. Worthington Jukes).

1 **paidā,** subst., profit, advantage; *kā paidā na bunn*, there is no advantage, 1595; *kā paidā na ess*, nothing comes of it, it is in vain, 1597; the word is probably borrowed from Pers. *fāidah*, and it is also written *faidā*; thus, *kai faidā butt*, what is the use of? 1141.

2 **paidā,** participle, produced; *paidā bolā*, it will be produced, 1170; *kā paidā na butt*, nothing is produced, nothing grows, 1723; *paidā kshī*, produce, 1075.

padrē, subst., bowels (?); *padrē ū prētt*, bowels (?) out go, I have diarrhœa, 349, 350.

padri, subst., an axe, 718 (acc.); *peḍṛī*, an axe, 1234 (nom.); gen. *petdrī dōṇ*, the handle of the axe, 615; cf. **pets.**

PAG, to get ripe, to ripen; the following forms occur:—

Infinitive, *pagasth dugā*, (the season) for getting ripe, 1250.

Past participle, *pagī*, ripened, ripe; *na pagī*, unripe, 1700 (attribute).

Present 3rd pers. *pagann*, ripens, ripen, 1179, 1435.

Perfect 3rd pers. *pagistai*, has ripened, is ripe, 1178.

n'piess (?), is not ripe, 209; cf. 2 **pi.**

Future 3rd pers. *na pagalā*, (the fruit) will not ripen, 1179.

pig in *đo pig*, thirsty, see 1 **PI.**

PUG, to wrap; *pugusth dugā sharr*, a cloth for wrapping (round your arm), 1726.

pgoluk (?) in *komlik pgoluk*, the golden oriole, 970.

pagior, pagiur, pagur, pagūrā, pagūro, adv. and postposition, down; under, underneath; (1) adverb, down; *ptul pagūr tāristai*, it beat down my crops, 1420; (2) postposition, *pagiōr*, *pagior*, to the foot of, down; *bado pagiōr*, down the hill, 1189; *bado pagior yār*, down to the foot of the hill, downhill, 1208; *pagiōr*, *pagūr*, under, p. 62; *ktol pagiur*, under the belly, 1445; *anī pagur*, under it, 1350; *prusht tā pagūr*, underneath the bed, 1576; *bado pagur*, at the foot of the hills, on the pass, 502; *badō pagūrā*, at the foot of the pass, 991; *pkūsh pgūro*, under the willow-tree, 1035; *pagār*, upon, p. 62; *b'brunzo pagūro*, on the polo ground, 1074; *tār pagur*, than; *wetsā tār pagur palāno lesst buttett*, tauchins are better than pubboos for snow (?), 1083; cf. **kūr.**

pūgess, has gone down, has set, 1266; see 2 **pū.**

poh, river, 7; see 3 **po.**

poh, footprint, 1541, 1542; see 4 **po.**

pōj, five, see **pōch.**

pujil, subst., a sheet, 1286 (acc.).

pkhul, adj., rotten, 1198 (predicate); *pkhulā*, rotten, 1254; cf. **pakkhel.**

p'khur, on the top of, 648; see **khur.**

pakhtalā, subst., a pass, 988, 989 (nom.); oblique, *pakhtalē tā*, (more difficult) than the pass, 989.

pakkī, subst., a flea, 493 (nom. plur.).

pakkhēl, adj., addled; *aikūn pakkhēl biss,* the egg is addled, 9.

p'kār, in need, needed, wanted, see **kār.**

p'kōr, in the ear, to the ear, see 1 **kor.**

p'krum, on the roof, see **krum.**

pēkshē, imperative, put; *ikiē tā dusht na pēkshē,* do not put the hand on it, do not touch it, 1537. The final *kshē* is probably the imperative of the base *KR.*

pkūsh, at the willow-tree, 1035; see **kūsh.**

palā, subst., watching, guarding; *palā krō,* do guarding, watch over, 1638; *chī palā krolam,* how much guarding shall I do? how many guards shall I put? 1639; *palā kullā,* they will do guarding, 1640; *palē tā torē,* near the sentry, 1327.

piōl, postposition, instead of, p. 62; *zū piōl,* instead of milk, 1052.

pōl, subst., ploughshare, 1033 (nom.).

pol, pul, subst., corn, grain; acc. *pol,* 1075; *pul,* 578, 590, 613, 811, 1365; *gum pul,* wheat grain, 1668 (nom.); *dros ăli pul ess,* the grapes (of my garden) are a big grain, are very big, 580.

puēli, down going, see 2 **pū.**

pālak (?), subst., spinach, 1372 (acc.).

pēlik, adv., at last, 768, p. 60.

palal, palol, subst., earth, clay; nom. *palol,* earth, clay (for making bricks), 257; acc. *palal,* earth, 1381; *palol,* earth, 400; oblique, *palol tā,* on the earth, on the ground, 593; *palelsht,* clods of earth, 265 (acc.).

palāno, subst., tauchins, a kind of boots, 1083 (nom.).

PALANG, to move, to walk; the following forms occur in the sentences:—

Infinitive, *piliangsth wokt biss,* it is time to march, to start, 1461; *piliangsth wēl tā,* at the time of marching, on the march, 1342; *pilingasth tā,* from marching, from journeying, 1084; *zīm tā pilingisth watsā,* pubboos for journeying over the snow 1082; *pilingstett tā shaiyē,* before marching, 405.

Verbal noun, *piliang tâ*, marching in, while marching, 745; *buru palangen na batt*, he cannot go downhill, 307; *pilingēn na batt*, he cannot go, p. 58.

Conjunctive participle, *pilingdī ann*, having walked comes, he is returning, 1624; *pilingitī ēllom*, having walked shall return, I shall return, 1734; *pilingītī atsalam*, I shall return, 1161.

2nd present 3rd pers. sing. *palangett*, (the dog) goes up and down, keeps watch, 71; (the horse) is moving, is rolling (on the ground), 593; *n'palangett*, he cannot walk, 288.

Past tense 1st pers. sing. *pilingam*, I walked about, 641.

3rd pers. sing. *n'palengā*, he has not moved, he is not walking up and down, 1626.

Perfect 1st pers. plur. *piliangsamish*, we have marched, 657.

Imperative, *palgā*, walk up and down, 70; *pilingiō*, walk about, 1480.

Causal verb, *pilangō*, to cause to walk; to succeed in using.

Infinitive, *ushp pilangōsth pott*, a path to make a horse go on, to take a horse, 992.

Verbal noun, *Bilian warī pilangon n'battam*, I cannot get the Chitrāli language to succeed, I cannot learn it, 781.

pelingiati, subst., the rafters of a house, 1115 (nom.).

pilir, adj., bay; *ushup pilīr ess*, the horse is a bay, 123.

palrāna, subst., the fourth month of a year, p. 65.

PILS, to rub, to polish.

Imperative, *pilsō*, rub, 1213.

PILT, to fall; the following forms occur:—

Infinitive, *piltisth*, to fall, pp. 18, 34; *b'bhīm piltisth dugà n'otē*, do not leave it to fall, to roll, on the ground, 1190.

Present participle, *piltil*, falling, p. 34; *piltalī ushp*, a falling, stumbling, horse, 679; *piltilī ushp*, a falling, stumbling, horse, p. 15; *piltil-tâ*, falling in, if he, they, fall, p. 35.

Conjunctive participle, *piltētī*, having fallen, p. 34.

Indefinite present 1st pers. sing. *piltim-dān*, if I fall, p. 35.

2nd pers. sing. *piltish-tâ*, if thou fallest, p. 35.

1st pers. plur. *piltēmá*, we fall, p. 34; *piltimish-tá*, if we fall, p. 35.

2nd pers. plur. *piltēr*, you fall, p. 34; *piltīr-dā*, if you fall, p. 35.

Present 1st pers. sing. *piltēnam*, I fall, p. 34.

2nd pers. sing. *piltanj*, thou fallest, p. 34.

3rd pers. sing. *piltann*, he falls, p. 34.

3rd pers. plur. *piltand*, they fall, p. 34.

Past tense 1st pers. sing. *piltiām*, I fell, 1208, 1260, 1535; *piltiā'm*, I fell, p. 34; *piltam*, I fell, 201.

2nd pers. sing. *piltiā'sh*, thou fellest, p. 34.

3rd pers. sing. *piltiā*, he fell, 352, 462, 463, p. 34.

1st pers. plur. *piltiāmish*, we fell, p. 34.

2nd pers. plur. *piltiār*, you fell, p. 34.

3rd pers. plur. *piltiā*, they fell, p. 34.

Imperfect 1st pers. sing. *piltinassam*, I was falling, p. 34.

2nd pers. sing. *piltinassish*, I was falling, p. 34.

3rd pers. sing. *piltinassī*, he was falling, p. 34.

1st pers. plur. *piltinassamish*, we were falling, p. 34.

2nd pers. plur. *piltinassār*, you were falling, p. 34.

3rd pers. plur. *piltinassī*, they were falling, p. 34.

Perfect and pluperfect 1st pers. sing. *paltiosam*, I fell, 828; *piltiosam*, I slipped, 360; *piltissam*, I fell, 1728; I had fallen, p. 34.

2nd pers. sing. *piltissish*, thou hadst fallen, p. 34.

3rd pers. sing. *piltiss*, he has fallen, 712; he fell, 1426, 1427; *piltissī*, he had fallen, p. 34.

1st pers. plur. *piltissamish*, we had fallen,, p. 34.

2nd pers. plur. *piltissār*, you had fallen, p. 34.

3rd pers. plur. *piltissī*, *piltistai*, they had fallen, p. 34.

Future 1st pers. sing. *piltilom*, I shall fall, p. 34.

2nd pers. sing. *piltilosh*, wilt fall, 407, 1181, p. 34.

3rd pers. sing. *piltilā*, he will fall, p. 34; *piltalī*, (the horse) is falling, will fall, 341, 1425; see present participle.

1st pers. plur. *piltilēmá*, we will fall, p. 34.

2nd pers. plur. *piltēlr*, you will fall, p. 34.

3rd pers. plur. *piltilā*, they will fall, p. 34.

Imperative 2nd pers. sing. *piltī*, fall, p. 35.

3rd pers. sing. *piltilā*, let him fall, p. 35.

1st pers. plur. *piltilēmá*, let us fall, p. 35.

2nd pers. plur. *piltēlār*, fall ye, p. 35.

3rd pers. plur. *piltilā*, let them fall, p. 35.

Causal verb, *piltō*, to cause to fall, to throw down.

Infinitive, *piltōsth*, to cause to fall, p. 56; *piltāosth*, to cause to fall, p. 18.

Present participle *piltōl* (?), causing to fall, p. 56.

Conjunctive participle, *pilteīti*, having caused to fall, p. 56.

Indefinite present 1st pers. sing. *piltōmbá*, if I cause to fall, p. 57.

2nd pers. sing. *piltōshbá*, if thou causest to fall, p. 57.

3rd pers. sing. *piltōbá*, if he causes to fall, p. 57.

1st pers. plur. *piltōmá*, we cause to fall, p. 56; *piltōmabá* (?), if we cause to fall, p. 57.

2nd pers. plur. *piltōr*, you cause to fall, p. 56; *piltōrbá*, if you cause to fall, p. 57.

Present 1st pers. sing. *piltōnam*, I cause to fall, p. 56.

2nd pers. sing. *piltōnanj*, thou causest to fall, p. 56.

3rd pers. sing. *piltōnn*, he causes to fall, p. 56.

3rd pers. plur. *piltōnd*, they cause to fall, p. 56.

Past 1st pers. sing. *piltēā'm*, I caused to fall, p. 56.

2nd pers. sing. *piltēā'sh*, thou causedst to fall, p. 56.

3rd pers. sing. *piltēā*, he caused to fall, threw down, 1679, p. 56; *piltiāo*, (a stone) knocked (me) over, 1169.

1st pers. plur. *pilteāmish*, we caused to fall, p. 56.

2nd pers. plur. *pilteār*, you caused to fall, p. 56.

3rd pers. plur. *piltēā*, they caused to fall, p. 56.

Imperfect 1st pers. sing. *piltōnassam*, I was causing to fall, p. 56.

2nd pers. sing. *piltōnassish*, thou wast causing to fall, p. 56.
3rd pers. sing. *piltōnassī*, he was causing to fall, p. 56.
1st pers. plur. *piltōnassamish*, we were causing to fall, p. 56.
2nd pers. plur. *piltōnassār*, you were causing to fall, p. 56.
3rd pers. plur. *piltōnassī*, they were causing to fall, p. 56.
Pluperfect 1st pers. sing *piltōssum*, I had caused to fall, p. 56.
2nd pers. sing. *piltōssish*, thou hadst caused to fall, p. 56.
3rd pers. sing. *piltōssī*, *piltōstai*, he had caused to fall, p. 56.
1st pers. plur. *piltōssumish*, we had caused to fall, p. 56.
2nd pers. plur. *piltōssār*, you had caused to fall, p. 56.
3rd pers. plur. *piltōssī*, *piltōstai*, they had caused to fall, p. 56.

Future 1st pers. sing. *piltōlom*, I shall cause to fall, p. 56.
2nd pers. sing. *piltōlosh*, thou wilt cause to fall, p. 56.
3rd pers. sing. *piltōlā*, he will cause to fall, p. 56.
1st pers. plur. *piltōlemmá*, we shall cause to fall, p. 56.
2nd pers. plur. *piltōlōr*, you will cause to fall, p. 56.
3rd pers. plur. *piltōlā*, they will cause to fall, p. 56; *piltōlabá*, if they cause to fall, p. 57.

Imperative 2nd pers. sing. *piltāō*, cause to fall, p. 57.
3rd pers. sing. *piltōlā*, let him cause to fall, p. 57.
1st pers. plur. *piltōmmá*, let us cause to fall, p. 57.
2nd pers. plur. *piltōlār*, cause ye to fall, p. 57.
3rd pers. plur. *piltōlā*, let them cause to fall, p. 57.

pulatan, subst., a widow, 1688 (nom.).

pāmē, adv., afterwards, p. 60.

p'amu, in the house, to the house, see **amu.**

p'mich, p'mij, p'mijhū, p'mish, in the midst of, in, between, see **mij.**

P'MISHT, to forget.

Present participle, *p'mishtal*, forgetting, forgetful, 525.

Conjunctive participle, *parmarshtētī*, having forgotten, forgetfully, 951; *pmishtētī*, having forgotten, having left, 1051, 1053.

Past 1st pers. sing. *p'mishtiā*, I have forgotten it, 524.

Perfect 1st pers. sing. *p'mishtiss*, I forgot, 1065; *p'mishtiassī*, I forgot, I left, 1076.

Future 1st pers. sing. *p'mishtalom*, I shall forget, 526; *n'pmishtēlam*, I will not forget, I will not pardon, 984.

p'mizhu, between, see **mij.**

pano, subst., a trough or aqueduct; *pano ão piāo*, make them drink water of the trough, 1555. The word is perhaps a compound containing the preposition *pa*.

panoī, adv., in front, p. 60; *panoī bā*, be in front, lead, 776, 777.

pin, drinks, in *tin pin*, he is a drunkard, 383; see **PI.**

pōnduk, subst., a boil, 67, 68 (nom.).

pondr, adj., round; *pondr n'kshīr*, do not make it round, 1384; *pandur asht*, they are round, 1201.

pondrik, subst., a bullet, 1323 (nom.); *tapkiē pondrik prōr bissishā*, wast thou wounded by the bullet of a gun? 1724; cf. **pondr, purik.**

painji, subst., in *grish painjī*, the time from 3 p.m. till evening, p. 64.

pōnj, numeral, five, 69, 969, 1058; see **pōch.**

pinjebā, when goes down; *sū pinjebā*, at sunset, 672, 1437; cf. 2 **pū.**

p'nilē, panilē, on the lake, see **nilē.**

panishr, first, in front, see **nishr.**

p'pshu, of the forest, see **pshu.**

p'apshē, at the mill, see **apshē.**

p'ptī, on the back, see **ptī.**

pūptā, was damaged, see 3 **pū.**

p'pott, p'putt, on the road, see **pott.**

1 **PRE,** to go, to come. The following forms of this verb occur in the sentences:—

Infinitive, *sū chī presth wokt tā*, sun up going time in, at sunrise, 1436.

Verbal noun, *pā*, to go, 4, 223, 378, 451, 454, 773, 1545, p 58; *pē n'balosh*, thou canst not go (across the precipice), 1062;

pē botten na bann, she cannot walk on, 1708 (perhaps *p'pott en na bann,* she cannot go on the road).

Conjunctive participle, *wōtt tā pū prētī,* stone on damaged going, having stumbled against a stone, 1427.

Indefinite present 1st pers. sing. *ō paṛimdā,* when I arrived, p. 4.

2nd pers. sing. *kai Chandrāl pariẕhbā,* when thou goest to, reachest, Chitrāl, 1563; *tū preishtā,* when arrivedst, p. 4.

1st pers. plur. *Shdrāl promā,* we shall reach Chitrāl, 1437.

Present 3rd pers. sing. *sū na prēnn,* the sun does not come, 1598.

Second present 3rd pers. sing. *prētt,* is going, 829; *agol prētt,* rain comes, there is rain, 302, 1117; *zīm prētt,* snow falls, 1117; *padrē ū prētt,* bowels (?) out come, there is diarrhœa, 349, 350; *mōs n'waṛon prētt,* moon not seen goes, the moon is not visible, 876.

pretann (?), he is going, 583; *wāī prēttett,* wind comes (into my right arm), I get rheumatism, 1166; *agal pittabā,* when rain falls, 1118; *zīm pittabā,* when snow falls, 1120.

Past 3rd pers. sing. *ptā,* came; *agol ptā,* rain has fallen, 441; *indrish ptā,* there was an earthquake, 401; there were earthquakes, 1717; *zīm ptā,* snow fell, 380, 399, 443.

sū ptī, the sun has come, has risen, 1180; time of the sun's appearance, p. 65.

po pū-ptā, my leg damaged went, I broke my leg, 1208; *zān pa wott pū-pta,* my knee was hurt against a stone, 745.

praptā, (a stone) hit (me), 1169; *preptū,* (a bullet) hit, 1323; *kuī wōtt praptawā,* when the stone hit, 1260; *Bastī tā preptī,* (the gun) hit Basti, 3.

Perfect 3rd pers. sing. *inḍrōn chī ptess,* a big rainbow has come, there is a big rainbow, 1121.

Future 3rd pers. *prāl,* he will go, will arrive, 889; *prēlā,* will come, will fall, 1002, 1533; they will come, they will alight, 1042.

Imperative, *partsī,* go, get thee gone, 1275; *prēts,* come, 519, p. 58; go, get out, 646, 1249; *prets,* go, p. 23; *pṛēts,* go on, 559. The above forms are probably derived from more than one base.

2 **PRE**, to give.

Infinitive, *prēsth*, to give, pp. 18, 44; *presth dugā*, for giving, 1393.

Present participle, *prēl* (?), giving, pp. 18, 44.

Conjunctive participle, *prētī*, having given, 1023, pp. 18, 44; *mārī prētī-giats*, money having given fetch, buy, 219, 558 (*maṛī p. gats*); *maṛī prētī ngūsth*, to buy, 566.

Indefinite present 1st pers. sing. *prom*, I will give, 607, p. 18; *prōm*, I will give, p. 44.

2nd pers. sing. *prēchī*, givest, 84.

1st pers. plur. *prēmá*, we give, p. 44.

2nd pers. plur. *prẽr*, you give, p. 44.

Present 1st pers. sing. *prēnam*, I give, pp. 18, 44.

2nd pers. sing. *prēnjī*, givest, p. 44; *prēnjībá*, if givest, 555; *n'prenjībá*, if dost not give, 185.

3rd pers. sing. *prēnn*, gives, 590, p. 44.

3rd pers. plur. *prēnd*, they give, p. 44; they give, they take (silk to Peshāwar), 1310; *n'prend*, they will not give, produce (eggs), 409.

Second present 3rd pers. *prētt*, he gives, he is in the habit of giving, 726, 1131, p. 44; *prett*, he gives, 192; *prēttett*, they give, 995, 1163.

Past tense, *ptā*, gave, p. 18.

1st pers. sing. *ptā*, I gave, I have given, 420, 556, 841; *ptā'm*, I gave, p. 44; *ptā'sh*, I gave to thee, 1149, p. 11; *pta'sh*, I gave to thee, 85.

2nd pers. sing. *ptā*, gavest, hast given, 1068, p. 12; *ptā'sh*, gavest, p. 44; *ptā'm*, gavest, hast given, to me, 794, 1148, 1474, p. 11.

3rd pers. sing. *ptā*, he gave, pp. 12, 44; *tutī ptā*, he gave, made, excuses, 768; *ptā'm*, he gave to me, p. 12; *ptā'sh*, he gave to thee, p. 12; *ptā'sh-ī*, he gave to thee, 1016, pp. 12, 17.

1st pers. plur. *ptāmish*, we gave, p. 44; *ptā*, we gave to him, p. 12; *ptā'sh*, we gave to thee, p. 12.

2nd pers. plur. *ptâr*, you gave, p. 44; *ptā*, you gave to him, p. 12; *ptā'm*, you gave to me, p. 12.

3rd pers. plur. *ptā*, they gave, they gave to him, pp. 12, 44; *ptā'm*, they gave to me, p. 12; *ptā'sh*, they gave to thee, p. 12.

Imperfect 1st pers. sing. *prēnazzam*, I was giving, pp. 18, 44.

2nd pers. sing. *prēnazzish*, wast giving, p. 44.

3rd pers. sing. *prēnazzī*, he was giving, p. 44.

1st pers. plur. *prēnazzamish*, we were giving, p. 44.

2nd pers. plur. *prēnazzār*, you were giving, p. 44.

3rd pers. plur. *prēnazzī*, they were giving, p. 44.

Perfect and pluperfect 1st pers. sing. *ptā-sh-uss*, I gave to thee, 969; *ptāssiam*, I had given, pp. 18, 44.

2nd pers. sing. *ptās'm*, hast given to me, 678, p. 11; *ptāssish*, hadst given, p. 44.

3rd pers. sing. *ptās'm*, he gave to me, 318, 677; *hukm ptāsam-ish* (i.e. *ptāsa-mish*), he gave order to us, 1221; *ku ptese-sh*, who has given to thee, p. 4 (Abdul Hakīm Khān); *ptāssī*, he had given, p. 44; *ptēss*, he gave, 1038; *ptess*, he gave, p. 3; *ptossī*, he has given, has sent, 1259; *ptustai*, he had given, p. 44.

1st pers. plur. *ptāssamish*, we had given, p. 44.

2nd pers. plur. *ptāssār*, you had given, p. 44.

3rd pers. plur. *ptāssī*, *ptustai*, they had given, p. 44.

Future 1st pers. sing. *prēlom*, I will give, 44, 194, 479, 554, 703, 933, 1029, 1063, 1077, 1149, 1164, 1210, 1477, pp. 11, 18, 44; *kai n'prēlom*, I will not give anything (to you), I will not be friends, I will not forgive, 919; *wā prēlom*, I will give back, return, 1161; *prēlombá*, if I give, pp. 18, 45.

2nd pers. sing. *prēlosh*, wilt give, p. 44; *prēloshbá*, if thou givest, p. 45.

3rd pers. sing. *prēlā*, he will give, p. 44; *prēlābá*, if he gives, p. 45.

1st pers. plur. *prēmá*, we will give, p. 44; *prēlomishbá*, if we give, p. 45.

2nd pers. plur. *prēlr*, you will give, p. 44; *prēlōrbá*, if you give, p. 45.

3rd pers. plur. *prēlā*, they will give, p. 44; *prēlābá*, if they give, p. 45.

Imperative 2nd pers. sing. *prē*, give, 176, 395, 811, 812, 1009, 1049, 1245, 1333, pp. 18, 45; *ptē*, give, 811; put, 1230, 1350; *n'ētē*, don't give, 811; cf. **TE.**

3rd pers. sing. *prēlā*, let him give, p. 45.

1st pers. plur. *prēmá*, let us give, p. 45.

2nd pers. plur. *prēlr*, give ye, p. 45.

3rd pers. plur. *prēlā*, let them give, p. 45.

PAR, to irrigate.

Infinitive, *parēst dugā*, in order to irrigate, 717.

pãr, pãr, postposition, beyond, on the other side, p. 61 (*pãr*); *Dryus pãr*, on the other side of Droz, 153; *pōē pãr*, across the river, 992; *áo tã pãr*, across the river, 1702; apparently used as an adverb in *sū pãr lang biā*, the sun has got to the other side, the sun has set, 274; the postposition is also written *pẽr*, p. 61; thus, *poi pẽr*, on the opposite bank of the river, 965; *poh pẽr*, across the river, 7; *áo tã pẽr*, on the other side of the water, 1305; *ushtiwā tã pẽr ī*, go to the other side of, cross, the precipice road, 1181.

1 **pãṛ,** subst., a ravine, *ikyē pãṛ*, in that ravine, 1126.

2 **pãṛ,** in *dashpãṛ purstha*, (flat) like the handback (?), 492.

para, parē, parī, adj., filled, full; *áo para kshī*, make water filled, fill it with water, 474; *palol parakshī*, fill it with earth, 400; *áo parē kaṛsā zū parē kaṛsā*, has water or milk been filled in? is it full of water or milk? 544; *dūm parē assā*, it is full of smoke, 1339; *dros parē ktī*, having filled with grapes, 1259; *rits parē kshī*, fill it with barley, 1216; *áo parī kshī*, fill it with water, 1052; cf. **puru.**

parē, adj., each, 282, 395, 1609 (attribute); *parē wōr*, each time, always, 654, p. 60.

paṛē, subst., a verandah, 1605 (acc.).

PEṚ, PEṬ, to split, to cut, to break; the following forms of this base occur in the sentences:—

Infinitive, *pochētr peṛisth*, to break the fast, 453; *peṭasthā*, for cutting (meat), 746; doubtful is *pēṭegā* in *hukm ptās'm tū duī pēṭegā*, he gave me order to cut thy hand off, 318.

Conjunctive participle, *pṛētī*, having cut off, 1329; *pēṭī briss*, having cut he took away, 1087; *peṭī giats*, cut and bring, 1035; *peṭṭi giats*, cut and bring, 480.

Present 2nd pers. sing. *peṛinjībā*, if thou breakest, 187.

3rd pers. sing. *basnā na peṭann*, (the scissors) will not cut the cloth, 1243.

Past 3rd pers. *dātik peṛiā*, he lost his wager, 1620; *peṭiā*, he cut off (my hand), 612; *pēṛiā*, they cut down (the vine-trees), 1610.

Perfect 3rd pers. *peṛiss*, has cut, cut, 308, 1314, 1509; *pēṭess*, he cut off, 317; *peṭiss*, he cut off, 1703; *pēṭiss*, he broke, 371.

Future 1st pers. sing. *peṭalam*, I shall cut, 1487.

Imperative 2nd pers. sing. *peṭā*, break, 179; *pēṭē*, break up, 784; *peṭṭ*, break, 13; *peṭan*, cut, 316; *pēṭang*, cut, 820; cf. *pēṭegā*, to cut, 318.

Passive verb formed from a verbal noun ending in *n*, by adding forms of the bases *I* and *GŪ*, to go.

Past tense 3rd pers. *peṛingā*, was broken, 1488; *peṛongā*, was broken, 202, 1194; *māṛī paṛengī*, my stick broke, 201; *māṛī peṛongī*, the stick is broken, pp. 2, 59.

peṭangā, is broken, 633; *peṭangwā*, (the skin) is cut, is come off, 641; is broken, 723, p. 59; *pēṭangwā*, (my lips) are split, 809; *pēṭangawā*, is broken, 66.

Perfect and pluperfect 3rd pers. *peṛingess*, is broken, was broken, 869, 1535; *pṛētangess*, is broken, 49; *peṭangess*, is broken, 198, 307, 615, 860, 1033, 1138, p. 59; *peṭang ess* (i.e. *peṭan gess*), is broken, 196, 599; *pēṭanguss*, is broken, 240; *peṭangūs*, is broken, p. 59; *peṭṭangus*, is broken, 175; *peṭṭ ons*, is broken, 189 (*tōtt kūr peṭṭ ons*, my father's leg is broken, my father has broken his leg).

Future 3rd pers. *peṛeng ēlā* (i.e. *peṛen gēlā*), will break, 1190; *peṭang ellā* (i.e. *peṭan gellā*), will break, p. 59.

peṭanlā,(the leg) will be broken, p. 59; *peṭanlō*, will break, 190.

n'pṛēliss, (the wood) will not break, 946.

pelingiatī peṭanless, the rafters will break, are weak, 1115.

kuī wīk pochētr na peṭlon ennā, until the fast is not broken, till the end of the fast. 1413.

Another passive participle or noun is *pitzen*, broken; thus, *pitzen biss*, (my box) is broken, 188; *n'pitzen kshē*, do not make it broken, do not break it, 186.

pēr, across, beyond, see **pār.**

Pir Khān, subst., Pir Khān, name of a man, 647 (gen.); *Pirkhān*, 790 (nom.).

pōr, subst., direction, way, side; *akī pōr kāst azzā*, how is the far side? 1331; commonly used in adverbial expressions; thus, *akī pōr*, that way, in that direction, 1647, 1648, p. 61; *akīā pōr*, that way, 1476; *anī pōr*, this way, in this direction, 1476, 1647, 1648, 1662, p. 61; *inā pōr*, this way, p. 61.

sū chunzlī pōr, sunrise way, east, 402, 403, p. 65; *sū puēlī pōr*, sunset way, west, 402 (*puēli*), 403, p. 65; *sū puesth pōr*, sunset way, west, p. 65; *sū pū esth pōr stē*, from the west, 1663; *sū puettan pōr*, west, 1662, p. 65; *prusht pōr*, Great Bear way, north, p. 65.

Very common as a postposition, in the direction of, towards, 1162, 1310, 1476, 1538, 1539, 1563, 1566, p. 62.

Note *dū ē pōr*, twofold, p. 64; *duts ē pōr*, tenfold, p. 64.

ē pur bittā tā, one direction becoming in, at the junction of (two rivers), 728.

poṛ, subst., a leaf, 93, 787 (nom. plur.); *stūm poṛ bā*, tree leaves became, the trees have become green, 587.

pur, purū, subst., leave, permission; *iā pur n'grussish*, I did not give thee leave, 783; *purū grosam*, I have got leave, I am allowed to depart, 37; *tu purū n'gattam*, I do not give thee leave, 784; *tū iā koī purū kolaibá*, when thou wilt give me leave, 1003.

iā puru-gul bosellā, I leave-getting (?) shall be? do you allow me to depart? 36.

puru, adj. or subst., full, fullness; in *iā mēsh puru kshī,* me with fullness make, help me, 644; *mrai puru kshī,* make bricks full, complete, 193; *sang warī puru-ketī walach,* thou sayest every word full making, in full manner, quite true, 1110; cf. **para.**

PARCH, to burn.

Second present 3rd pers. sing. *parchitta,* it burns, 729; *na parchitt,* it does not burn, 243.

Causal verb imperative 2nd pers. sing. *parchiō,* cause (the fire) to burn, blow (the fire), 166; 3rd pers. sing. *parchiālā,* let him light (the fire), 806; cf. **PASH.**

paṛchē, subst., a polo-stick, 1400 (acc.); *parchev mishisth,* to play polo, 1039, 1040.

parochi, adv., all night, 590.

puruchkāl, adv., early this morning, 356.

purdū, purdik, subst., an old person, an old man; nom. *purdū,* an old person, 1352; *purdik,* an old man, 163, 1209; an old woman, 1654, 1708; acc. *purduka,* the old man, 221; gen *purdikē,* of an old man, 1727.

purugul, leave to depart, see **pur, purū.**

paṛhī, subst., a book, 1129; a letter, 1258, 1557, 1729.

PURJ, to recognize, to know, to think; the following forms of this base occur in the sentences:—

Conjunctive participle, *purjītī,* having known, purposely, intentionally, 1091.

Present 1st pers. sing. *purjanam,* I am sure, I think, 531, 593, 1121, 1246, 1313, 1326, 1335, 1523; *lesst purjanam,* I well know, I am quite sure, 1615; *purjonam,* I think, 1122, 1137, 1203, 1281, 1425 (I am sure), 1495; *purjinam,* I think, 1254, 1437; *purzhanam,* I think, I expect, 1323; *purzanam,* I am sure, 983.

Second present 1st pers. sing. *purjitam,* I am sure, 916; I understand, 1235; *purjītam,* I think, 1080; *purjitom,* I think, 839; *purjittam,* I suppose, 1212.

2nd pers. sing. *purjitish-ā*, doest thou think? 1105, p. 17.

Perfect (?) 1st pers. sing. *tū warī n'purjosam*, I cannot understand (lit. I did not understand) thy speech, 854.

parkī, adv., alone; *parkī edsam*, I am left alone, 456; *parkī afzoshā*, art thou coming alone? 38; *parkiē*, alone, apart; *parkie ats*, come here apart, 59.

purik, subst., a bullet, 778 (acc. plur.); probabl only a various writing of **pondrik**.

Pirkhān, Pir Khān, see **Pir**.

puruketī, truly, 1110; see **puru**.

paṛōl, subst., a vulture, 1617 (nom. plur.).

prāl, prēlā, will come, see 1 **PRE**.

prēlā, will give, see 2 **PRE**.

pṛēliss, it will break, see **PEṚ**, passive.

prama, adj., small; *amu prama ess*, the house is small, 1334; see **parmen**.

prēmā, we will give; **prom**, I will give, see 2 **PRE**.

promā, we will come; **parimdā**, when I arrived, see 1 **PRE**.

parmen, adj., small, little; used as an attribute, 154, 309, 1469; and as a predicate, 1493, 1499; also written *prama*; thus, *amu prama ess*, the house is small, 1334; *parmen* is also used as a noun, child, boy, 529 (nom.). In this sense it more commonly takes a form ending in *r*; thus, *parmēr*, boys, 1026 (nom.); *paṛmiṛ*, boy, 1439 (acc.); *paṛmire dugē*, for a boy, for a child, 512; see **parmenstuk**.

parmenstuk, adj., small, little; used as an attribute, 512, 971, 1185 (*inā parmenstuk mazharlē ano*, this little ram's flesh, this bit of ram's flesh), 1218, 1333, 1389, p. 8; and as a predicate, 660, 765, 892, 941, 1295, 1296, 1335, 1405, 1428, 1668.

parmenstuk amu, a small house, a trap in the shape of a small house, 1543.

parmenstuk zira mēsh, with small heart, small-hearted, 658

prampor pradzī, subst., a crupper, 307 (nom.).

parmarshtētī, forgettingly, see **P'MISH**.

prang, adj., English, 418 (attribute).

praptā, hit, 1169; **preptā,** hit, 1323; **preptī,** hit, 3; **praptawā,** (when) it hit, 1260; see 1 PRE.

paṛṛ, subst., an apple; said to be a feminine, pp. 1, 7 (*āllī paṛṛ*, a big apple); cf. *ālī paṛṛ ess*, it is a big apple, 607; nom. *paṛṛ*, apple, 61; apples, 472, 727; acc. *paṛṛ*, 576 (apples); *paṛṛo*, 986 (apple); *paṛṛ pish*, apple flower, 1242.

prōr, subst., a blow, a wound; *aklī prōr biss*, to my skin a wound became, my skin is broken, 252; *gotr tā prōr biss*, on my upper arm there has been a blow, 1449; *tū kā prōr bissish, tarwoch prōr bissizhā, tapkiē pondrik prōr bissishā?* to thee what wound became-to-thee, sword wound became-to-thee, gun bullet wound became-to-thee? how wast thou wounded, by a sword or a bullet? 1724; also written *pṛoṛ* in *pṛoṛ kṛiss*, made a wound, wounded, 1358; *pror nizhan*, a wound mark, a scar, 1239.

puṛṛ, subst., smallpox; *tu puṛṛ bissiā*, to-thee smallpox was? hadst thou smallpox, 1335; *tu puṛṛ mugho ashī*, to-thee smallpox face-in is, thy face is pitted with smallpox, 1335.

Parish, subst., Asmār, name of a place, 1134 (to Asmār), 1153 (nom.); *Parish pōr*, Asmār way, towards Asmār, 1162; *Parish stē*, from Asmār, 1139.

parōsh, subst., the belt of a sword, 1455 (nom.).

prushkurē (?), in *giāmī prushkurē*, without thinking anything about it, 1456; lit. perhaps nothing having done asking, without asking any questions; cf. Sanskrit *praś*, to ask.

preishtā, when arrivest, p. 4; see 1 PRE.

prishta, adj., like, often added to substantives in order to form a kind of adjective, p. 9; the word occurs in several slightly different forms.

prishta, in *Morī divarā prishta wishtar*, broad like the Morī plain, 1022.

prishtha, like, p. 9.

purst, like to, p. 61 (adv.).

pūrst, like; *wrigī pūrst manchī*, a fox-like man, a clever man, 1368.

pristha, like; *ikīā argrū pristha argrū*, a beam equal to this beam, 422.

pirstha, like, p. 9; *vrikī pirstha manchī*, a fox-like, cunning, man, 333.

pursth, like; *ikyē basnā pursth*, like this cloth, 1225.

purstha, like; *ē purstha ai*, they are one like, they resemble each other, 1151; *ī purstha katī*, having done like me, like me, 1174; *dashpar purstha diwar*, flat like the hand, 492; *gum purstha manchī*, a rose-like, rosy-faced, man, 1197; *Mirak purstha shtār*, a thief like Mirak, 1721; *matsī purstha*, like a fish, 1451; *wrikī purstha*, fox-like, clever, p. 9.

1 **prusht**, subst., the constellation of the great bear, 128 (nom.); *prusht pōr*, towards the great bear, north, p. 65.

2 **prusht**, subst., a bed, 134, 135 (acc.); *prusht tā pagūr*, underneath the bed, 1576.

prushtī, a bed; *prushtī tā*, in the bed, 210.

pariss, subst., dust, 387 (nom.).

parēst, to irrigate, see **PAR.**

prētī, having come, see 1 **PRE.**

prētī, having given, see 2 **PRE.**

prētī, having cut off, see **PER.**

partī, subst., a part, portion; *inā parro trē partī kshī*, make this apple into three parts, 986.

partsī, go away, 1275; see 1 **PRE.**

prets, prēts, go, come, 519, 559, 646, 1249, pp. 23, 58; see 1 **PRE.**

prots, subst., a spot, 662, 1377 (nom. plur.).

PREZH, to sit down.

Imperative 1st pers. plur. *yū prezhamā*, let us sit down, let us take breath, 1332.

parizhbā, when thou arrivest, see 1 **PRE.**

purzhanam, purzanam, I think, I am sure, see **PURJ.**

psā (?), in *barpachargo psā* (?), hang (my pugri on the branch of that tree), 616.

paisa, subst., a pice, money; nom. *paisa,* money, 1044; acc. *paisa,* a pice, money, 933, 1257; also written *paiz,* in the nominative, 875, and in the accusative, 590, 841, 933.

p'sē, in the year, see **sē.**

psio, adj., sharp, 1036 (predicate).

PIS, to lose.

Past tense, *psiā,* was lost; *Tajī sarīen Bilian sarī psiā,* by the Badaks̲h̲s̲h̲ānī army the Chitrāl army was lost, the Badaks̲h̲s̲h̲ānī army defeated the Chitrāl army, 334; *sang keti psiā,* all (the goats) having said were lost, I lost all (the goats), 827; *bōr psiā,* his load was lost, 828.

Perfect 3rd pers. sing. *psess,* he has lost, 736; *psetai,* he lost, p. 2.

pis, piz, adj., lost; *pis-billiē,* let it be lost, do not try to save it, 1111; *piz bā,* (the goats) were lost, strayed, 1417; *piz biā,* is lost, 114, 381; *do p'mic̲h̲ pizbiā,* he was lost, drowned, in the water, 284; *piz bilā,* let it be lost, let it alone, 797. Also *puz*; thus, *puz biss,* is lost, 1237; (the horse) is lost, ran away (from the stable), 1385; *puz bistai,* (the goats) have been lost, 1217; cf. **piss.**

p'shai, p'shaio, on the head, see **s̲h̲ai.**

PS̲H̲Ī, to grind; the following forms of this base occur :—

Infinitive, *ps̲h̲īsth,* to grind, p. 50.

Present participle, *ps̲h̲īl* (?), grinding, p. 50.

Conjunctive participle, *ps̲h̲etī,* having ground, 501; *ps̲h̲ītī,* having ground, p. 50.

Indefinite present 2nd pers. sing. *ps̲h̲īs̲h̲bá* (?), if thou grindest, p. 51.

3rd pers. *ps̲h̲ībá,* if he, they, grind, p. 51.

1st pers. plur. *ps̲h̲īmis̲h̲,* we grind, p. 50; *ps̲h̲īmis̲h̲bá,* if we grind, p. 51.

2nd pers. plur. *ps̲h̲īr,* you grind, p. 50; *ps̲h̲īrbá,* if you grind, p. 51.

Present 1st pers. sing. *pshīnam*, I grind, p. 50; *pshīnambá*, if I grind, p. 51.

2nd pers. sing. *pshīnj*, grindest, p. 50.

3rd pers. sing. *pshinn*, he grinds, p. 50.

3rd pers. plur. *pshīnd*, they grind, p. 50.

Past tense 1st pers. sing. *pshā'm*, I ground, p. 50.

2nd pers. sing. *pshā'sh*, thou groundest, p. 50.

3rd pers. sing. *pshā*, he ground, p. 50.

1st pers. plur. *pshāmish*, we ground, p. 50.

2nd pers. plur. *pshăr*, you ground, p. 50.

3rd pers. plur. *pshā*, they ground, p. 50.

Imperfect 1st pers. sing. *pshīnazzam*, I was grinding, p. 50.

2nd pers. sing. *pshīnazzish*, wast grinding, p. 50.

3rd pers. sing. *pshīnazzī*, he was grinding, p. 50.

1st pers. plur. *pshīnazzamish*, we were grinding, p. 50.

2nd pers. plur. *pshīnazzăr*, you were grinding, p. 50.

3rd pers. plur. *pshīnazzī*, they were grinding, p. 50.

Perfect and pluperfect 1st pers. sing. *pshīssam*, I had ground, p. 50.

2nd pers. sing. *pshīssish*, thou hadst ground, p. 50.

3rd pers. sing. *pshīssī*, he had ground, p. 50.

1st pers. plur. *pshissī*, we have been grinding, 590; *pshīssamish*, we had ground, p. 50.

2nd pers. plur. *pshīssăr*, you had ground, p. 50.

3rd pers. plur. *pshīssī*, they had ground, p. 50.

Future 1st pers. sing. *pshīlom*, I shall grind, p. 50.

2nd pers. sing. *pshīlosh*, thou wilt grind, p. 50.

3rd pers. sing. *pshīlā*, he will grind, p. 50.

1st pers. plur. *pshīmá*, we shall grind, p. 50.

2nd pers. plur. *pshīlr*, you will grind, p. 50.

3rd pers. plur. *pshīlā*, they will grind, p. 50.

Imperative 2nd pers. sing. *pshī*, grind, p. 51; *pshio*, grind, 868.

3rd pers. sing. *pshīlā*, let him grind, p. 51.

1st pers. plur. *pshīmá*, let us grind, p. 51.

2nd pers. plur. *pshīlăr*, grind ye, p. 51.

3rd pers. plur. *pshīlā*, let them grind, p. 51.

1 **PSHU,** to sleep; the following forms of this base occur in the sentences:—

Verbal noun, *pshu*, sleeping; *pshu wēl*, time for sleep, 700; *pshuikan*, to sleep (?); *pshuikan n'ūtan*, do not let me sleep, 881; *pshuik*, to sleep; *pshuik n'battam*, I cannot sleep, 1013; *pshōn*, to sleep, in *pshōn n'battam*, I cannot sleep, 882.

Present participle, *pshuik*, inclined to sleep, drowsy, lazy; *pshuik oss*, thou art lazy, 701.

Conjunctive participle, *pshutī*, sleeping, having slept; *Mehar pshutī n'yett*, the Mehtar sleeping not-goes, cannot sleep, 928; *pshuttī gussā*, sleeping went, he fell asleep, 1261.

Perfect 2nd pers. sing. *n'pshusiā*, didst thou not sleep, 1733.

3rd pers. sing. *pshuiss*, he is asleep, 102; *pshuissā*, he was asleep, 1327.

2 **pshu,** subst., hill; *p'pshu lattrī*, a thing of the hills, a wild animal, 1689 (translated "a thing of the woods").

pashī, hill, mountain, 886 (nom.); *pashī tă*, on the hill, 845, 950.

pashu, hill, 618 (nom.); *pashū tă*, on hills, 1174.

askā pashuī tă, on that hill, 668 (translated "in that forest").

pazhun, the spur of a hill, 1382 (nom.).

PASH, to light.

Infinitive, *pashisth*, to light, p. 18; *pashiōsth dugă*, for lighting (the lamp), 942.

Conjunctive participle, *pashētī*, having lit, 1536.

Imperative, *pashāo*, relight (the fire), 1142; cf. **PARCH.**

pāsha, in *badi pāsha*, the fifth month of a year, p. 65.

pashē, adv., like, as; *dū manchīon pashē drgr*, as long as two men, 1193.

p'ashī, in the mouth, 174; see **ashi.**

pashi, pashu, hill, see 2 **pshu.**

PAOSH, POISH, PŪSH, to be accomplished, to be finished.

Past 3rd pers. sing. *paoshā*, is over, 1047; *tū koi kudūm poishabā*, when thy work has been finished, when you have finished work, 479; *koī kudūm pūshabā*, when you have ended your work, 415.

pish, subst., a flower, 1735 (acc.); plur. *pīsh*, flowers, 116 (nom.); *shingīra pīsh*, pretty flowers, p. 7; acc. *pīsh*, flowers, 1035; oblique, *sundī pish tā*, (the prettiest) of all flowers, 1195; *mulkhen pīsh ū osthai*, the violet flowers have come out, 1614; *parr pīsh*, the apple flower, 1242 (gen.); *tarī pīsh*, the dog-rose, 1196 (nom. plur., written *pish*), 1242, 1336, 1338, 1363 (gen. sing.); also written *pizh*; thus, *sirēn pizh bā*, of the trees flowers became, the trees are blossoming, 165.

piash, in the morning, see **iash**.

posh, subst., a noose, a trap, 1543, 1544 (acc.).

poishabâ, pūshabā, when finished, see **PAOSH**.

pashku, subst., a ewer, a water ewer, 427 (nom.), 474 (acc.), 1052 (into the ewer); *pashku tā*, from the ewer, 413, 1052; in the ewer, 544; a wooden platter, 1025 (nom.); *pashku giats dò pinam*, give me a metal cup to drink water, 313; the translation is probably wrong for "give me a ewer, I want to drink water".

pshuikbut, subst., a belch, eructation; *pshuikbut n'kshī*, do not belch, 142; looks like a compound with *pshuik*, drowsy.

pshīman, I fight; *iā shtur tā ē dī shūr n'ess, kaikotī pshīman?* in my quiver is not even one arrow, how can I fight? 1112. The form is quite abnormal; perhaps *pshīnam*.

pshin, subst., a grave; *pshin tā*, towards the grave, 583.

peshāni, subst., forehead; *peshāniā*, on (your) forehead, p. 5.

1 **pshar,** subst., a diviner, a wizard, 365 (nom.).

2 **pshar,** subst., a maternity hospital, 683 (nom.).

p'shur, pashur, in the swamp, in the forest, see **shur**.

Peshār, subst., Peshāwar, 923, 979 (to Peshāwar); *Peshār pōr*, towards Peshāwar, 1310; *Peshār stē*, from Peshāwar, 614, 1177, 1223, 1517.

pshīāsh, subst., a cat, 230 (nom.).

pashtug, subst., a bag; acc. *pashtug*, a bag, 111; *pashtuga*, a bag, 110; oblique, *pashtuga tā*, in the bag, 109; acc. plur. *pashtuk*, bags, sacks, 1583.

poshtrē, on the hill, 499; see **ashtrē.**

pshtarak, to-day, see **starak.**

pson, in the forest, see **son.**

p'sir, p'tsir, on the top of, upon, see **sir.**

psūṛ, subst., father-in-law; *psūṛ daṛ*, father-in-law troop, relations by marriage, 1139 (nom.).

pīss, subst., damage, harm; *biliuk pīss kṛiss*, they have done much damage (to my crops), 817; cf. **pis.**

psess, he has lost, see **PIS.**

postao, subst., hearth; *iā postao*, on my hearth, 636; the actual form of the word is doubtful; the initial *p* is perhaps the preposition **pa.**

psetai, he lost, see **PIS.**

puesth, to go down, see 2 **pū.**

psotr, in *ikiā dugā psotr*, therefore (because we do not understand the scales) we are robbed, 1238. The real meaning of the word is not clear.

pstarak, to-day, see **starak.**

psawai, adj., herding, *gdo psawai*, a cowherd, 295 (nom.).

1 **ptā,** came, see 1 **PRE.**

2 **ptā,** gave, see 2 **PRE.**

ptē, give, see 2 **PRE.**

1 **ptī,** subst., the back; nom. *ptī*, the back, 104; acc. *ptī*, 1276; oblique, *pa ptī*, on the back, 370; from the back, 375; *p'ptī tā*, on the back, 1377; from on the back, 1583; in *zīn ptitē*, put the saddle on, 1219, *pti* is written for *p'ptī*, and *tē* is the imper. of *TE*, to do, to make.

ptior, adv., at the back of, afterwards, p. 60; behind, 777, 907; *ptior otin ess*, he is left behind, 934; *ptior ats*, come back, 666; postposition, after, behind, p. 61; *tū p'amu ptior bhīm*, the ground behind thy house, 762; *ī pamu ptior*, at the back of, adjoining, my house, 772; *iā ptiōr*, after me, 14; *iā ptiora nishē*, sit behind me, 141.

pitur, adv., behind, after; *pitur-aisalam*, I will come after, 138.

ptiwar, adv., behind, after, p. 60; *ptiwar oss*, he came behind, he came second, 487; *ptiwar atsalā*, let him come behind, 506; *ptiwar utsolam*, I shall come behind, 776; *ptiwar utiness*, he is left behind, 1209; *ptiwor utin ess*, he is left behind, 1144; postposition, after, behind, p. 61; *bado ptiwar esth*, to go behind the pass, to cross the pass, 1023; *iā ptiwar*, behind me, 14; *ē mōs ptiwar*, after one month, 1136; cf. 15, 16, 17, 1161; *trē ptiwar* (?), third; *witsī ptiwar* (?), twentieth; *pōch witsī ptiwar* (?), hundredth, p. 64.

ptiwor, see *ptiwar*.

ptibar, adv., afterwards, p. 60; postposition, after; *shu sē ptibar*, after six years, 1734; *panishr stē ptibar*, after the first, second, p. 64; *ptibr*, hindquarters, see separately.

tibar, adv., behind, after; *tibar ēsth dugā*, for going after, for pursuing, 1092; postposition, after, behind, p. 61; *iā tibar*, after me, 14; *pit tibar*, on the other side of the hillock, 659.

2 **ptī**, subst., paper, 713 (nom.).

patī, a written petition, 770 (acc.); a letter, 798 (acc.).

pattī, a letter, p. 4.

1 **PATĪ**, to believe; 2nd present 1st pers. sing. *n'patītom*, I do not believe, 143, 144.

2 **patī**, subst., the shoulder-blade, 1298 (nom.); cf. 1 **ptī**.

paito, subst., puttees, 1096 (nom.).

PEṬ, to break, see **PEṚ**.

pit, subst., a hillock; *pit tibar*, behind, on the other side of, the hillock, 659.

potā, subst., a stirrup leather; *potā tā drgṛ kshī*, lengthen the stirrup leather, 1405.

ptibr, subst., the hindquarters of a horse, 662.

ptibar, behind, see **1 ptī.**

petdrī, subst., an axe, 615 ; see **padrī.**

puṭik, subst., a flower, 502 (nom. plur.).

ptol, in the pot, see **tol.**

ptul, in the field, see **tul.**

patel, subst., a cave; *patel kaṛoh,* in that cave, 235; seems to contain the preposition *pa*; the actual form of the word is not certain.

p'åotre, at the ford, 519; see **åotre.**

piṭr, puṭr, subst., a son; nom. *piṭr,* 28, 39, 102, 595, 692, 706, 1361; *puṭr,* 1358; acc. *piṭr,* 100, p. 4; *puṭr,* 1358; agent, *piṭr,* p. 2 (wrongly translated "father"); dat. *piṭr,* 607; gen. *piṭr,* 566; nom. plur. *piṭr,* 1318; *Pirkhān piṭrs,* Pirkhān son-his, Pirkhān's son, 647; *piṭras,* his son, p. 4 (acc.); *piṭress,* his son, p. 11; *Bastī puṭress,* Bastī's son, 1573 (acc.); *piṭran's,* his sons, p. 11; *ikīost puṭriness,* his own sons, 1398.

chir piṭr, a foster-child, 529 (nom.).

tottī piṭr (?), my cousin, 293 (dat. of possession).

PUTR, to go across, to cross.

Verbal noun, *kaikote putr bamå,* how can we cross? 1345; *petṛ-n banam,* I cannot cross, 1321; *putrē n'bamå,* we cannot cross, 1147; *patren na bamish,* we cannot cross, 332; *putrēn n'dronn* (?), he does not venture to cross, 1520.

Indefinite present 2nd pers. sing. *kuī putarijbå,* when thou hast crossed, 1331.

Future 1st pers. plur. *putremå,* we will cross, 1436; *petrēmå,* we will cross, 1618.

Imperative 1st pers. plur. *patrem,* let us go across, 519.

patramjuk, subst., night, p. 65; *dus p'tramjuk,* last night, 532; perhaps "at the lamp", "at the time of the lamp" cf. **tremchuk.**

p'tremshuk, subst., a lamp, 942; see **tremchuk.**

pituraisalam, I will come after, 138; see **1 ptī.**

patsā, adj., herding; *patsā mochī*, the shepherd, 1287 (agent); *gáo patsā*, cowherd, 295 (nom.); *ushp patso*, a groom, 591 (acc.).

patōs, on my shoulder, see **tōs**.

pets, subst., an axe, 103 (nom.), 961 (acc.); *pots*, an axe, 978 (nom.); cf. **padrī**.

pits, to drink, see 1 **PI**.

pitshun, in war, see **tshun**.

potsantestā, subst., a pillow, 1013 (nom.).

pitsenwā, adj., cold; *kūr pitsenwā*, my feet are cold, 273; cf., however, **pitzen**.

p'tsir, upon, see **sir**.

ptistuk, in *inī bangut shto ptistuk kshīr*, make this sangar wall four-sided, square, 1384; see **ptiwā**.

paṭṭā, subst., brow; *achē-paṭṭā*, eyebrow, 433 (nom.).

pattī, subst., a letter, p. 4; see 2 **pti**.

pott, putt, subst., a road, path; said to be feminine, p. 1; nom. *pott*, 340, 404, 885, 992, 993, 1043, 1401; *putt*, 889 (*p. digrī ess*, is bad), 907 (*aruṇī ess*, is narrow), 908, 924, 1184, 1200 (*digrī ess*, is bad), 1300, 1686 (*vishtrī*, broad), p. 7 (*digrī p.*, *wishtrī p.*; cf. footnote stating that the qualifying adjective is sometimes also masculine); acc. *putt*, 1536; oblique, *putt dugā*, for the road, for the journey, 1081; *pott tā atsand*, they are coming on the road, 531; *askā potta tā*, on that road, 355; *putt tā*, on the road, 386; *puttan*, i.e. *putt tā*, on the road, 947; *p'pott*, on the road, 495; *pott*, i.e. *p'pott* (?), on the road, 462; *potto*, i.e. *p'pott tā* or *pott tā*, on the road, 476; *pa putt*, on the road, 1548; *p'putt*, on the road, 352, 1164, 1245, 1629; *p'putt tā*, on the road, 1233; *p'putt tār*, on the road, 1541; *ē gujr pott, dū gajr pott, trai gajr pott*, one day's road, march, two days' march, three days' march, 846; *ē wōs pott*, one day's march, 327; *chī wōs pott*, how many days' march? how many stages? 1387; *p'putt lattrī ngal*, on road property taking, highway robber, p. 9; *p'putt lattrī ngalā*, highway robber, 1188; *p'putt lattrī rangal*, on road property taking, highway robber, p. 9; *pott zāṛl*, road knowing, a guide, 518, p. 9 (*zaṛl*).

ptitē, imper., saddle; *ushp tā zīn ptitē,* saddle the horse, lit. horse on saddle (on) back put, 1219; see 1 **ptī** and **TE.**

pittabā, if comes, if falls, see 1 **PRE.**

pottm, adverb, on foot; *pottm n'aietam,* I do not go on foot, 40.

potten, subst., a measure of length, a pace; *ē potten,* one pace, p. 64.

puettan, down going, see 2 **pū.**

ptīwā, in *shtowa ptīwā,* four-sided, square, 1201 (pred.); perhaps having four backs; cf. **ptī** and **ptistuk.**

ptīwar, after, behind, see **ptī.**

pitzen, broken; *pitzen biss,* (my box) is broken, 188; *n'pitzen kshē,* do not make it broken, do not break, 186; cf. **PEṚ.**

paiz, subst., money, see **paisa.**

piz, puz, lost, see **pis.**

1 **pazhē,** adv., near; *pazhē n'ai,* do not come near, 407; *emā pazhī stē winämish,* us near from struck us, they attacked us, 1429; read perhaps *p'azhē.*

2 **pazhē,** subst. (?), skull (?); *pondrik spāhī pazhē preptā,* a bullet hit the sepoy's skull, 1323; read perhaps *p'azhē.*

pazhu, subst., a place, 1301 (acc.); *askā pazhu tā,* in that place, 1301; read perhaps *p'azhu.*

pizh, subst., blossom, flower, see **pish.**

pashun, subst., the spur of a hill, 1382 (nom.); see 2 **pshu.**

R

r, pronominal suffix of the 2nd person plural, used to denote the subject with verbs. The following instances of its use occur, mostly in the paradigms of verbs: *ēr,* you go, you will go, p. 22; *ēnazzār,* you were going, p. 22; *elār,* you will go, p. 59; *ēr,* go ye, p. 23; *achūr,* you run, p. 36; *achūrbā,* if you run, p. 37; *achūniār,* you ran, p. 36; *achūnazzār,* you were running, p. 36; *achūnissār,* you had run, p. 36; *achūnlṛ,* you will run, p. 36; *achūnlār,* run, p. 37; *amjīr,* you put on, p. 48; *amjiār,* you did put on, p. 48; *amjinazzār*, you were putting on, p. 48; *amjissār*, you had put on, p. 48; *amjīlr*, you will put on, p. 48; *amjīlrbá*, if you put on, p. 49; *amjīlār*, put ye on, p. 49; *azār*, you are, you were; *azē̤rbá*, if you are, p. 19; *azzirā*, are you? 1659; *otār*, you remain; *otīr*, you remained, p. 38; *otīrbá*, if you remain, p. 39; *otinazzār*, you were remaining; *otinassār*, you had remained, p. 38; *otīlār*, remain ye, p. 39; *awē̄r*, you bring; *awē̤rār* (?), you brought, p. 46; *awa̤rē̄rbá*, if you bring, p. 47; *awenazzār*, you were bringing; *awa̤rissār* (?), you had brought; *awē̄lr*, you will bring, p. 46; *bīrdá*, if you are, p. 21; *bā̄r*, you are; *bōr*, you were; *būnazār*, you were becoming; *bissār*, you had been, p. 20; *bissār*, you have become, you are, 1315; *bulōr*, you will become, p. 20; *bulāzrbá*, if you become, p. 21; *bō̄r*, be ye, 777; *bā̄r*, become ye, 1439, p. 21; *gār*, you went, p. 22; *gussē̄r*, you went, 1737; *gūssē̄r*, you had gone, p. 22; *gā̤rbá*, if you go, p. 23; *gatsār*, bring ye, p. 47; *kā̄r*, you do, p. 24; *kunazzār*, you were doing; *kālr*, you will do, p. 24; *k<u>sh</u>ē̄r*, do ye, 364; *k<u>sh</u>ī̄r*, do ye, 515, 516, 640, 1221, 1309, 1384, 1543, p. 25; *k<u>sh</u>ōr*, pull ye, 1529; *lu<u>zh</u>ē̄r*, you are frostbitten; *lu<u>zh</u>engār*, you were frostbitten; *lu<u>zh</u>ènazzā̄r*, you were being frostbitten; *lu<u>zh</u>engussār*, you had been frostbitten; *lu<u>zh</u>ē̄lr*, you will be frostbitten, p. 30; *lu<u>zh</u>tē̄rtān* (?), if you are frostbitten; *lu<u>zh</u>ē̄lē̄r*, be frostbitten, p. 31; *mr̥ē̄r*, you die, you will die; *mr̥ā̄r*, you died; *mr̥ēnazzār*, you were dying; *mr̥issār*, you had died, p. 26; *mr̥ēr*, *mr̥ē̄r*, die ye, p. 27; *mi<u>zh</u>ōr*, you tell lies; *mi<u>zh</u>iār*, you lied; *mi<u>zh</u>ōnazzār*, you were lying; *mi<u>zh</u>essār*, you had lied; *mi<u>zh</u>ōlr*, you will lie, p. 28; *mi<u>zh</u>ōlār*, lie ye, p. 29; *ngār*, you take; *ngūtār*, you took; *ngānazzār*, you were taking; *ngūtūssār*, you had taken; *ngālr*, you will take, p. 42; *ngālrbá* (?), if you take; *ngār*, take ye, p. 43; *ngār*, take ye, 1458; *ni<u>zh</u>ē̄r*, you sit; *ni<u>zh</u>inazzār*, you were sitting; *ni<u>zh</u>ēnassār*, you had sat; *ni<u>zh</u>ē̄lr*, you will sit, p. 32; *ni<u>zh</u>ē̄lrbá*, if you sit; *ni<u>zh</u>ē̄lr*, sit ye, p. 33; *ni<u>zh</u>ōr*, you set; *ni<u>sh</u>ē̄r*, you did sit; *ni<u>zh</u>ōnazzār*, you were setting, p. 54; *ni<u>zh</u>ālezr̄bá*, if you were setting, p. 55;

nizhōnassār, you had set; *nizhōlr*, you will set, p. 54; *nizhōr*, set ye, p. 55; *piltēr*, you fall, p. 34; *piltirdā*, if you fall, p. 35; *piltiār*, you fell; *piltinassār*, you were falling; *piltissār*, you had fallen; *piltēlr*, you will fall, p. 34; *piltēlār*, fall ye, p. 35; *piltōr*, you fell, p. 56; *piltōrbā* (?), if you fell, p. 57; *pilteār*, you felled; *piltōnassār*, you were felling; *piltōssār*, you had felled; *piltōlōr*, you will fell, p. 56; *piltōlār*, fell ye, p. 57; *prēr*, you give; *ptār*, you gave; *prēnazzār*, you were giving; *ptāssār*, you had given; *prēlr*, you will give, p. 44; *prēlōrbā*, if you give; *prēlr*, give ye, p. 45; *pshīr*, you grind, p. 50; *pshīrbā*, if you grind, p. 51; *pshār*, you ground; *pshīnazzār*, you were grinding; *pshīssār*, you had ground; *pshīlr*, you will grind, p. 50; *pshīlār*, grind ye, p. 51; *wīr*, you strike, p. 52; *wīrbā* (?), if you strike, p. 53; *winār*, you struck; *winazzār*, you were striking; *winossār*, you had struck; *wilōr*, you will strike, p. 52; *wilōr*, strike ye, p. 53; *yūr*, you eat, p. 40; *yūrbā*, if you eat, p. 41; *yūnazzār*, you were eating; *iārissār*, you had eaten; *yūlr*, you will eat, p. 40; *yūr*, eat ye, p. 41; it will be seen that there is usually a nasalization of this *r* or of the preceding vowel. The actual form of the suffix is therefore a cerebral *ṇ*.

RU, to reap, to cut; future 1st pers. plur. *gum kaikotē ruimā*, how can we cut the wheat? 1304; see **URU.**

ruch, subst., light, illumination, 785 (nom.); *ruch bā*, light became, daylight, p. 64; *ruch bibā*, when light comes, at daylight, 785; *ruzh bibā*, when light comes, at daylight, 329.

radhar, radar, subst., night; the last vowel occurs as *a*, *o*, *ō*, and *u*; instead of *d* we occasionally find *t*; thus, *rōtr*, to-night, 1441; *rōtar brābar*, midnight, p. 64; the word is used as a noun, *dū rador bulozhbā*, if thou stayest for two nights, 1395; in most instances, however, it is an adverb; thus, *radhar*, by night, at night, 650, 721, 925; *radar*, at night, p. 60; *rador*, at night, 976, 1251; *radur*, at night, 461, 1087; *radhar*, to-night, 1441; *rador*, to-night, 1638, 1639; *rōtr*, to-night, 1441; *rador*, last night, 401, 830, 1327; *radhar brābar*, midnight, p. 64; *rador* *barbōr*, at midnight, 865; *rōtar brābar*, midnight, p. 64; *dus radhar*, yesterday night, last night, 1510; *dus radar*, last night, 371, 901; *dus rador*, last night, 766, 1627, 1733; *dūs rador*, last night, 1615; *dus radōr*, last night, 1691, 1706; *dus radur*, last night, 1090, 1385, 1386; *shtarak radōr*, to-night, 1533; *strak rador*, to-night, 1495.

radsâ, subst., rhubarb, 1167 (nom.).

RAG, to ask for, to demand, to require; cf. **WAG.** The following forms of this base occur in the sentences :—

Indefinite present 2nd pers. sing. *ragach*, askest, 1149; *starak dī ragacha*, doest thou ask to-day again? 1149; *kai dugã ragachī*, why doest thou demand? 1175.

Present 2nd pers. sing. *raganjā*, doest thou require? 1629.

3rd pers. plur. *ragand*, they will require, 531.

Second present 1st pers. sing. *ragattam*, I demand (money), I ask for, 1257.

2nd pers. sing. *hukm n'ragattā*, doest not ask for, obey, his command, 1205.

3rd pers. sing. *ragat*, asks for, requires, 1150; *ragatt*, asks for, requires, 1352, 1353.

Imperfect 2nd pers. sing. *raganasuch*, wast asking for, 1149.

Future 1st pers. sing. *ragalam*, I will ask (as a price), 1211.

ruganâ, subst., a fir-tree, 480 (nom. plur.).

rok, subst., a certain vegetable, 1168.

rakūs, subst., a hare; *rakūs ano*, hare's flesh, 620.

Rāolī-gor, subst., the Lawari Pass, 988, 989.

ramo, subst., a willow; *ramo kāno*, willow-trees, 1690 (nom.).

ruimâ, we shall cut, see **URU.**

romēn, subst., an aspen-tree; *romēn dār*, the aspen-tree wood, 81.

randsol, sick of fever, see **RANZ.**

rang, subst., colour; *adr rang azzā*, he is yellow-coloured, 1378; *mulkhen rang*, violet colour, 1613 (nom.); *erangst ess*, are of one colour, are of the same kind, of the same price, 1282.

rangal, participle, taking, p. 9; see **NGĀ**.

RANZ, to shake, to tremble.

Present participle, *randsol,* shaking, feverish, sick of fever; *randsol bitī mṛsī,* having become feverish died. died of fever, 470; *randsōl bitī mṛā,* they have died of fever, 467; *tu ranzol assā,* art thou feverish? 1290; *ranzul assa,* art thou feverish? 1552; *ranzul biss,* she is feverish, she has fever, 1317.

Present 3rd pers. sing. *ṛanzann,* (the tree) shakes, 1271.

Second present 3rd. pers. sing. *shtūan ranzat,* the pillar shakes, is weak, 1012; *ranzott,* (the body) trembles, 1552.

Causal verb, past 1st pers. sing. *ṛanzēī,* I did not shake (the tree), 1271.

Imperative, *ṛanzāo,* shake (the tree), 1270.

rāṛā, onomatopoetic, subst., noise; *rāṛā kṛiss,* they made a noise, 901; the neighing of a horse; *rāṛā kutt,* he is neighing, 916.

rāṛā-wā, noisy, quarrelsome, 1103 (attrib.).

rāṛṛa, the braying of an ass, 183 (obj.); cf. **ṚAṬṬ**.

rashtā, subst., a star, 1392 (nom. plur.).

ṛiti, adj., yellow, 1035 (attrib.).

rotr, rōtar, at night, see **radhar**.

1 **rits,** subst., barley; nom. *rīts,* 118, 1365; acc. *rits,* 1222; *rits,* 868, 1216; gen. *rits,* 1583; oblique, *rīts dugā,* for barley, 760.

2 **rits,** subst., a bear, 1123; see **its**.

ṚAṬṬ, to bark; second present 3rd pers. sing. *ṛaṭṭatt,* he is barking, 117, 774.

ruzh, subst., light, 329; see **ruch**.

S

s, ss, a suffix of the 3rd pers. sing.; added in order to indicate a genitive; thus, *ju-s,* his daughter, p. 4; *kunzā jū-s,* the queen her daughter, the princess, 1073; *iā nawōs ju-s,* my nephew's daughter, 918; *mochī-s,* his master, 1325, 1326; *nōn's,* his mother, 971; *piṭras,* his son, p. 4; *Pir Khān piṭr-s,* Pir Khān's son, 647, *piṭress,* his son, p. 11; *Bastī puṭress,* Bastī's son, 1573; *piṭran's,* his sons, p. 11; *ikīost puṭriness,* his sons, 1398; *tŏtt's,* his father, 583, 900, 971, p. 11; *shtri-ss-ē* or *ishtrī-s-ē,* to his wife, 726; *wāo's,* his grandfather, 900.

sa, subst., year, see 1 **sē.**

1 **sai,** subst., a man; nom. plur. *sai,* 1207; agent plur. *sai,* 207, 1714.

2 **sai,** subst., sun, see **sū.**

1 **sē,** subst., a year; occasionally written *sa* (452, 467); common in adverbial expressions and in idioms such as *chi sē biss,* how many years became? how long? 569; plural, *sē,* years, 19, 383, 393, 406, 452 (*sa*), 569, 1072, 1073, 1097, 1153, 1581, 1709; *shu sē ptibar,* after six years, 1734; *pōch sē wīk,* until five years, 1191; *dumā sē,* a dry year, a drought, 380 (*duma*), 1428; *inā sē,* this year, 6, 65, 95, 118, 212, 247, 286, 390, 399, 472, 538, 541, 698, 699, 727, 923, 997, 1012, 1032, 1167, 1170, 1179, 1221, 1228, 1240, 1428, 1628, 1668, p. 9; *pō sē,* last year, 503, 623, 648, 794, 850, 895 (*se*), 1208, 1289, 1316, 1488, 1635, p. 60; *pō sē stē,* than last year, 1240, p. 9 (*po*); *sōr sē tă,* next year, 923; *shtarak sē,* this year, 1498; *starka sē,* this year, 596; *starak sē,* this year, 272, 302, 467 (*sa*), 504, 557, 621, 622, 623, 848, 1032, 1064; *starak p'sē,* this year, 441, 1668.

2 **sē,** subst., a bag; *sē tă,* in the bag, 1029; of the bag, 1049.

3 **sē,** sun, see **sū.**

4 **sē,** is, 227; see **AS.**

siu, sū, sūī, subst., a bridge, nom. *sū,* 196, p. 59; acc. *sū,* 195, 480; *sūī,* 465; nom. plur. *siu,* 197.

so, adv., well; *so enjī,* goest well, fare well, good-bye, 1162, p. 63.

sū, subst., the sun, 274, 328, 1266, 1434, 1438; *sū na prēnn,* sun does not come, it gets no sun, 1598; *sū ptī,* the sun has come, has risen, 1180, p. 65 (time of the sun's appearance); note the following idioms: *sū chī presth wokt tă,* sun up going time in, at sunrise, 1436; *sū chunzlī,* sunrise, p. 65; *sū chunzlī pōr,* sunrise way, east, 402, 403, p. 65; *sū garo yaristhē dugā*, owing to an eclipse eating the sun, 325; *sū garo n'yāriss*, an eclipse has not eaten the sun, there has been no eclipse, 406; *sū puēlī*, sunset, p. 65; *sū puēlī pōr*, sunset direction, west, 402 (*puēli*), 403, p. 65; *sū puesth pōr*, sunset direction, west, 1663 (*pū esth*), p. 65; *sū puettan pōr*, sunset direction, west, 1662 (*pū ettan*), p. 65; *sū pinjebā*, when the sun sets, at sunset, 672, 1437; *sū tsāwen bibā*, when the sun goes down, sunset, p. 65; *sai yār wīk*, sun down till, till sundown, 1245; *sē yār*, sundown, p. 65.

sabhu, subst., wild rhubarb, 1168 (nom.).

sabjun, subst., saliva, spit (?); *sabjun wisth*, to spit, 1373.

sāch, dwellest, 389; see **AS.**

sachī, subst., the wrist; *dusht sachī witrpiss*, the wrist of my hand is damaged, 1728.

sachung, subst., a spider, 1371 (nom. plur.).

sād wasā, subst., Saturday, p. 65.

sodāgar, subst., a merchant, 1177 (*suodāgar*, nom.), 1310 (nom. plur.); *sodāgar tā*, to the merchant, 1177; *sodāgarā tā stē*, from with the merchant, from the merchant's, 1066; *sodāgar-o tā stē*, from the merchant, 1286; cf. **sādawai.**

sudat, numeral, ninety, p. 63 footnote (from the collection of the Rev. Worthington Jukes).

sādawai, subst., a merchant, 862 (nom.); cf. **sodagar.**

SAGĀ, to clean, to sweep, see **SKĀ.**

sagon, subst., a broom, 1447 (acc.); see **skā.**

sh, pronominal suffix of the 2nd pers. sing. It can be added to nouns in order to denote the genitive of the pronoun, but is more frequently appended to verbal forms in order to indicate the subject, a direct or an indirect object. There are two forms of the suffix, viz. *ch* and its substitute *j* on one side, and *sh* and *zh* on the other. An *ī* can be added in all cases. The following examples occur in the sentences:—

ch, chī, j, jī; the form *ch, chī* is sometimes added to nouns ending in *t*, which latter consonant can then be dropped; thus, *tott-chī*, thy father, 278, p. 11; *to-chī*, thy father, 1492. In the conjugation of verbs this suffix is regularly used in the indefinite present formed directly from the base, while *j* is used instead in the first present formed by adding the suffix *n*. *j* is also substituted for *ch*, when *b* follows. The only exceptions to these rules are *banch*, canst, 1534 (but *banj*, p. 58; *banjī*, 1054), *sanganch*, hearest, obeyest, 1307, and *walanch*, sayest, 1188, 1463. The suffix *ch* is occasionally used to denote an object; thus, *tū ī lē zānchībá*, if I know thee as good, if thou pleasest me, 1029; more commonly, however, it denotes the subject. The following examples occur: *os̲h̲ich*, knittest, 747; *otich*, risest, 1180; *awēguch*, demandest, considerest, 940; *awēguchī*, demandest, 933; *az̲h̲ichī*, art, 1366; *bachā*, canst, 1214, p. 58; *bachī*, canst, 1311; *banch*, canst, 1534 (see above); *buch*, becomest, art, 813, 1101, p. 20; *ditkichī*, tremblest, 1290; *tū jidd kai dugā̃ ditkiochī*? why is thy body trembling for thee? 1552; *kuch*, makest, 80, 224 (*kuc̲h̲*), 1000; *kuchā*, *kuchiā*, makest? 510; *kuchī*, makest, 941; *kudoch*, askest, 1105; *kanich*, laughest, 771; *kusoch*, smokest, 1340; *ks̲h̲áchī*, makest, 1307; *laraichī*, liest, 144; *larēchī*, liest, 430; *larich*, liest, 52; *manīchī*, meanest, 854; *mārechī*, sayest, 1235; *mis̲h̲och*, liest, 802; *mis̲h̲ochī*, liest, 1175; *prēchī*, givest, 84; *ragach*, *ragacha*, askest, demandest, 1149; *ragachī*, demandest, 1175; *sách*, dwellest, 389; *sanganch*, hearest, obeyest, 1307 (see above); *s̲h̲tārchī*, art groaning, 880; *vich*, beatest, pushest, 737, 1093; *vichī*, kickest, 738; *wich*, beatest, p. 52; *vichībá*, if pushest, 1093; *wagachī*, demandest, 1175; *walach*, sayest, 51, 1108, 1110; *walanch*, sayest, 1188, 1463 (see above); *yūchī*, eatest, 1232, p. 40; *z̲h̲uchī*, grievest, 589; *zāṛchā*, knowest? 1277; as already stated *j* is regularly used instead of *ch* after *n* and before *b*. It also occurs before *ā* in the past tense in *vino-j-ā*, did I beat thee? 1312; cf. *z̲h̲* below. It is occasionally used to denote an object; thus, *mukinjebá*, if I flee from thee, 495; *vinojā*, did I beat thee? 1312. Usually, however, it denotes the subject; thus, *achūnanj*, runnest, p. 36; *amjinj*, puttest on clothes, p. 48; *anjī*, comest, 952; *anjībá*, if comest, 106, p. 58; *enjā*, goest, wilt go, p. 22; *ēnjā*, goest? 1132; *enjī*, goest, 1162, p. 63; *ēnjī*, goest, 1134, p. 22; *enjībá*, if goest, 1582; *otinj*, remainest, p. 38; *atsanjī*, art coming, 1672; *awēnj*, bringest, p. 46; *awenjībá*, if comest, 1354; (*baron*) *azinj*, art vomiting, 1616; *uzzamanj*, yawnest, 1733; *banj*, canst, p. 58; *banjī*, canst, 1054; *bunjī*, becomest, p. 20; *gujbá*, if goest, 46, 1202, 1411; *gūjbá*, if goest, p. 33; *kunjī*, makest, 1605, 1608; *kūnjī*, makest, p. 24; *kunjībá*, if makest, p. 25; *kshonji*, dost, p. 24; *kshonjī*, dost, 408; *kshonjībá*, if makest, p. 25; *kulojbā*, if wilt make, p. 25; *kulājbá*, if wilt make, 1396 (perhaps wrong for *kulozhbá*, *kulāzhbá*, respectively); *luzhenj*, art frostbitten, p. 30; *mrojbá*, if diest, p. 27; *mrenjī*, diest, p. 27; *mizhōnjī*, liest, p. 28; *nganj*, takest, p. 42; *nizhenj*, sittest, p. 32; *nizhōnj*, settest, p. 54; *piltanj*, fallest, p. 34; *piltonanj*, causest to fall, p. 56; *prēnjī*, givest, p. 44; *prēnjībá*, if givest, 185 (*prenjībá*), 555; *perinjībá*, if breakest, 187; *pshīnj*, grindest, p. 50; *putarijbá*, when crossest, 1331; *raganjā*, dost thou want? 1629; *samarijbá*, when startest, 1067; *widharanj*, fearest, 1684; *vinj*, beatest, p. 13; *winj*, beatest, p. 52; *yūnjī*, eatest, p. 40; *yūnjbá*, if eatest, p. 41.

sh, *shī*, *zh*, *zhī*:—the *sh* form occurs in some isolated cases, especially from the root *AS*; thus, *assish*, art. It is further the regular suffix in the *t*-present, in all forms of the past (indefinite past, imperfect, perfect, and pluperfect), and in the future. The form *pshīshbá*, if grindest, p. 51, is given with a query, and should probably be *pshījbá*. Before *b*, *sh* interchanges with *zh*, and this latter form is sometimes also used before vowels; thus, *winio-zh-ā*, has anyone hit you? 1470; *bro-zhī*, thy brother's, 294.

sh, *shī* is often used to denote a direct or indirect object; thus, *utēa-sh*, I have awakened thee, 1180; *bissish*, became to thee, 853, 1724; *karā'sh*, made thee, for thee, p. 12; *karā-sh*, made thee, 1312; *karo-sh*, made for thee, 1273, 1570, 1665;

karsi-sh, have made for thee, 794, 1063, p. 11; *ptā'sh*, gave thee, 85 (*pta'sh*), 1149, pp. 11, 12; *ptā'shī*, (who) gave thee? 1016; *ptā'sh-ī*, (who) gave thee? pp. 12, 17; *ptese-sh*, he has given thee, p. 4; *vinā'sh*, struck thee, p. 12; *winā'sh*, struck thee, p. 11; *vinosā-sh*, have beaten thee, 1312, p. 11 (*vinosā'sh*); *vinossi'sh*, have beaten thee, p. 12; the examples of the use of this form in order to denote the subject are numerous,—*aiyo-sh*, camest, 769, 770, p. 58 (*aiyō-sh*); *ēti-sh*, goest, 439, 1134, p. 22; *ēti-shi-ā*, goest? 1132; *etti-shi-ā*, goest? p. 17; *ēnazzi-sh*, wast going, p. 19; *elosh*, wilt go, 863; *ēlosh*, wilt go, 561, 1181, 1531, p. 22; *achūnashbá*, if runnest, p. 37 (irregular); *achūniā'sh* (?), rannest, p. 36; *achūnazzi-sh*, wast running, p. 36; *achūnissi-sh*, hadst run, p. 36; *achūnlo-sh*, wilt run, p. 36; *afzō-sh-ā*, didst thou come? 38; *amjiā'sh*, didst put on (clothes), p. 48; *amjinazzi-sh*, wast putting on, p. 48; *amjissi-sh*, hadst put on, p. 48; *amjilo-sh*, wilt put on, p. 48; *amjilosh-bá*, if thou wilt put on, p. 48; *vinagan ungalo-sh*, wilt be beaten, p. 59; *ashā*, art? 1736; *ashī*, art, 707, 852, 1054, 1335, 1534, 1692, 1693, p. 19; *ashiā*, art? 1307, 1366; *oshī*, art, 703, p. 19; *ashībá*, if thou art, 617, p. 19; *oshībá*, if thou art, 617; all these forms of the base *AS* are very uncertain, as the *sh* can belong to the base and is not necessarily the suffix of the second person; *osi-sh*, art, 99; *oshi-sh*, art, p. 19; *assi-sh*, art, 105, 190, 224, 457, 525, 586, 611, 670, 700, 708, 720, 740, 919, 927, 940, 968, 974, 983, 994, 1000, 1018, 1080, 1088, 1103, 1171, 1176, 1262, 1273, 1275, 1311, 1486; *azzi-sh*, art, p. 19; *azzu-sh*, wast, p. 19; *otilo-sh*, wilt remain, p. 38; *otiniā'sh*, remainedst, p. 38; *otino-sh*, art dead beat, 1523; *otinazzi-sh*, wast remaining, p. 38; *otinassi-sh*, hadst remained, p. 38; *atiō-sh*, pour out, 1052 (uncertain); *awērā'sh*, broughtest, p. 46; *awēnazzi-sh*, wast bringing, p. 46; *awarissi-sh*, hadst brought, p. 46; *awēlo-sh*, wilt bring, p. 46; *awēlo-sh-bá*, if bringest, 1164; *biti-sh*, becomest, 1360; *bā'sh*, becamest, p. 20; *bā-sh*, becamest, 1716; *bo-sh*, *bō-sh*, becamest, 234, p. 20; *bishtá*, if becamest, p. 21 (uncertain); *bulazzi-sh-bá*, if thou art becoming,

p. 21; *būnazzi-sh*, wast becoming, p. 20; *bosi-sh*, hast, hadst become, p. 20; *bissi-sh*, hast, hadst become, 107, 543, 701, 843, 985, 1157, 1217, 1503, 1523, 1667, p. 20; *bissi-sh-ā*, didst become ? 1307; *bulo-sh*, wilt become, 1080, 1160, p. 20 (*būlo-sh*); *balo-sh*, wilt be able, canst, 1062, p. 58; *bilo-sh*, wilt be able, 378; *gā'sh*, wentest, p. 22; *gā-osh*, hast gone, 783; *gosāo-sh*, wentest, 1660; *gūssi-sh*, hast gone, 1519; *n'grussish*, hast not got, 783; *jānṛeti-sh*, knowest, 1176; *jārlo-sh*, wilt kill. 1160; *koti-sh*, dost, 863; *kuti-sh*, dost, 1108; (*koshi*, makest, 92, is uncertain); *kunazzi-sh*, wast doing, p. 24; *kulo-sh*, wilt do, p. 24; *lunelo-sh*, wilt fall, 190; *luzhenga-sh*, wast frostbitten, p. 30; *luzhēnazzi-sh*, wast being frostbitten, p. 30; *luzhengossi-sh*, hadst been frostbitten, p. 30; *luzhēnelo-sh*, wilt be frostbitten, p. 30; *mṛā'sh*, diedst, p. 26; *mṛēnazzi-sh*, wast dying, p. 26; *mṛissi-sh*, hadst died, p. 26; *mṛlo-sh*, wilt die, 73, 350, 439, p. 26 (*mṛlōsh*); *mārnazu-sh*, wast speaking, p. 4; *mizhiā'sh*, didst lie, p. 28; *mizhōnazzi-sh*, wast telling lies, p. 28; *mizhōla-sh*, wilt tell lies, p. 28; *ngūtā'sh*, tookest, p. 42; *ngānazzi-sh*, wast taking, p. 42; *ngūtūssi-sh*, hadst taken, p. 42; *ngālo-sh*, wilt take, p. 42; *nishiā'sh* (?), sattest, p. 32; *nizhinazzi-sh*, wast sitting, p. 32; *nizhēnassi-sh*, hadst sat, p. 32; *nishēā'sh*, didst set, p. 54; *nizhōnazzi-sh*, wast setting, p. 54; *nizhōnassi-sh*, hadst set, p. 54; *nizhōlo-sh*, wilt set, p. 54; *nizhālezi-sh-bá*, if settest, p. 54; *piltiā'sh*, didst fall, p. 34; *piltinassi-sh*, wast falling, p. 34; *piltissi-sh*, hadst fallen, p. 34; *piltilo-sh*, wilt fall, 407, 1181, p. 34; *piltēā'sh*, felledest, p. 56; *piltōnassi-sh*, wast felling, p. 56; *piltōssi-sh*, hadst felled, p. 56; *piltōlo-sh*, wilt fell, p. 56; *piltō-sh-bá*, if thou didst fell, p. 57; *purjiti-sh-ā*, dost thou think ? 1105, p. 17; *ptā'sh*, gavest, p. 44; *prēnazzi-sh*, wast giving, p. 44; *ptāssi-sh*, hadst given, p. 44; *prēlo-sh*, wilt give, p. 44; *prēlo-sh-bá*, if thou wilt give, p. 45; *pshā'sh*, groundest, p. 50; *pshīnazzi-sh*, wast grinding, p. 50; *pshīssi-sh*, hadst ground, p. 50; *pshīlo-sh*, wilt grind, p. 50; *pshī-sh-bá* (?), if grindest, p. 51 (see above); *silkilo-sh*, wilt slip,

1130; *samarlo-sh*, wilt set out, 1546; *winā'sh*, didst beat, p. 52; *wino-sh-bá*, if beatest, p. 53; *winazzi-sh*, wast beating, p. 52; *winossi-sh*, hadst beaten, p. 52; *vilo-sh*, wilt beat, p. 13; *wilo-sh*, wilt beat, p. 52; *walēti-sh*, art talking, 929; *yūnazzi-sh*, wast eating, p. 40; *iārissi-sh*, hadst eaten, p. 40; *yūlo-sh*, wilt eat, 73, p. 40; *zhārti-sh*, knowest, 611; *zaronlo-sh*, wilt learn, 408.

It has already been remarked that *zh* is sometimes substituted for *sh* before vowels and the consonant *b*. *zh* occurs with nouns; thus, *bro-zhī*, thy brother's, 294; it denotes a direct or indirect object; thus, *bissi-zh-ā*, has it become to thee? 1724; *wino-zh-ā*, has (anybody) hit you? 1470; and it is added in order to denote a subject of the 2nd person singular; thus, *i-zhī-bá*, you may go, 1157; *otina-zh-bá*, if thou remainest, p. 39; *bo-zhā*, becamest, p. 20; *bulo-zh-bá*, if thou wilt be, 1395; *nizhēla-zh-bá*, if thou sittest, p. 33; *pari-zh-bá*, when thou hast arrived, 1563; *zārla-zh-ā*, dost thou understand? 1577.

1 **shâ**, pronoun of 2nd pers. plur., you; nom. *shá*, you, 777, 1315, 1659, 1737, pp. 10, 59; voc. *shá*, O you, p. 10; agent, *shá*, you, pp. 4, 10, 12; acc. *shá*, you, 1740, p. 10; gen. *shá*, your, 573; *shá'st*, your, 1743, p. 10; *shāsta*, your, p. 8 (Abdul Hakīm Khān); oblique, *shá mēsh*, from you, p. 10; *shátā*, to you, p. 10; *shá yōt zara*, you yourselves, p. 13.

2 **shâ**, subst., night; *starak shá-o anī wisilom*, this night I shall spend here, 1370.

shai, subst., head; nom. *shai*, head, 5, 671, 952, 1344; acc. *shai*, head, 1319; *shaī*, my head, p. 12; gen. *she*, of the head, 605; oblique, *shai tá*, on the head, 1260; *shai wrē*, on the head, 952; *pshai*, on the head, 650; *p'shai p'mīju*, on my head, 949; *pshai* is said to mean 'head', and to have an accusative *pshaio*, p. 5; *shai yār*, head down, upside down, 1591; *shiē yār bitī*, head being downwards, 712; *dō shai*, the top of the hill, 657 (nom.); *badō shai*, on the top of the pass, 827, 955, 1331; on the top of the mountain, 795 (*bado*), 920, 1589, 1671; *bado shai putrē*, to cross on the top of the pass, to get across the pass, 1147; *bado shaiē stē*, from the crest of the hill, 299; *bado shai tā*, at the top of the pass, on crossing the pass, 303.

1 **she,** head, see **shai.**

2 **shē,** subst., frost, black frost; nom. *shē*, black frost, 541; acc. *shie*, frost, ice, 698; commonly used with *TI*; thus, *shē tin*, frozen, 534, 858, 1034 (used as a pred.); *shī tin*, frozen, 1330; *ďo shē tinn*, the water becomes frozen, 1698; *ďo shē n'tilā*, the water will not freeze, 533.

1 **shī,** subst., a horn (of an ibex), 673 (nom.).

2 **shī,** subst., a carpet, p. 7; cf. *zhō*, carpets, 606.

3 **shī,** subst., frost, see 2 **shē.**

shiāo, subst., a saw, 1234 (acc.).

1 **shie,** subst., ice, 698; see 2 **shē.**

2 **shiē,** subst., head; *shiē yūr bīti*, head getting downwards, 712; see **shai.**

shō, subst., food; *shō le iaṛō*, I have eaten (too) much food, 145; *ishá tyor kshī*, get food ready, 507.

1 **SHU,** to sew. Infinitive, *shusth*, to sew, 1267, 1504; *shusthē dugā*, for sewing, 1138; *shewesth dugā*, for sewing, 782.

Present participle, *basná shul*, clothes sewing, a tailor, 1243, 1289.

Perfect 3rd pers. sing. *shusī*, he sewed, 1289.

Imperative 2nd pers. sing. *shiwē*, sew, 859.

2 **shu,** subst., hairs, wool, 1731; see **zhū.**

3 **shu,** numeral, six, 1256, 1285, 1734, p. 63.

4 **shū,** subst., knowledge, information; *shū n'ess*, there is no information, one does not know, 749, 830, 921; *shu n'azzī tan dā* (?), knowledge not being in, suddenly, 1429; *shū bā*, did knowledge come (to thee)? didst thou feel? 1510; *shū awēl manchī*, information, news, bringing man, a spy, 1383, p. 14 (*mōch*); the man who took the news, p. 15; *kuī shū awēn na bachī*, thou canst not bring any information, thou wilt not do as a spy, 1311; *shū aweṛā*, he has brought information, 1383;

shū kudosth, to bring information, to scout, 1245; *shū ngal*, news-taker, spy, 1665; *shū ngal manchī*, spy, 1723.

5 **shū**, subst., breathing, sigh; *ikīā tā shū ness*, there is no breathing, life, in it, 803; *shū kshāchī*, art making sighs, 1307; *shus*, breath; *shus kalon*, let him take breath, 191; *shūs-kett*, he is taking breath, is gasping, out of breath, 548.

6 **shū**, subst., a rose, 1195, 1196, p. 7 (nom.); said to be feminine, p. 1.

shuā, adj., escaped, rescued; *shuā bāsh*, wast rescued, didst escape, 1716.

sāhib, subst., a gentleman, master, sahib; nom. *sāhib*, 531 (nom. plur.), 906, 1011, 1150, 1353, 1624; vocative, *sāhib*, sir, 414, 515, 590, 801, 1083, 1087, 1264, 1644; *sāhibo*, sir, 277. gen. *sāhib-ē*, the sahib's, 1298.

shōch, subst., a fight, a battle; *shōch kusth*, to make fight, to fight, 471; *shuch krā*, they fought, 1600; *shuj biss*, there was a battle, 121; *shuj kuldi*, they fight, 122; *shush kusthū*, for fighting, 336.

shodr, subst., a servant, 852, 856, 1081, 1262, 1263, 1644 (nom.); 736 (agent); *tū ī shodr karāsh*, I made thee my servant, 1312, p. 11; *shodr kulom*, I will make (thee) my servant, 1693; *Mehar'st shodr*, the Mehtar's servants, subjects, 1154 (nom.).

shodarī, subst., service, 1264 (nom.), 1265 (acc.).

shedrukral, adj., pink, 1014 (attr.).

Shdrāl, subst., Chitrāl, name of a place; nom. *Shdrāl*, 2, 449, 1046; gen. *Shdrāl*, 527, 834, 926; oblique, *Shdrāl*, in Chitrāl, 861, 903, 1178; to Chitrāl, 180, 327, 560, 564, 565, 846, 1387, 1437; *Shdrāl Bruz p'mij*, between Chitrāl and Brōz, 151; *Shdrāl stē*, from Chitrāl, 447, 540 (*stē*), 785 (*stā*); also written *Shtrāl*, to Chitrāl, 1132; *Shtrālo stā*, from Chitral, 146; cf. **Chandrāl**.

shagī, subst., galloping; *shagī tā*, from galloping, 1004; cf. **SHIG**.

SHIG, to be quick, to race:—

Present participle, *shigil,* fast, quick, 682, p. 8 (pred.); causal verb second present 3rd pers. plur. *shigiottett,* they are racing (their horses), 1114.

Shogoi, subst., Shoghōt, name of a place, 447 (nom.); oblique, *Shogōr,* to Shoghōt, 1530.

shugā, subst., a coat, a cloak, a choga; nom. *shugā,* 254, 429, 1116, 1164, 1248, 1357, 1482, 1491, 1576; acc. *shugā,* 269, 747, 1116, 1161, 1251, 1481, 1715; gen. *shugā,* 1329; nom. plur. *shugā,* 255.

shigil, fast, swift, see **SHIG.**

Shogōr, to Shoghōt, see **Shogoi.**

shigiottett, they are racing, see **SHIG.**

shuj, subst., battle, see **shōch.**

shak, subst., vegetables, 1603 (acc.); *shiak bī,* vegetable seeds, 1516; *shiok p'mij,* out of my vegetables, 1653.

shkorī, adj., crooked; *manoī shkorī biss,* my walking-stick is crooked, 301.

shaksh, adj., wrinkled; *miok shakshiss,* the forehead is wrinkled, 1727.

shal, cold, see **shil.**

shali, adj., in foal: *ushp shalī n'ess,* my mare is not in foal, 504.

shāli, subst., rice crop, rice, 1170 (nom.), 1697 (acc.).

shil, adj., cool, cold, 26, 292, 533, 540 (pred.); also written *shal,* 1663; cf. **shillā.**

shilā, subst., smallpox; *ikīā manchī-ē tuk shilā biss, tū tā dī shilā,* this man has got smallpox, you will also catch smallpox, 1462.

shiāl, subst., a jackal, 721 (nom. plur.).

shul, sewing, see **SHU.**

1 **shall,** subst., a wolf, 1706 (agent); cf. **shiāl.**

2 **shall,** subst., a cattle-shed; *shall stē,* from the cattle-shed, 1284.

shillā, subst., cold, 18, 272, 274, 865, 1431; *iā shillā biss*, to me cold has become, I am cold, 1320; *shillā biss*, art thou cold? 1552; *tū shillē bissā*, art thou cold, 1290; *shillē*, owing to the cold, 297, 936; *shillē tā*, owing to the cold, 397, 809; *shillē tā*, owing to the cold, 538; also *shallā*; thus, *shallā bonā*, cold has become, it is cold, 654; cf. **shil**.

shalum (?), subst., turnip, 1569 (acc.).

shom, subst., revenue (of a village), 1163 (acc.).

shamash, interjection, well! bravo! 182, p. 63; *shamash kusth*, to applaud, to thank, 582, 1474.

shion, subst., life; *shion nuksâlam*, I will hurt his life, take away his life, 1090.

shangiē, adv., early, soon, 1435; *shangyē*, early, soon, p. 60; *shangyē zamāna tā*, early in the time, formerly, 1206, p. 60.

shangūr, adj., numb; *angur shangūr bistai*, my fingers have become numb, 936.

pū shinguṛ bunn, my leg has become numb, is asleep, 1328.

shingar, adj., pretty, handsome, lovely; occurs in several slightly different forms, viz. *shingar*, 133 (pred.); *shingara basnâ*, pretty clothes, 1066; *gol shingarī ass*, my country is pretty, 292; *shingir*, pretty, 502 (pred.); *shingīr*, pretty, p. 7; *dī shingīr oss*, the sky is lovely, clear, 1324; *shingīra basnâ*, pretty clothes, p. 7; *shingīra brunz*, a pretty lawn, 772, p. 7; *shingīra darestān*, a pretty garden, p. 7; *shingīra pīsh*, pretty flowers, p. 7; *darestā shingīra bā*, my garden is pretty, 831; *shū shingīra ess*, the rose is pretty, p. 7; *nizhā shingiera assā*, the wood is pretty, 1711; *shū sundī pīsh tā shingierai azz*, the rose is pretty among all flowers, the prettiest of all flowers, 1195; *brâ shingorā assā*, my brother is handsome, 1028, p. 8; *shingur ossā*, (the bird) is pretty, 970.

shinguṛ, numb, see **shangūṛ**.

shangyē, early, soon, see **shangiē**.

shpah, subst., Monday, p. 65.

shar, a turban, see **sharr**.

shāra, subst., autumn, 94 (nom.); *shāro*, in autumn, 93.

shārū, subst., *Capra falconeri*, Mārkhor, 848 (nom. plur.), 1214 (acc. plur.).

sher, numeral, hundred, p. 63; *pōch sher*, five hundred, 897.

Shēr Malik, subst., Shēr Malik, name of a man, 1066 (agent), 1456 (*Sher Malik*, nom.).

shiṛ, subst., a crop, 596 (nom.).

shor, shur, subst., (1) *shur*, mud, 522, 893, 902; *pott shur biss*, to the road mud has come, the road is sticky, 1401; (2) *shor*, *shur*, low, marshy land, a marsh, a swamp; *Shdrāl shor assā*, Chitrāl is low land, 1046; *shor tā̃*, in the low land, in the valley, 763; *ikī shur tawarē̃*, near that swamp, 1137; *shur tā̃*, in a marsh, 851; *shur tār*, in a marsh, 1098; *p'shur tā̃*, in a marsh, 1443; *tū pa-shur tā̃*, in thy marshes (translated 'forest'), 1006; (3) *shur*, dung, purging (?), *shur lāsett*, I have dysentery, 394.

shūr, subst., an arrow, 72 (acc.), 1112 (nom.).

shiṛēn, adv., too much; *buṛī shiṛēn n'āyū*, do not eat too much food, 586.

sharr, subst., a strip of cloth, 1725 (acc.); a pagri, a turban, 616 (acc.), 1561 (*sharr*, nom.); *shar*, a pagri, a turban, 1084 (nom.).

shaṛṛ, subst., a goat, 1705 (acc. plur.); *sharon dugā̃*, for goats, 1167.

shirr, subst., a loin cloth, 821 (nom.).

shuṛṛ, subst., a waistband, 1622 (acc.).

shartrī, subst., a hunter, 959 (nom.).

shurṭṛ, subst., hunting, sport; *shurṭṛ kusth*, to make sport, to hunt, 694.

sherwa, in *wariān sherwa*, the tenth month of a year, p. 66.

shus, subst., breath; *shus kalon*, let him take breath, 191;

shusi, he sewed, see **SHU**.

shūs-kett, he is taking breath, he is gasping, 548; see 5 **shū**.

Shīshī, subst., Shīshī, name of a place, 562 (to Shīshī); *Shīshī*, to Shīshī, 1737; *Shīshī b'gol*, in the Shīshī valley, 1599.

shosh, subst., a witness, 1705 (nom.).

shush, subst., fighting, see **shōch**.

shūskett, he is breathing, gasping, 548; see 5 **shū**.

shā'st, shāsta, your, see **shā**.

shisthā, for sowing, 310; see **AJI**.

shusth, to sew, see **SHU**.

shtā, adj., clean, pure; *nuṛī shtā n'biss*, the butter is not clean, 218; *āo shtā assā*, the water is pure, 1418.

shtī, subst., a cliff, 261 (nom.).

shto, numeral, four, 16, 469, 873, 1279, 1458, p. 63; *shto kuro-ett*, he goes on four legs, he is creeping, 298; *shto ptistuk*, having four backs, square, 1384; *shto kazhē*, four kazhē, sixty seers, p. 64; *shto witsī*, four twenties, eighty, p. 63; *shto witsī duts*, four twenties ten, ninety, p. 63; the numeral also occurs in the form *shtowa*, 376, 465, 466, 549, 552, 754, 777, 1049, 1098, 1153; *shtowa ptīwā*, having four backs, square, 1201; *shtowa vissī*, four twenties, eighty, 1211.

shūt, subst., the second month of a year, p. 65.

shtak, to-day, see **starak**.

shotik, subst. (?), in *iā shotik n'ess*, it is not my fault, 1128; *iā shotik n'bā*, (this cloth) is not to my taste, 242; *Mehr shotik n'ess*, the Mehtar has no leisure, 770.

shtal, adj., true; *shtal manchī*, a true, trustworthy, man, 1021, 1557; *shtal warī*, true words, the truth, 365, 1131 (*varī*), 1416, 1558; *shtal warī-wā*, of true words, truthful, p. 5; *shtalī n'ess*, it is not true, 1486.

shtal, certainly, really, 350, 417.

shtalē, certainly, verily, of course, 1018, 1148, 1579; *shtalē ēsth tū wōr assā*, it is indeed thy turn to go, 1355; *shtalē tyor*, surely, certainly, 1359.

shtalē̃, certainly, 475; *shtalē̃ walanch*, thou speakest truly, the truth, 1188.

shtalē, probably, perhaps, 1002, 1091, 1104, 1174; *shtalē*, perhaps, p. 2; *shtalē̃*, perhaps, 244, 567, 1184, 1472, p. 61; *shtalē̃ ī nasib n'azilabā*, perhaps my luck may not be, if my luck is bad, 436; the particle *bá* can be dropped, and we find *shtalē*, if, 1160; *shtalē*, if, 526, 1090, 1132, 1222, 1315, without any such addition to the verb.

shtom, subst., a tree, 179 (gen.); *shtoma-tā*, from the trees, 787; also written *stūm*, 587 (nom. plur.).

1 **shtan,** subst., a stick, 215 (acc.).

2 **shtan,** subst., a thief, 536; see **shtār.**

shtūan, subst., a wooden pillar, 1012 (nom.).

shâtin, shotin, adj., contented, glad; *shâtin-istā* (?), they are glad, 351; *n'shotin-esta-bá*, if (anybody) is dissatisfied, 841; probably a present participle; cf. **shotik.**

shtrī, a wife, see **ishtrī.**

SHTĀR, to utter inarticulate sounds.

Indefinite present 2nd pers. sing. *shtārchī*, thou art eructating (and wilt vomit), 880.

Second present 3rd pers. sing. *shtārt*, he is groaning, 593.

shtār, subst., a thief; nom. sing. *shtār*, 42, 298, 372, 373, 410 425, 428, 670, 810, 845, 862, 985, 1088, 1105, 1187, 1188, 1261 1275, 1407, 1412, 1486, 1538, 1682, 1721 (*shtār*), p. 17; *shtan*, 536; agent sing. *shtār*, 371, 612, 1329; *shtāro*, 111; acc. sing. *shtār*, p. 3; gen. sing. *shtār*, 1542; *shtārē*, 511; nom. plur. *shtār*, 117, 537, 845, 925, 947 (*shtār*), p. 3; oblique plur. *shtār dugā*, on account of thieves, 1247; *shtār dugē*, on account of thieves, 460; *shtār kusth*, to do thieving, to steal, 1087, 1186, 1396, 1487; *shtār ktī*, having done theft, having stolen, 1087 (*shtāra*), 1261 (*katī*), 1322, 1389 (*kati*).

shtarī, female, see **ishtrī.**

shtor, subst., a quiver, 1293 (nom., wrongly translated 'arrow'); *shtur tā*, in the quiver, 1112.

shtur, a camel, see **ushtar.**

shtarak, starak, adv., now, at this time; the following forms occur in the sentences, *ishtrak*, now, p. 4; *starak*, now, 331, 730, 767, 890, 934, 1117, 1206, 1589, 1599; *starak na*, now not, not yet, 1136; *p'starak stē*, at now from, henceforth, 646; *shtarak* *wīk na*, up to now not, not yet, 1739; *starak wīk*, up to now, hitherto, 664, p. 60; *starak wīk na*, not yet, 1178; *pstarak wīk*, up to now, 657; the adverb is often combined with words denoting time; thus, *shtarak gujr*, now in the day, to-day, 351; *struk gujr*, to-day, 756; *starak gajar*, to-day, 878; *starak gujar*, to-day, 443; *starak gujr*, to-day, 271, 327, 404, 959, 1063, 1104, 1121, 1497; *starak piāsh*, now in the morning, this morning, 1038; *shtarak radōr*, to-night, 1533; *starak rador*, to-night, 1495, 1639; *starak shā*, to-night, 1370; *shtarak sē*, this year, 1498; *starka sē*, this year, 596; *starak sa*, this year, 443, 467; *starak sē*, this year, 272, 302, 504, 557, 621, 622, 623, 848, 1064; *starak p'sē*, this year, 441, 1668; our adverb is often used alone, without the addition of *gujr*, in the meaning of to-day; thus, *shtak*, to-day, 26, p. 60; *shtrak*, to-day, 1059; *shtarak*, to-day, 26, 27, 244, 561, 1317; *p'shtarak*, to-day, 26, p. 60; *starak*, to-day, 533, 754, 792, 1149, 1215, 1217, 1219, 1316, 1527, 1612, 1681, p. 60; *pstarak*, to-day, 734, p. 60; *ēsth dugā starak matakshi*, decide the day for starting, 1031.

Shtrāl, subst., Chitrāl, 1132; *Shtrālo stā*, from Chitrāl, 146; see **Shdrāl**.

shatrami, adj., swift; *ushp shatramī ess*, the horse is swift, 451, 773; also *shataramī*, 1450.

shatrim, adj., clever, cunning, 1542 (attrib.), 1544 (predic.).

shtring, adj., spotted; *krūī shtring na ass*, the dog is not spotted, 1378.

shtrissē, his wife, 726; see **ishtrī**.

shtrits, numeral, fourteen, p. 63.

shets, numeral, sixteen, p. 63; *shets sē bā*, sixteen years became, since sixteen years, 1581.

shotsa, numeral, eighty, p. 63, footnote (from the collection of the Rev. Worthington Jukes).

shott, shutt, subst., an oath; *shott chīm*, I take an oath, 939 (perhaps Khōwār idiom); *shott kulom*, I take an oath, 144 *shutt dibī*, I take an oath, 939.

shtett, is blowing, 387; see **OSHT.**

shtowa, numeral, four, see **shto.**

shiwē, shewesth, sew, to sew, see **SHU.**

Shāwal, subst., name of a pass; *Shāwal bado wīk*, to the Shāwal Pass, 1619; *Shāwalo bado*, on the Shāwal Pass, 155.

shaiyē, adv., before, p. 60; *pilingstett tā shaiyē*, marching from before, before marching, 405; cf. **shangiē.**

SKĀ, to clean, to sweep.

Past 3rd pers. sing. *sagāya*, he has cleaned (my gun), p. 4 (Abdul Hakīm Khān).

Imperative, *sagāō*, sweep, 1447; *skā*, wipe, sweep, 199, 386, 636, 1699; *skā*, sweep, 1447.

skā, subst., a broom; acc. *skā*, 199; oblique, *skā mēsh*, with a broom, 386, 636 (*mesh*); also *sagon*, a broom, 1447 (acc.).

skā, subst., arsenic, 73 (acc.).

sali, in *trūtsan salī*, scissors, 1243.

suli, subst., friend, 536 (nom.).

silibo, in *tū mishoch silibo wilom*, if thou liest I will beat thee, 802; lit. perhaps 'thou liest, if that be the case, I will beat'.

SILK, to slip, to be slippery.

Present participle, *silkin*, slippery; *bhīm silkin biss*, the ground is slippery, 1330.

Second present 3rd pers. *silkiottett*, boots slip (on the snow), 1082.

Future 2nd pers. sing. *silkilosh*, thou wilt slip, 1330.

salkēn, subst. (?), night, evening; *dalkiē salkēn wār*, to-morrow evening time, to-morrow evening, 877; *salka-war*, at evening time, in the evening, 424.

sell, participle, working; *dāo sell*, a wood-worker, a carpenter, 227, 238 (nom., read *dāo sell asē*); *dāo sellē giats*, get a carpenter, 860.

salām, subst., salutation, greetings, compliments, 37 (acc.).

SAMĒ, to let go, to allow to go, to send.

Future 1st pers. sing. *samīlam*, I will let you go, I will give you leave, 784.

Imperative 2nd pers. sing. *samē*, send (two men), 1024; cf. **SAMAR.**

siūm, adj., old, p. 7; *siūm biss*, has grown old, 1165, 1220, 1289; *siūm bistai*, are become old, 943; *shī siūm*, an old carpet, p. 7; *siūm kālo*, the old fort, 834; *siūmē kālo tā*, than the old fort, 527, p. 7 (*kālē*).

sum, in *gatrā butī ayā sum*, tired having become come am, I am tired, 134; see **Ā.**

SAMAR, to start, to be off (on a journey).

Conjunctive participle, *samartī*, having started, 1517.

Indefinite present 2nd pers. sing. *samrī-bā*, when thou startest, 786; *koī samarij-bā*, when thou startest, 1067.

Second present 1st pers. sing. *samiritsam*. I am starting, I am off, 733.

Perfect 3rd pers. sing. *samriss*, he has started, he is off, 1011.

Future 2nd pers. sing. *kuī samarlosh*, when thou wilt start, set out, 1546; cf. **SAMĒ.**

Samar, subst., name of a man, 906; agent, *Samar*, 899, 1306; gen. *Samar*, 1509.

sain, subst., an army, 69 (nom.); cf. **sarī.**

1 **son,** in *amnī dū brā-son*, these two brothers, 1102. The *s* is perhaps the suffix of the pronoun of the third person.

2 **sōn,** subst., (1) a forest; *ikīā p-sōn*, in this forest, 825; *p-son p'mich*, in the woods, 1122; (2) pasture land, 991 (nom.).

3 **sōn,** subst., gold, 570.

4 **sōn,** subst., cloth, 1146 (acc.).

sundī, adj., whole, all, 85, 86, 87 (acc.); 900, 1125, 1154, 1201, 1209, 1254, 1522, 1528, 1610, 1649, 1659, 1720, 1740, p. 4 (nom. plur.); often used as an attribute, 4 (whole), 6, 588, 602, 669, 683 757, 997, 1069, 1092, 1135, 1139, 1163, 1195, 1209, 1217, 1223, 1229, 1233, 1334, 1502, 1529, pp. 8 (*sundi*), 9; *sundī*, always, 34, 1416.

sandok, subst., a box, 285 (acc.); *sanduka*, a box, 176.

sang, adj., all, 31, 32, 33, 181, 212, 232, 279, 358, 421, 538, 545, 566, 600, 608, 645, 827, 972, p. 7; can also be translated 'both', 579; often used as an attribute, 183, 239, 247, 351, 425, 532, 546, 587, 743, 761, 832, 905, 1074, 1079, 1081, 1110; *sang gujr*, every day, daily, 320, p. 60; *sang wōr*, every time, always, 862; *sang*, always, 40.

SANGA, to hear, to notice.

Present 2nd pers. sing. *warī na sanganch*, dost not notice my word, dost not obey, 1570.

Past 1st pers. sing. *sangāyā*, I heard, 833; *n'sangāyā*, I did not hear, 807.

Perfect 1st pers. sing. *tu vari sangāisi*, I heard thy speech, p. 4 (Abdul Hakīm Khān).

Future 3rd pers. *sangalā*, (the enemy) will hear, 1309.

suntrō, adj., mixed; *āo mish suntrō katī*, having made mixed, having mixed, with water, 874.

sānawotan, subst., waist, 1621 (nom.).

spī, subst., a quilt, a bed-cloth; nom. *spī*, 1165, 1204; *spio*, 1109.

sap, sip, sop, sup, onamatopoetic particle.

sap-sip, quickly, 1106; *sapp*, immediately, p. 60; usually *zapp*, immediately, quickly, 1127, 1229, 1381, 1455, 1468, 1600, p. 60; soon, shortly, 1249, p. 60.

sōp sip manchī, a pertinacious man, 1005.

sup-kott, he makes *sup*, he stammers, 1390.

spāhī, subst., a soldier, a sepoy; nom. sing. *spāhī*, 29, 150, 253, 495 (*spāhi*), 1051, 1343, 1626; agent sing. *spāhī*, 317, 1703; gen. sing. *spāhī*, 1323; nom. plur. *spāhī*, 63, 181, 277, 280, 418, 486, 515, 552, 600, 824, 981, 1288, 1348, 1536, 1550, 1664 (*spahī*), 1726, pp. 19, 59; acc. plur. *spāhī*, 276; oblique plur. *spāhī dugā*, for the soldiers, 956; *spāhien dugā*, for the soldiers, 1473.

sapits, numeral, seventeen, pp. 12, 63.

sar, in *mikiyā-sar* (i.e. *mikiyāsar*), they have run away, 460; see **MUG.**

sari, subst., an army, 334 (acc.), 335 (nom.); agent sing. *sarīen*, 334; perhaps wrong for *sārī*; cf. **sain.**

serī, subst., an apricot; nom. plur. *serī*, 1179; *sarren*, 65.

1 **sir,** subst., a seer, 1282.

2 **sir, tsir,** subst., head; used as a postposition, on, upon; thus, *ushp sir manchī*, horse on man, a mounted man, 1037; *ushp-o sir manchī*, a mounted man, 889; *ushp sir nishisth*, to sit on a horse, to ride, 1173; in most cases *sir, tsir* is then preceded by the preposition *p*; thus, *ango p'tsiru*, on the fire, 233; *ushp p'sir*, on a horse, on horseback, 885, 1173, 1174, 1625; *ushp p'sir nishēl*, sitting on horseback, a horseman, 1174; *ushp p'sir nizhisth*, to sit on horseback, to ride, 1173; *ushp p'tsir*, on the horse, 1617; *ushp p'tsir nishēl*, a rider, p. 9; *ushp p'tsir stē*, from on horseback, 1488; *ashtrē p'sir*, on the top of the mountain, 887; *dusht p'tsir*, on (around) the arm, 1725; *kunā ptsir*, on the table, 948; *vōtt p'sir*, on the stone, 1319; *zim tă p'sir*, on the snow, 1381; *zīn p'tsir bazisnă*, saddle on cloth, saddlecloth, 1220.

sōr, adj., next, coming; *sōr mōsa tă*, next month, 922; *sōr sē tă*, next year, 923.

sarkār, subst., Government; gen. *sarkāro*, of Government, belonging to Government, 181, 897; *sirkāro*, 824, 1288 (*sirkār-o*), p. 5.

sirēn, subst., tree; *sirēn pizh bā*, the trees are blossoming, 165.

sarren, apricots, see **serī.**

sirtă, subst., highland, 540 (nom. translated 'frontier'); *sarētă*, in the highlands, 654; *srētă*, in the highlands, 903; *sirtan tă*, in the highlands, 763.

sarēz, subst., juniper; *sarēz dāo*, the wood of the juniper, 729.

ss, suffix of the pronoun of the third person, see **s.**

ses, in *ses kra*, the eleventh month of a year, p. 66.

sōs, soss, subst., purpose, mind (?); *sōs katī*, mind making, seizing the opportunity, 964; *kai soss tă*, in what purpose? why? 816.

sús, subst., a sister; *sus tā ranzul biss,* my sister has fever, 1317; *chir sūs,* foster-sister, 530 (nom. plur.).

susni, subst., a kerchief, a drying cloth; *hōst susnī,* a handkerchief, 614 (acc. plur.); the word seems to be feminine; thus, *host susnī awaṛī,* I have brought a handkerchief, p. 3.

soss, purpose, see **sōs.**

stā, pronoun, that he, 178; commonly used as an adjective before a noun, 109, 113, 115, 131, 260, 296, 297, 392, 411, 435, 446, 487, 535 (translated 'this'), 837, 839.

stē, postposition of the ablative, from, pp. 5, 62; other forms are *stā,* 146; *stā̃,* 785; *ste,* 1619, p. 62; *stĕ,* 517, 540; *stē̃,* 848, 1139, p. 62, and *stha,* 160; the postposition is added immediately after proper nouns; thus, *Mirak stē,* from Mirak, 1186, 1187; similarly after names of places, 447, 614, 785 (*stā̃*), 1177, 1223, 1387, 1473, 1496, 1517, 1546, 1547, 1619 (*ste*); note *Dryus stē Bruz p'mizhu,* between Drōsh and Brōz, 1200; *Dryus stē Gairath p'mīsh,* between Drōsh and Gairath, 1184; *Badakshā Shdrāl stē p'mich,* between Badakhshān and Chitrāl, 540; the postposition is also added immediately after pronouns and pronominal adverbs; thus, *akīē stē,* from there, 1481; *kuī stē,* since when? p. 60; since, 1227; *kōr stē,* wherefrom? 1672, p. 61; wherever from, 1354; without the addition of any other preposition or postposition we also find *stē* forming an ablative of comparison; thus, *pō sē stē chogh,* more scarce than last year, 1240, p. 9 (*chāgh*); *Shtrālo stā nīr,* below Chitrāl, 146.

stē is sometimes also added immediately after ordinary nouns; thus, *apsiss stē,* from the tumour, 1560; *bāzār stē,* from the bazaar, 1294, 1376 (perhaps wrong instead of *b'bāzār stē,* cf. 558); *sū pū esth pōr stē,* from the direction of the setting sun, 1663; *shall stē,* from the shed, 1284; usually, however, the preposition *b, p* is added before the noun; thus, *bado shaiē stē,* from the crest of the hill, 299; *ba-di-stē* (?), from the sky, 396; *p'amu stē,* from the house, 410; similarly, 160 (*stha*), 517 (*stĕ*), 552, 558, 646, 848 (*stē*), 1429, 1488, 1568; sometimes we also find the postposition *tā̆* added after the governed noun; thus, *ushp-amu tā̃ stē*, from the stable, 1385; *sodāgarā tā̆ stē*, from the merchant's, 1066, *sodāgar-o tā̆ stē*, from the merchant's, 1286.

SATĒ, to perform (?).

Imperative, *kāna satē*, perform burial, bury, 216.

satkiya, subst., in *wutsa satkiyā*, the twelfth month of the year, p. 66.

stūm, subst., a tree, 587; see **shtom.**

STRA, to write.

Infinitive, *strasth dugā̆*, in order to write, 1729.

Verbal noun, *strān na banam*, I cannot write, 1729.

satr, subst., the maina bird; *satr marangats*, mainas, 903 (nom. plur.).

strak, starak, adv., now, to-day, see **shtarak.**

sots, subst., pain; *achiē̃ sots kuttett*, the eyes ache, 980.

sett, is, 763; see **AS.**

sott, numeral, seven, 293, 556; *sutt*, 1161, 1346, pp. 12, 63.

sawer, subst., *sawer wasā*, Wednesday, p. 65.

T

ta, thy, see **tū.**

tā̃, postposition, in, on, to, from, occurs in various forms, such as *tā*, *tā̆r* (p. 62, footnote), *tā̆*, *to*, etc.

(1) in, on, into (denoting place), 67 (*tā*), 109, 141, 197, 210, 213, 217, 297, 304, 348, 355, 386, 389, 435, 445, 522, 531, 544, 570, 573, 575, 576, 593, 596, 616, 662, 668, 691, 697, 743, 745, 763, 813, 816, 842, 845, 847 (*tā*), 851, 883, 902, 935, 950, 1017, 1029, 1042, 1052, 1082, 1097, 1112, 1123, 1166, 1174, 1216, 1219, 1253, 1268, 1301, 1339, 1363, 1380, 1412, 1427, 1438, 1455, 1470, 1501, 1506, 1507, 1516, 1537, 1591, 1618, 1634, 1636, 1652, 1657, 1712, 1713, 1721, pp. 7, 62; *tōst bidī tā̆*, in, according to, thy wish, 1369; *ushp tā̆ zīn ptitē*, put the saddle on the

horse, 1219; *ashtrē tă ūwē*, to climb on the hill, 436; *jilamă tă*, at my tent, 1638.

In (denoting time), 472, 793, 831, 881, 922, 923, 995, 1147, 1158, 1161, 1198, 1206, 1342, 1436, 1480, 1630, 1670, 1717, p. 60.

Some nouns followed by this *tă* are used as postpositions; thus, *chiwol tă*, in the neighbourhood of, near, 1226; *tawarē tă*, near to, p. 62; *pamu torē tă*, near the house, 1562.

(2) With, together with, 1101, 1553, 1667, p. 62; *iă tă nishē*, sit with, near, me, 911.

(3) To (denoting locality), 415, 583, 697, 863, 1177, 1498, 1508, 1524, 1542; *iă tă gun ann*, smell comes to me, I smell, 1336.

(4) To; used to denote an indirect object, 516, 524, 905, 906, 1018, 1077, 1161, 1175, 1210, 1309, 1315, 1319, 1430, 1474, 1477, 1571, 1665, pp. 2, 5, 12.

Also used to denote a dativus commodi; thus, *iă tă kūr bradzott*, to me the foot pains, my foot pains, 130; *stā manchī tă dāṛi kazhīra bissă*, to that man the beard has become white, 131; *ushp tă lazhom peṭangess*, to the horse the bridle has become broken, 198; cf. further 104, 240, 307, 534, 553, 593, 642, 671 842, 933, 1033, 1405, 1449, 1627; thus commonly with verbs meaning to be, to become, forming a dative of possession; thus, *tōtta tă chok sē bissă*, to the father how many years have become? what is your father's age? 19; *emă tă tūs ass*, to us is bhūsa, we have bhūsa, 149; cf. 478, 803 (*tā*), 933, 1116, 1172 (*tā*), 1203 (*tā*), 1234, 1304, 1317, 1367, 1423, 1424, 1462, 1466; *tă* can further be used to form a kind of genitive and be translated 'of', p. 62; thus, *iă watan tă manchī*, the men of my country, 601; *tott bră tă nanwṛi*, the head of the clan, 631; *to chitt tă manchī*, (thou art) a man of thy own mind, an independent, headstrong, man, 707, 1692 (*mōch*); *zīm tă bōr*, a load of snow, 815; *ano tă gun*, the smell of meat, 1001.

(5) In, to, used to denote the direct object; thus, *Bastī tă preptī*, it hit Bastī, 3; *kūr tă atamshi*, bit the leg, 1342, 1501

(*atamshiss*, the translation given is wrong); cf. 89, 904, 1049, 1169, 1260, 1321, 1405, 1618.

(6) From, denoting place, 78, 161, 340, 360, 413, 730, 758, 775, 787, 933, 1052, 1532.

(7) From, forming an ablative of comparison; thus, *Brōza tă chĭr*, up from Brōz, higher than, above, Brōz, 2; *siūmē kālo tă lesst*, good from the old fort, better than the old fort, 527; *Bastī tā drgr*, longer than Bastī, 1464; cf. 417, 446, 585 (*tā*), 889, 898, 1170, 1242, 1450, 1464 (*tā*), 1742, p. 9; thus also, *sundī amu tă bilugh âla*, all houses from (or, in) much large, the largest of all houses, 1334; *sundī pīsh tă shingierai*, the prettiest of all flowers, 1195.

(8) From, by reason of, p. 61; on account of, p. 62; thus, *agol tă*, from the rain, 239; *shillē tă*, from cold, 397, 538 (*shillĕ*), 809; cf. 937, 1004, 1084, 1271, 1528.

(9) *tă* is often used before other postpositions and adverbs; thus, *adrē tă atĕr*, inside the box, 713; *nasur tā atĕr*, inside the nostril, 931; *kālo tă atūr*, inside the fort, 637; *kunī tă atūr*, inside the jar, 722; *âo tă ĭr*, on this side of the river, 1305; *duī tă brobar*, like the hand, 996; similarly, *tă p'mich*, within, in, 1316; *tă păr*, on the other side of, across, 1702; *tă pĕr*, on the other side of, across, 1181, 1305; *tă pagūr*, under, 1576; *tă p'sir*, on, upon, 1381; *tă shaiyē*, before, 405; *tă stē*, from, 1066, 1286, 1385; *tă torĕ*, near, 1327.

(10) In a similar way *tă* is used after a noun preceded by the preposition *b*, *p*; thus, *ba-do shai tă*, on crossing the pass, 303; *b'dusht tă*, from the hand, 1343; *b'gul tă*, in the nullah, 1183, 1196, 1224; *p'ptī tă*, on the back, 1377; from the back, 1583; *p'putt tă*, on the road, 1233; *p'shur tă*, in a marsh, 1443; *pa-shur tă*, in the marshes, 1006; *b'zul tă*, in the jungle, 1485.

Sometimes we find this idiom before postpositions or adverbial expressions; thus, *p'amu tă nirgo*, in front of the house, 386; *b'dū tă torĕ*, in front of the door, 1399.

(11) *tă* is often combined with verbal forms; thus, *ē pur bitta tă*, one direction becoming in, at the junction, 728; *ushp tă wāo atsa-ta-m*, at the time of my coming down from the horse, 360; *ĩ en tă*, at the time of my going, p. 17; *tū preish-tă*, when thou arrivedst, p. 4; *Mirak āzittă*, when Mirak arrived, p. 4; *bim-tă*, my becoming in, if I become, p. 21; *bittă*, if he, they, become, p. 21.

Other forms of the same postposition are, *dă*, *dă*, in from; thus, *ushpă dă*, from the horse, p. 8; *paṛim-dă*, when I arrived, p. 4; *piltim-dăn*, if I fall; *piltīr-dă*, if you fall, p. 35; *en dă*, at the time of going, p. 17; *atsan-dă*, when coming, 1535; *shū n'azzī tan dă* (?), news not being in, suddenly, 1429; *dá*; thus, *bīr-dá*, if you become, p. 21; *ien-dá*, at the time of going, 1057; it will be seen that the *d* forms only occur after nasals.

tá, in, occurs with verbal forms in the so-called conditional mood; thus, *bis-tá*, if thou hadst been, 1700; *bish-tá*, if thou becomest, p. 21; *bimis-tá*, if we become, p. 21; *piltish-tá*, if fallest; *piltil-tá*, if he, they, fall; *piltimish-tá*, if we fall, p. 35.

to, in, from; *manchī to-dī bilugh kshul*, male from even very clever, cleverer than the male, 464; *inā kuttā-to-m*, this saying-in-to-me, when he asked me, 51.

tĕ, to; *tă tĕ*, to thee, 969.

tan, *tān*, in; *puttan* (i.e. *putt tă*), on the road, 947; *tān* is used in the so-called conditional mood, pp. 17, 29, footnote; thus, *lushtim-tān*, if I am frostbitten; *lushtich-tān*, if thou art frostbitten; *lushtinn-tān*, if he, (they (?)), is, are, frostbitten; *lushtemish-tān* (?), if we are frostbitten; *lushtēr-tān* (?), if you are frostbitten, p. 31; *mizhē-tān*, if tell lies, p. 29.

tăr, in, to, from, p. 62 footnote; in, 1098 (*tăr*), 1282; *kāstē tăr*, what in? when? p. 60; to, 1085, 1103, 1570 (dative); from; *watsă tăr* (*pagur*) *lesst*, good from pubboos, better than pubboos, 1083; with prepositions and adverbs, *p-amu tăr*, at the house, 1413; *p'putt tăr*, on the road, 1541; *wōtt tăr torĕ*, near the stone, 1410.

ta, te, conjunction, or; *dalkiš ēmá ta n'ēmá*, shall we go or shall we not go to-morrow? 714; *Chandrāl pōr gwā te Ashrett pōr gūssā*, did he go towards Chitrāl or has he gone towards Ashrett? 1538; *te*, or, p. 62.

1 **TE,** to make, to do.

Infinitive, *sū testh dugē*, for building a bridge, 480.

Verbal noun, *barū-ten*, to let out, to fire a gun, 1293.

Conjunctive participle, *wōr tētī*, doing turns, alternately, 1640.

Present 1st pers. sing. *kar tēnum*, I make ear, I hear, 244 (Abdul Hakīm Khān).

Future 1st pers. sing. *gāno telam*, I will make, give, charity, 244.

Imperative 2nd pers. sing. *ushp tā zīn ptitē*, i.e. perhaps *p'ptī tē*, put the saddle on the back of the horse, 1219; cf. *ptē, ētē*, under 2 **PRĒ**.

1st pers. plur. *sū tamu*, let us make a bridge, 195.

2 **te,** or, see **ta.**

TI, an auxiliary verb of uncertain meaning, perhaps identical with *TE*; the following forms occur in the sentences:—

Present participle, *tin*; thus, *kuduma tin nu kuch*, work doing not dost, dost not take care, 224; *dom tin-ess*, was herding, 648; *shē tin ess*, is frozen, 534, 755 (*ass*), 858, 1034; *shī tin ass*, is frozen, 1330.

Conjunctive participle, *dom tittī*, herding, 499.

Present 3rd pers. *shē tinn*, it freezes, 1698.

Future 3rd pers. *shē n'tilā*, (the water) will not freeze, 533.

1 **to, tō,** thy, see **tū.**

2 **to,** in, see **tā.**

tū, pronoun, thou; the following forms occur in the sentences:—

Nominative, *to, tō*, thou, p. 10; *tu*, thou, 185, 187, 190, 843, 941, 1107, 1290, 1301, 1616, 1660, pp. 4, 10, 13, 59; *tū*, thou, 38, 44, 51, 52, 80, 84, 87, 92, 99, 105, 106, 107, 138, 141, 144, 224, 225, 234, 350, 389, 408, 420, 430, 431, 439, 457, 475, 477, 506, 507, 510, 525, 539, 542, 543, 554, 555, 561, 586, 589,

611, 617, 619, 670, 701, 702, 703, 707, 720, 737, 738, 740, 747, 769, 770, 771, 775, 776, 783, 802, 813, 852, 854, 863, 911, 919, 927, 929, 933, 940, 941, 952, 968, 974, 985, 994, 1000, 1003, 1018, 1031, 1054, 1062, 1065, 1080, 1088, 1093, 1095, 1101, 1105, 1106, 1107, 1108, 1110, 1132, 1134, 1137, 1143, 1149, 1157, 1160, 1164, 1171, 1175, 1176, 1180, 1181, 1188, 1201, 1202, 1205, 1217, 1232, 1235, 1249, 1273, 1274, 1275, 1277, 1290, 1307, 1308, 1311, 1330, 1335, 1340, 1347, 1360, 1366, 1410, 1411, 1416, 1461, 1462, 1463, 1486, 1487, 1503, 1519, 1523, 1531, 1534, 1546, 1564, 1570, 1577, 1582, 1586, 1602, 1605, 1608, 1629, 1667, 1671, 1672, 1684, 1692, 1693, 1700, 1704, 1716, 1733, 1736, pp. 10, 13, 17.

Vocative, *tū*, O thou, p. 10.

Agent, *tu*, thou, p. 3; *tū*, thou, 87, 346, 384, 479, 582, 678, 794, 816, 880, 951, 984, 1023, 1068, 1077, 1103, 1127, 1136, 1148, 1232, 1255, 1262, 1363, 1375, 1444, 1471, 1474, 1591, 1616, 1658, 1669, pp. 10, 11, 12.

Case of direct object, *tō*, thee, 1262; *tu*, thee, 132; *tū*, thee, 107, 695, 707, 737, 738, 784, 941, 1023, 1029, 1088, 1093, 1103, 1180, 1205, 1299, 1312, 1375, 1396, 1444, 1486, pp. 10, 11, 12, 13.

Case of indirect object, *tū*, to thee, 607, 784, 793, 853, 919, 933, 1016, 1063, 1149, pp. 11, 12, 17; similarly, *tū lestabalā*, it will be good for thee, 21 (dativus commodi).

Dative of possession, *tu*, to thee, 1335; *tū*, to thee, 430, 528, 569, 670, 714, 843, 1273, 1335, 1510, 1554, 1724.

Genitive, *tā*, thy, 259, 1510, 1652; *to*, thy, 493, 707, 763, 836, 983, 1030, 1152, 1692, p. 2; *tō*, thy, 455, 715, p. 10; *tu*, thy, p. 4; *tū*, thy, 38, 144, 183, 203, 258, 294, 305, 318, 342, 451, 463, 475, 521, 522, 542, 585, 589, 607, 635, 649, 656, 660, 685, 762, 770, 773, 847, 852, 854, 911, 985, 1006, 1028, 1029, 1036, 1160, 1192, 1199, 1217, 1235, 1334, 1337, 1355, 1361, 1450, 1470, 1552, 1639, 1646, 1674, 1676, 1701, 1719, 1725, p. 9; *tus*, thy, p. 8 (Abdul Hakīm Khān); *tusā*, *tūsā*, thy, p. 10; *tusē*, thy, p. 10; *tū-sē*, thy, 1744; *to'st*, thy, p. 2; *tost*, thy, 1493, 1644; *tō'st*, thy, 1377,

p. 10; *tōst*, thy, 341, 369, 675, 1264, 1369, 1394, 1413, 1560, 1561, 1741; *tostā*, thy, 952; *tōstā*, thy, p. 10; *tu'st*, thy, 1161.

Oblique, *tă tĕ*, to thee, 969; *to gē*, to thee, p. 4; *tū dugă*, for thee, 769, 798 (*dugā*), 1259, 1395, 1569; *tū gă*, thee, 84; *tū mēsh*, with thee, 978; *tū mēsh*, from thee, p. 10; *tu p'nishr*, in front of thee, 666; *tū panishr*, in front of thee, 1107; *tū ptiwar*, after thee, 776; *tū tă*, to thee, 478, 843, 1063, 1101, 1161, 1172 (*tā*), 1175, 1210, 1462, 1665, pp. 10, 12; *tū tăr*, to thee, 1570.

tuiā, in *less tuiā* (i.e. *lesstuiā*), is (your harvest) good? 621; see 3 **ā, ai.**

tāb, subst., heat, 637 (nom.); *tabī*, adj., hot, 654, 684, 1268; see **tāp, tapī.**

tabib, subst., a doctor, a surgeon, 1560; *tapip*, a doctor, 695 (nom.), 1106 (acc.).

tabal, adj., rubbed on; *tabal kshī*, rub it on, 1594.

tibar, after, behind, see 1 **ptī.**

tich, tīch, tĭch, tĭ̄ch, tinch, tīnch, tinj, (1) adj., certain, true; equal; *inā warī tich na bunn*, this word is not true, 1187; *tinj bitī*, having become certain, on purpose, 3 (*bitī*), 951; *tīch badūr*, equally far, 447; *emă mēsh tīch katī ettett*, they go having made it equal with us, they are marching even with us, 965; (2) subst., certainty, knowledge; *tīch n'ess*, there is no knowledge, I do not know, 1357; *tīch n'bunn*, I do not know, 1417; *tīch na bunn*, I do not believe, 1472; *tinch n'ess*, I do not know, 373; *tinch n'bā*, I do not know, 1078; *tīnch n'ess*, I do not know, 1125; also written *tīsh*; thus, *tīsh n'butt*, I do not understand, 945.

toch, tuch, subst., lead; *epol toch*, flat lead, a flat bullet, 213 (nom.); acc. *tuch*, lead, bullets, 1550 (wrongly translated 'powder'); *tūch*, lead, 778; *ashtrutt tuch*, lead stone, 871; *kallā tuch*, tin, 1521; *tuch*, tin, 1522 (after *kallā tuch kaṛ*); *kallā tuch kaṛ*, a tinsmith, 1522.

tochī, thy father, see **tott.**

tchkur, adj., steep, 340 (pred.); cf. **ukaṛ.**

thū thū, interjection, for shame! 1273, p. 63.

thuṛus, subst., a precipice, 324 (nom.).

tajī, adj., Badakhshānī; *tajī sarīen*, the Badakhshānī army, 334.

tuk, subst., a scar, pock; *tuk shilā*, scar smallpox, smallpox, 1462.

tikā, for the sake of, p. 62; see **dugā**.

TIKHĒ, to subside, to be caught.

Future 2nd pers. sing. *tikhēlosh*, thou wilt be caught (in the quicksand), 1107.

tokūm, subst., a namda, saddlecloth, 937 (nom.); said to be feminine, p. 1 (*tokum*).

talā, subst., a torch, 1536 (acc. plur.).

tēl, subst., oil, 942 (nom.); *iā tel kaikotī ruch n'buttosal*, why is there not light in my oil? why does not my lamp give a light? 759.

tol, subst., a cauldron, a pot, 412 (nom.); 233, 1257 (acc.); *ptol tā*, into the pot, 1052.

tul, subst., field; *ptul*, (what is) in the field, crop, 302, 515, 604, 817, 870, 895, 1133, 1420, 1428; *ptul kudūm*, in field work, agriculture, 22; *ptul pachūrē*, around the field, 640; *ptul p'mich*, in the field, 227, 1241 (*p'mīch*); *ptul tā*, in the field, 596, 717.

telam, I will make, I will give, see **TE**.

tamu, let us make, see **TE**.

tamkio, subst., tobacco; *tamkio kusth*, to smoke tobacco, 315; *tamkio n'ksholam*, I do not smoke tobacco, 603; *tamkio n'kshātam*, I do not smoke tobacco, 1015; *tamkio n'kusoch*, (why) dost thou not smoke? 1340; *tamkio n'kshond*, they do not smoke, 1526; *tamkio lestā kshī*, do not smoke, avoid tobacco, 98.

taman, subst., the skirt of a garment, trousers, pyjamas, 1513 (nom.); 1097, 1146, 1225 (translated 'shirt'), 1687 (acc.); 1341 (gen.), p. 7; *taman dugā*, for trousers, 1613.

tan, tān, in, see **tā**.

1 **tin**, subst., wine, liquor, 1695 (nom.), 383 (acc.), 1201 (gen.).

2 **tin,** auxiliary, see **TI.**

tinch, certain, certainty, see **tich.**

tang, subst., a rupee, money; nom. sing. *tang,* a rupee, 1175; acc. sing. *tang,* a rupee, 395, 793, 794, 1063, 1077, 1149, 1164, 1210, 1352, 1474, 1477, p. 11; gen. sing. *ē tang digṛī,* one rupee's worth of cloth, 219; *eo tangē pul,* one rupee's worth of grain, 578; nom. plur. *tang,* rupees, money, 1116, 1172; acc. plur. *tang,* rupees, 556, 1175, 1186, 1211, p. 12; money, 1369; *tanga,* rupees, 554, 995; *tangē,* rupees, 975.

tong, tōng, subst., a pear; nom. plur. *tōng,* pears, 997; acc. plur. *tong,* pears, 576.

tinj, certain, see **tich.**

tēnum, I do, see **TE.**

tinn, in *s̲h̲ē tinn,* it freezes, see **TI.**

TAP, to be hot, to get warm.

Second present 3rd pers. sing. *tapett,* (the body) gets warm, 999.

Causal verb, *tapē, tipā,* to make hot, to warm.

Conjunctive participle, *tapētī,* having heated, 638.

Indefinite present 1st pers. sing. *kaikotī tipām,* how can I warm (the water)? 1645.

Second present 3rd pers. sing. *tipát,* (the sun) heats, melts (the snow), 328.

Perfect 1st pers. sing. *tipess,* I have warmed (the water), 1644.

Imperative, *tipāo,* warm, boil (the water), 173, 1642; *tipāō,* warm, melt (the ghī), 858.

tāp, subst., heat, warmth; nom. *tāp,* 699; *tāb,* 637; *tōp,* 272, 865.

tapī, hot, 1433, 1438 (pred.); 1632 (attr.); *kuī tū tā tapī onzībá,* when it comes hot to you, when you get fever, 1466; *tapī kunn,* (the fire) makes it hot, gives warmth, 1633; *tapī waktā,* in the hot season, in summer, 1123.

tabī, hot, 654, 684, 1268 (pred.).

tapā, participle, killed, shot; *tapā gwā,* they were killed, p. 59; cf. **tapk.**

tapē, subst., in *drun tapē,* a pistol, 1016 (acc.), lit. perhaps 'bow gun'.

tapk, tapak, tapik, subst., a gun; nom. *tapk,* 1293, 1367 (plur.); *tapak,* 3, 514, p. 18; *tapik,* 624, 626, 627, 860, 1744; acc. *tapka,* p. 4 (Abdul Hakīm Khān); *tapkiē,* 1699; *tapik,* 816, 1261; acc. plur. *tapak,* 600; *tapkīen,* 1301; gen. *tapkē,* 635; *tapkiē,* 1724; *tapkiē,* 902; oblique, *tapik dugā,* for my gun, 1053.

du tapka barkstaṛa, he fired two guns, p. 4 (Abdul Hakīm Khān); *tapk barūten,* to fire a gun, 1293; *tapik damitt,* he is seizing his gun, he is aiming, 25; *tapkiē wisth,* to hit with a gun, to shoot, 1047; *tapkē witī,* having hit, having shot, with a gun, 673; *tapkiē vitī,* with a gun, 1396; *tapkiē witī,* with a gun, 1091; *tapkiē lesst vind,* they strike well with the guns, they shoot straight, 1348.

tapol, adj., sticking; *s͟hur tapol biss,* mud is adhering, 522; *luī tapola biss,* blood is adhering, 164.

tipām, I may make warm, see **TAP.**

tapip, a doctor, see **tabib.**

tuppdun, subst., a flag, 490 (acc.).

tipess, I have heated; **tipāt,** melts; **tapēti,** having heated; **tapett,** it gets warm, see **TAP.**

tupetich, adj., impatient; *tupetich manchī,* an impatient fellow, 994.

trā, trai, trē, troi, numeral, three; *trai,* 846; *trē,* 452, 629, 986, 990, 995, p. 63; *troi,* 16, 206, 349, 383, 855, 873, 955, 1157, 1180, 1185; *dā troi,* two or three, some few, 1157; *yō trā trē,* each three three, three by three, p. 64; *trē witsī,* three twenties, sixty, p. 63; *trē witsī duts,* three twenties ten, seventy, p. 63; *trē ptiwar* (?), third, p. 64; *troi wosthā oss,* he came third, 487.

TAR, to place, to put.

Perfect 2nd pers. sing. *tarissā,* thou hast put, 1591.

3rd pers. *pagūr tāristai,* (the mud stream) has put down, beaten down my crops, 1420.

Imperative, *angā taṛā,* set fire to, 1386.

tā̆r, in, to, see **tā̆.**

taṛ, ejecting, see **TOṚ.**

taṛē, subst., a looking-glass, 823 (nom.); acc. plur. *taṛe,* 558.

taṛī, subst., the dog rose; *taṛī pīsh,* the dog rose flower, 1196 (*vish*), 1242, 1336, 1338, 1363; cf. **tarīn.**

TOṚ, TUṚ, TAṚ, to break, to throw away, to dismiss.

Past participle, *taṛā,* dismissed, left; *taṛā kshī,* leave behind, 786.

tōṛ, toṛ, tuṛ, taṛ is often used with *AJI,* to throw; thus, *tōṛ azhēlom,* I will throw off, I will dismiss, 1262, 1375; *toṛ azhēlam,* I shall ruin you, 1205; *tuṛ azhā,* they have ejected, 1135; *tardzho,* drive him out, 379; *taṛ-zhār,* turn him out, 517; similarly, *tōṛ kṛā,* I turned him out, 1568.

torē, turē, tawarē, adv., near, p. 60; *torē,* near, 440, 1462, 1465; *tur,* near, 453; *turē,* near, 932; *tavaraī,* near, 158; *tavaraī,* near, 324; *tawarē,* near, 449, 685, 846; *tawarē,* near 1212.

torē, tawarē, is also used as a postposition, sometimes together with the preposition *b, p,* and with the postposition *tā̆*; thus, *Bruts torē,* near Brōz, 1690; *jilamā jāgā torē,* near the tent ground, 1639; *p-amu torē,* near the house, 844; *b'dū tā̆ torē,* near the door, 1399; *palē tā̆ torē,* near the sentry, 1327; *wōtt tā̆r torē,* near the stones, 1410; *do tawarē,* near the river, on the bank, 116; *iā̆ tawarē,* near me, 448; *shur tawarē,* near the swamp, 1137; *p-amu tawarē,* near the house, 958; *tawarē tā̆,* near to, p. 62; *p'amu torē tā̆,* near the house, 1562.

TUR, to weigh.

Infinitive, *tursth dugā,* for weighing, 1656.

Present 3rd pers. sing. *turann,* he is weighing, 1655.

Imperfect 3rd pers. sing. *turnajī* (i.e. *turnazzī*), he was weighing, 1655.

1 **tūr,** subst., a mountain ash; *tūr dār,* the wood of the mountain ash, 77.

2 **tūr,** subst., a ford, 518; *kūir tūr tā̆,* in, by, the foot ford, by wading, 1618.

turē, near, see **torē.**

trăchi, adj., guarding, caretaking, careful; *trăchī manchī*, a caretaking man, a sentinel, 1261; *trăchī bō*, be careful, take care, 439, 1330; *tarăchī bō*, take care, 127, 171, 225, p. 63 (*bo*); *tarāchī bō*, take care, 1108; *taraīchī bō*, take care, 152, 666; *tṛăchī bŭr*, be ye careful, 1439; *trăchī bō dugă*, for the purpose 'take care', in order to guard, 597.

tarja, subst., scales; *tarja nizhān*, the marks on the scales, 1238; cf. **TUR.**

tārak, subst., a poplar; *tārak kāno*, poplar-trees, 1046.

tremchuk, subst., a lamp, 433 (by the lamp; perhaps miswritten for *p'tremchuk*, in the lamp); *dus p'tramjuk*, yesterday at lamp, at the lamp time, last night, 532; *ptremshuk pashiosth dugă*, for lighting on the lamp, for lighting the lamp, 942; this word is probably also contained in *patramjuk*, night, p. 65, lit. at lamp (time).

trmir, subst., an inflated skin for crossing (a river), 1321 (*tarmir*), 1452, 1702, 1704; see **ăotrmir** and 2 **tŭr.**

tarin, subst., a thorn bush; *tarīn watarawa* (?), a hedge of thorn bushes, 640; see **taṛī.**

trang, subst., a girth (of a horse), 826 (nom.).

turungo, adj., thin; used of clothes and boots, 1199, 1291, 1491 (pred.); *ăo turungo ass*, the water is thin, shallow, 1272.

turnaji, turann, was weighing, is weighing, see **TUR.**

turus, subst., an avalanche, 95 (nom. plur.).

trasu, subst., household; *trasu lattrī*, household property, 573; *tŭrsŭn-lattrī*, household property, 1079.

trashtu, subst., an onion; *ĕ bōr trashtu*, a load of onions, 956.

tarissă, tăristai, hast put, has beaten (down), see **TAR.**

tursth, to weigh, see **TUR.**

trits, numeral, thirteen, 1413, pp. 12, 63; *ierits*, 326.

trūtsan salī, subst., scissors, 1243 (nom.).

tarwach, tarwoch, tarwaj, tarwāz, subst., a sword; nom. *tarwach*, 514, 1454; *tarwaj*, 626; acc. *tarwach*, 1213; gen.

tarwach, 1455; *tarwách*, 1237; *tarwoch*, 1036, 1724; *trowōch*, 660; instrumental, *tarwochē wil*, striking with sword, a swordsman, 1456; *tarwochē wīl*, sword beating, p. 9; *tarwechen vītī*, having struck with a sword, 1573; *iāsī kūr tarwāz-ē-m petiss*, my leg sword-with-my (?) cut, he cut my leg off with a sword, 1703; oblique, *tarwach brobar*, like, as, my sword, 1280; *tarwochī mēsh witī*, having struck with the sword, 1074.

tarázho, tar-zhār, turn out, see **TOR.**

tsá, subst., a branch; *tsá tā*, on the branch, 616.

tseo, tsiā, adj., sharp; *tseo kshī*, make (my sword) sharp, 1454; *katá tsiā assā*, my knife is sharp, 1280.

tsu, subst., sand, 1226 (nom.).

tsuiē, adv., empty-handed; *tsuiē ettett*, they march empty-handed, 573.

tōs, subst., a shoulder, *iā pa-tōs*, on my shoulder, 1297.

tūs, subst., chopped straw, chaff, 58, 149, 239; said to be feminine, p. 1; cf. 239.

tus, tusā, tusē, thy, see **tū.**

tish, knowledge, certainty, see **tich.**

tshun, subst., war; *pi-tshun*, in war, 1630, 1631.

tsamar, subst., rust, 1213 (agent).

tsir, top, see **sir.**

tsiren, subst., a peach, 472 (nom. plur.).

tsarr, subst., an orphan, 971 (nom.).

tōst, tōstā, tust, thy, see **tū.**

testh, to make, see **TE.**

tsawē, subst., shadow, shade; *tsawē tā*, in the shade, 1268 (*tsāwē*), 1438; *sū tsāwen bibā*, when the sun gets in shadow, sunset, p. 65

tēti, doing, see **TE.**

tot, father, see **tōtt.**

tuti, subst., excuse; *bilugh tuti ptā*, he made many excuses, 768.

titsa, subst., a skin-bag (for carrying flour), 1322 (acc.).

ttsitt [*sic*], subst., dung, 386 (nom.).

tittī, having made, see **TI.**

tōtt, subst., father; nom. *tott,* 12; *tōtt,* 20, 45, 48, 57, 148, 206, 244, 323, 456, 462, 463, 468, 567, 672, 765, 1086, 1113, 1398, 1464, 1497, 1685, 1743, pp. 6, 13; acc. *tōtt,* 1394, p. 6; voc. *tōtt-ā,* O father, p. 5; *tōttiā,* O father, p. 6 (O my father?); dative of possession, *tōttia,* to my father, 24; *tōttio,* to my father, 749; agent, *tot,* p. 4; *tōtt,* 319, 347, 1255; *tōtt-ē,* p. 6; gen. *tōtt,* 189, 259; *tōttā,* 749; *tōtti,* 545 (my father's), p. 6; *tōttio,* pp. 5, 6; *tōtto,* 676; *tōtt's,* p. 6; oblique, *tōtt dugā,* for my father, 290; *tōtt stē,* from a father, p. 6; *tōtt tā,* from the father, than the father, 1464; *tōtta tā,* to your father, 19; *tōttē tā,* to a father, p. 6; nom. plur. *tōtt,* p. 6; acc. plur. *tōttān* (?), p. 6; voc. plur. *tottiā,* p. 6; agent plur. *tōtt* (?), p. 6; gen. plur. *tōttān, tōttān'st,* p. 6; oblique plural, *tōttān stē,* from fathers; *tōttān* (?) *tā,* to fathers, p. 6.

tōtt-ī, my father, p. 11; my uncle's, 293; *tōtti,* my father's, 545, 605; *tōttia,* to my father, 24; *tōttio,* to my father, 749.

tōtt-chī, thy father, p. 11; thy father's, 278; *tochī,* thy father's, 1492.

tōtt's, his father, 900, 971, p. 11; his father's, 583.

jash tōtt, paternal uncle, 1573 (ag.); *tōttī piṭr,* my uncle's son, my cousin, 293.

nōn tōtt, mother, father, parents, 985, 1086.

tōtt brā, father brothers, family, clan, 256, 421, 1139, p. 7 (nom.); *tōtt brā tā,* to the clan, 631.

tōtt wāo, father, grandfather, ancestors, 549, 603.

tavaraī, tawarē, near, see **torē.**

twā ditus, numeral, fifty, p. 63, footnote (from the collection of the Rev. Worthington Jukes).

tawarik, subst., a fly, 497 (nom. plur.).

tyor, (1) adj., ready, prepared, 1130, 1383 (pred.); *tyor kusth,* to make ready, to prepare, produce, 507, 551, 601, 743, 1229, 1354, 1694.

(2) Adverb, certainly, surely, 632, 1465, 1527, 1533; *shtalē tyor,* certainly, surely, 1359.

V, W

1 **wā,** adv., (1) out; *wā-kshess,* he tore (the nose) out, off, 930; *wa-kshol,* pull out, 376; also written *ū*; thus, *dusht ū kshī,* put your hand out, show your hand, 1308; *u-kshosth dugā,* in order to drag out, 1008, 1098; *padrē ū prētt,* the bowels (?) go out, there is diarrhœa, 349, 350; *pīsh ū osthai,* the flowers have come out, 1614; instead of *ū* we find *ō* in *achē oksh,* show your eye, 434; a third form *wō* occurs in *ṇa wō ass,* (the seed) is not out, 1253.

(2) Down; *wā osth,* to come down, to descend, 341; *wā-kshō,* get down, unload, 1583; *wa-kshá,* take off, p. 8; also written *wao, wāo, wāwo, wō*; *wē̃, wia, viyan*; *wār, viār*; thus, *wao,* downwards, p. 60; *wao-ksho,* take down, 375; *wāo atsatam,* when I came down, when dismounting, 360; *wāo atsolam,* I shall get down (from the horse), 775; *wāw·ats,* dismount, 665; *wāwo etsatī,* having come down, 340; *wō,* down, 758, 1009; *wē̃ attalāō,* thrown down, 1508; *wia-ziā,* (the leaves) are falling, 787; *viyanyā,* (the leaves) are falling, 93; *wār,* downwards, p. 60; *wār ossam,* I fell down, 1488; *viār n'ūtē,* do not throw down, 225.

(3) Back, p. 60; *wā prēlom,* I will give back, I will return, 1161.

2 **wā,** onomatopoetic, the sound *wā*; *wā-wā-wā kutt,* he makes *wā-wā-wā,* he mumbles, 945.

3 **wā,** particle, a suffix denoting uncertainty; *kuī wōtt prapta-wā,* when the stone hit, 1260; see **bâ.**

4 **wā, wai, o,** suffix forming adjectives of possession, p. 5; *aruz-wā,* sweetness having, sweet, 764; *aruz-wai,* sweet, 727, 910; *arūzdo,* sweet, 1448; *ál bidī-wā,* high heart having, high-hearted, 361, 927 (*bidio*), 1055 (*bidiwā*), p. 5; *digar bidī-o,* bad heart having, evil-minded, 619; *lē bidī-wā,* good heart having, of good intention, 740, p. 5; *bar-wai,* load having, a coolie, 74, 75, 112, 184, 227, 276, 277, 279, 284, 291, 339, 374, 395, 639, 712, 805, 815, 819, 822, 832, 837, 846, 905,

928, 932, 934, 953, 1018, 1049, 1055, 1130, 1131, 1144, 1185, 1296, 1397, 1423, 1432, 1566, 1567, 1650; *bradso-wā*, illness having, ill, 632, 983, 1359, 1502, 1720; *bradsw-aio*, he is ill, 1236; *bradzo-wā*, ill, 475 (*-wo*), 767, 1104, 1307; *bradzo-w-ai*, he is ill, 589; *bradzo-w-ås*, he was ill, 331; *damkol-wā*, dry, 286; *drushtī-wā*, poverty having, poor, 343, 690, 823, p. 5; *duṛ-wā* (?), a musician, 901; *gāno-wā*, heavy, 1218, 1414; *gāwā*, heavy, 805; *jerik-na-wā*, shame not having, shameless, 1275; *kā-no-wā*, anything not having, poor, worthless, 1155, 1580, 1590, 1649; *kai-no-wā*, poor, of no account, 875, 966, 1109, 1171, 1172; *kaṛ-wā*, strong, 206, 658, 1612; *kusul-wā*, skilful, careful, 225; *lattrī-wā*, property having, rich, 1070, 1155, 1171, 1415, p. 5; *marapsawai* (?), a falconer, 438; *naluz-o*, misery having, subdued, peaceful, 90; *naluz-w-ås*, he is a beggar, 140; *nashtar-wai*, being in front, 138, 506, 539, p. 60; *pitzen-wā*, cold, 273; *shtowa ptī-wā*, four backs having, square, 1201; *sådawai*, a merchant, 862; *tapik na w-åi*, guns not having-are, they have no guns, 627; *shtal warī-wā*, true words having, truthful, 1559, p. 5; *warī-na-wā*, words not having, dumb, 1366; *ål zira-wā*, high heart having, noble, 927; *digar zira-wā*, bad heart having, of bad heart, 724, p. 5; *zora-wā*, strength having, firm, 486; *zor-w-ai*, they are strong, p. 19; *zūr-w-ai*, they are strong, 181.

Several of the above examples show how this suffix can be followed by a verb substantive. The form *wōs*, was, p. 19, is probably the suffix *wā* followed by the base *as*; this word seems to occur in several instances, cf. *bradzo-w-ås*, he was ill, 331; *naluz-w-ås*, he is a beggar, 140; *tapik-w-ås*, gun having is, he has a gun, 624, p. 58 (*tapak wås*); *dush n'wåsam*, fault not having am, I have no fault, 711, 731, p. 58; *tarwaj wåsam tapik na wåsam*, sword having am gun not having am, I have a sword but not a gun, 626; *ē shī wåssiā*, one horn having was, he had only one horn, 673; *paisa n'wåttettamish*, money not having are we, we have no money, 1044.

WAI, to get.

Second present 1st pers. sing. *waietum*, I am getting, 180.

1 **wāi,** subst., wind, rheumatism; *wāī prēttett*, the wind comes (into), I get rheumatism, 1166.

2 **wāi,** subst., grandmother, 579 (*wāi*, nom.); an old woman, 945, 1247 (nom.); see 1 **wāo.**

1 **wāo,** subst., a grandfather, 550, 579 (nom.); *tōtt wāo*, father, grandfather, forefathers, 549, 603 (nom.); *wāo's*, his grandfather, 900 (nom.); *wāo*, of an old man, 945.

2 **wāo,** down; see 1 **wā** (2).

3 **wāo mushtar,** subst., a hunchback, 692.

WĒ, to go, to get along.

Present participle, *kur wēl ass*, a donkey going is, a donkey can get along, 1184.

Present definite 3rd pers. sing. *shtalẽ ushp wēlī ushtar na wēlī*, perhaps a horse can go, a camel cannot go, 1184.

wē, subst., a sheep, 1285 (nom. plur.); *wez*, a ewe; *wāk*, a lamb, 1285; *wakī*, a lamb, 756, p. 7.

wẽ, down, see 1 **wā** (2).

WI, VI, to beat, to strike; used in several idioms such as *oren vī*, to push; *chá, chō, wī*, to make a noise, to howl; *dōtt wī*, to beat a drum; *kon vī*, to hit with an arrow; *katō vī*, to hit with a dagger; *pá wī*, to kick; *sabjun wī*, to spit; *tapkiẽ wī*, to strike with a gun, to shoot; *tarwochẽ wī*, to strike with a sword. The following forms occur:—

Infinitive, *vīsth*, to beat, p. 52; *ikīā visth ass*, his beating is, he should be punished, 1156, p. 15 (*ikiē*); *wisth*, to beat, p. 52; *sabjun wisth*, to spit, 1373; *tapkiē wisth dugā*, for shooting, 1047.

Present participle, *wīl*, beating, p. 52; *tarwochẽ wīl*, sword beating, a swordsman, 1456 (*wil*), p. 9 (*tarwochē*).

Conjunctive participle, *wītī*, having beaten, p. 52; *chō wītī*, shouting, 1299; *cho wītī*, loudly, 1463; *kon vītī*, having hit with an arrow, 1579; *katō vītī*, having hit with a dagger, 319; *tapkiẽ vitī*, having hit with a gun, 1396; *tapkẽ witī*, having hit with a gun, 673, 1091 (*tapkiē*); *tarwechen vītī*, having hit with a sword, 1573; *tarwochī mēsh witī*, having hit with a sword, 1074.

Passive participle or verbal noun, *vina*, beaten; *ots vina vina kaṛesam*, me beaten beaten hast made me, I am beaten, 132, p. 59 (*kaṛessum*); *vina-gan*, beaten going, beaten; *tu vinagan ungalosh*, thou wilt be beaten, p. 59; *ika vinagan ungalazī*, he would have been beaten, p. 59; *emá vinagan ungutussī*, we have been beaten, p. 59.

Indefinite present 2nd pers. sing. *wich*, beatest, p. 52; *oṛen vich*, pushest, 1093; *pá vich*, kickest, 737; *pá vichī*, kickest, 738; *oṛen vichībá*, if pushest, 1093.

1st pers. plur. *wimish*, we beat, p. 52.

2nd pers. plur. *wīr*, you beat, p. 52; *wīrbá* (?), if you beat, p. 53.

Present 1st pers. sing. *vinom*, I beat, p. 13; *winom*, I beat, p. 52; *winambá*, if I beat, p. 53.

2nd pers. sing. *vinj*, beatest, p. 13; *winj*, beatest, p. 52; *winoshbá*, if beatest, p. 53.

3rd pers. sing. *vinn*, beats, p. 13; *winn*, beats, p. 52; *winabá*, if he beats, p. 53.

1st pers. plur. *winamishbá* (?), if we beat, p. 53.

3rd pers. plur. *tapkiē vind*, they shoot, 1348; *wind*, they strike, p. 52; *winabá*, if they strike, p. 53.

Second present 3rd pers. sing. *witt*, he beats, p. 52; *chá witt*, he is howling, 689; he makes noise, 721.

Past tense 1st pers. sing. *winā'm*, I struck, p. 52; *vino-j-ā*, did I ever beat thee? 1312; *winā'sh*, I have beaten thee, p. 11.

2nd pers. sing. *vinā*, hast beaten, p. 12; *winā'sh*, hast beaten, p. 52.

3rd pers. sing. *winā*, he beat, p. 52; *winā'm*, he beat me, 1306; *vinā'sh*, he beat thee, p. 12; *kū wino-zh-ā*, has anyone hit thee? 1470.

1st pers. plur. *vinā*, we beat him, p. 12; *vinā'sh*, we beat you, p. 12; *wināmish*, we beat, p. 52.

2nd pers. plur. *vinā*, you beat him, p. 12; *vinā'm*, you beat me, p. 12; *winār*, you beat, p. 52.

3rd pers. plur. *winā*, they beat, p. 52; *winām'ish* (?), i.e. *winā-mish*, they beat us, they attacked us, 1429; *vinā'sh*, they have beaten thee, p. 12.

Imperfect 1st pers. sing. *winazzam*, I was beating, p. 52

2nd pers. sing. *winazzish*, wast beating, p. 52.

3rd pers. sing. *winazzī*, was beating, p. 52.

1st pers. plur. *winazzamish*, we were beating, p. 52.

2nd pers. plur. *winazzār*, you were beating, p. 52.

3rd pers. plur. *winazzī*, they were beating, p. 52.

Perfect and pluperfect 1st pers. sing. *winossam*, I had beaten, p. 52; *n'vinosā'sh*, I have never beaten thee, 1312, p. 11.

2nd pers. sing. *vinossā*, hast beaten, p. 12; *winossish*, hadst beaten, p. 52.

3rd pers. sing. *winossī*, he had beaten, p. 52; *vinās'm*, he beat me, p. 12; *vinoss'm*, he beat me, p. 12; *vinossi'sh*, he beat thee, p. 12; *wanā's*, he has beaten me, 630.

1st pers. plur. *vinossā*, we beat him, p. 12; *vinossi'sh*, we beat thee, p. 12; *winossamish*, we had beaten, p. 52.

2nd pers. plur. *vinossā*, you have beaten him, p. 12; *vinossa'm*, you have beaten me, p. 12; *winossār*, you had beaten, p. 52.

3rd pers. plur. *winossī*, they had beaten, p. 52; *vinossa'm*, they have beaten me, p. 12; *vinossi'sh*, they have beaten thee, p. 12; *tapkē wanisthā*, they have fired a gun, 635.

Future 1st pers. sing. *vilom*, I will beat, 132, p. 13; *pā vilom*, I will kick, 737; *wilom*, I will beat, 738, 802, 1422, 1486, p. 52; I will punish, 707, 1088.

2nd pers. sing. *vilosh*, wilt beat, p. 13; *wilosh*, wilt beat, p. 52.

3rd pers. sing. *vilā*, will beat, p. 13; *wilā*, will beat, p. 52.

1st pers. plur. *wimā*, we will beat, p. 52.

2nd pers. plur. *wilōr*, you will beat, p. 52.

3rd pers. plur. *wilā*, they will beat, p. 52.

Imperative 2nd pers. sing. *vī*, punish, 1089; *wī*, beat, p. 53; punish, 1087; *na wī*, don't beat, 1479.

3rd pers. sing. *wilā*, let him beat, p. 53.

1st pers. plur. *wimá*, let us beat, p. 53.

2nd pers. plur. *wilōr*, beat ye, p. 53; *dōtt wāṛ*, beat a drum, 382.

3rd pers. plur. *wilā*, let them beat, p. 53.

wō, out, see 1 **wā** (1).

wū, subst., sister-in-law; gen. *wū-o*, of a sister-in-law, 1318 (dative of possession), p. 5.

wui, subst., a scabbard, 1237 (nom.).

wich, vich, beatest, see **WI.**

wichá, subst., a guest, a traveller, 598 (nom.); *wichá-zmi<u>sh</u>*, we are travellers, we shall travel, 1059; also written *wischā*, *wischio*; thus, *wischio*, a traveller, 1061 (nom.); *wischīo*, a traveller, 584 (agent); *wischā manchī*, travellers, 1547 (nom.); *wischio dugā*, for travellers, 1061.

wide<u>gh</u>, subst., fear, 458 (nom.).

WIDHAR, to fear, see **WIDAR.**

Widing, subst., name of a man, 906, 964, 1021, 1670 (nom.); 1512 (agent); 1277, 1615 (gen.).

WIDAR, to fear; the following forms of this verb, many of them written with *dh* instead of *d*, occur in the sentences:—

Infinitive, *kai widerasth n'ess*, there is nothing to fear, 1181.

Present participle, *widarl*, fearing, timid, p. 9; *widharal*, timid, 1520.

Conjunctive participle, *vidruitī*, having feared, 460; *widarthī*, having feared, 1325; *widhertī*, having feared, 1139.

Indefinite present 1st pers. sing. *wideram*, I fear, 1144, 1181.

Present 1st pers. sing. *widarnam*, I fear, 459, 494; *vidarnom*, I fear, 619; *widarnom*, I fear, 1233; *widernam*, I fear, 1198; *widharnam*, I fear, 1695.

2nd pers. sing. *widharanj*, art afraid, 1684.

3rd pers. plur. *widharand*, they fear, 1398.

Second present 1st pers. sing. *widerthum*, I fear, 137, 367; *widarēttum*, I fear, 954.

3rd pers. sing. *widarett*, she fears, 1247.

Past 1st pers. sing. *widaram*, I was frightened, 401.

Causal verb, infinitive, *widarosth dugē*, in order to frighten, 537.

wodaran-chut, subst., thunder, 1510 (nom.); cf. **uḍeṛl.**

WAG, to demand, require; this base is apparently identical with *RAG*; the following forms occur in the sentences:—

Indefinite present 2nd pers. sing. *wagachī*, (why) dost thou demand? 1175; *ragach*, askest, 1149; *starak dī ragacha*, dost thou demand again to-day? 1149; *ragachī*, (why) dost thou demand? 1175; *tū iā tā paisa awēguchī*, thou askest money from me, 933; *warī n'awēguch*, dost not obey, 940.

Present 2nd pers. sing. *raganjā*, dost thou require? 1629.

3rd pers. plur. *ragand*, they will require, 531.

Second present 1st pers. sing. *ushu wagattam*, I want medicine, 290; *ragattam*, I demand, I ask for, 1257.

2nd pers. sing. *hukm n'ragattā*, dost not ask for, dost not obey, his command, 1205.

3rd pers. sing. *ragat*, asks for, requires, 1150; *ragatt*, asks for, requires, 1352, 1353; *kai awegutā*, what does he beg for? 139.

3rd pers. plur. *warī n'wagattett*, they do not ask for word, they do not obey, 516.

Imperfect 2nd pers. sing. *raganasuch*, wast asking for, 1149.

Future 1st pers. sing. *wagalom*, I shall require, hire, 663; I will ask, 1211.

Imperative, *iā warī wagā*, agree to, obey, my words, 21.

WIG, to rest:—

Infinitive, *wisth*, to rest, p. 18; *wigasth dugā*, for resting, 1269.

Conjunctive participle, *wigī*, having rested; *ikiā p'amu wigī aīsh kshī*, having rested in that house examination do, 76.

Past 2nd pers. sing. *kui wigiā*, when thou art rested, 1157.

Imperative 2nd pers. sing. *wigiō*, rest, take a rest, 1157, 1503.

Causal verb, infinitive, *wiāsth*, to cause to rest, p. 18.

Future 1st pers. sing. *wiālam*, I will let him rest, 1219.

wāgcha, subst., the ninth month of a year, p. 65.

1 **wāk,** subst., a lamb, 1285; *wakī*, a lamb, 756, p. 7; see **wē.**

2 **wak,** in *dangariwak*, lazy, 1424.

wēk, subst., a moth, 883 (nom. pl.).

wīk, postposition, until, up to, p. 62.

Used to denote place, thus, *Dīr wīk*, up to, to, Dīr, 1557; *Drāsan wīk*, up to, as far as, Drāsan, 1458; *Dryūs wīk*, to Drōsh, 1496; *Konisht wik*, to Ranbur, 1283; *Shāwal bado wīk*, up to the Shāwal Pass top, 1619; similarly, *kachkruī wīk*, up to the armpits, 1345: *pa chuk wīk*, up to the chest, 1183.

It also denotes time, thus, *pōch sē wīk*, up to five years, 1191; *sai yār wīk*, till sundown, 1245; *starak wīk*, up to now, hitherto, 664, 1178, p. 60; *shtarak wīk*, up to now, 1739; *pstarak wīk*, up to now, 657; *atsiṛ wīk*, until thou returnest, 1586; *waṛan wīk*, until thou seest, 1624; *kuī wik*, up till when, 1669; *iā kuī atsir wīk*, until I return, 1143; *kuī wīk pochētr na peṭlon ennā*, until the fast is not broken, up to the end of the fast, 1413.

wakshā, wākshō, take down, unload, see 1 **wā** (2).

wōkshal, subst., a doctor, 367 (acc.); *wokshhal*, a doctor, 314.

wākshess, he tore off, see 1 **wā** (1).

wakt, season, see **wokt.**

wokt, subst., time, season, 1250, 1461, 1516 (nom.); *kai wokt*, what time? when? p. 60; *wosut wokt*, in springtime, 1189; *waktā, woktā*, i.e. perhaps *wokt tā*, at the time; *achok woktā*, few times, rarely, 1124, p. 60; *tapī waktā*, at summer-time, 1123; *wokt tā*, at the time; *bosut wokt tā*, at the time of spring, 831; *askī wokt tā*, at that time, 1480; *sū chī presth wokt tā*, at the time of the going up of the sun, 1436.

WAL, to say, to speak; to read; to call, to summon:—

Infinitive, *paṛhī walesth dugā̆*, for reading books, 1129.

Verbal noun, *paṛhī walan*, to read books, 1129.

Present participle, *wari walal manchī*, a words-speaking, jabbering, man, 720.

Indefinite present 1st pers. sing. *kaikotī wilām-bá*, as I say, 1594.

2nd pers. sing. *wạlach*, sayest, 1108, 1110.

Present 2nd pers. sing. *walanch*, sayest, 1188, 1463.

3rd pers. sing. *walann*, says, tells, 365, 1472, 1675; *walonn*, he is calling, 1299.

Second present 1st pers. sing. *walatom*, I say, 52 (translated 'I answered').

2nd pers. sing. *walĕtish*, art talking, 929.

3rd pers. sing. *walett*, he says, talks, 839, 945.

3rd pers. plur. *walettett*, they say, speak, 339, 437, 819.

Past 2nd pers. sing. *kā walach*, what didst thou say? 51.

Perfect 1st pers. sing. *waliosam*, I said, 52.

3rd pers. sing. *kudūm iā̆ tā̆ wiliāsim*, he told me (to do) a work, 524, p. 12 (*wiliās'm*).

Imperative 2nd pers. sing. *walō*, say, speak, tell, 282, 822, 905, 906, 1235, 1299; call, summon, 221, 376, 591, 610 (*walo*), 806, 953, 1729.

3rd pers. sing. *ī walā*, let him tell me, 841.

wēl, subst., time, season, opportunity; *inā wēl pshu wēl n'ess*, this time is not the time for sleep, 700; *piliangsth wēl tā̆*, at the time of marching, 1342; *yazhī wēl tā̆*, in the morning, 881, 1147.

wēl, wēlī, going, will go, see **WĒ**.

welī, in *welī kshī*, ask for, 1085.

wīl, wilā, wilom, beating, will beat, see **WI**.

WILI, to melt:—

Conjunctive participle, *zīm wilitī*, the snow having melted, from the melting of snow, 500.

Present 3rd pers. sing. *wilinn*, (the snow) melts, 1381; *zīm vilna-bá*, when the snow melts, 1183.

wiālam, I will let him rest, see **WIG.**

wilāmbá, I say, see **WAL.**

wilōr, wilosh, you will beat, wilt beat, see **WI.**

wiliāsim, he told me, see **WAL.**

wālti, subdued; *wālti kshī*, subdue (the fire), 481.

wōm, subst., time, leisure, 792, 1518 (nom.).

winā, struck, see **WI.**

WONA, to make, prepare; imperative, *posh woná*, set a trap, 1543 (translated 'let us set a trap').

WANAM, to catch, to hold:—

Infinitive, *wanomasth dugā*, in order to catch, 1543.

Conjunctive participle, *wanamdī*, having caught, having seized, held, 396, 788.

Past 3rd pers. sing. *ku wanemiā*, who has caught (the thieves)? p. 3.

1st pers. plur. *emá wanemia*, we have caught, p. 3.

Perfect 3rd pers. sing. *wanamess*, he has seized (is carrying a flag), 490; *wanamiss*, he caught, 1287, 1358, 1549.

Future 1st pers. sing. *wanomalom*, I will catch him, 1090.

3rd pers. sing. *wanamelā*, he will catch (me), 495.

Imperative, *wanamā*, hold (the horse), 665.

vinrēni, adv., downstream, 374, p. 60; cf. 1 **wā** (2).

wanā's, he struck me, see **WI.**

wanisthā, they have fired, see **WI.**

wanzī, subst., a holly-tree, 958 (nom. plur.); *wanzī kāno*, holly-trees, 668.

wanzo, subst., an axe; *wanzo mēsh*, with axes, 1610.

wopsan, wopsin, adj., left behind; *wopsin ess*, he is left behind, 790; *wopsan-asum*, I am left behind, I am at the end of my strength, 644; *wopsan-ossum*, I was left behind, 955.

vrē, wrā̃, wrē̃, warē, postposition, with, by means of; also written *wrā̃*, *wrē̃*, *warē̃*, p. 62; *achē̃ vrē*, with the eyes, 667; *achē̃* *warē*, with the eyes, 1126 (*achēn*), 1579, 1624; *angur warē wāṛō*, show with thy finger, 1037; *kūr wrā*, by means of the legs, on the legs, 952; *kūir warē*, on the legs, 1625; *shai wrē na anjī*, dost not march by means of the head, 952; *tsū warē pilsō*, rub it with sand, 1213.

vrī, word, see **warī.**

WAR, to grow; Present 3rd pers. *shiṛ warand*, my crops grow, 596.

wār, time, see **wōr.**

wār, down, see 1 **wā** (2).

WAṚ, to see; the following forms of this base occur in the sentences:—

Verbal noun, *wāṛ n'bamā*, we cannot see, 657; *wār* (sic) *n'bammā*, we cannot see, p. 58; *wṛan na band*, they cannot see, 1536; *waṛantan n'buttett*, one cannot see, 872.

Conjunctive participle, *ikīē waṛantī widheṛand*, having seen him they fear, they are afraid of him, 1398.

Indefinite present 2nd pers. sing. *kuī waṛi-m-bā*, when thou seest me, 1671.

Present 1st pers. sing. *vaṛion*, I see, 124.

2nd pers. sing. *waṛan wīk*; till thou seest, 1624; *waṛin-bā*, if seest, 1347; *kuī waṛin-bā*, when seest, 1308; *koī waṛī-bā*, when seest, 822.

Second present 1st pers. sing. *waṛanṭam*, can I see? 60; *n'wṛantum*, I cannot see, 539; *n'wṛantam*, I will not see, 646; *n'waṛentam*, I do not see, 1037.

Past 1st pers. sing. *waṛiām*, I saw, 287 (*waṛiā'm*), 476 (I found), 807, 930, 1124, 1246, 1252, 1327, 1579, 1655; I have seen, 667, 698, 932; *waṛiā*, I have seen, 385.

2nd pers. sing. *tū waṛiām* (?), didst thou see? 1471; *waṛiān*, hast thou seen? 1255.

Perfect 1st pers. sing. *waṛīs*, I have seen, 921, 1234 (*waṛins*), 1255 (*waṛīns*); *waṛainsā*, I have seen, 347.

2nd pers. sing. *waṛainsā*, hast thou seen? 346

3rd pers. sing. *waṛiāns*, he has seen, 1255; *waṛains*, he has seen, 377.

Future 3rd pers. sing. *n'vṛēlā*, will not see, 651.

Imperative 3rd pers. sing. *n'vṛēlā*, let him not see, 652.

Present passive, *waṛon enn*, he is seen, he appears, 1607; *na waṛon end*, they cannot be seen, 1392; *waṛon ett*, is visible, 1180, 1212, 1434; *waṛion butt*, is visible, 128; *waṛon prētt*, is visible, 876; *n'waṛoins*, is not visible, 657; *waṛantus*, is visible, appears in view, 299.

Casual verb, infinitive, *waṛōsth dugē*, in order to show, 518.

Future 1st pers. sing. *wṛālom*, I will show, 1301.

Imperative 2nd pers. sing. *wāṛo*, show, 434, 1319; *wāṛō*, show, 1037, 1300.

wārā, adj., another, p. 14; also written *wārē* and *var*; used as an attribute; thus, *ē var manchī*, another man, 50; a foreigner, 520; *wārā s̲h̲ū*, other roses, 1196; *wārā s̲h̲tār n'as̲h̲t*, another thief is not, there is no thief besides, 372; *wārē us̲h̲p*, another horse, 663; *wārē kāno*, other trees, 958, 668; *wārē s̲h̲ugā*, another cloak, 1116; *wārā* is also used as a noun, another, anybody else, 428, 706, 957, 1129; *wārā kāch*, anybody else, 148, 1209 (*kā*); *wārā*, anything else, 149, 289, 437, 1206 (nom.); 880 (acc.); *wārē kā*, anything else, 955 (acc.); gen. *warants assē*, is it another's? 1078; note, *khazonn ngandu wārē dorē tuch ngandā*, do they take treasure? else (or) do they take gunpowder and bullets? 1550.

wāṛā, subst. (?), in *wāṛā lettrī*, bribes, 192 (acc.).

wā̃ṛa, subst., in *mā̃r wā̃ṛa*, the fourteenth month of a year, p. 66.

warē, with, by means of, see **wrā̃**.

1 **warī, varī, vrī**, subst., a word; nom. *warī*, 911; acc. *warī*, 649, 1110; often meaning 'word', 'speech'; nom. *varī*, 1585; *warī*, 259, 1585; *varī less*, his speech, his advice, is good, 11, 12; *inā warī tich na bunn*, this speech, statement, is not true, 1187; *drgr warī*, a long story, p. 7; acc. *varī*, 1577, p. 4 (*vari*); *warī*, 143 (*warīa*), 144, 854, 945, 1235.

vari, warī, speech, dialect; nom. *warī*, 732, 764; acc. *varī*, 1467; *warī*, 750, 781, 1000, 1518.

varī, warī, a story, matter; *derbūn varī ess*, it is a wonderful story, it is marvellous, 1717; *lē varī*, an amazing matter, 41; *kai warī bosel*, what the matter may be, 830; *tū kai warī ess*, what matter is it for thee, 1160; *warī kuttā kusth*, to make a matter done, to follow up an intention, 91, 92.

varī, warī, voice; nom. *warī* (sound), 830; *varī chut*, the sound of the voice, the voice, 1615.

varī, warī is often used in idioms with certain verbs; thus, *varī bakshiō*, forgive my word, my crime, 300; *varī dam*, to take one's word, to allow, permit, 35; *vrī kusth*, to make word, to speak, tell, 1299, 1471, 1680; *varī kusth*, 1494, 1665; *warī kusth*, 639, 1000, 1055, 1163, 1299, 1308, 1309, 1315, 1366; *dl vrī na kshī*, don't speak loud, 1680; *eo nargī varī kshī*, say one word at a time, 1718; *shtal varī kshī*, speak the truth, 1131; *shtal warī kshī*, speak the truth, 1416, 1558; *yo nirikē warī kshī*, speak each word separately, 1235; *warī sang*, to listen to one's word, to obey, 1570; *warī wag* (*awēg*), to take one's word, to obey, 21, 516 (*varī*), 940; *warī wal*, to speak words, to speak, 339, 1675; *biliuk warī walach*, many words sayest, talkest too much, 1108; *biluk warī walal manchī*, many words saying, a jabbering, man, 720; *drgr warī walann*, he is telling a long story, 1472; *lesst warī na walett*, she does not speak well, clear, 945; *parē warī kūrē kūrē walō*, say every word separately, 282; *shtal warī walann*, he speaks the truth, 365.

utilī-wār, quarrelling speech, boasting, 1602 (acc.).

warī-na-wā, words not having, dumb, 1366.

shtal warī-wā, true words having, truthful, 1559, p. 5.

2 **wari, wāri**, a suffix corresponding to Hindōstānī *wālā*, implying possession or relation generally; cf. **4 wā**; thus—

amo-wārī, the owner of a house, 979.

ush-warī manchī, a horseman, 1092.

Brōz wārī, an inhabitant of Brōs, 709.
kil-warīān, quarrelling, 353 (nom. plur.).
mashu warī, an enemy, 281, 496 (nom.).
nalus warīān, the poor ones, 1045 (acc.).
pachan warī, an enemy, see separately.

wīr, you strike, see **WI.**

wōr, subst., time, turn; *ē wōr*, one time, once, 954, p. 60; at the same time, 1529, p. 60; *dū wōr*, twice, 1570, pp. 11, 60; *troi wōr*, three times, 1180; *pōch wōr*, five times, 1056, 1058 (*pōnj*), 1061; *duts wōr*, ten times, p. 60; *chī wōr*, how many times, 1519; *parē wōr*, each time, always, 654, p. 60; *sang wōr*, each time, always, 862; also *wār*; thus, *dalkiē salkēn wār*, to-morrow at evening time, 877.

iāst wōr n'ess, it is not my turn, 1567; *tū wōr assā*, it is thy turn, 1355; *wōr tētī*, doing turns, by turns, alternately, 1640.

waṛibâ, when see, see **WAṚ.**

wrēch, subst., selling, giving out, giving away; *baziensâ wrēch kuttam paisa ragattam, tol na wrēch kunam*, I am habitually selling clothes and getting money, I do not sell pots, 1257; *vrīch kshī*, give out, spend (the money), 1369.

VRAGH, to get, to receive.

Perfect 1st pers. sing. *vrāghuttus*, I have received, 1136.
2nd pers. sing. *vrāghuttasā*, hast thou received? 1136.
Future 1st pers. sing. *vrāghalam*, I shall receive, 1136.

wrikī, vrikī, wrigi, subst., a fox; nom. *wrigī*, 1287; acc. *wrigī*, 1287; agent, *wrigī*, 532; oblique, *wrigī purst manchī*, a fox-like, clever man, 1368; *wrikī ayūr, wrikī pursthа*, fox-like, clever, p. 9; *iwrakī ayūr ess*, he is cunning, 312; *vrikī pirstha manchī*, a cunning man, 333.

warūk, subst., wool; nom. *waruk*, 1715; acc. *warūk*, 1283.

wṛālom, I will show; **waṛiām,** I saw; **waṛimbâ,** when you see; **waṛan,** seest, sees, etc., see **WAṚ.**

warand, they grow, see **WAR.**

WRANGĀ, to snatch, to take by force.

Conjunctive participle, *vrangātī*, having taken by force, 1256; *wrangātī*, 1460; *wrangītī*, having snatched, 1343.

waronstai, in *dutt waronstai*, the teeth have fallen out, 945.

warants, belonging to another, see **wārā.**

WURSHI, to sink, stick, to be caught, cf. **4 yū.**

Past 3rd pers. sing. *wurshiā*, (the horse) has got bogged (in a marsh), 851.

Perfect 3rd pers. sing. *woshchisa*, (my horse) is caught (in a quagmire), 1098.

wāo's, his grandfather, see **1 wāo.**

WAS, to remain, to spend the night, to halt.

Future 1st pers. sing. *wisilom*, I will remain, 1370.

1st pers. plur. *wasemá*, we will halt, 608.

wâs, wōs, was, is, see **4 wā.**

wasā, day, see **wōs.**

wōs, subst., a day; *ē wōs tā*, in one day, 1717; *askē wōs tā*, on that day, 1161; *kai wōs tā*, on any day, at any time, p. 60; *kuī wōs tā*, some day, 1198, p. 60; ever, p. 60; *pōch wōs ptiwar*, after five days, 15; cf. 16, 17, 1161; *ē wōs pott*, one day's way, one stage, 327; *chī wōs pott*, how many days' way? how many stages? 1387.

Often used in adverbial expressions, thus, *pōch wōs tā ē wōs*, (to rest) one day in five days, 1158; *pōj wōs*, for five days, 99; *chē wōs*, for how many days? 1150; similarly 855, 955, 1157, 1413; with a similar meaning we find expressions such as *troi wōs butt*, three days become, for three days, 349; *latta wōs bā*, many days became, for many days, 350; *shto wōs bā*, for four days, 469; *sutt wōs bā*, for seven days, 1346.

Another form, *oss*, occurs in *mōs pichis oss bitī dū oss dī biss*, moon fifteen days having become two days also became, it is two days after full moon, 879.

A third form, *wasā*, occurs in *sawer wasā*, Wednesday, *namach wasā*, prayer day, Thursday; *sād wasā*, Saturday, p. 65.

wischio, subst., a traveller; nom. *wischio,* 1061; agent, *wischīo,* 584; nom. plur. *wischā,* 1547; *wischio dugā,* for travellers, 1061; see **wichā.**

wish, subst., (1) poison, 1038, 1122 (acc.); (2) medicine, p. 3, see **ushā.**

vishi, subst., a neighbour; *amu vishī,* house neighbour, neighbour, 917 (nom.).

wōsh, subst., a pickaxe, 1008 (acc.); *woshī mēsh,* with an axe, 13; *wezō,* an axe, 978 (nom.).

wushē, medicine, 874; see **ushā.**

woshchiss, he is caught (in a quagmire), 1098; see **WURSHI.**

wishirworh, subst., figure, shape, bodily appearance; nom. *wishirworh,* 473; acc. *wizhirwor,* 1277.

WISHT, to tighten, to make stiff.

Past participle, *wishtī ass,* (the girth) is tight, 821.

Imperative 2nd pers. sing. *weshto,* tighten (the girth), 1514; *wishtē,* tighten (the girth), 553, 826.

Passive voice perfect 3rd pers. sing. *wishtan-gess,* it has become stiff, 1402.

vishti, having feigned, see **VIZH.**

WUSHTA, to consider, to think.

Indefinite present 1st pers. sing. *washītam,* I think, 567, 1002 (*washitam*).

Second present 1st pers. sing. *wūshtātum,* I think, I am afraid (my father is dying), 57; *woshtettam,* I think, 699.

Imperfect 1st pers. sing. *wushtatāsum,* I considered, thought, 281; cf. **WIZHA.**

washītam, I think, see **WUSHTA.**

wishtr, adj., broad, wide, 254, 1292 (pred.); *vishtr taman,* wide trousers, 1687, p. 7 (*wishtr*); *divarā wishtar ass,* the plain is broad, 1022; *wishtrī putt,* a broad, wide, road, p. 7; *putt wishtrī assā,* the road is wide, 1686; (*parōsh*) *wishtrī kshī,* make my sword-belt wide, loosen it, 1455.

wishtawal, adj., boastful, 170 (pred.).

wisilom, wasemâ, I will remain, we will halt, see **WAS.**

wâsam, I have, see 4 **wā.**

WASN, WASANR, to assemble, collect.

Perfect 3rd pers. *wasanṛistai,* is collected, heaped up, 844; are assembled, 545, 849, 1047; *wasn westai,* are collected, 277.

Imperative 2nd pers. sing. *wasnāo,* collect, 276; *wasanṛā,* collect, 1229; *wasanṛāō,* collect, 1409, 1469; *wasanṛō,* collect, 1092; *wasankṛo* (?), collect, 276.

wâssiā, he had, see 4 **wā.**

wissī, vissī, numeral, twenty, 1230 (*vissī*); *s̱htowa vissī,* four twenties, eighty, 1211; *pōch vissī,* five twenties, hundred, 1419, 1439; *pōc̱h wissī,* hundred, 1515; *witsī, watsa,* twenty; *witsī eo,* twenty-one; *witsa duts,* twenty ten, thirty; *du witsī,* two twenties, forty; *du witsī duts,* two twenties ten, fifty; *trē witsī,* three twenties, sixty; *trē witsī duts,* three twenties ten, seventy; *s̱hto witsī,* four twenties, eighty; *s̱hto witsī duts,* four twenties ten, ninety; *pōch witsī,* five twenties, hundred; *duts witsī,* ten twenties, two hundred; *pachits witsī,* fifteen twenties, three hundred; *diu azār je duts witsī,* two four hundred and ten twenties, thousand, p. 63; *witsī ptiwar* (?), twentieth; *pōch witsī ptiwar* (?), hundredth, p. 64; *pōnj watsa,* hundred, 69.

wasut, subst., spring; nom. *wasut,* 165; *wosut,* 310, 587, 1516; *wasut,* in spring, 96, 1379; *wosut,* in spring, 970; *wazut,* in spring, 162; *wosut wokt,* in spring, 1189; *bosut* (*sic*) *wokt tā,* in spring, 831.

westai, in *wasn westai,* they are collected, see **WASN.**

wiāsth, to come to rest, see **WIG.**

1 **visth, wisth,** to beat, see **WI.**

2 **wisth,** to rest, see **WIG.**

wostha, in *troi wostha,* third, 487; see **tre.**

watē, put, 233; see **OTI.**

witī, having struck, see **WI.**

WATL, WITL, to fall; cf. **ATL.**

Past participle, *watla wōtt,* fallen stones, a stone shoot, 1410.

Future 3rd pers. *witlalā*, it will fall, 440; *witlilī*, it will fall, 1012; *witlalī*, they will fall, 1115; *vitlelī*, they will fall, 1198.

WIṬLO, to cut.

Infinitive, *witlosth dugā̃*, in order to cut (your tumour), 1560.

waiētum, I am getting, see **WAI.**

watan, subst., country, native country, home, 492 (nom.); *iā̃ watan tā̃*, in my country, 601, 935; *emā́ watan tā̃*, in our country, 1097; *inā watan tā̃*, in this country, 575.

wotinam, I am dead beat, 1276; see **OTI.**

vetr, wutr, subst., a fairy, 437 (nom. plur.).

WETARO, to turn, to turn aside.

Infinitive, *wetarosth dugā̃*, in order to turn (the coolies towards Bragamantal), 1566.

WOTṚ, WUTAR, to be left, to be lying.

Perfect 3rd pers. sing. *wutarst*, it is left, 948; *wotṛiss*, (a corpse) is lying, 803.

witrl, adj., ruined, old; *witrliss*, (the house) has got in ruins, 944.

witrpiss, is damaged; *dushṭ sachī witrpiss*, the wrist of my hand is damaged, 1728; cf. **pīss.**

wōtṛiss, is lying, 803; see **WŌTṚ.**

wutarst, it is left, 948; see **WOTṚ.**

WATS, to sing (of a bird).

Second present 3rd pers. sing. *watsett*, he sings, 970.

watsa, twenty, see **wissi.**

watsā́, wetsā́, wetzā́, subst., grass sandals, pubboos; acc. *watsā́*, 1082; *wetso*, 782; oblique, *watsā́ tā̃r lesst*, better than pubboos, 1083.

kashk wetzā́, shoes, 1291 (nom.).

ushpe wetzā́, a horseshoe, 1292 (nom.); *ushp watsā́ amchol*, horseshoe fastening, a farrier, 450 (*wetsā́*), 571, p. 15 (*wetsu*).

witsi, twenty, see **wissī.**

wutsa satkiya, subst., the twelfth month of a year, p. 66.

watesth, in *watesth dār*, firewood, 485; cf. Pers. *ātesh.*

wotasth, to raise, to pitch, see **OSHT.**

watsett, he is singing, 970; see **WATS.**

watta, subst., the eighteenth month of a year, p. 66.

witt, strikes, beats, see **WI.**

1 **vott, wott,** subst., a stone; according to p. 7 *wōtt* is masculine; nom. sing. *vōtt,* 308, 1189; *wōtt,* 1169, 1260; acc. sing. *vōtt,* 1187; nom. plur. *vōtt,* 96; *wōtt,* 1100; *vott athalon,* stones will fall, 171 (translated 'there is a bog ahead of you'); acc. plur. *wōtt,* stones, 207, 1008, 1409, 1656; oblique, *vōtt p'sir,* on the stone, 1319; *wōtt tã,* against a stone, 1427; *watla wōtt tãr torē̃,* near the fallen stone, 1410; *pa wott,* on a stone, 745.

2 **wott,** in *Gāgra wott,* 502; *Gāgrī-wott,* 989, 991 (the Gangal-watt Pass); cf. **pott.**

wottestai, (the provisions) have been got ready, 1081.

wâttettamish, we possess, 1044; sêe **4 wā.**

wetzâ, sandals, pubboos, see **wetsâ.**

wāwo, down; *wāwats,* to come down, to dismount, see **1 wā 2.**

viyanyā, (the leaves) fall, 93; see **1 wā 2.**

wez, subst., an ewe, 1285 (nom.); *wazest chamo,* a goat's skin, 1320; see **wē.**

wezō̃, subst., an axe, 978 (nom.); see **wōsh** and **pets.**

wiaziā, (the leaves) are falling, 787; see **1 wā 2.**

wazdor, wizdor, subst., summer; nom. *wizdōr,* summer, 787; *wazdōr,* in summer, 699, 1371; *wazdur,* in summer, 1183, 1433; *wizdor,* in summer, 348, 825; *wizdōr,* in summer, 55 (wrongly translated 'in spring'), 883, 1244.

VIZH, to feign.

Conjunctive participle, *mṛalogoṃ vizhom,* having feigned dead, 461; *maṛelgō̃ vishtī,* having feigned dead, 1358.

wizhu, adj., unsewn, undone of sewing; *shugā wizhu, biss* (?), the seam (?) of my choga has become undone, 1248.

WIZHA, to think, to believe.

Present 1st pers. sing. *wezhanam,* I think, I fear, 1115; *wizhanam,* I believe, 803; cf. **WUSHTA.**

vizheri, adj., pretty; *jū vizheri n'aza,* (my) daughter is not pretty, p. 8 (Abdul Hakīm Khān).

wizhirwor, subst., figure, shape, 1277; see **wishirworh.**

wazest, a goat's, see **wez.**

wazut, spring, see **wasut.**

Y

ya, conjunction, or; *nah krūī ya shtarī krūī,* a male dog or a female dog, 369.

1 **yā,** subst., food; nom. *yash,* 789 (translated 'meat'); acc. *yā,* 142; *yash,* 789, 1081 (translated 'provisions'), p. 4; *yashī,* bread, 184.

2 **yā,** yourselves, see 3 **yō.**

1 **yō, yū,** subst., a water channel; acc. *yō,* 717; *yū,* 1419; gen. *yū,* 1643.

2 **yō, yu,** numeral, one, 63; *inā barwai yo chok prē,* these coolies one a bit give, give each coolie one portion, 1049; similarly, *yō, yo, yu* often means one each, each; cf. Sanskrit *ēkaika*; thus, *yo kūrē,* each separately, one by one, pp. 14, 64 (*yō kūrē*), 953 (*yu kūrē*); *yo narē,* one each, p. 14; *yō narī kutt,* one tower each, 1609; *yō narik,* one by one, p. 64; *yo nirikē,* one by one, separately, p. 60; *yo nirikē warī kshī,* speak each word separately, speak distinctly, 1235; *yō do-dun,* each two two, two by two, p. 64; *yō trā-trē,* three by three, p. 64; *yō cha-shton,* four by four, p. 64; cf. 3 **ē.**

3 **yō, yōt,** pronoun, self; *yō zārē,* by myself, 1729, p. 14 (*yo zarē*); *yot zara, yōt zara,* self, p. 13; *iā yōt zara,* I myself; *tū yōt zara,* thou thyself; *tōtt yōt zara,* the father himself; *emā yōt zara,* we ourselves; *shā yōt zara,* you yourselves; *amnā yōt zara,* they themselves, p. 13.

Gen. *yost,* my own, 667, 1126, 1579; *yo'st,* thy own, p. 13; *yost,* thy own, 1319, 1605, 1624, 1658, 1671; *yost,* their own, 1209.

Oblique, *yā p'mich,* between yourselves, 364.

4 **yō**, eat, see **YŪ.**

YŪ, to eat. Many forms of this base begin with an *i*. In the conjunctive participle *y* interchanges with <u>zh</u>. The following forms occur:—

Infinitive, *iasth*, to eat, 405, p. 40; *iāsth*, to eat, 419; *yosth*, to eat, p. 15, 40; *yosthā*, for the sake of eating, p. 15; *yosth dugē*, for eating, 488; *yusth*, to eat, p. 40; *yusth dugā less*, good to eat, 1099; *yusthā*, for the sake of eating, p. 62; *yusthē dugā lesst*, good to eat, 1167; *yūsth*, to eat, 1569, p. 40; *sū garo yaristhe dugā*, on account of an eclipse eating the sun, 325.

Verbal noun, *yū*, to eat; *yū n'banam*, I cannot eat, 1574.

Present participle, *yūl*, eating, p. 40.

Conjunctive participle, *yūtī*, having eaten, p. 40; *yūs yūtī laga biss*, grass having eaten applied became, the grass is eaten up, p. 59; *<u>zh</u>ūtī*, having eaten, 142, p. 40 (*zhūtī*).

Indefinite present 2nd pers. sing. *yūchī*, eatest, 1232, p. 40.

1st pers. plur. *yūmi<u>sh</u>*, we eat, 1086, p. 40; *yūmi<u>sh</u>bá*, if we eat, p. 41.

2nd pers. plur. *yūr*, you eat, p. 40; *yūrba*, if you eat, p. 41.

Present 1st pers. sing. *yūnam*, I eat, p. 40; *yūnambá*, if I eat, p. 41.

2nd pers. sing. *yūnjī*, eatest, p. 40; *yūnjbá*, if eatest, p. 41.

3rd pers. sing. *yūnn*, eats, p. 40; *u<u>sh</u>pe yus yuno*, the horse is eating the grass, p. 4 (Abdul Hakīm <u>Kh</u>ān); *yūnabá*, if he eats, p. 41.

3rd pers. plur. *yūnd*, they eat, p. 40; *yūndabá*, if they eat, p. 41.

Second present 1st pers. sing. *aietam*, I eat, 987, p. 40.

3rd pers. sing. *yutt*, he eats, 629; *yūtt*, he eats, 581, 840, p. 40; *yūttett*, he eats, p. 40.

3rd pers. plur. *yūtt*, *yūttett*, they eat, p. 40; *kō bilu<u>gh</u> yūttett*, mosquitoes eat, bite, much, 882; *n'yūttett*, they do not bite, 493.

Present definite 3rd pers. plur. *yūlai*, they are eating, 1086.

Past 1st pers. sing. *iyā*, I ate, 86, p. 40; *iār*, I have eaten,

I ate, 275, 855, 955; *iūrā*, I have eaten, I ate, 419, 857, p. 40; *iūro*, I have eaten, 394; *iaṛō*, I have eaten, 145; *ōts dātik kusth iūron*, I wager making ate, I won my wager, 1620.

2nd pers. sing. *iyānā*, didst thou eat? 87; *iūr*, hast eaten, 880; *iūrā*, atest, hast eaten, 85, 1616, p. 40.

3rd pers. sing. *iyā*, ate, p. 40; *iūr*, has eaten, ate, 1365; *iūrā*, has eaten, ate, 1408, pp. 3, 40; *iūro*, has eaten, 789; *iūrabā*, if one has eaten, by eating, 999, 1372, 1431.

1st pers. plur. *iūramish* (?), we ate, p. 40.

2nd pers. plur. *iūr*, you ate, p. 40.

3rd pers. plur. *iūr*, they have eaten, 669; *iūrā*, they ate, p. 40.

Imperfect 1st pers. sing. *yūnazzam*, *yūlazzam*, I was eating, p. 40.

2nd pers. sing. *yūnazzish*, *yūlazzish*, wast eating, p. 40; *na yulozish*, wouldst not have eaten, 1700.

3rd pers. sing. *yūnazzī*, *yūlazzī*, was eating, p. 40.

1st pers. plur. *yūnazzamish*, *yūlazzamish*, we were eating, p. 40.

2nd pers. plur. *yūnazzūr*, *yūlazzūr*, you were eating, p. 40.

3rd pers. plur. *yūnazzī*, *yūlazzī*, they were eating, p. 40.

Perfect and pluperfect 1st pers. sing. *iūsht*, I ate, 356; *iūrissam*, I had eaten, p. 40; *na yūressi*, I had not eaten, p. 4.

2nd pers. sing. *iūrissā*, has eaten, 1444; *iūrissish*, hadst eaten, p. 40.

3rd pers. sing. *iyāsht*, he ate, p. 40; *iūrs*, has eaten, 1122; *sū garo n'yūriss*, an eclipse has not eaten the sun, 406; *iūrissī*, he had eaten, p. 40; *yūṛissi*, he had eaten, p. 4; *yūrissī*, has eaten, p. 4.

1st pers. plur. *iūrissamish*, we had eaten, p. 40.

2nd pers. plur. *iūrissūr*, you had eaten, p. 40.

3rd pers. plur. *iūriss*, they have eaten, 1722; *iūrissī*, they had eaten, p. 40.

Future 1st pers. sing. *yūlom*, I shall eat, p. 40; *ano n'yūlom*, I cannot eat meat, 1048.

2nd pers. sing. *yūlosh*, thou wilt eat, 73, p. 40.

3rd pers. sing. *yūlā*, he will eat, p. 40.

1st pers. plur. *yūmá*, we shall eat, p. 40.

2nd pers. plur. *yūlr*, you will eat, p. 40.

3rd pers. plur. *yūlā*, they will eat, 246, p. 40.

Imperative 2nd pers. sing. *iō, āyū, yō, yū*, eat, p. 41; *wārā n'yū*, don't eat more, 880; *n'āyū*, don't eat, 586.

3rd pers. *yūlā*, let him eat, let them eat, p. 41.

1st pers. plur. *yūmá*, let us eat, p. 41.

2nd pers. plur. *yūr*, eat ye, p. 41.

2 **yū,** an irrigation channel, see 1 **yō.**

3 **yu,** one, each, see 2 **yō.**

4 **yū,** adv., down; *yū prezhamá*, let us sit down, let us take breath, 1332.

yūr, down, 848, 1169, 1208, 1535, p. 60; *kuī agal yūr onzībá*, when rain comes down, when it rains, 1166; *yūr ellā*, (the fruit) will come down, will drop, 1270; *yūr gūssam*, I went down, I sank (in the snow), 1316; *sē yūr*, sundown, evening, twilight, p. 65; *sai yūr wīk*, till sundown, 1245; *shai yūr*, head down, upside down, 1591; *shiē yūr bītī*, head down having become, head downwards, 712; cf. 1 **wā** 2.

yūr seems to be used as a verb in *yūrshā*, (the horses) have got down, are stuck (in the swamp), 1443; *wurshiā*, has stuck, 851; *woshchiss*, is caught (in a quagmire), 1098.

yābū, subst., a pony, a small horse, 1043 (acc.).

yūchi, eatest, see **YŪ.**

yuds, cold, is cold, 271; see **yuts.**

yagī, subst., a rebel, 1135 (nom. plur.).

yūl, yūmá, eating, we eat, etc., see **YŪ.**

yamna, adj., double, two; *yamna gōr*, two handfuls, 1222; *yāmna bitī*, having become pairs, in pairs, two abreast, 907; *yamnā butī*, in pairs, 981.

yuno, is eating; **yund,** they eat, see **YŪ.**

yangut, subst., the headstall of a horse, 633 (nom.).

yanits, numeral, eleven, 1301, pp. 12, 63.

yōr, adj. (?), like; *ē yōr asht,* they are exactly alike. 808; cf. **agūr** and **chor.**

yūr, subst., sunshine, 1179 (nom.).

yūr, adv., down, see **4 yū.**

yūrbá, if you eat, see **YŪ.**

yūrshā, (the horses) are stuck, 1443; see 4 **yū.**

yāṛessi, has eaten, see **YŪ.**

YAS, to extinguish, to blow out.

Imperative, *yāsē,* blow out, 168.

Passive voice, *yassa ettā,* (the fire) has gone out, 1142.

yus, yūs, subst., grass, fodder; said to be feminine, p. 1; nom. *yūs,* 950, 1032, 1064, 1635, 1653, p. 59; acc. *yus,* 200, 205, 206, p. 4; *yūs,* 505; gen. *yūs,* 1386.

brunz yūs, turf, 1562 (nom.).

darī yus, dry grass, hay, 581, 629 (*yūs*).

naṛukī drigrī yus tawarē, near the reeds and long grass. near the reeds, 1137.

zhila yus, green grass, 581 (acc.), p. 8 (nom.).

yash, subst., food, meat, 789 (nom. and acc.), p. 4 (acc.); food supply, provisions, 1081 (acc.); *yashī,* food, bread, 184 (acc.); see 1 **yā.**

yush, adj., idle; *yush assish,* thou art idle, 700.

yūsh, subst., a devil, 345 (nom.), 346, 347 (acc.).

yūsht, subst., a lip, 809 (nom. plur.).

yassa, extinguished, see **YAS.**

1 **yost, yosth, yūsth,** to eat, see **YŪ.**

2 **yost,** own, see 3 **yō.**

yot, self, see 3 **yō.**

yâtsá, adj., ragged; *yâtsá biss,* (my cloak) has become ragged, 1116.

yuts, adj., cold; *yuts áo,* cold water, 1379; *yuts dumī,* cold wind, 542; *yūts damu,* cold winds, 1178.

dumī yuds, the breeze is cold, 271; cf. **yazh.**

yett, goes; *pshutī n'yett,* sleeping not goes, he cannot sleep, 928; see **I.**

yutt, yuttett, eats, see **YŪ.**

yazh, in *yazh duma,* a whirlwind, 1679.

yazhī, subst., morning; *yazhī wēl,* morning time, 881, 1147, p. 65; see **iash.**

Z

zā, are; *cho manchīzā,* how many men are there; 62, p. 19; see **AS.**

zu, zū, subst., milk; nom. *zū,* 1282; acc. *zu,* 866; *zū,* 320, 544, 1052, 1067.

zūgh, subst., in *zūgh gâo,* a yak, 1732 (nom.).

zh, zhī, suffix of the pronoun of the 2nd pers., see **sh.**

1 **zhī,** adj., black, dark, 159, 264, 435, 662, 1219, 1357, 1377, 1576 (attr.); 294, 588, 998, 1457 (pred.); *zhī kor,* dark-faced, 1197; *zhī marē,* a black bird, an eagle, 396; a kite, 744, p. 3; a lammergeer, 758.

2 **zhī,** in *na zhī ett,* see **nazh.**

zho, zhu, subst., hair; said to be fem., p. 1; cf. *kazhīrī zhū,* white hair, p. 7; nom. *zhū,* 605, 606; *mariok tā zho,* the hair in the neck, the mane, 842; also written *shu*; thus, *inā basnā shu atēr assā,* the hairs of this cloth are inside, this is the wrong side of the cloth, 842; cf. **zhō, zhūr,** and **dro.**

zhō, subst., a carpet, a rug (of goat's hair); nom. *zhūr,* 1204; acc. *zhō,* 606; cf. 2 **shi.**

ZHU, to grieve, to weep, to cry.

Conjunctive participle, *zhundī,* weeping, 1654.

Indefinite present 2nd pers. sing. *zhuchī,* (why) dost thou grieve, 589.

Present 3rd pers. sing. *zhun,* she cries, 1654.

Second present 3rd pers. sing. *zhutt,* he cries, 309.

zhū, hair, see **zho.**

zhuk, subst., salt, 1223 (nom.).

zhil, zhila, adj., wet, damp; *zhil bhīm,* damp soil, p. 8; *bhīm zhil ess,* the ground is damp, 321, 594, 1664 (*ass*).

zhila dār, wet, green wood, 384 (*zhilā*), p. 8; *zhila yus,* wet, fresh grass, 581; *zhilā biss,* (the namda) is wet, 937.

zhilē ano, wet, underdone, meat, 1574.

zhilī burī, wet, half-baked, bread, p. 8.

buṛī zhillī ess, the bread is wet, insufficiently baked, 1127.

zhum, subst., buckwheat, 209; cf. **gum.**

zhūr, a rug, 1204; see **zhō.**

zharṛ, subst., a noise, 928, 929 (acc.).

zhūti, having eaten, see **YŪ.**

zajir, adj., waste, uncultivated, 762 (pred.).

1 **zul,** subst., jungle; *b'zul lattrī,* a thing of the jungle, wild, 1689; *bi-zul attā,* in the jungle, 1126; *b'zul stē,* from the jungle, 1429; *ikīā bzul tā,* in that jungle, 1485; also written *zsul,* 523 (nom.).

2 **zul,** adj., muddy; *ào zul biss,* the water is muddy, 1643.

zalimcha, subst., a carpet, 1204 (nom.).

ZŌLAS, to stumble.

Conjunctive participle, *zōlastī,* having stumbled, 1426.

Second present 3rd pers. sing. *zōlazzatt* (?), (my horse) stumbles, 1425.

zim, subst., snow, 34, 272, 380, 399, 442, 443, 500 (*zim*), 684, 887, 920, 1064, 1117, 1120, 1147, 1183, 1345, 1533, 1548, 1589, 1599, 1635, p. 5 (nom.); acc. *zīmo,* 328, p. 5; *zīm yūr gūssam,* I went down, I sank, in the snow, 1316; *zīm dugā,* on account of the snow, 1346; *zīm tā,* in the snow, 1082; from the snow, from the cold, 1528; *zīm tā p'sir,* on the snow, 1381; *zīm-o tā,* on account of the snow, 273; *zīma-tā bōr,* a load of snow, 815.

zamān, subst., son-in-law, 1359 (nom.).

zamāna, subst., time; *shangyē zamāna tā,* in former times, formerly, 1206, p. 60.

zamāni, subst., a Kabuli rupee, 1211 (acc. plur.).

ZIMĪT, to snow.

Past 3rd pers. sing. *zīm zimītā*, snow, snowed, snow fell, 442.

1 **zāñ,** subst., a knee, 745 (nom.).

2 **zān,** subst., harm, damage, see **ziān.**

zīn, subst., a saddle, 1190, 1218, p. 59 (nom.); 1218, 1219 (acc.); *zina*, saddles, p. 8 (acc. plur.); *zīn bramighten*, a saddle girth, 1514; *zīn p'tsir bazisnā*, saddle on cloth, saddle cloth, 1220; *zin tokūm*, saddle cloth, 937.

ziān, subst., harm, damage; *ziān na kulom*, I will not do harm, 1444; *ziān kaṛol*, harm-making, destructive, malicious, harmful, 1374, p. 9 (*kaṛōl*); also written *zān*; thus, *ikīē zān biss*, to her damage became, she is hurt, 1281.

zanzīr, subst., ruin, 1206 (nom.).

1 **zapp,** subst., a cloth, 266 (nom.); 264, 824 (acc.).

2 **zapp,** adv., quickly, immediately, 1127, 1229, 1249, 1381, 1455, 1468, 1600, p. 60; see **sap.**

ZĀṚ, to know, to learn; some forms of this base occur with an initial *j* or *zh*; the following forms occur in the sentences:—

Infinitive, *zārasth*, to learn, 1518; *n'zāṛasth*, not to learn, unlearnable, hard to learn, 732.

Present participle, *kō kai n'jānṛl*, anybody not knowing, proud, 1080; *pott zaṛl*, road knowing, p. 9; *pott zāṛl manchī*, a road knowing man, a guide, 518.

Indefinite present 1st pers. sing. *tū ī lē zānchībā*, if I know thee as good, if thou pleasest me, 1029.

2nd pers. sing. *zāṛchā*, dost thou know? 1277.

1st pers. plur. *na jānṛamish*, we do not know, understand, 1238.

Second present 1st pers. sing. *n'zāṛtam*, I do not know, 591; *na zāṛētam*, I do not know, 1293; *na jānṛetam*, I do not know, 1173.

2nd pers. sing. *n'zhāṛtish*, dost not know, 611; *na jānṛetish*, dost not know, 1176.

3rd pers. plur. *n'zā̆ṛtett*, they do not know, 643; *n'zā̆tett*, they do not know, 915.

Present definite 1st pers. sing. *n'zā̆ṛlsam*, I do not know, 750; *n'jā̆ṛlsam*, I do not know, 751.

2nd pers. sing. *zā̆ṛlaz͟hā*, dost thou understand? 1577.

3rd pers. sing. *jā̆ṛlann*, he knows, 1002.

Future 2nd pers. sing. *zaṛonlos͟h*, (how) wilt thou learn? 408.

Imperative, *zā̆ṛ*, know; *jerik na zā̆ṛ*, do not know shame, do not be ashamed, 1274.

Causal verb infinitive, *zā̆ṛōsth*, to teach, 1467.

zār, adj., dyed, see **zīr.**

1 **zara,** subst., heart, see **zira.**

2 **zara,** in *yot zara, yōt zara*, self, p. 13; *yō zarē*, by myself, 1729, p. 14; see 3 **yō**; perhaps identical with the preceding, so that *yot zara* literally means 'own heart'.

zīr, adj., yellow, red; *zīr hōst susnī*, a red handkerchief, 614; *zīr krūī*, a yellow dog, 786; *zīṛā digṛī*, red shirts, 1651; also written *zār*; thus, *zār koṛis͟htai*, he has made red, dyed (his beard), 392.

zira, subst., heart, chest, 248 (nom.); *parmenstuk zira mēs͟h*, with small heart, small-hearted, 658; *āl zira-wā*, high heart having, noble, 927; *digar zira-wā*, evil heart having, bad-hearted, jealous, 724, p. 5; *bazira padrē ū prētt*, in the chest (?) intestines (?) out come, I have diarrhœa, 349; also written *zara*, heart, 1313 (nom.).

zor, zur, subst., strength, force, violence; *emā zur bā*, to us oppression became, we are oppressed, 1430; *zor kusth*, to make oppression, to use violence, 1430; *zur kusth*, to make oppression, to use violence, 1571, 1611; *zorawā*, strength having, firm, 486; *zor-wai*, they are having strength, they are strong, p. 19; *zūr-w-ai*, they are brave, 181.

zur, adj., hard, severe, difficult; *zur assā*, it is hard. 781, 1141 (*ass*), 1719 (*essā*).

zarīn, adj., yellow, 1735 (attr.).

zarur, adj., necessary; *zarur n'ess,* it is not necessary, 1061.

ziritiliā, subst., the forequarters of a horse; *ziritiliā tā,* on the forequarters, 522.

zorawā, firm, 486; see **zor.**

zsul, subst., jungle, forest, 523; see **zul.**

zass, is produced; *iamru mana na zass,* walnuts have not been produced, 1628.

zōtr, subst., a friend, a relation; nom. sing. *zōtr,* 1140; nom. plur. *zotr,* friends, 938.

zātett, they know, see **ZĀ̆Ṛ.**

zawōr, adv., in winter, 54, 497, 1698; *zawor,* in winter, 999; *ziwōr,* in winter, 380, 493, 890, 1125, 1244, 1598; *ziwor,* in winter, 988.